Career Frontiers

Career Frontiers: New Conceptions of Working Lives

Edited by

MAURY A. PEIPERL, MICHAEL B. ARTHUR,
ROB GOFFEE, AND TIMOTHY MORRIS

Centre for Organisational Research, London Business School

OXFORD
UNIVERSITY PRESS

OXFORD

UNIVERSITY PRESS

Great Clarendon Street, Oxford OX2 6DP

Oxford University Press is a department of the University of Oxford.
It furthers the University's objective of excellence in research, scholarship,
and education by publishing worldwide in

Oxford New York

Athens Auckland Bangkok Bogotá Buenos Aires Calcutta
Cape Town Chennai Dar es Salaam Delhi Florence Hong Kong Istanbul
Karachi Kuala Lumpur Madrid Melbourne Mexico City Mumbai
Nairobi Paris São Paulo Singapore Taipei Tokyo Toronto Warsaw
and associated companies in Berlin Ibadan

Oxford is a registered trade mark of Oxford University Press
in the UK and certain other countries

Published in the United States
by Oxford University Press Inc., New York

British Library Cataloguing in Publication Data

Data available

Library of Congress Cataloging-in-Publication Data

Career frontiers: new conceptions of working lives/edited by Maury Peiperl . . . [et al.].
    p. cm.
Includes bibliographical references and index.
1. Career development. I. Peiperl, Maury.
HF5549.5.C35 C367 2000   331.7 21–dc21   99–045715
ISBN 0–19–829691–6
     0–19–829692–4 (pbk.)

1 3 5 7 9 10 8 6 4 2

Typeset by J&L Composition Ltd, Filey, North Yorkshire
Printed in Great Britain
on acid-free paper by
Biddles Ltd, Guildford & Kings Lynn

To the memory of a few great teachers
whose guidance and example helped to
shape our own careers

Arthur Amtower
Roger Brown
Daniel Levinson
Shelley Weston Stowe

PREFACE

The other evening, in an MBA course on managing change, one of our students was commenting on the downside of a very successful change case. The company in question had eliminated several layers of management and reorganized into a project-based structure in which no one had permanent assignments or titles. People were expected to become multi-skilled and to move around among different jobs. Productivity, flexibility, and innovation had all been greatly enhanced, and employees felt more empowered, efficient, and effective than ever before. Yet the second-year student, who must even then have been engaged in his own job search, responded with great concern in his voice: 'They have eliminated careers!'

What the student meant, of course, was that the company had eliminated vertical career paths. The widely accepted academic view that careers need not imply vertical mobility—such as Hall's definition of career as 'the individually perceived sequence of attitudes and behaviors associated with work-related experiences and activities over the span of a person's life'—was not in evidence. Nor was the more recent suggestion that 'boundaryless careers' should include crossing lines, rather than climbing ladders, within or between companies. To that student, and to many others, a career is still what you get when you join a firm, and if the firm has no 'careers' to offer, you don't join.

If elites like London Business School MBAs have not yet come around to the individual, 'protean' view of careers, then how much has really changed in the last twenty years, and how 'post-corporate' have careers really become? The implications of these questions, in both practical and theoretical terms, are substantial. They run all the way from the practice of work in corporations, including firms' obligations to employees, to the nature of an individual's working life, including what is and is not considered work, and from there all the way to the purpose and conduct of modern life itself.

In 1998 the Centre for Organisational Research at London Business School convened its first Career Realities Conference to explore the nature of careers, consider how and where they were changing, and analyze new and emergent career forms. A small group of careers researchers from around the world mingled with an interested set of human resource directors and career practitioners to discuss recent experience and thinking in the field. Drawing on a host of different disciplines, we presented and discussed empirical research, considered new concepts and theories, and attempted to build an international and comparative perspective while addressing themes relevant to both academic and practitioner audiences.

A longer-term purpose of the conference, now a biannual event, was to make London Business School and the Centre for Organisational Research the venue for an ongoing set of scholarly conversations about careers and career theory. We are fortunate to have been helped in this by the outstanding group of scholars who joined our conference, many of whom have contributed to this subsequent volume. The chapters included here combine some of the best-known names in careers with many newer ones, and with others from related fields. Here you will find represented researchers from six countries and at least as many disciplines: Psychology, Sociology, Organizational Behavior, Human Resource Management, Education, and Counseling, to name the most obvious. The study of careers is rich in its disciplinary anchors, and this book both draws from and speaks to many of them.

The book draws upon and extends a number of existing debates in the area of careers, the basic dimensions of which are laid out in Chapter 1. Its pages also contain the beginnings of several new dialogues, which we hope to see extended in future work. To this end, we envision not only a biannual conference but also future volumes, drawing upon an even more diverse set of contributors and ideas, to act as a kind of ongoing stream of conversations in career theory. We encourage the reader to join in those conversations in whatever way you choose. For example, all the authors in this volume would be pleased to hear comments on their work, and all are listed, with their contact details. Readers interested in the work of the Centre for Organisational Research at London Business School, including future conferences and other events, are encouraged to visit the Centre's web site (www.lbs.ac.uk/cor). Finally, there are a number of professional associations active in the study of careers; these include the Careers Division of the Academy of Management (www.aom.pace.edu) the European Association for Work and Organizational Psychology (ursus.jun.alaska.edu/lists/eawop.html), the Society for Industrial and Organizational Psychology (www.siop.org), the American Sociologial Association (depts.washington.edu/socmeth2), and the International Consortium for Executive Development Research (www.icedr.org/gpub.html).

Acknowledgements

This book was made possible, first and foremost, by the thoughtful and diligent work of our contributors, without whom it would not exist. We acknowledge their creativity, their openness to criticism, and in particular their willingness to engage with one another, a fact verified by the many cross references among chapters in this volume. We would also like to acknowledge the contributions of the following people, each of whom made one or more elements of the conference and/or the book possible: Jeanne Brett, Barbara Bryant, Florence Chan, Susan Cohen, Chris Earley, Laura Empson, Miriam Erez, Robert DeFillippi, Jennifer Georgia, Lynda Gratton, Gay Haskins, Veronica Hope Hailey, Brittany Jones, Toshihiro Kanai, Victoria Medvec, Phil Mirvis, David Musson, Rosemary Nixon, Ashly Pinnington, Angie Quest, Joyce Renney, Rosemary Robertson, Anthony Senior, Linda Stroh, Rose Trevelyan, Lidewey van der Sluis, Hilary Walford, and Paul Willman. Finally, we would like to thank the Centre for Management Development at London Business School and Korn/Ferry International, both of which helped to sponsor the conference, and the Economic and Social Research Council (UK) which has generously supported and continues to sponsor research in careers and related subjects in the Centre for Organisational Research at London Business School.

We hope you will find this volume useful and thought-provoking. If so, the contributing authors, and the others mentioned above, deserve most of the credit.

M. A. P.
M. B. A.
R. G.
T. M.

London, 1999

CONTENTS

LIST OF CONTRIBUTORS

José Luis Alvarez has a joint appointment in the departments of General Management and Organizational Behavior at IESE, International Graduate School of Management (Barcelona, Spain). His basic research theme has been managerial tasks and jobs. An earlier approach to this topic, started as his doctoral dissertation at Harvard University, was made through the Institutional School of Organizational Theory, which underlined the external restrictions to managerial discretion. He is currently working on a more micro-approach, provided by theories of action, which emphasizes a more active and tactical view of managerial activities, and more fluid notions of executive careers. He can be reached at alvarez@iese.edu.

Michael B. Arthur is Professor of Management at the Sawyer School of Management, Suffolk University, Boston. His books include the *Handbook of Career Theory* (1989), *The Boundaryless Career* (1996), and *The New Careers* (1999). He has contributed to both popular and scholarly journals on the subject of contemporary careers, and is presently engaged in exploring how career experiences stimulate both individual and collective learning. He has been a Visiting Professor at University of Warwick, UK, and University of Auckland, New Zealand, and is a continuing Visiting Professor at London Business School. Michael holds MBA and Ph.D. degrees from the School of Management at Cranfield University. He can be reached at marthur@ suffolk.edu.

Anne-Françoise Bailly-Bender is Assistant Professor of Human Resource Management at ESCEM, Graduate School of Management, Tours, France, and CNAM (Conservatoire des Arts et Métiers). A graduate of the ESSEC School of Management in Paris, she earned a Ph.D. in Human Resource Management at the Université Paris 1—Sorbonne in 1998, after a four-year working experience with a French bank. Her research interests are the new trends in career management and, more generally, the current changes in employment practices in companies. She also works on the impact of national cultures on management practices. She can be contacted at afbender@escem.fr.

Lotte Bailyn is the T. Wilson (1953) Professor of Management at MIT's Sloan School of Management. Her research deals with the interrelation between managerial practice and employee lives, and has dealt with such workplace innovations as telecommuting, flexible scheduling, family benefits, and work redesign. She is the author of *Living with Technology: Issues at Mid-Career* (1980), co-author of *Working with Careers* (1984), and, most recently, the author of *Breaking the Mold: Women, Men, and Time in the New Corporate World* (1993) and co-author of *Relinking Life and Work: Toward a Better Future* (1996). She can be reached at lbailyn@mit.edu.

Richard E. Boyatzis is a psychologist, Professor and Chair of the Department of Organizational Behavior at the Weatherhead School of Management, Case Western Reserve University. Formerly the president of McBer and Company, where his work focused on managerial competencies, his research since 1987 has been devoted to lifelong, adult, and competency development. His e-mail address is reb2@po.cwru.edu.

Loïc Cadin is Associate Professor at the École Supérieure de Commerce de Paris (ESCP). He holds a doctorate in management from ESSEC (Paris). Before becoming a full time professor he had different positions in the Human Resource Management function in several companies. His current research deals with careers and international comparisons of Human Research Management practices. He has also published on the topic of organizations and competency development. He recently contributed to a book edited by D. M. Rousseau and R. Schalk, *International Psychological Contracts* (1999) with a chapter entitled 'Does the Psychological Contract Theory work in France?' He can be reached at cadin@escp.fr.

Susan C. Eaton is an Assistant Professor of Public Policy at the John F. Kennedy School of Government at Harvard University in Cambridge, Mass. Her Ph.D. is from the Sloan School of Management, at MIT. Her research interests include service-sector work, careers and innovation, health-care work organization, work and family integration, labor–management relations, and gender. Eaton worked twelve years as an organizer, negotiator, educator, and top-level manager for the Service Employees International Union (SEIU), AFL-CIO, CLC. Her M. P. A. is from Harvard and her A. B. is from Harvard-Radcliffe. Contact: www.ksg.harvard.edu.

Martin Evans received his bachelor's and master's degrees from the University of Manchester (but met his co-authors only at Toronto!). He received a Ph.D. in 1968 in Administrative Sciences from Yale University. He is currently Professor of Organizational Behaviour at the Rotman School of Management at the University of Toronto (web site: http://www.mgmt.utoronto.ca/~evans/). He has been exploring issues in, around, and about organizations for more than thirty-five years. His most recent work, as well as examining career issues, includes an examination of the structure of IQ, the implications of evolutionary psychology for management, and the impact of downsizing. Recent publications include articles in *Managerial and Decision Economics*, *Academy of Management Executive*, and *Academy of Management Journal*. He has always been interested in methodology and causal inference and has published in these areas since 1969. He can be reached at evans@fmgmt.mgmt.utoronto.ca. and also recommends the Academy of Management Research Methods web page at http://www.aom. pace.edu/rmd.

Rob Goffee is Professor of Organisational Behaviour at London Business School. He has been Chair of the Organisational Behaviour Group, a Member of the Governing Body, and Director of several executive programs. His research interests include entrepreneurship, managerial careers, and cultural change. His most recent book is *The Character of a Corporation* with Gareth Jones (1998). His e-mail address is RGoffee@lbs.ac.uk.

Hugh Gunz trained as a chemist in New Zealand, and has Ph.D.s in both Chemistry and Organizational Behavior. His career started in the petro-chemical industry, and he has taught on the faculties of Manchester Business School and the University of Toronto. He has published papers on the careers of managers, professionals, and others, the management of technical professionals, and management education. He is the author of the book *Careers and Corporate Cultures* (1989). His research interests include the structure of managerial careers in and between organizations and their impact on firms' strategic management, the application of complexity science to careers, and ethical dilemmas experienced by employed professionals. His e-mail address is gunz@mgmt.utoronto.ca.

Michael Jalland is Associate Professor of Strategic Management at the University of Toronto. He has a Ph.D. in strategic management from the University of Manchester, based on studies of planning in multidivisional organizations. His recent research has examined the relationships between organizational career streams and strategies, which has resulted in contributions to books and publications in the *Academy of Management Review*, *Academy of Management Executive*, and *Advances in Strategic Management*. He can be reached at jalland@mgmt.utoronto.ca.

Candace Jones is an Assistant Professor of Organization Studies at the Carroll School of Management at Boston College. She received her Ph.D. from the University of Utah. Her research interests include inter-firm networks, project-based organizing, and careers, primarily in cultural industries and professional services. Her most recent publications include articles in *Organization Science*, *Academy of Management Review*, *Academy of Management Executive*, and *Industrielle Beziehungen*. She can be reached at jonescq@bc.edu.

Gareth Jones is the BT Professor of Organizational Development at Henley Management College and visiting Professor of Organizational Behavior at Insead. He is the author of books and articles dealing with organizational change, gender at work, and organizational culture. He is, with Rob Goffee, a founding partner of Creative Management Associates and works with a number of organizations that see creativity as a source of competitive advantage.

David A. Kolb is a learning theorist and Professor of Organizational Behavior at the Weatherhead School of Management, Case Western Reserve University. He is best known for his research in experiential learning and learning styles. His research continues to be focused on learning processes, including conversation, adaptation, and flexibility in learning. His e-mail address is dak5@po.cwru.edu.

Benyamin M. Bergmann Lichtenstein is Assistant Professor of Management and Entrepreneurship at the University of Hartford. Using metaphors from evolutionary biology and complexity theory, he has developed a four-stage model of non-linear dynamic change that emphasizes how increases in organizing capacity and performance can be achieved through self-organizing processes. His model has been applied to entrepreneurial stage transitions, organizational transformation, organizational learning, and career research. He is also exploring the validity of 'new' management paradigms, and how they can help improve organizational research as well as business and society at large. He can be reached at Benyamin@mail.hartford.edu.

Judi Marshall is Professor of Organizational Behaviour in the School of Management, University of Bath, UK. She started her academic career at UMIST, Manchester, UK, undertaking research on managerial job stress for her Ph.D. and publishing significantly in this field with Cary L. Cooper. She joined Bath University in 1978. Her main research interests since then have been women in management, organizational cultures, and career development. She has published two books on women in management: *Women Managers: Travellers in a Male World* (1984) and *Women Managers Moving On: Exploring Career and Life Choices* (1995). She has also contributed to research methodology through the development of self-reflective sense-making approaches and action-oriented inquiry practices. She is a member of the School of Management's Centre for Action Research in Professional Practice, and the Director of Studies for the M.Sc. in Responsibility and Business Practice. Her e-mail address is J.Marshall@bath.ac.uk.

Timothy Morris works in the Centre for Organisational Research, London Business School. His main research interest is in the management of professional service firms and he has published papers on promotion systems, profit sharing, the evaluation of professionals, and the management of change in these organizations. His current work focuses on three areas: knowledge management, particularly in consulting firms, the governance consequences of the partnership form of ownership, and career patterns of professional staff. He can be reached at Tmorris@lbs.ac.uk.

Nigel Nicholson is Professor of Organisational Behaviour at London Business School. His current work applying evolutionary psychology to business and management has been represented in a recent *Harvard Business Review* article, and is the subject of a forthcoming book. His current research falls in two main areas: personality and leadership, and risk and decision making in finance. He has published ten books and over 100 articles in these and other areas, including employee performance, careers, and organizational change. He has held visiting appointments at European and North American universities, and been honored with an award from the Academy of Management for his contribution to theory. He can be reached at NNicholson@lbs.ac.uk.

Polly Parker has worked as an educator, counselor, and career consultant. In recent postgraduate studies she developed a card-sort instrument to assess 'intelligent-career' behavior. This instrument has since been refined and applied extensively in practice. Her interests include a comparison of traditional and contemporary approaches to research and leadership coaching and development. She holds a Master of Philosophy degree from the University of Auckland and is currently enrolled in the University's Ph.D. program. Her thesis is entitled 'Career Communities: Organizing in Contemporary Work Arrangements'. She can be reached via e-mail at p.parker@auckland.ac.nz.

Maury A. Peiperl is Assistant Professor of Organisational Behaviour in the Centre for Organisational Research at London Business School. He holds a BSE in electrical engineering and computer science from Princeton and an MBA, AM in psychology, and Ph.D. in OB from Harvard. His work on careers has been published in *Academy of Management Review, Human Resource Management*, and *Organizational Dynamics*, among others. His current research includes an international longitudinal study of managerial careers, an analysis of the changing role of the CEO in Europe, and several theoretical and empirical papers on peer appraisal. Before entering academia he worked as a programmer and engineer at IBM, a Project Manager at Merrill Lynch Capital Markets, and a strategy consultant at LIEIK Partnership (UK). He has also been on the boards of several small, high-technology companies. His e-mail address is MPeiperl@lbs.ac.uk.

Véronique de Saint-Giniez is an Assistant Professor of Business and Economics at Marne-la-Vallée University. She received her Ph.D. in Human Resource Management from Aix-en-Provence University, France, and ESSEC Business School. Her research interests are in the areas of potential assessment and development and career development and dynamics.

1

Topics for Conversation: Career Themes Old and New

Maury A. Peiperl and Michael B. Arthur

The millennium is an opportune time to consider the concept of career—what it means, how it has evolved, and how it may be changing. A thousand years ago careers were largely left to the individual. With the exception of the church, the military, and to a lesser extent governments, few bureaucracies existed. Most people's work was closely tied to their family and community. And although there were no psychologists, sociologists, or careers researchers (that we know of) to report it, there was a certain work–life balance. That is, those 'working to live' so far outnumbered those 'living to work' that we can be reasonably assured that working lives and personal lives were in synch: they were part and parcel of each other. People were usually artisans, farmers, laborers, or domestic servants, their families were intertwined with their work, and their work was intertwined with their community.

It is surprising to see, given how different from this picture have been the past 150 years or so (at least in the West) that many in the careers field now seem to be envisioning a very similar picture for the future: individual, person-centered careers in balance with family and community, less dependent on large bureaucracies (Arthur and Rousseau 1996; Hall and Associates 1996). Clearly, much has changed in the last 1,000 years—infrastructure, longevity, standard of living, technology, and travel, to name a few—but human nature, for the most part, has not. And in the ongoing human struggle to grow and achieve, the individual may once again be emerging dominant. Contemporary ideas about the organizing of work, whether they emphasize dynamic inter-firm network arrangements (Handy 1989; Miles and Snow 1994) or decentralized, 'individualized' corporations (Ghoshal and Bartlett, 1997), rely on the individual's ability to learn and adapt rather than perform as required.

We are indebted to Candace Jones for helpful comments on an earlier version of this chapter.

Another marker of the passing millennium is the Magna Carta, the ground-ing document for individual liberty signed in England in the early thirteenth century. Since then, there have been eras of relative freedom and constraint. However, as we look ahead it appears that individual freedom may be ascending once more, as a function of changing political systems, the fall of communism, the rise of entrepreneurial and free-market ideals, and the (relative) decline of barriers in global communication and trade. The latest trend, at least for most members of the workforce, is freedom—for better or worse—from lifetime employment. It is possible that the mid-twentieth-century corporate career (Whyte 1956) with which so many of us grew up as a norm was in fact an anomaly in the larger history of human work.

Are we, then, in a 'post-bureaucratic' era? In one sense we are. However, in another sense we are not. There is an increasing complexity to work and careers that seems to indicate more than a simple shift back from bureau-cracies toward individuals. Rather, there appears to be a shift taking place, toward multiple mechanisms through which the coordination of careers comes about. It involves more dynamic, non-traditional forms of coordina-tion. It is a shift worthy of some conversation.

Is Career Theory Converging or Diverging?

The progression of a field of study, across both the natural and social sciences, typically occurs incrementally. Scholars at different points in the field focus their separate lenses on what are presumed to be the same phenomena, and their separate insights converge into a refined body of knowledge. Occasionally, however, the assumptions of all a field's partici-pants get called into question and a period of divergence emerges. Physical scientists went on for several centuries accepting Newton's theory of gravity before Einstein (and others) pointed out its limitations. Various other branches of science have recently been adjusting to evidence about non-linear systems their disciplines were unaccustomed to explain (Capra 1996). When divergence occurs, the nature of debate changes. The question of the state of career theory, and of whether it is characterized by convergence, is complicated by both the disciplines of study involved and the times in which we live.

The four principal fields contributing to career theory are Psychology, Sociology, Education, and Management. Each of these fields has traditionally experienced its own convergence around the constructs of personality, social structure, vocation, and the organization of work, respectively. Each field has also enjoyed a relatively long run of convergence, as the ideas of, for example, Freud (1953), Weber (1947), Strong (1943), and Barnard (1938) served as anchors for within-field refinements that followed. Each field has also played a largely complementary role to the others in what Galbraith (1971) called the 'industrial state' of the post-1945 era. Stable personalities were seen to give rise to enduring vocational choice; vocational choice was seen to occur in a relatively stable employment structure; organizations were seen as the mechanisms through which the employment structure attained largely pre-dictable economic productivity. There was a shared understanding about the way careers came about.

The emergence of what may be termed the 'new economy' (Arthur *et al.* 1999) has meant that the traditional convergence both within and between fields has broken down. Schein once warned of the price involved in 'mem-bers of each subset of (careers) researchers' not building theory 'on broad enough bases to be relevant to the academic community at large or to practitioners' (Schein 1986: 315). Writing some fifteen years later, we would reverse Schein's emphasis, from anti-fragmentation to cross-fertilization. The time for convergence has passed. What is most important now is to keep the academic community and practitioners in touch with one another, to keep the conversation alive, as we strain to build and share a new appre-ciation of what is going on.

Without convergence, though, what can be done to help hold the careers field together? If we cannot unify it, how can we better see the forces for changes that are at work, and the connections among those forces? At the outset, we can at least map the fault lines along which the rifts have appeared, and characterize the debates related to those rifts. Beyond this, we can encourage and participate in further debates that at a minimum will increase understanding and that, eventually, may cause some of the rifts to start to close.

Four Lines of Debate

We see four lines of debate, or contrasts, which frame the conversation about careers as we enter the twenty-first century. Some aspects of the debate reflect long-standing issues in the field of careers, while others derive from more recent developments, both theoretical and practical. The lines of debate are structure versus action, stasis versus adaptation, universalism versus particularism, and institutional knowledge versus indi-vidual knowledge. We set them out here in anticipation of the chapters that follow.

Structure versus action

To what extent are careers the product of established structures, versus that of individual actions? That is, do careers unfold primarily within structures, such as the institutional frameworks of governments, occupations, or employer companies? Or do careers largely enact their own paths, creating new structures as they go?

The structured view is fundamentally expressed in Weber's work on bureaucracy, offering an essentially static even if respectful view of employer institutions. Bureaucracies were administrative systems built upon the wisdom of experience. Bureaucracies were intended to emphasize 'precision, speed, clarity, regularity, reliability and efficiency achieved through the creation of a fixed division of tasks, hierarchical supervision, and detailed rules and regulations' (Morgan 1986: 25). The emergent structure of bureaucracies also provided a career system of progressively more responsible positions through which a person's career could progress. A similar view may be taken on the professions—like the crafts of earlier times—sustaining a relatively static and permanent place for themselves near the top of the occupational structure (Cipolla 1980). The professions, too, have long had levels of prestige that were assigned, much like bureaucracies, to indicate relative status among members.

A related and persistent twentieth-century theme concerns the concentration of power. Various arguments about the role of colonialism, central government, class, bureaucracy, and the corporate state (Galbraith 1971) each ascribed power to relatively few centralized organizations. These organizations in both public and private sectors were seen to be better at planning than their smaller counterparts, and entrusted to do that on society's behalf. As an extension of the bureaucratic principle, experience within such an organization became seen as a prerequisite for becoming a senior power-holder within it. Frequently, the routes to power were—and still are—overtly or covertly reserved for a limited number of 'high-potential' employees whose careers were nurtured through a series of experiences designed to prepare them for senior office (Derr *et al.* 1988). Other workers were left to join a lesser 'tournament' (Rosenbaum 1984) than the one played out by these elites as they vied for the very top positions in the hierarchy.

By contrast, action-based views of careers take individual action as the independent variable and structure as the dependent variable. A prominent example stems from humanistic psychology through the work of Maslow (1954) and his associates. The 'hierarchy of needs' offered a path to prospective 'self-actualization' where the person was seen to be psychologically beyond external influences on his or her behavior. The hierarchy provides a clear basis for an action-based view of the career, and various attempts have been made to use this basis in company settings. However, the attempts commonly missed much of the point. Self-actualization, it seemed, was available only through the work the company needed to have done (Shepard 1984). Ideas about self-actualization took greater hold in independent career advising outside any employment arena, although even there the working assumption was often that the person would need to adjust to existing employment opportunities.

A parallel sociological challenge to mainstream assumptions about career structures came somewhat earlier from Hughes and his colleagues at the University of Chicago. They saw career behavior in unconventional terms, spanning work and non-work, and eschewed formal organizations and upward mobility within them as principal constructs in their inquiries (Hughes 1958). Careers were the paths through which people's subjective selves met the outside world, and drew coherence from it. However, the influence between structure and action was seen as two-way, with careers having a recursive role in the shaping of institutions. Careers were seen 'to provide access to the empirical relation between social action and social structure' (Barley 1989: 52). A link may be drawn to subsequent ideas on structuration (Giddens 1984)—that is, on 'how specific institutions are maintained or altered by careers' capacities to organize the sequence and meaning of people's lives' (Barley 1989: 53–4).

Various stage-based views of career may also be seen to mediate between structure and action. Inspired by the work of both psychologists and sociologists, the general idea was that people's career behavior predictably altered according to their emergent career stage. Original models tended to follow 'life-stage' thinking fairly closely, suggesting there was a time for career experimentation, advancement, maturity, and even decline. Later versions allowed more variance in when the stages occurred and how many of them a person might experience, in turn allowing for more variation in the nature of people's careers (Dalton and Thompson 1986; Super 1992). Stage-based views suggested cohort effects, including generational and inter-generational effects, upon society and its employment institutions through which careers unfold.

Much recent work has been inspired by the 'organizational-career' approach initiated in the mid-1970s (Hall 1976; Van Maanen 1977). The approach set out to explore the nuances of individual career experiences as they evolved within a single organizational setting, and how those experiences could be improved for mutual benefit. It has led to the emergence of considerable literatures on, among other topics, socialization, mentoring, dual-career paths, accommodation of diversity, the interplay of work and family, and the utility of 'career anchors' intended to connect organizational and individual needs (Sullivan 1999). Although the original work on organizational careers was careful to downplay orthodox assumptions about hierarchy and upward progression, much of the later work in the field has not followed that lead. In the process, the later work has tended to subordinate ideas about action to structural constraints.

In direct contrast to the organizational-career perspective stands that of the 'boundaryless career' (Arthur and Rousseau 1996). The boundaryless-career perspective can be used as a platform to explore prospective losses that a lack of structure entails, such as the demise of a 'civil society' delivered largely through the workplace (Perrow 1996). However, most work from this perspective emphasizes an action-based view. The definition of boundaryless careers as 'sequences of job opportunities that go beyond the boundaries of single employment settings' (DeFillippi and Arthur 1994: 307) places the ownership of careers primarily in the hands of individual actors rather than institutions. Much boundaryless theory goes further, characterizing this approach as strongly positive, suggesting that, in a complex world of often-shifting work arrangements, it is a good thing for everyone to take ownership of his or her own career.

Critics of the boundaryless approach ask to what extent individuals' careers really do transcend boundaries, particularly those of work organizations. Instability has affected many careers, but it is not clear how much overall patterns of inter-firm mobility have changed. Nor is it clear whether the experiencing of boundaryless careers makes their owners better off (Hirsch and Shanley 1996). What is clear is that very large firms still dominate many industries and often operate from an 'organizational-career' perspective, attempting to determine career options within their own employment structures, even though those structures may be changing (Gratton and Hope Hailey 1999).

A recent approach linking organizational-career and boundaryless-career principles concerns the enactment of careers (Weick 1996). The enactment perspective on careers begins with the observation that organizational structures are 'weakening', and in turn traditional career paths are becoming less reliable. People are encouraged to act on the ambiguity they experience, to engage in self-organizing, to exercise agency on their own, and to build community with others, leading in turn to new structural effects. Thus 'boundaryless careers in boundaryless organizations shape one other' (Weick 1996: 42) in an interplay of structure and action that begins to take us beyond the basic dichotomy between them. The enactment perspective offers a new approach to appreciating the way careers both shape and are shaped by the economic institutions of our time (Arthur *et al.* 1999).

The boundaryless career and enactment perspectives play down the importance of host structures for people's careers. However, in doing so they suggest a new role for structures—that is, for their role in the *processes* through which careers unfold. This brings us to our next dichotomy.

Stasis versus adaptation

Related to the structure-versus-action perspective, this next dichotomy refers to how much the world of careers is presumed to stay the same rather than change. This can apply to individuals, particular jobs, or entire firms, occupations, industries, or networks.

Freud and his followers saw the structure of the mind—the psyche—as essentially complete by the time adulthood was reached, and conveniently static over the years of work to follow. Thus, we find from the early to mid-twentieth century a set of models and instruments designed to match people with certain characteristics to jobs and career paths in well-defined places.

The Strong Interest Inventory (Hansen 1992), Holland's (1985) theory of vocational choices, and a range of related approaches all seek to match people's personalities to the world of occupations, and to provide appropriate counseling for job-seekers (Osipow 1990). Schein's (1978, 1996) theory of 'career anchors' attempts something similar after the early years of work experience. Although the matching approach has been questioned in recent years (Brown and Brooks 1996), it remains popular. When it is applied, static assumptions prevail on both sides of the matching exercise—about the person and about the world of work.

We have already mentioned the Weberian view of bureaucracy, suggesting both a firmly structured and a largely static employment unit. This in turn was embedded in our larger notions of 'the organizational society', viewed as a collection of efficient bureaucracies with similar features. The organization, of course, hosted a variety of different functions and within them a variety of occupational positions, providing an appropriately static counterpoint to the static view of the psyche. A further aspect of this, at least for a while, was to view all employer organizations as essentially similar. This was the spirit of the landmark 'Aston studies', which focused on what was common across multiple organizations, rather than on what may be different (Starbuck 1993). In turn, the field of 'Organization Behavior' evolved largely with a single stereotype of what the organization was, or what it ought to be. It may be argued that this way of thinking prevailed up to and through the widely popularized search for company 'excellence' (Peters and Waterman 1982) and for ideal careers within such a company.

However, the so-called 'search for excellence' was also influenced by more adaptive views, including sociological views concerned about 'organic' rather than 'mechanistic' organizational forms (Burns and Stalker 1961). There soon emerged the notion of the 'self-designing organization,' explicitly intended for adaptability rather than stasis, and for survival in a changing, innovation-driven world (Hedberg *et al.* 1976). If one pushed the point, it could be seen that organizations designed for uncertainty called for careers designed for uncertainty too (Weick and Berlinger 1989). Yet the idea ran against the popularity of 'job security' as a fundamental company benefit, so that in practice career adaptation was often practiced after the fact of company adaptation—through downsizing, restructuring, merging, or receivership—and seen as a painful exception to the job-stability norm (Leana and Feldman 1992). Many people still view career adaptation that way.

Another way to mediate between stasis and adaptation is to think in terms of different company types, and of different kinds of career systems within them. For example, Sonnenfeld and Peiperl (1988) follow a popular typology of company strategies to evolve a matching typology of career systems—fortresses, clubs, academies, and baseball teams—with different levels of readiness for adaptation and inter-firm mobility. Gunz, Jalland, and Evans (1998) offer a typology of career streams—command-centered, constitutional, and evolutionary—stemming from experiences involving increased accountability, diversity of experience, and entrepreneurial opportunities respectively. The focus of research into such typologies is essentially to generate contingency theories of career systems, aimed at getting beyond 'one best practice' models to provide more practical approaches to firms and individuals with different attributes.

Stage-based models of company development are another way of trying to accommodate static-versus-adaptive views about careers and employment. Some models are directly predictive of sequences of phases and challenges companies will face, from early innovation to late maturity, and look distinctly like the career-stage models cited earlier (Quinn and Campbell 1983). However, other models are open to differences, simply saying that 'punctuated equilibrium' is the norm, for careers and companies as well as for work groups and larger social arrangements, because equilibrium sustains its own resistance to change and in turn change happens suddenly and sharply when it occurs (Romanelli and Tushman 1994). One of the quandaries of the careers field is whether we are approaching some new form of equilibrium, in which work arrangements, although far greater in variety than in previous eras, are none the less 'settling down'. Are individuals and firms working out new arrangements for a new era, or are we witnessing a shift toward a permanently more adaptive employment arena?

Another approach related to the above is the study of career transitions—that is, the punctuation of careers as they unfold. Transitions involve both individual transformation to accommodate the demands of a new role, and role development to accommodate the uniqueness of the person (Nicholson 1984). It has been observed that organizations often miss the adaptation opportunities that transitions offer, and in particular the opportunities from inter-company transitions, upon which most companies may be ill-equipped to capitalize (Nicholson and West 1989). However, the more dynamic employment picture of recent times, as well as new arguments about the benefits of inter-firm mobility in concentrated industry regions (Saxenian 1996) suggest good reason to re-examine this observation.

Recently, increased attention has been given to what may fall between transitions—namely, the projects that seem increasingly to define the contemporary workplace. Projects—for example, in construction, software writing, management consulting, new product development, and research—provide temporary structures to accommodate individual action. In an extreme example, a company is little more than the projects its career actors are presently pursuing (Gould 1994). In other cases—for example, in independent film-making—projects provide intermediate structures between the career actor and the host industry, and the company is a temporary and legal convenience that gets disbanded on project completion (DeFillippi and Arthur 1998).

Part of the debate comes back to human nature, and the capacity of people for change. Despite increased attention to the lifelong development of individuals and the growing evidence in favor of more adaptive forms of company, we still see many company leaders and their advisers making assumptions that people long used to the old career structures cannot successfully make the transition to new ones. Is this merely unenlightened thinking, or are some individuals and firms constitutionally or situationally less adaptive than others? This kind of question leads us to our third dichotomy, about how broadly applicable career theory can be.

Universalism versus particularism

A common thread to both structural and static approaches to career is their emphasis on the search for or assumption of universal truths, about both people and institutions. This reflects, in large part, social science's traditional reliance on the physical sciences for both inspiration and legitimacy. However, that reliance is being increasingly questioned.

A universalist standpoint relates to much of what has been said about both structural and static views of career. The simple argument is that organizations and people are the same the world over; that we can probe ever more deeply for nuances that we did not appreciate before. If there are multiple organizational or career types, these can be catalogued and their differences understood. Observations accumulate into an 'orthodox consensus' (Atkinson 1971) about the world of employment. A 'functional' mindset prevails, and the point of careers is to contribute to what is functional—that is, to serve the employing institution on behalf of the greater economic good (Clegg and Hardy 1996a). Being at the frontier of careers research, from this standpoint, means promoting careers that help a company or institution to function better.

The universalist thesis is very much supported by what has been termed 'normal science' (Burrell 1996), derived from the traditional approach to the study of the physical sciences. It is a science concerned with the search for universal truths, and for uncovering them through the testing of formal hypotheses, clear distinction between independent and dependent variables, the control of intervening variables, insistence on reliability and replicability, and the gradual accumulation and refinement of the overall body of knowledge as a collection of enduring cause–effect relationships. Readers will recognize that normal science has been the principal inspiration for the social and behavioral sciences, even if that inspiration holds a little less sway than it did.

The social-science derivative of normal science is deeply ingrained in recommendations for social-research inquiry (Campbell and Stanley 1966; Kerlinger 1986). Careers research has typically deferred to the universalist position, even if most authors hastily point out that the generalizability of their findings is limited by sample size or demographics, lack of a longitudinal database, or the possible (although undocumented) presence of unexplored moderating variables. For example, a universalist approach might look for accumulating evidence about the relationship between people's 'career anchors', the jobs the people perform, and the company performance ratings that result. The idea would be to apply the concept of career anchors more effectively in promoting superior company performance.

Two branches of alternative social science take particular aim at normal science. One is critical theory, which seeks to reveal 'structures and processes of power and domination hidden in the legitimate and taken-for-granted aspects of our social world' (Clegg and Hardy 1996b: 12). As such, it challenges what many career writers see as a universal and benevolent career system. Critical theory also goes further by challenging the worker's consent toward the established career system. New, less confining employment and career systems are seen to be more urgently needed than equal opportunity within existing systems (Alvesson and Deetz 1996).

A related branch of alternative social science is postmodernism, where 'modern' may be loosely seen as the ideal form of the 'industrial state' introduced earlier. Postmodernism emphasizes what is local and idiosyncratic to the players involved, rather than what is generalizable. Like the Chicago School before them, proponents of postmodernism emphasize the subjective self, and its interdependence with the host environment. However, rather than affirming a role for institutions, postmodern ideas offer 'a celebration of multiple perspectives and a carnival of positions and structurings' (Alvesson and Deetz 1996: 195). The threads of individual careers are seen as the cause of any apparently broader tapestry, and the grounding principles behind mainstream vocational guidance practice are considered suspect (Young et al. 1996).

Although it came about largely independently, there is an another alternative model emerging from the natural sciences, sometimes called new science, which brings a new respectability to ideas about interdependence. New ideas in physics, biology, and chemistry propose a more holistic understanding of systems—such as weather systems, the cells of the body, and DNA systems—involving 'an entirely new landscape of connections, of phenomena that cannot be reduced to simple cause and effect, and of the constant flux of dynamic processes' (Wheatley 1992: 9). By analogy, the universal 'hidden order' (Holland 1995) of an employment system may be seen to stem from the behavior over time of the system's people—that is, from the particulars of people's individual careers—in a fashion too complex to be understood, much less predicted, by deterministic models.

The hidden order behind prevailing employment systems may also be linked to the influence of personal networks. It has long been understood that personal networks can make a difference to people's job-search activities, and thereby to the distribution of who fills what institutional role. However, a more particular interpretation extends to seeing how the nature of a person's networks—the range of ties, their frequency, and their duration—influence his or her ability to acquire a repertory of role models and opportunities for experimentation. Drawing from the accumulating repertory in turn leads to internalization of new roles, identity development, and reputation building through the person's unfolding career (Ibarra 1999).

Both universalist and particularist approaches have proved popular in careers research. Yet they have coexisted, in general, somewhat uncomfortably, reflecting perhaps the nature of the traditional difference between the academic theorist searching for general principles and the practitioner searching for a solution to a particular problem. The current dichotomy is sharpened by the fact that many academics too—perhaps more than in recent decades—now once again see particularist approaches as important to an understanding of career phenomena. This may be partly because the distinction between universal and particular interpretations has a bearing on the way we see knowledge. To what extent does knowledge reside in the person rather than in more aggregate forms of organization, such as the employer companies through which careers come about? Or, to what extent is company knowledge affected by the career flows of people across its boundaries? We turn to our last distinction.

Institutional knowledge versus individual knowledge

A legacy of all three of the above distinctions, one way or another, is our view of knowledge. Structural, static, and universal views tend to support one another in suggesting that knowledge can be explored as a feature of institutions. Action-centered, adaptive, and particular views see knowledge as more explicitly residing in the individual. Both sets of views raise the question of what is knowledge, and what purpose does it serve in the unfolding of contemporary careers.

A traditional view sees knowledge as explicit, codified, and subdivided by specialization. This view underlies the evolution of the professions, and their role in people's careers. Those in the professions—accountants, doctors, lawyers, psychologists, and many others—have always claimed jurisdiction over expert knowledge in return for privileged status in society. The claim underlies the wider process of professionalization, in which groups of career actors press similar claims to knowledge and seek special recognition in return (Freidson 1986). The same kind of bargain was alive in the early craft unions, and survives, with varying levels of comfort, in the modern-day trade union. The professional or occupational association makes a central claim over both people's career investments and the institutionalization of knowledge.

The traditional approach of the company, abetted by formal job arrangements, is to recruit professional or occupational knowledge into one of its functional 'stovepipes' for accountants, engineers, production specialists, and the like. In this way the company defers to occupational associations in determining what knowledge is important and how it is to be recognized. Once recruited, however, the person also accumulates company-specific knowledge from the work he or she performs, and from interactions with others inside and outside his or her specialization. A further emphasis may be placed on company knowledge when 'organizational careers' provide opportunities for cross-functional transfer to occur, and with it the exchange of information in the company at large. Many companies would claim to have internal career systems designed to encourage just this kind of learning (Hall and Associates 1986).

The picture so far is one of explicit knowledge that can be codified, built into the job specifications that make up a career system, and directly communicated. However, careers also commonly involve a tacit learning component where people—analogously to Polanyi's (1966) classic examples of people who have learned to swim or to ride a bike—are unable to directly explain what they know to others. One of the tensions in the organizational-careers-versus-boundaryless-careers debate concerns how useful this tacit knowledge is within the company, as opposed to beyond it. Complicating the debate is the question of shared knowledge, and how much of this may also be tacit, in the sense that it is mutually understood but never expressed (Bird 1996).

The notion of shared knowledge brings with it the recently popular idea of organizational learning (Cohen and Sproul 1996). It is easy to appreciate that careers are the conduits for this kind of learning as people interact over time. It is more difficult to grasp what the relationship between individual career learning and collective organizational learning really is. A popular view sees organizational learning through cycles of tacit-to-explicit knowledge accumulation, as workers engage with and solve problems and in turn become able to explain what they learned (Nonaka and Takeuchi 1995). However, most such views tend not to be explicit about career implications, and in turn about where the learning goes and how it helps the individual as further learning cycles unfold.

In particular, most treatments of organizational learning neglect the role of career mobility in both intra- and inter-company learning possibilities. This neglect seems problematic in the contemporary era, with its image of *employability* security rather than employment security, and the widespread exhortation that people ought to accumulate knowledge and manage their careers to provide for transferability between companies. The issue for companies is to become better at knowledge capture, to take greater advantage of new knowledge when recruits come in, as well as to retain knowledge when leavers move on. Some of the major management consulting companies, with their traditions of high consultant turnover, are trying hardest to solve the knowledge-capture problem, but so far it seems with limited success.

Organizations are not the only institutions that learn, and an argument may be made that other kinds of institutions, notably the institutions of occupations and whole industries, learn faster when mobility is relatively high. Porter (1990) argues that industry regions sustain themselves through knowledge flows among adjacent firms, whether through employment mobility or networking among proximate personnel, providing a 'regional advantage' from which most participant firms can benefit. California's Silicon Valley is one well-known exemplar of that argument (Saxenian 1996). However, it remains relatively rare for employers to celebrate this kind of inter-firm mobility, and many companies' employment benefits still discriminate against it through pension vesting and vacation-time arrangements (Lucero and Allen 1994).

A final issue in the arena of institutional knowledge versus individual knowledge concerns the role of networks. Most discussion of innovation sees it as a function of the firm (Utterback 1994), or sometimes as a function of inter-firm collaboration (Gomez-Mejia and Lawless 1995). However, recent ideas and evidence are pointing to the role of interpersonal networks in contributing to overall patterns of industry innovation (Powell 1998). These are networks that people accumulate during the course of their careers, and that remain available even as the career unfolds across alternative firms, or into self-employment. Whatever their institutional provenance, they are individually held sets of knowledge and relationships, which are largely non-transferable.

In some respects this dichotomy raises issues from economics, such as how to value labor when labor itself contributes to the human capital people and firms can possess (Quinn 1992). Firms investing in large-scale, knowledge-capturing systems are implicitly taking one view, and firms (or individuals) relying on individuals to use their own knowledge are taking another view. The question for both firms and individuals is what kind of work arrangements to seek, and over what kind of term.

Looking Ahead from Here

The chapters that follow explore these contrasts, and a few others, in some depth. This book is organized into three parts, each with a brief preview, and the four debates we have outlined run through each part. There is no simple relationship between any chapter and any one debate, but rather an unfolding of insight across all four debates as the book unfolds. Thus, the connections between the debates and the chapters indicated below are illustrative rather than exclusive.

Part I, 'Career Theory: Where do We Go from Here?', delves further into the question of how best to model and conduct research on careers in an increasingly complex world. Hugh Gunz, Martin Evans, and Michael Jalland consider the structure-versus-action issue in their observations on the nature of boundaries, and show how one professional labor market seems, at the least, very sticky. Nigel Nicholson speaks to stasis versus adaptation in his model of individual drivers, selection decisions, and career behavior based on evolutionary psychology, which suggests that long-standing human attributes and some of the traditional structures that derive from them will continue to have their effect. Richard Boyatzis and David Kolb construct a 'three-mode' growth and learning theory that gives us a new lens with which to understand work behavior and career motivation. Finally, Polly Parker and Michael Arthur illustrate a methodology for eliciting the subjective career and propose ten types of 'career community' through which people can self-organize around mutual interests.

Part II, 'Knowledge Workers: Professionals in the Post-Corporate Age', moves from models to protagonists. Although all authors speak to the contrast between institutional and individual knowledge, they also address other debates. José Luis Alvarez summarizes the stream of sociological research on managerial action and shows how this may be used to characterize the structuring of careers in idiosyncratic ways. Timothy Morris shows how a near-universal up-or-out model of promotion in professional service firms is misaligned with the idea of firm-specific knowledge, as well as with the desire among younger and dual-career professionals to balance work and family. Candace Jones and Benyamin Lichtenstein use the choices made by partners in architectural firms to define alternative 'dominant logics' behind company adaptation and link these to partners' career competencies. Finally, Susan Eaton and Lotte Bailyn use examples from the US biopharmaceuticals industry to show how particular work factors interact with broader social settings to create complex and often fluid careers.

Part III, 'Work and Non-Work, Boundaries and Cultures', considers the contexts in which careers unfold. Judi Marshall uses selected narratives from women managers who have been through career transitions or re-evaluations to show how choices are made within complex contexts, and extends the concept of career beyond work to incorporate the broader scope of individual lives. Loïc Cadin, Anne-Françoise Bailly-Bender, and Véronique de Saint-Giniez give us a model of five different types of career actors, derived from interviews and experience in what is reported as a relatively static French employment context. Finally, Rob Goffee and Gareth Jones delineate the relatively universal implications of four different corporate contexts for the evolution and management of careers within work organizations.

Whatever their place in the organization of this book, all the chapters take an independent approach to the topic of careers, and all engage the underlying questions of how careers evolve, and how better to study and understand them. In addition, all the chapters make reference to one another in genuinely open conversation—a continuation of the conference in which most of the authors participated as a microcosm of the careers field. Although we can claim no comprehensive coverage of all the important topics relating to careers, we believe the conversations contained here provide new insights and connections about key issues in our field.

In a recent Harvard Business Review article entitled 'Managing Oneself' management sage Peter Drucker (1999) reflects on the importance of career actors learning from others through 'feedback analysis'. Although it may sound cutting edge, this approach was apparently invented in the fourteenth century by an obscure German theologian and later adopted by John Calvin and Ignatius Loyola, founders of the Calvinist Church and Jesuit Order, respectively. In turn, feedback analysis is reported to have been behind the emergent domination of those two institutions over Europe in the thirty years that followed. The way in which this occurred suggests an interplay across all four of the contrasts suggested in this chapter. The approach worked within the structure of the two host institutions to encourage more effective individual action. Despite the static traditions of religious institutions and their hierarchies, the feedback system led to rapid large-scale adaptation. In addition, the universal beliefs of the two institutions promoted particular investments in personal career behavior. And, finally, institutional knowledge was apparently nurtured from the seedlings of individual knowledge that were generated.

It looks as if the framework for our suggested conversation has been around for a long time, and has been useful before in linking theory and practice. We trust it will be useful again.

References

Alvesson, M., and Deetz, S. (1996), 'Critical Theory and Postmodernism Approaches to Organizational Studies', in S. R. Clegg, C. Hardy, and W. R. Nord (eds.), *Handbook of Organization Studies* (London: Sage).

Arthur, M. B., and Rousseau, D. M. (1996) (eds.), *The Boundaryless Career: A New Employment Principle for a New Organizational Era* (New York: Oxford University Press).

—— Hall, D. T., and Lawrence, B. S. (1989) (eds.), *Handbook of Career Theory* (New York: Cambridge University Press).

—— Inkson, K., and Pringle, J. K. (1999), *The New Careers: Individual Action and Economic Change* (London: Sage).

Atkinson, M. (1971), *Orthodox Consensus and Radical Alternative: A Study in Sociological Theory* (London: Heinemann).

Baker, P. L. (1993), 'Chaos, Order and Sociological Theory', *Sociological Inquiry,* 63/2: 123–49.

Barley, S. R. (1989), 'Careers, Identities, and Institutions: The Legacy of the Chicago School of Sociology', in M. B. Arthur, D. T. Hall, and B. S. Lawrence (eds.), *Handbook of Career Theory* (New York: Cambridge University Press).

Barnard, C. (1938), *The Functions of the Executive* (Cambridge, Mass.: Harvard University Press).

Bird, A. (1996), 'Careers as Repositories of Knowledge', in M. B. Arthur and D. M. Rousseau (eds.), *The Boundaryless Career: A New Employment Principle for a New Organizational Era* (New York: Oxford University Press).

Brown, D., and Brooks, L. (1996), 'Introduction to Theories of Career Development and Choice: Origins, Evolution and Current Efforts', in D. Brown and L. Brooks (eds.), *Career Choice and Development* (3rd edn., San Francisco: Jossey-Bass).

Burns, T., and Stalker, G. M. (1961), *The Management of Innovation* (London: Tavistock).

Burrell, G. (1996), 'Normal Science, Metaphors, Discourses and Genealogies of Analysis', in S. R. Clegg, C. Hardy, and W. R. Nord (eds.), *Handbook of Organization Studies* (London: Sage).

Campbell, D. T., and Stanley, J. C. (1966), *Experimental and Quasi-Experimental Designs for Research* (Chicago: Rand McNally).

Capra, F. (1996), *The Web of Life* (New York: Anchor Books).

Cipolla, C. M. (1980), *Before the Industrial Revolution: European Society and Economy, 1000–1700* (2nd edn., New York: Norton).

Clegg, S. R., and Hardy, C. (1996a), 'Conclusion: Representations', in S. R. Clegg, C. Hardy and W. R. Nord (eds.), *Handbook of Organization Studies* (London: Sage).

—— —— (1996b), 'Organizations, Organization and Organizing', in S. R. Clegg, C. Hardy, and W. R. Nord (eds.), *Handbook of Organization Studies* (London, Sage).

Cohen, M. D., and Sproul, L. S. (1996), *Organizational Learning* (Thousand Oaks, Calif.: Sage).

Dalton, G., and Thompson, P. (1986), *Novations: Strategies for Career Development* (Glenview, Ill.: Scott Foresman).

DeFillippi, R. J., and Arthur, M. B. (1994), 'The Boundaryless Career: A Competency-Based Perspective', *Journal of Organizational Behavior*, 15: 307–24.

—— —— (1996), 'Boundaryless Contexts and Careers: A Competency-Based Perspective', in M. B. Arthur and D. M. Rousseau (eds.), *The Boundaryless Career: A New Employment Principle for a New Organizational Era* (New York: Oxford University Press).

—— —— (1998), 'Paradox in Project-Based Enterprise: The Case of Film Making', *California Management Review*, 40/2: 125–39.

Derr, C. B., Jones, C., and Toomey, E. L. (1988), 'Managing High-Potential Employees: Current Practices in 33 US Corporations', *Human Resource Management*, 27/3: 273–90.

Drucker, P. F. (1999), 'Managing Oneself', *Harvard Business Review*, 77/2: 64–74.

Freidson, E. (1986), *Professional Powers* (Chicago: University of Chicago Press).

Freud, S. (1953), *The Complete Psychological Works of Sigmund Freud* (London: Hogarth Press).

Galbraith, J. K. (1971), *The New Industrial State* (2nd edn., New York: Houghton Mifflin).

Ghoshal, S., and Bartlett, C.A. (1997), *The Individualized Corporation: A Fundamentally New Approach to Management* (London: Heinemann).

Giddens, A. (1984), *The Constitution of Society* (Berkeley and Los Angeles: University of California Press).

Gomez-Mejia, L. R., and Lawless, M. W. (1995) (eds.), *Advances in Global High Technology Management: Strategic Alliances in High Technology* (Greenwich, Conn.: JAI Press).

Gould, M. (1994), *Revolution at Oticon A/S (A and B cases)* (Lausanne, Switzerland: Institute for Management Development).

Gratton, L., and Hope Hailey, V. (1999), 'The Rhetoric and Reality of "New Careers"', in L. Gratton, V. Hope Hailey, P. Stiles, and C. Truss, *Strategic Human Resource Management* (Oxford: Oxford University Press).

Gunz, H. P., Jalland, M., and Evans, M. G. (1998), 'New Strategies, Wrong Managers? What you Need to Know about Career Streams', *Academy of Management Executive*, 12/2: 21–37.

Hall, D. T. (1976), *Careers in Organizations* (Santa Monica, Calif.: Goodyear).

—— and Associates (1986), *Career Development in Organizations* (San Francisco: Jossey-Bass).

—— and Associates (1996), *The Career is Dead: Long Live the Career* (San Francisco: Jossey-Bass).

Handy, C. (1989), *The Age of Unreason* (Boston: Harvard Business School Press).

Hansen, J. C. (1992), *User's Guide for the Strong Interest Inventory* (rev. edn., Stanford, Calif.: Stanford University Press).

Hedberg, B. L. T., Nystrom, P. C., and Starbuck, W. H. (1976), 'Camping on Seesaws: Prescriptions for a Self-Designing Organization', *Administrative Science Quarterly*, 21: 41–65.

Hirsch, P. M., and Shanley, M. (1996), 'The Rhetoric of Boundaryless—or How the Newly Empowered Managerial Class Bought into its own Marginalization', in M. B. Arthur, and D. M. Rousseau (eds.), *The Boundaryless Career: A New Employment Principle for a New Organizational Era* (New York, Oxford University Press).

Holland, J. L. (1985), *Making Vocational Choices: A Theory of Vocational Personalities and Work Environments* (2nd edn., Englewood Cliffs, NJ: Prentice Hall).

Holland, J. H. (1995), *Hidden Order: How Adaptation Builds Complexity* (Reading, Mass.: Addison-Wesley).

Hughes, E. C. (1958), *Men and their Work* (Glencoe, Ill.: Free Press).

Ibarra, H. (1999), 'Professional Selves: Experimenting with Image and Identity in Professional Adaptation', working paper, Harvard Business School.

Kerlinger, F. N. (1986), *Foundations of Behavioral Research* (3rd edn., New York: Holt, Rinehart & Wilson).

Leana, C. R., and Feldman, D. C. (1992), *Coping with Job Loss* (New York: Lexington Books).

Lucero, M. A., and Allen, R. E. (1994), 'Employee Benefits: A Growing Source of Psychological Contract Violations', *Human Resource Management*, 33: 425–46.

Miles, R. E., and Snow, C. C. (1994), *Fit, Failure and the Hall of Fame: How Companies Succeed or Fail* (New York: Free Press).

Maslow, A. H. (1954), *Motivation and Personality* (New York: Harper & Row).

Morgan, G. (1986), *Images of Organization* (Beverly Hills, Calif.: Sage).

Nicholson, N. (1984), 'A Theory of Work Role Transitions', *Administrative Science Quarterly*, 29: 172–91.

—— and West, M. (1989), 'Transitions, Work Histories, and Careers', in M. B. Arthur, D. T. Hall, and B. S. Lawrence (eds.), *Handbook of Career Theory* (New York: Cambridge University Press).

Nonaka, I., and Takeuchi, H. (1995), *The Knowledge-Creating Company* (New York: Oxford University Press).

Osipow, S. H. (1990), 'Convergence in Theories of Career Choice and Development', *Journal of Vocational Behavior*, 36: 122–31.

Peiperl, M., and Baruch, Y. (1997), 'Back to Square Zero: The Post-Corporate Career', *Organizational Dynamics* (Spring), 7–22.

Perrow, C. (1996), 'The Bounded Career and the Demise of Civil Society', in M. B.

Arthur and D. M. Rousseau (eds.), *The Boundaryless Career: A New Employment Principle for a New Organizational Era* (New York: Oxford University Press).

Peters, T. J., and Waterman, R. H. (1982), *In Search of Excellence* (New York: Harper & Row).

Polanyi, M. (1966), *The Tacit Dimension* (London: Routledge & Kegan Paul).

Porter, M. E. (1990), *The Competitive Advantage of Nations* (New York: Free Press).

Powell, W. W. (1998), 'Learning from Collaboration: Knowledge and Networks in the Biotechnology and Pharmaceutical Industries', *California Management Review*, 40/3: 228–40.

Quinn, J. B. (1992), *Intelligent Enterprise* (New York: Free Press).

Quinn, R. E., and Campbell, K. (1983), 'Organizational Life Cycles and Shifting Criteria of Effectiveness: Some Preliminary Evidence', *Management Science*, 29/1: 33–51.

Rosenbaum, J. E. (1984), *Career Mobility in a Corporate Hierarchy* (New York: Academic Press).

Romanelli, E., and Tushman, M. L. (1994), 'Organizational Transformation and Punctuated Equilibrium: an Empirical Test', *Academy of Management Journal*, 37/5: 1141–66.

Saxenian, A. L. (1996), 'Beyond Boundaries: Open Labor Markets and Learning in Silicon Valley', in M. B. Arthur and D. M. Rousseau (eds.), *The Boundaryless Career: A New Employment Principle for a New Organizational Era* (New York: Oxford University Press).

Schein, E. H. (1978), *Career Dynamics: Matching Individual and Organizational Needs* (Reading, Mass.: Addison-Wesley).

—— (1986), 'A Critical Look at Current Career Theory and Research', in D. T. Hall and Associates, *Career Development in Organizations* (San Francisco: Jossey-Bass).

—— (1996), 'Career Anchors Revised: Implications for Career Development in the 21st Century', *Academy of Management Executive* 10/4: 80–8.

Shepard, H. A. (1984), 'On the Realization of Human Potential: A Path with Heart', in M. B. Arthur, L. Bailyn, D. J. Levinson, and H. A. Shepard, *Working with Careers* (New York: Columbia University Graduate School of Business).

Sonnenfeld, J. A., and Peiperl, M. A. (1988), 'Staffing Policy as a Strategic Response: A Typology of Career Systems', *Academy of Management Review*, 13: 588–600.

Starbuck, W. H. (1993), 'Keeping a Butterfly and an Elephant in a House of Cards: The Elements of Exceptional Success', *Journal of Management Studies*, 30/6: 885–921.

Strong, E. K., Jr. (1943), *Vocational Interests of Men and Women* (Stanford, Calif.: Stanford University Press).

Sullivan, S. (1999), 'The Changing Nature of Work: A Review and Research Agenda', *Journal of Management*, 25: 457–84.

Super, D. E. (1992), 'Toward a Comprehensive Theory of Career Development', in D. H. Montross and C. J. Shinkman (eds.), *Career Development: Theory and Practice* (Springfield, Ill.: Charles C. Thomas).

Utterback, J. M. (1994), *Mastering the Dynamics of Innovation* (Boston: Harvard Business School Press).

Van Maanen, J. (1977), *Organizational Careers: Some New Perspectives* (New York: Wiley International).

Weber, M. (1947; original 1922), *The Theory of Social and Economic Organization*, trans. A. D. Henderson and T. Parsons (New York: Free Press).

Weick, K. E. (1996), 'Enactment and the Boundaryless Career: Organizing as we Work', in M. B. Arthur and D. M. Rousseau (eds.), *The Boundaryless Career: A New Employment Principle for a New Organizational Era* (New York: Oxford University Press).

—— and Berlinger, L. (1989), 'Career Improvisation in Self-Designing Organizations', in M. B. Arthur, D. T. Hall, and B. S. Lawrence (eds.), *Handbook of Career Theory* (New York: Cambridge University Press).

Wheatley, M. J. (1992), *Leadership and the New Science* (San Francisco, Calif.: Berrett–Koehler Publishers).

Whyte, W. H., Jr. (1956), *The Organization Man* (New York: Simon & Schuster).

Young, R. A., Valach, L., and Colin, A. (1996), 'A Contextual Explanation of Career', in D. Brown, L Brooks, and Associates (eds.), *Career Choice and Development* (San Francisco: Jossey-Bass).

I

CAREER THEORY: WHERE DO WE GO FROM HERE?

In a field fragmented by wide diversity both of interests as well as of under-lying phenomena, the development of theory that is widely applicable is a tremendous challenge. This section contains four chapters, all of which go a substantial way toward meeting that challenge. Each provides a new lens with which to view the landscape of careers, from a 'telephoto' focus on boundaries in Canadian biotechnology, resulting in the beginnings of a contingency theory of career boundaries (Chapter 2 by Gunz, Evans, and Jalland) to the very widest angle of a general typology of career communities (Chapter 5 by Parker and Arthur). Along the way, familiar questions of boundaries, motivations, and choices appear, bringing into sharp relief the aforementioned dichotomies of the careers field: structure versus action, stasis versus adaptation, universalism versus particularism, and institutional knowledge versus individual knowledge.

The problem of how to study careers has long been one of how to marry the plethora of theoretical ideas with the more realistic, although often anecdotal, world of practice. Theories are more useful if their practical implications are clear; practical experience is more understandable and transferable if lessons and patterns can be distilled from it. When the raw material of such theory and practice is the stuff of working life itself, the research takes on a highly salient quality—nearly everyone can relate to it, and nearly everyone has an opinion. Supporting and maintaining a clear, intelligible, and intelligent voice in the resulting cacophony is a difficult task, particularly when we still wish to engage in conversations, and not merely monologues, about theories of the present reality, and the future shape, of careers.

Each of the four chapters in this section maintains such a voice, and gives us a way forward toward a richer understanding of careers, in open con-versation with other chapters and other previous research. In Chapter 2, Gunz, Evans, and Jalland explore the boundaries, structural and personal, that constrain the individual's career path. They take a labor-market per-spective of boundaries as an imperfection in the free and unfettered flow of labor. Drawing on data from the Canadian biotechnology industry, they find both similarities and differences between this industry and the Silicon Valley exemplar of boundarylessness in the extent to which different kinds of boundaries exist. They use these similarities and differences to begin the process of developing a contingency theory of career boundaries. That is, they propose, not a world of boundaryless careers, but one of careers that are bounded in ways that emerge from the striving of actors to make sense of their place in the world.

Chapter 3 proposes a compelling model of human nature and the nature of social interactions. Nicholson's Motivation–Selection–Connection model draws on ideas from the new discipline of evolutionary psychology to analyze the enduring motives that drive careers, the selective forces embedded in social and organizational structures, and the perceptual and social biases influencing the connections people achieve in career develop- ment. The model is used to analyze the persistent and widening inequalities of opportunity in society, the causes of differing forms of career mobility, the development of leaders, and what Nicholson terms 'the problematic status of the "boundaryless career"'. He concludes that more organic alternatives to traditional mechanistic career systems are now possible, but that traditional patterns and themes in the careers literature will continue to be relevant and important because, essentially, we are wired to enact them. This argument suggests that career change is a much more difficult and serendipitous process than the 'new orthodoxy of the portmanteau career' would have us believe.

In Chapter 4, Boyatzis and Kolb assert that current developmental theories do not adequately describe or explain the dynamics of today's lifelong search for growth and adaptation. They propose a theory in which a person is said to be in one of three 'modes' at any one time in his or her life or career. These are the Performance Mode as the quest for mastery, the Learning Mode as the quest for novelty, and the Development Mode as the quest for meaning. The theory was developed to elaborate and reconstruct experiential learning theory by applying it to lifelong adaptation, and thereby to integrate the development process of competency acquisition. The theory differs from others in two major ways. First, it proposes a recursive, non-hierarchical schema, in which there is no 'best' or ultimate stage, phase, or place to be. Secondly, it integrates personal and career transitions into a holistic context. The practical roots of the theory in the authors' many years of consulting and educational work, as well as the clear implications of the theory for educa- tion and human resource development, place this chapter squarely in the integrative space between theory and practice mentioned above.

Chapter 5 by Parker and Arthur explores the connection between career behavior and the community attachments that career actors make. The related notions of 'intelligent careers' and 'communities of practice' are combined to suggest that community and inter-community relations, rather than formal employment arrangements, underlie the organizing of work. The chapter proposes a typology of 'career communities' through which career actors relate to one another. The authors argue that the career communities with which people associate are typically combinations of pure community types, and that particular combinations predict the kind of investments and returns members make and receive. Using evidence from an example work situation, they illustrate the model in both pure and combined types, providing a clear taking-off point for further research into the often complex world of the contemporary career.

2

Career Boundaries in a 'Boundaryless' World

Hugh Gunz, Martin Evans, and Michael Jalland

Boundarylessness has become a fashionable concept in organizational analysis, perhaps because it fits the *Zeitgeist*. Globalization, we are constantly reminded, was the central theme of the latter part of the twentieth century. Those who do not become citizens of a boundaryless, nationless world will lose their place in it.

Echoes of this theme, although without the global canvas, can be identified in recent work identifying a new boundarylessness in careers (Arthur and Rousseau 1996). In brief, the thesis can be stated as follows: to flourish in this new environment one must become self-reliant, losing one's dependence on the organization as the prime provider of structure to a career. Boundarylessness in careers means developing new competencies and a new architecture to careers (Arthur *et al.* 1995; De Fillippi and Arthur 1998).

Yet it is a curious paradox that globalization has been accompanied by a powerful localization movement. Business has certainly become global, free trade zones have grown, and regulations governing the movement of goods, services, and capital have become liberalized. But, at the same time, nineteenth-century empires have crumbled, and many countries formed during the twentieth century are disintegrating. Movements asserting the nationhood of much older ethnic groupings are gathering strength (or have not lost it), and it has been argued that the city state—or, at least, the large

The authors are grateful to Fred Haynes of Contact International for permitting us access to his data on the Canadian biotechnology industry, to Joel Baum, the project director, and to Movin Moukbel for help with data processing and collection. Portions of this paper were written while the second author was a visiting scholar at Northeastern University and Suffolk University. The hospitality of these institutions is greatly appreciated; the second author also thanks Richard Hackman for his continuing support.

urban unit—will become the focus for economic development in future (Bergman *et al.* 1991; Ohmae 1995; Keating and Loughlin 1997; Storper 1997). Everyone wants a Walkman, but they want to be able to use it to listen to their own music. The more that boundaries are knocked down, it seems, the more people put up new ones. How true might this be of boundaryless careers?

In this chapter we shall be arguing that careers have not become boundaryless in any absolute sense. Rather, career boundaries have become considerably more complex and multifaceted in nature. The past two decades have seen an increasing permeability of organizational boundaries, resulting in different kinds of boundaries becoming salient. We shall explore some of these complexities, drawing on some data on managerial careers from the Canadian biotechnology industry.

Boundaries in Careers

We know very little of the extent of boundarylessness in careers. It is now conventional wisdom that everyone will have several 'careers' during his or her lifetime, but this idea is not new: over twenty years ago Hall (1976) coined the term 'protean' to describe careers that involve periodic personal reinvention. This was, in part, a reaction to the changes that were then beginning to become evident in the business world of the Western developed economies.

Organizational careers in Western developed economies have been profoundly affected by the growth of the large organizations that have risen to such significance. If industrial concentration is low, firms are not large enough to sustain internal labor markets of any complexity. A merger wave, such as that which swept the UK cotton industry in the early part of the twentieth century, changes the picture dramatically. The large firms that resulted had well-developed and complex managerial labor markets, so many managers who started their careers moving regularly between small companies ended their careers by moving regularly within one large firm (Gunz 1989) that resulted from the merger.

The post-Second World War period involved steady economic growth for the Western economies, and this was accompanied by continued growth in the size of the corporations that provided employment. As the companies grew, so did the chances of a corporate career. But by the early 1970s the periodic business cycle downturns were becoming more worrisome, and it was increasingly being said that people could no longer count on spending their careers with one employer. Many, of course, had begun their careers in the Depression, so this was nothing new for them. But the shock of managers in mid-career abandoned by the companies that they had come to believe would look after them from cradle to grave was profound, and it was this mood that Hall addressed so influentially. It is clearly, too, the mood addressed by the boundarylessness movement and the intelligent-career concept to which we shall refer in greater detail in a moment. The waves of downsizing that swept many developed economies in the early to mid-1990s generated great feelings of insecurity and made attractive any ideas that helped people find a place in this confusing, threatening world.

At its simplest, the boundaryless-career hypothesis holds that careers are no longer constrained by organizational boundaries. People in the new order move freely between firms, relying on competencies that are transferable between companies. Some of these competencies are the technical skills and expertise that make, for example, an electronics engineer mobile between computer companies, and some are more generalizable. Looking beyond managerial careers to careers in general, Arthur *et al.* (1995) focus on the competencies they label *knowing-why* (knowing why the work is important), *knowing-how* (how to do the work), and *knowing-whom* (having a rich network of contacts), and argue that these are central to the successful 'intelligent career', the career model that is best suited to modern boundarylessness.[1]

Recent work has explored these issues further. Cadin *et al.* (Chapter 11) suggest that similar career patterns occur in France. Their informants range from those whose lives are spent wholly in one firm, to those who move through a variety of firms, to those with only a casual attachment to the workforce. Because of the small-sample, exploratory nature of the study, the authors do not report the proportions falling into each of their five classes, nor do they make any claims that their findings are representative of the French labor force.

It is clear, however, that few writers claim that careers can be completely boundaryless. In what seems often to be the most prototypical of boundaryless careers, that of the Silicon Valley engineer, there is a clear geographical and industrial boundary constraining the engineers' movement that can be contrasted with the organization boundaries that constrain the movement of their colleagues working in Boston's Route 128 development (Saxenian 1996). Yet even Silicon Valley, by virtue of the frequency with which it is used as an example, may not be typical of anything. Indeed it has a most unusual genesis, the result of the confluence of a particular kind of technology emerging from the laboratories of a particularly entrepreneurial group of academics with access to exactly the right company at the right time (Rogers and Larson 1984). The point of Saxenian's (1996) comparison is that these conditions did not apply to all electronics companies everywhere. Route 128 companies had organizational boundaries that were too closed, and the early attempt of Cambridge (UK) to develop a similar industry foundered on the rocks of a lack of an indigenous market for the products of fledgling companies (Saxenian 1989; it has been more successful latterly, however).

The complex nature of career boundaries is nicely illustrated in the contributions to Arthur and Rousseau's (1996) book on *The Boundaryless Career* (Table 2.1). Many of its authors assume that the only boundaries that matter

Table 2.1. *Boundaries discussed in Arthur and Rousseau (1996)*

Chapter authors	Boundaries identified
Arthur and Rousseau	Firm
Saxenian	Geography
	Industry
Weick	Firm
Jones	Firm
	Functional specialists
Robinson and Miner	Firm
Miles and Snow	Specialism
	Firm
DeFillippi and Arthur	Firm
	Industry
	Occupation
Baker and Aldrich	Firm
Bird	Firm
Ellig and Thatchenkery	Firm
	Profession
Raider and Burt	Firm
Granrose and Chua	Firm
Hirsch and Shanley	Firm
	Profession
Mirvis and Hall	Firm
	Specialism
Fletcher and Bailyn	Firm
	Function
Thomas and Higgins	Firm
Fondas	Not Stated
Perrow	Firm
Best and Forrant	Geography
	Firm
Tolbert	Firm
	Occupation
Rosenbaum and Miller	Firm

are organizational. In nineteen of the twenty-two chapters the explicit statement is made that boundarylessness means that firms' boundaries are irrelevant to careers. Two other kinds of boundaries are referred to, but more controversially. Two chapters imply that, even if careers are unconstrained by organizational boundaries, they are constrained geographically, while two others imply that they are not. Five chapters argue that careers that are unconstrained by organizational boundaries are still constrained by professional boundaries, viewing the incumbent in the traditional cosmopolitan role (Gouldner 1957); six argue that professional boundaries do not exist, because individuals have to reinvent themselves in terms of skills over the course of their career.

We shall argue here that boundaries, in career terms, have both a subjective and an objective existence. In the mind of the person experiencing a career, there may be perceived boundaries that are assumed to limit her or his career opportunities. These subjective boundaries may be the limits of the firm, they may be the limits of the industry, they may be geographic boundaries, or they may be professional in scope. In each case, unless forced by circumstance, the individual may not test the reality of those limits, so that they become self-fulfilling boundaries to career movement. On the objective side, there may be real barriers to mobility imposed by the nature of the territory that the careerist is traversing. These barriers may be between firms (for example, where hiring is only at the entry level), between industries ('we only hire people with five years of industry experience'), or between professions ('we would never hire someone with that kind of background').

Perspectives on Career Boundaries

We cannot discuss career boundaries without a concept of the landscape on which they are drawn. It is hard to escape the concept of role in this connection: the networks of roles that define an organization, a project group, or an occupational group. In these terms, boundaries can be observed in at least three different ways: as a labor-market phenomenon, as a demand-side phenomenon (for example, a reluctance to select), and as a supply-side phenomenon (for example, a reluctance to move). We shall examine each in turn.

As a labor-market phenomenon, a boundary is an imperfection in the market, observable by the relative lack of movement that takes place between certain groups of roles. For example, if a company has a strong internal labor market that is typically accessed at entry level only (Sonnenfeld and Peiperl 1988), the existence of an organizational career boundary can be inferred by an observer who sees very few people moving into senior positions from outside the organization. Similarly, there may be internal organizational boundaries inferred by observing intraorganizational mobility. Gunz (1989) describes three types of internal boundary structure: *command-centered*, in which boundaries surround occupational groups, *evolutionary*, in which boundaries surround organizational divisions (typically SBUs), and *constructional*, in which such boundaries as do exist are very permeable to the elite who are on a fast track to senior positions.[2]

Labor-market boundaries are simply constructs inferred from empirical data on labor mobility. At the collective level of analysis, they can be correlated with other collective-level phenomena such as organizational structure and organizational mode of growth (Gunz 1989), or the way in which effective organizational membership is assessed and rewarded (Sonnenfeld and Peiperl 1988). Labor market boundaries are amenable to exploration using the tools of microeconomics, because they define populations to which the costs and benefits can be assigned of, for example, internal *versus* external hires. These labor-market imperfections can be understood in terms of the second and third ways of conceptualization: a reluctance to select and a reluctance to move. Here, we are dealing with barriers that exist in the minds of the actors who make the decisions that underpin the labor market: selectors and career-owners.

A *reluctance to select* people who lack certain kinds of experience or expertise—for example, experience of the organization for which the selector works, or expertise of the kind needed by a project group—leads to the creation of a boundary in the mind of the selector. A reluctance to hire externally may be based on a rational analysis of the search and replacement costs of an external hire *versus* an internal hire, which is the standard explanation for the existence of internal labor markets (see e.g. Tolbert 1996).[3] The boundary may be without substance in the sense that it is not, in fact, as good a discriminator as the selector thinks, and it is common to encounter vigorous controversy about the nature of such boundaries. The literature is completely confused, for example, on whether it is better, and under which circumstances it might be, to hire insider or outsider CEOs (Gunz and Jalland 1996).

A *reluctance to move* is the Janus-like obverse of a reluctance to select, and in many ways it forms the foundation of the boundaryless career movement.[4] It refers to the boundaries that career-owners construct in their minds, which constrain careers: the limits we place on ourselves when we wonder what we could possibly do. Someone's despair at being laid off may be explained in part in terms of the boundaries she has in her mind which make it hard for her to see who else might value her services. Someone else's confidence in a similar situation may spring from the ease with which she believes she can move into a new job or occupation, in other words, from the absence of mental barriers. The intelligent-career analysis, thinking about why, how, and with whom one can do things, addresses these mental barriers directly by encouraging the individual to think about features of themselves and the things that they can do that emphasize their mobility. A reluctance to move is not simply the creation of the career-owner: it may be deliberately manipulated by other actors. University deans do this regularly when they try to stop star members of their faculty from leaving by doing their best to match external offers.

To summarize, we view boundaries here as labor-market imperfections driven by the reluctance of selectors to allow certain kinds of people to make given moves, and the reluctance on the part of career-owners to move to certain kinds of jobs.

The Industry as Career Boundary

Earlier we noted that, in boundaryless careers, moves are no longer constrained by organizational boundaries. In order to provide some structure to
the discussion that follows and the data that will be examined, we shall
adopt the position that it is possible to view labor markets in terms of so-
called industry careers.

In boundaryless careers, managers move freely between firms, relying on
competencies that are transferable between companies. One important
dimension of such transferable knowledge and skills is their application in
specific industry contexts. Managers are often hired[5] because they are familiar with an industry and have experience in dealing with characteristic
problems and opportunities. They may bring know-how associated with
products, customers, or technologies. Alternatively there may be some
unique features of an industry, or features at least perceived as unique,
that demand specialized skills. Thus nuclear power generation relies, *inter
alia*, on specialized knowledge of unique features of the industry associated
with the extremely hazardous nature of radioactive materials, their indes-
tructibility, and the extraordinarily long half-lives of many of them. This
makes it more likely, other things being equal, that selectors and career-
owners will seek each other out. More generally, selectors are also likely to be
influenced by contemporary thinking, which requires human resource management (HRM) strategy to be linked to overall business strategy: relevant
know-how and speed of integration have become important criteria in hiring
decisions.

There are, of course, definitional issues in any discussion of industries
(Abell 1980). However, the influence of the language of economics, the dis-
semination of ideas about competitive strategy and the frequent use of the
concept of a market have led to a ready acceptance of the notion of a set of
firms with competencies that allow them to compete in providing value for
customers. This business-level analysis assumes that there is a shared definition of the suppliers and customers and the nature of the boundaries of
value beyond which products or services will be perceived as only partial
substitutes. There are several levels of aggregation, reflected in published
statistics, that preserve overall assumptions about shared characteristics at
each level. Thus SIC codes successively group industries with common
characteristics.

Inevitably, discussions of careers refer to industry categories: we talk about
retail careers or careers in the textile industry. This means that mobility
between firms in these categories is likely to be easier and more typical
than movement outside them: the labor market is coterminous with the
type of product market—that is, the most significant boundaries for careers
are those of the industry category. Similarly subdivisions, or segments, of
industries with shared characteristics among competitors might be expected

to lead to higher labor-market mobility within segment boundaries: Silicon Valley is one such example, and is particularly interesting for the purposes of our analysis.

Boundaries in High-Technology Industries

We noted above that Silicon Valley (SV) seems to be taken almost universally as the locus of the paradigmatic case of the modern, boundaryless career. Yet Saxenian (1996) argues that critics who suggest that it is simply typical of an industry in its start-up phase miss the point: it is ideally suited to the needs of that particular industry. She draws on comparisons with the much more bounded companies of Route 128 to show that it is a more viable model of organizing for industries of that type.

As late as the 1980s, the most desirable career path on Route 128 was to move up the corporate ladder of a large company with a good reputation. Whereas interfirm mobility was by then a way of life in Silicon Valley, Route 128 executives were more likely to consider job-hopping unacceptable and to express a preference for professionals who were 'in it for the long term'. . . .

In short, Route 128 firms like DEC strictly defended their corporate boundaries at a time when job mobility and open information sharing were widely accepted practices in Silicon Valley. Network and informal exchanges on Route 128 occurred almost exclusively within the large firms, not between them. As a result, information about labor and product markets remained trapped within the boundaries of individual firms, rather than being diffused rapidly through local social and professional networks, as in Silicon Valley. This insularity deprived the Route 128 region of many of the opportunities for collective learning that distinguish Silicon Valley.   (Saxenian 1996: 32–6)

Saxenian's argument is that this difference explains a great deal of why SV is thriving while Route 128 companies are not: the SV labor market meets the needs of the industry, while the Route 128 labor market does not. Saxenian argues that boundarylessness was the reason for Hewlett-Packard, a classic SV company, outgrowing DEC as a computer manufacturer. Although she is careful not to fall into the trap of overgeneralizing from her findings, much of the boundarylessness movement seems to extrapolate from the SV experience and assume that careers, henceforth, should be boundaryless, especially in SV-like knowledge-based industries.

What Saxenian is drawing, in effect, is a set of inferences about the relationships between labor-market conditions, supply-side configurations, and success: specifically between labor mobility, high-technology supply chains, and growth rates. This offers a way of examining the boundarylessness phenomenon using a grounded approach that builds on existing observations. If it is possible to demonstrate that higher mobility can indeed be associated with supply-side configurations that benefit from knowledge sharing, then we may have the beginnings of a theory about boundaries that links industries and labor markets.

This thinking led to our choice of the biotechnology industry[6] as one that might provide a suitable comparative industry setting: it was high-tech, it was growing fast, had a supply-chain configuration that had some similarities to the computer industry, and appeared to share many of the labor shortages experienced by firms in SV. It also had the advantage that it was well documented. We also later gained access to a database on firms and managers in the Canadian biotechnology industry (CBI), which provided an opportunity for some exploratory work, some of which is reported here.

Why the Biotechnology Industry?

The biotechnology industry has a great deal in common with microelectronics. Both industries result from Nobel-prizewinning scientific discoveries (the discovery of the transistor effect, and the elucidation of the double helix structure of DNA), and neither industry was realistically imaginable before the mid-1940s. In both cases there are close intellectual links between the world of academic research and the commercial firms that exploit the research, because of each industry's fundamental dependence on knowledge creation: the development of each industry is in the hands of highly qualified scientists and engineers to a much greater extent than in a great many other industries. In each case the cost of research is such that major basic advances are not limited to the academic world: a great deal of basic research takes place in industrial R&D laboratories, tightening the links between academe and industry.

In consequence, it is easy to see a strong *prima-facie* argument for boundaryless careers in both industries. The highly trained professionals on whom they depend are precisely the kind of people who are likely to benefit from mobility between projects, and the need for firms to keep at the forefront of technological developments leads us to expect a well-developed market for their skills and knowledge. So is there evidence for the same kind of boundarylessness in biotechnology that is so evident in microelectronics in Silicon Valley?

Careers in Canadian Biotechnology: Some Preliminary Findings

Since 1991, *Canadian Biotechnology* has published an annual yearbook of Canadian firms that operate in the biotechnology industry. The Canadian biotechnology industry is made up of relatively small firms compared to those in the USA and Japan. Most biotechnology firms are located in Ontario, followed by Quebec and British Columbia. Following the international trend, many CBI firms have sought alliances with large multinational firms. From 1989 to 1993, total sales of biotechnology products in Canada grew at an average annual rate of 24 per cent, exports at 19 per cent, and employment at 14 per cent, all of which were the highest among all industrial sectors (Baum and Silverman 1998). Each entry in the yearbook lists the top management team (TMT) of the company,[7] enabling a year-by-year review of the movement of people between firms between 1991 and 1997.

The data provide a longitudinal sample of the managers of an industry population, and an opportunity to test the extent to which these managers move freely between firms. If careers in the industry are as boundaryless as we expect them to be by analogy with SV, there should be plenty of evidence of movement within the sample. Inevitably the data do have some limitations: only a subset of the managerial employees of each firm is listed, and non-managerial roles are not included.

The database contains information on 606 firms, for the period from 1991 to 1997. Every company does not appear in each edition of the yearbook, partly because firms were founded or foundered during this time, and partly because not every firm may have chosen to be listed (or, perhaps, was not approached by the yearbook editors) every year. Of the five TMT members listed each year for each company, there are often fewer than five different people shown, because one person often occupies more than one role. In all, there are 2,270 people listed in the database, and a total of 12,173 mentions of these people, so that each person is listed an average of 5.4 times.

We decided to measure elapsed time for which data were available on each individual by the difference between the earliest and latest years in which the person was listed in any company in the database. Thus someone who first appeared in 1991 and last appeared in 1997 was assigned 'time in database' of six years. Of the 2,270 people in the database, 641 (28 per cent) were in the database for the full six years (Table 2.2).

The database covers the years 1991 to 1997. Some firms were in the database for this whole period. Some firms appeared after 1991, some disappeared before 1997; some did both. Many managers appeared in and disappeared from the database at the same time as their firms did.

For the purpose of analysis the population was divided into four groups (Fig. 2.1):

- *joiners*: 495 (22 per cent) managers who joined the database after the beginning of the period *and* after their firm joined the database;
- *leavers*: 367 (16 per cent) managers who left the database before the end of the period *and* before their firm left the database;
- *transients*: 237 (10 per cent) managers who both joined the database during the study period after their firm did, and left it before their firm did;

Table 2.2. *Elapsed times for which people are listed in the database*

Elapsed years in database	n	%
0[a]	530	23.3
1	256	11.3
2	276	12.2
3	286	12.6
4	163	7.2
5	118	5.2
6	641	28.2
Total	2,270	100.0

[a] People who appeared only once in the database.

- *stayers*, the 1,171 (52 per cent) managers who did not fit the other categories. Stayers may have moved from one company in the database to another company in the database. However, their appearance in and disappearance from the database was the result of their *company* joining or leaving, and not the consequence of their *own individual action* (at least, as far as we could tell from the data). They were of three types: people who appeared with the same firm for the whole period; those

		Left database		
		Yes	No	Total
Joined database	Yes	237 (transients)	495 (joiners)	732
	No	367 (leavers)	1,171 (stayers)	1,538
	Total	604	1,666	2,270

Fig. 2.1. Managers grouped by appearance in database

whose stay was coterminous with the years the firm appeared in the database; and those who stayed in the database working sequentially for different firms during the duration of those firms' presence in the database.

Joining the database after the beginning of the period, or leaving it before its end, does not necessarily imply a change of company (although it was possible for joiners, leavers, and transients to change companies during their time in the database). For example, joining after the period's beginning could be the consequence of joining the company from another firm not in the database, perhaps an American biotechnology company or another firm with no links to the biotechnology industry. Equally, however, it might indicate (a) a first job after, for example, postdoctoral study or completing an MBA, (b) promotion into one of the five roles listed in the database, (c) a reorganization resulting in the person's appearance in one of the five roles, or (d) internal moves from another part of the company outside Canada or outside the biotechnology industry. Similarly, disappearance before the end of the period could be the consequence of leaving the firm or the industry. However, it could also be the result of (a) retirement, (b) demotion, (c) reorganization, or (d) moving to another part of the company.

Each person in the database was coded for the number of moves he or she made between employers. A move was inferred to be forced on the individual if the company had 'died' at the time the individual moved elsewhere; otherwise, the move was inferred to be at the individual's volition ('free' move (Table 2.3)). This probably overstates the proportion of free moves, because no data are available on the motivation for the move. For

Table 2.3. *Moves between companies: stayers*

Elapsed years in database	No. of people	Moves[a]		
		Forced	Free	Total
0	97	3[b]	0	3
1	67	0	0	
2	107	0	0	
3	49	3	0	3
4	142	0	0	
5	68	1	0	1
6	641	11	7	18
Total	1,171	18	7	25

[a] No person made more than one move, so the numbers are equivalent to people.
[b] The three forced moves reflect the fact that three of the ninety-seven people worked for companies that disappeared after these three people made their first and last appearance.

example, the individual's employment might have been terminated by his or her former employer.

We focus first on the group for which we do have comparatively complete information, the 1,171 stayers. Table 2.3 shows the breakdown of forced and free moves by length of time in the database. Very little forced movement has taken place, but even less free movement: seven moves in total. In other words, to choose an arbitrary denominator of those who had been in the database for four to six years (the 'long stayers'), 0.8 per cent had made a voluntary move between companies in that time. This does not represent a lot of free movement between companies: half of the CBI's managers simply have not moved between companies of their own volition in four to six years.

We next reviewed the remainder of the population of managers, the joiners, leavers, and transients, to see if there was anything that could be inferred about the nature of their mobility (Table 2.4; data on stayers are included here for comparison). First, the firms were examined for differences. We examined potential differences by firm size,[8] geographic location (first letter of postcode), industry sector, and the alliances in which the firms were involved. The only variables that showed any significant differences among the four groups were the number and distribution of alliances with which the firms were involved (Table 2.5). Alliances could be with institutions of the following sort: biotechnology companies, pharmaceutical companies, chemical companies, colleges and universities, research institutes, government laboratories, hospitals, as well as other types of institution. The outlying group were the transients: they were found in firms with more alliances and with a tendency toward a greater variety of alliances than the other groups. In Table 2.5 we show the number and variation for alliances associated with each type of person. Organizations through which the transients

Table 2.4. *Free moves between companies*

		Elapsed years in database							Total
		0	1	2	3	4	5	6	
Joiners	Non-movers	196	167	9	100	21	0	0	493
	Movers	0	0	0	2	0	0	0	2
Leavers	Non-movers	33	18	135	129	0	48	0	363
	Movers	0	0	0	2	0	2	0	4
Transients	Non-movers	204	4	24	4	0	0	0	236
	Movers	0	0	1	0	0	0	0	1
Stayers	Non-movers	97	67	107	49	142	68	634	1,164
	Movers	0	0	0	0	0	0	7	7
Total	Non-movers	530	256	275	282	163	116	634	2,256
	Movers	0	0	1	4	0	2	7	14

Note: No person made more than one move, so the numbers are equivalent to people.

Table 2.5. *Association of type of move and alliance frequency and variability*

	Type of Move				Differences	
	Transients	Leavers	Joiners	Stayers	Parametric	Non-Parametric
Number of Alliances (*n* = 2,009)	5.50 (6.08)	4.09 (3.49)	4.46 (5.08)	4.09 (4.29)	Transients > rest[a] (p < .001)	Transients > rest
SD of alliances (*n* = 1,812)	1.20 (1.51)	0.90 (0.63)	1.00 (1.32)	0.91 (1.02)	Transients > rest	Not significant[a]
Herfindahl–Hirschman Index for alliances (*n* = 1,811)	0.42 (0.28)	0.39 (0.28)	0.36 (0.29)	0.36 (0.29)	Transients > leavers and stayers Transients = joiners Joiners = leavers and stayers[a] (p > .05)	Not significant

Note. Figures in parentheses are standard deviations.
[a] Using appropriate test.

flowed tended to have more alliances (5.5 versus 4.2) than the other groups (joiners, leavers, and stayers).[9] The data were more equivocal for the variation. We used two measures, the standard deviation of the number of alliances in each firm and the Herfindahl–Hirschman Index.[10] Both are higher if the firm engages in more different kinds of alliance. Our data are not conclusive; the firms employing the transient group show a trend to having more variety in their alliances, but the effect is weak.[11]

To summarize, the transients' firms, in particular, were involved in a greater variety of alliances, more evenly spread over different kinds of alliance, than the other groups, in particular the stayers' firms. One interpretation of these findings is that this is evidence of alliances being cemented by personnel transfers: firms use personnel moves as a means of managing alliances and making them work (Pfeffer and Leblebici 1973).

In addition to these inferences from the database, some follow-up checks were made to see what proportion of joiners really belonged in this category. Joiners were selected for the preliminary checks because they were more likely to be easily traceable than leavers and transients. Attempts were made to contact all joiners in the database who worked for companies in the local telephone dialing area for Toronto; forty-six people were identified in nineteen companies that responded. Of these, just under a quarter seemed to be 'true joiners' (i.e. they had joined the company during the study period (Table 2.6)). The largest single group had either been promoted into the job that had got them the listing in the database, had moved internally to that job, were associated with the company (i.e. had not really joined it), or had joined as the result of a merger, or this was their first job after completing their MBA. In one case the company was small, so the managers of the company shared the roles around and it was somewhat arbitrary as to who

Table 2.6. *Follow-up interviews with sample of 'joiners'*

Classification	Number	% all cases
True joiner[a]	11	23.9
Joiner: first job after education	1	2.2
Leaver	0	0.0
Stayer[b]	5	10.9
Stayer: promoted or moved into job[b]	18	39.1
Stayer: associated with company[b]	1	2.2
Stayer: company merged in[b]	2	4.3
Transient	1	2.2
No information: retired	2	4.3
No information: left	5	10.9
Total	46	100.0

[a] See text.
[b] Inclusive stayer (see text).

was listed for which position in the database. Of the thirty-nine people about whom information could be collected, 69 per cent, for these reasons, would have been better classified as stayers. This group are called here the 'inclusive stayers.'

Furthermore the non-stayers were not evenly distributed across the companies. Five firms had ten of the 'true joiners' and half of these went to one firm: Company 21 (Table 2.7). Further investigation showed why this was the case: the firm went through a period of major organizational change. It was incorporated in September 1986, and an Initial Public Offering (IPO) took place in October 1991. The firm went through a turnaround in May 1996 when a new president was hired. New management was brought in, largely from outside the industry, after the firm had to suspend clinical trials because its major product (for cancer treatment) was shown to have quality-control measurement problems.

The numbers of the follow-up sample are small, of course, limiting the extent from which its findings can be generalized. If it were the case that they were representative, 342 of the 495 joiners in the database would need to be reclassified as stayers, leaving 153 'true joiners', representing 7 per cent of the people in the database.[12] Furthermore it seems likely that these people would not be evenly distributed across the companies, and that two factors may influence their concentration in a subset of firms: (a) the firms' alliances with other companies, and (b) periods of rapid growth or other organizational change experienced by those firms.

To summarize the findings from this analysis of inter-organizational mobility in the CBI: surprisingly little movement seems to be taking place. Although there is a great deal still to be learned about whatever movement is

Table 2.7. *Distribution of 'inclusive stayers' and non-stayers by company, follow-up sample*

Company code number	Inclusive stayers	Non-stayers	No information: left
1	2	0	0
2	2	0	1
5	3	0	0
14	2	1	0
18	3	0	0
19	3	1	0
21	0	5	0
22	0	2	3
28	2	0	0
29	3	0	0
35	2	1	0
Total	22	10	4

happening within the industry, there are indications that much of it is related to inter-firm alliances or organizational change. In other words, it is beginning to look as if career boundaries in the CBI are very different from those in Silicon Valley. Although it is clearly the case that careers are not made rigidly within one employer on the Route 128 model, it also seems to be the case that they do not have the fluid boundarylessness of SV.

Next, we reflect on these findings and suggest a number of possible explanations. We shall attempt, in effect, to begin putting together a contingency theory of inter-organizational career structures by generalizing from each point of contrast in a series of propositions.

Boundaries, Mobility, and Labor Markets

We noted above that the definition of boundaries was problematic in the literature: many writers treat the organizational boundary as the important hurdle for the manager and the focus for analysis. We selected imperfections in managerial labor markets as the key to our perspective on boundaries. Then we added questions about the linkage between industries and mobility in labor markets. This approach leads inevitably to questions of labor-market behavior and what the mechanisms might be that facilitate or inhibit mobility.

The starting point for our thinking was a conventional one: that markets are arenas for value exchange, and that labor markets exhibit the same characteristics as product markets in that price and quality judgments by buyers and sellers shape behavior. In labor markets, managers choose to enter the market at various points in their careers. Sometimes they are willing sellers, while at other times events such as downsizing may make them unwilling ones. Similarly firms enter the labor market driven, for example, by the requirements of their strategies and by the departure of managerial resources. In both cases exchange behavior is a function of the way that the parties assess value, based on experience of market behavior and their maps of the relevant factors and participants. Imperfections in knowledge create opportunities for extra returns.

It follows that supply-side behavior, including the decision by a manager to enter the labor market, is affected by several factors, some of which are under his or her control, and others of which are driven by market forces. For the manager, the challenge is to develop a good understanding of the value equation in the relevant labor market. The aim is to accept commensurate risk and avoid uncertainty in the assessment of future returns, and in comparison with what the current job provides. Thus perceptions of the characteristics of the labor market are an important influence on behavior. The current employment may also be revalued as an employer makes a bid to keep the employee: the mobility decision may be influenced by exit barriers.

While some managers keep their résumés polished and their interview skills practiced, most probably bring their attention to bear on labor markets only when the circumstances demand or opportunity beckons. Inevitably, some labor markets are more amenable to evaluation than others, and our key assumption is that they differ in the extent to which they present barriers to understanding (Baker and Aldrich 1996; Bird 1996; DeFillippi and Arthur 1996).

It then becomes possible to search for characteristics of industries that might make understanding more difficult and in which we therefore expect mobility to be lower. Any factors that work to fragment activities in the industry would be candidates for investigation. Similarly, where there are strong forces for change, perceptions of employment risks are likely to be higher. Such features could, of course, be offset by others, so that rewards rise to offset the risks, or patterns of change become recognizable through learning effects. Conversely we can also look for 'boundarylessness': this implies a set of related labor markets such that managers can make sense of the value offerings in each of them and are motivated to move. From our perspective it also may imply a relatedness in the characteristics of the industries that form the context for the labor markets.

A similar logic can be applied to demand-side behavior: the selectors who are doing the hiring also have the task of understanding labor markets, and need to judge the relevance of other labor markets in assessing the value of a candidate. The industry characteristics that make understanding of labor markets difficult and lead to information asymmetries apply here too.

Contrasting SV with the CBI: Towards a Contingency Theory of Inter-Organizational Career Boundaries

Given this framing of the conceptual issues, we can proceed to examine the two industries that are the focus of our exploratory work. They differ in a number of important respects, among them the stage of their respective life cycles, their characteristic project timescales, their geographies and the nature of the linkages between the firms, their levels of secrecy, the extent to which they are subject to regulation, and their intellectual differentiation and specialization.

Stage in life cycle

Although both industries are growing, SV is at a much more mature stage than the CBI. The first commercial transistor radio appeared in 1954; integrated circuits became a practical possibility in the 1960s, and large-scale integration leading to the microchip came in the 1970s. By contrast, the first commercial biotechnological products are only now reaching the market, and few if any firms were active before the 1980s; their mean age is 15.6 years (Fig. 2.2; Baum and Silverman 1998). The CBI has a large number of small start-up ventures, many of which are still closely connected with the university or other research institute from which they originated. The microelectronics industry has well-established, positive cash flows, while the dearth of commercial biotechnological products means that most bio-technological companies are still cash negative.

The relatively immature state of the CBI means that it has a great need for personnel with managerial skills, as opposed to the highly sophisticated scientific or technological skills needed to understand and work with the technology. There is no established labor market for biotechnology man-agers, because there are so few people with managerial experience in the CBI. In a smaller sample, drawn from firms in the Vancouver area, often managers interviewed had joined start-up firms in top management posi-tions after long careers in management elsewhere. One had spent thirty years in one company, rising to be president of the Canadian subsidiary of a large pharmaceutical company (essentially a firm-bounded career). Another had moved through a variety of engineering and management positions in a number of firms. Venture capital providers are extremely concerned about this issue, and play an important role in encouraging firms to search outside the industry for appropriate managerial skills. Uncertainty in labor markets is high and it takes more to tempt a manager to move.

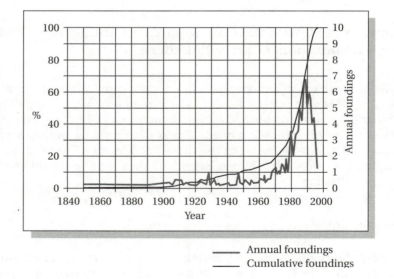

————— Annual foundings
————— Cumulative foundings

Fig. 2.2. Canadian biotechnology industry: annual foundings of firms, and cumulative foundings, as percentage of firms in database

We generalize these observations in the following propositions:

P1: In an immature industry, management positions will be filled from a wider variety of sources inside and outside the industry than in a mature industry.

P2: In an immature industry, there will be less inter-company and intra-industry movement between management jobs than in a mature industry.[13]

Project timescales

Careers are, by definition, time-based phenomena. A work career is typically limited to a span of, at most, half a century, and the longer a person spends in the education system, the shorter his or her work career becomes. High-technology industries are peopled with highly qualified workers, who, especially if they have completed postdoctoral fellowships before taking their first contract, joining their first employer, or starting their first company, may be retiring after thirty years' work or less.

The defining characteristic of both electronics and biotechnology industries is innovation: firms survive, and the industry develops, as a result of a stream of new products or processes reaching the market. The unit of analysis for the innovation process is the project. One of the most striking differences between the two industries is the timescale of their projects. Project lengths in electronics vary, but are typically measured in months. Even a major project such as writing an operating system may take three years or less. This is illustrated by the narrowing gaps between the introduction of 'new' versions of applications software (see e.g. Markoff 1996; Garud et al. 1997). So the kind of people who populate SV can look forward to a string of projects: as each project reaches its completion, it becomes time to look for the next project (cf. the film industry (Jones 1996)). SV is distinguished from Route 128 by the social institutions that encourage its denizens to seek projects anywhere in SV, not just in the same organization.

Biotechnological R&D project lives, by contrast, are much longer, literally measured in decades. Not only is the research much more speculative, but the sensitivities that surround genetic engineering are such that the development process is highly regulated. The stages a product must pass through before it can be tested in humans are many and lengthy. Even conventional pharmaceutical products take a minimum of twelve years between the discovery of a chemical entity with therapeutic effect and its release to markets such as those in the USA, and the risk of failing one of the screening tests is high at each stage. As we have seen, very few 'biotech' products have emerged from this lengthy process yet, which is why the CBI is, overall, still cash negative. So the greatest number of innovation projects any given individual is likely to see through from beginning to end is likely to be very small; it is conceivable that someone who has bad luck may not see any. Furthermore, because workers in the industry do not continually experience their projects coming to an end, there is not the same temporary feel to their employment situation. Projects do end unexpectedly, of course; biotechnology is a high-risk industry. But employees lack the continual impetus to move on that is experienced by workers in industries with much shorter project lives.

Eaton and Bailyn suggest in Chapter 9 that the long time frame of biotechnology projects reduces the day-to-day pressure of work for the scientific workforce. This makes the industry accommodating to people with parental, spousal, or filial responsibilities. They can arrange more flexible work arrangements than might be possible in university settings. This reduces the pressure to leave the organization.

Differences in project timescales affect mobility because of a learning effect: when projects are short, people moving around get to know what the jobs involve and what the risks of the typical contract are. If no one moves, then it is very difficult to assess what the risks are in moving: there are few successes both in terms of projects and in terms of careers. Further, the *absence* of the pressure of the looming project end removes a need to move, so that an industry such as biotechnology, which otherwise appears to be of a kind that would foster boundarylessness, is less likely to experience it.

> P3: Managers in industries with long project lives are more likely to be reluctant to move, because they do not continually experience the disconnection with organization that a project end represents.

Geography and the nature of inter-firm connections

The SV electronics industry, by definition, occupies a defined and contained geographical space in mid-California. This geographical concentration has made it possible for the social institutions—for example, the Homebrew Computer Club—to cement many of the close linkages between companies. It owes its origins to two local founding institutions, Stanford University and Fairchild Semiconductor. Indeed since about 1980 there have been many examples of attempts, some successful and some not, to build clusters of high-technology industries around entrepreneurial universities. The aim has been to provide an environment that encourages the birth of small, high-technology businesses drawing on the ideas from the university, which in turn nurtures their growth. The implication is that linkages between firms are based on, and derive from, geographical proximity in much the same way that the financial world tends to cluster geographically in centers such as London, New York, and Tokyo.

It is easy to see examples of geographical clustering in the CBI, too. For example, the University of Toronto has been the source of considerable innovation in the industry, and a number of firms have grown up in the Greater Toronto area as a result. However, the interconnections within the biotechnology industry are very different from those of the electronics industry as found in locations such as SV. The alliances take advantage of the different strengths of large and small firms. For example, small firms, often emerging from the work of a small group of academic scientists, are well positioned to work on the early stages of an innovation. They lack the resources for the later phases of the work, involving expensive trials with the product, and this is normally undertaken by the large partners. So, although some clustering is evident because of the way start-up firms have been spun off from university laboratories, many of the linkages between firms in the biotechnology industry are the outcome of alliances between companies specializing in different stages of the innovation process, and geographical proximity is not a major factor in determining their success. This, in turn, makes it less likely that the very free movement between firms seen in SV will be found in the CBI.

Geographic proximity of firms has three effects. Two are associated with the ease of surveillance. On the one hand, individuals are made aware of the opportunities available in other firms; on the other, firms are made aware of the bright 'stars' twinkling in other firms. Finally, because a change of firm does not mean an uprooting of spouse and children, movement is facilitated. These can be formalized as follows:

P4: Geographic proximity increases the willingness to move between firms.

Secrecy

One of the most fascinating features of SV is the freedom with which information is shared between SV people working for competing firms:

Competitors consulted each other on technical matters with a frequency unheard of in other areas of the country . . . The CEO of a semiconductor-materials firm noted: 'There are people gathered together once a month or once every two months to discuss every area of common scientific interest in the Valley. Around every technological subject, or every engineering concern, you have meeting groups that tend to foster new ideas and innovate. People rub shoulders and share ideas.'   (Saxenian 1996: 26)

Although there are, of course, well-developed scientific communities in the biotechnology world as well, there is a much greater degree of secrecy. For example, a company whose product is the base sequence of a section of the human genome guards its intellectual property with immense care. The competitive benefits of many years' work can be lost in an instant if information is leaked about the chemical structure of a promising lead, or the results of a critical series of tests. Secrecy is very much part of the biotechnological world, as it has been in the pharmaceuticals business for a long time. The need to protect intellectual property has never been an insuperable barrier to movement in industries of this kind, but the issue is managed with care to ensure that people do not take trade secrets from one firm to the next. Such secrecy also results in a lack of free interchange between people about the job opportunities available, especially the technical specifics about what the job entails, and makes new jobs difficult to evaluate.

Much of the difference between the two industries lies in the difference in project timescales discussed above. Even in microelectronics, in which timescales are short, there is much to lose if a competitor steals an idea. But in biotechnology, the consequences of having an idea stolen after a decade of development work are potentially catastrophic:

P5: Organizations operating in industries in which there is a strong need for commercial secrecy are more likely to attempt to generate a reluctance to move among their employees than firms in industries lacking this need for secrecy.

Regulatory controls

The two industries are strikingly different in the extent to which their activities are regulated. A microelectronics product has to pass a variety of tests imposed by the jurisdictions in which it is to be sold, involving, for example, electrical safety, energy efficiency, and radio transmission characteristics. The software industry is notorious for the lack of any effective controls over product standards. By contrast, biotechnology is regulated almost to the point of paralysis. Indeed it is not uncommon to hear stories of genetically modified plants or other organisms that cannot be tested commercially because of complaints about potential dangers if they are accidentally released to the environment. Pharmaceuticals firms have been familiar, for several decades now, with very close regulation of their developmental activities. For example, any product that is intended for most Western markets must show a comprehensive and auditable paper trail covering every test done during its development, wherever that test was done.

As with the secrecy issue, the regulated nature of the biotechnology industry is not an impermeable barrier to movement. However, in addition to all the other reasons for not wanting staff to leave a firm, the need to maintain a complete audit trail governing every aspect of a project is likely to make a firm even less keen for its staff to leave. Thus firms raise the barriers to exit from the old job, and this changes the value equation in the labor market when the old is compared to the new job. Overall the effect of regulation on mobility is to reinforce any tendencies to fragmentation and specialization, and make labor markets more differentiated.

P6: Organizations operating in highly regulated industries are more likely to attempt to generate a reluctance to move among their employees than firms in less-regulated industries.

Intellectual differentiation and specialization

The social reasons for the concentration of microelectronics firms in SV have been widely discussed. It is usual to trace the development of SV to Fairchild Semiconductor and the engineers who started with Fairchild and left to develop their own businesses (Rogers and Larson 1984). It is possible to go back further, to the Stanford Dean of Engineering in the 1940s who promoted a culture of collaboration and helped many of the founders of SV to flourish. But intellectually, SV owes its origins to a comparatively limited number of trains of events. The most obvious started with the discovery of the transistor effect and the development of a commercial transistor (Shockley, in fact, left Bell Telephone Labs in 1956 to found Shockley Transistor Corp. in Palo Alto), and continued through the construction of integrated circuits, the precursor of the microchip. Another train of events had its origins in the development of the stored program digital computer and the software that comprised the programs. Yet another was the development of protocols that allowed the digital transmission of data over long distances. The history of SV is of building on discoveries and concepts, finding uses for them, elaborating the products that resulted, adding layers of complexity by combining the results of other discoveries, and developing novel products as a result. Furthermore, the need for these products to be able to work together has reinforced the normal tendency for standards to develop in a new industry, resulting in a rapid convergence, so that the great variety of initial ideas and innovations have come together in a surprisingly narrow range of standardized products. So, for example, in the case of PC-based systems the Windows®/Intel platform has become the *de facto* standard worldwide.

Biotechnology certainly has its intellectual roots in one highly significant event: Crick and Watson's discovery of the double helix structure of DNA, already known to be the store of the genetic code. But it has progressed by learning more about the genetic code and the way it is expressed in living organisms, which means digging into every imaginable corner of the animal and vegetable kingdoms looking for problems to solve and products to develop. The names of companies within the CBI illustrate this nicely: among the to-be-expected pharmaceuticals and agrochemicals firms, companies specializing in diagnostics and other services to medicine and veterinary science, there are firms that specialize in forestry products (Pacific Forest Products), seeds (Canadian Seed Coaters Ltd.), fish farming (Atlantic Fish Health Inc.), poultry breeding (Hybrid Turkeys), and many more (e.g. Sea Forest Plantation Co. Ltd.). It would not be surprising if there were to be something of a reluctance to move between firms in such a highly differentiated industry, given that each component is so dependent on highly specific expertise:

> P7: The more intellectually differentiated an industry, the more reluctant people will be to move between firms in different parts and the more reluctant hirers will be to take people from different parts.

The extent to which passports to mobility remain is an interesting empirical question that deserves further investigation. Some competencies are likely to be regarded as transferable, but their valuation is likely to differ, unless some 'pedigrees' have been established that are widely recognized, like the training that Procter & Gamble provides for managers in the fast-moving consumer goods industry. One further refinement in the knowledge arena is the extent to which knowledge is codified or 'tacit'. We referred above to the differentiation between fields of codified knowledge, which is very high in the biotechnology industry. Tacit knowledge is also likely to be highly differentiated between firms (it is often viewed as 'firm-specific knowledge'), so is likely to raise the barrier to inter-firm and inter-industry mobility. Thus the greater the extent to which firms rely on this knowledge, the more likely people are to remain within the firm. Professional services firms (see Chapters 7 and 8) rely on intimate knowledge of the characteristics of their clientele and so are likely to keep their managers, with one exception: the placement of their employees within client firms.

Discussion

We started this chapter with the assertion that the concept of the boundary-less career, fitting as it does the spirit of the times, has become an object of great interest to many students of careers. But the boundarylessness concept, on closer inspection, turns out to be not really boundarylessness at all, but a disappearance of organizational boundaries as important shapers of careers. That, in turn, suggests that career boundaries still exist, but that they have changed. If, that is, they *have* changed. The trouble with the boundary-lessness hypothesis is that it is still just that: a hypothesis. For example, Rosenbaum and Rafiullah Miller (1996: 350) assert that 'The company man, if not entirely extinct, is a rapidly dying species.' They continue with a fascinating account of career attainment signaling, but we are left wondering: how do we *know* that the species is, in fact, heading for extinction? What if it isn't?

There is no question that there are places where firm boundaries seem to have little relevance to people's work careers. Silicon Valley (SV) seems to be one such, and there are others—for example, the film industry. But the film industry is not a new one, and there are many features of SV-type careers that can be seen in other well-established industries, such as the cotton industry of the early twentieth century, advertising, investment banking, and software design. The interesting argument for the spread of boundaryless careers is based on assumptions about the changing nature of work, away from the care and tending of large machine bureaucracies, toward flexible, project-based structures.

Yet it is not clear that this is true of any but a small proportion of jobs. Perrow (1996) traces the reasons for the dependence of the majority of the US population on large organizations, and most of his arguments (with the exception of health-care dependencies) can be extrapolated to other developed economies. We have been struck, in our own fieldwork, by the force with which managers have made it clear to us that their aim is *not* to lose their employees, because of the great costs and uncertainties involved in replacing them. The boundaryless world is not supposed to be like that.

Clearly, we need more information about what is really happening to careers in modern organizations. In this chapter we reported on a very preliminary look at an industrial sector, the Canadian biotechnology industry (CBI), which superficially has much in common with the similarly high-technology world of SV. It turns out that a surprising proportion of the managers for whom we had data stayed with their companies, at least for the six to seven years for which data were available. It is possible, further, that many of the inter-company moves that did occur were driven by two organizational-level phenomena. First, there is indication that some mobility is positively related to inter-company alliances. Secondly, yet more mobility is certainly the consequence of organizational change: the growth and shake-outs to which a fledgling industry of this type is bound to be subject.

Of course, we have no comparable data for SV managers, so, although the anecdotal material available speaks strongly to a high degree of mobility, it is not possible to know, for example, what proportion of senior SV managers would still be working for the same company for six to seven years continuously. Nevertheless it looks as if the situation in the CBI is different, and that careers are differently bounded, which led us to ask why this might be, and to suggest a number of reasons for the differences.

This approach has ignored the obvious—namely, that an industry that consists chiefly of small firms is not likely to be supportive of organizational careers: the firms are too small to have meaningful labor markets. This is, of course, the chief driver of what would now be called boundaryless careers in, for example, that part of the software design industry populated by small firms, and we have already referred to its importance in the UK cotton industry in the early part of this century. We concentrated on six factors that seemed to differentiate between SV and the CBI: the stage of their respective life cycles, their characteristic project timescales, their geographies and the nature of the linkages between the firms, their levels of secrecy, the extent to which they are subject to regulation, and their intellectual differentiation and specialization. The arguments were summarized as a series of propositions that might form the beginnings of a contingency theory of inter-organizational careers.

We view boundaries here as labor-market imperfections caused by the reluctance of selectors to allow certain kinds of people to make given moves, and the reluctance on the part of career-owners to move to certain kinds of jobs (perhaps as the result of their managers' attempts to make the status quo more attractive). The discussion above explored the idea that exchanges of value in labor markets provided a useful and interesting way of framing the issues surrounding mobility. In addition we set out an interpretation of the differences between SV and CBI that identified generalizable contextual factors that influence behavior in job seeking and selection. At the heart of the model is the idea of asymmetries in information and more fundamentally in perceptions of the labor market. This in turns leads us into questions about the definition of labor-market boundaries.

We followed this argument because of our belief that boundaries are to do with making sense of one's place in the world. Weick (1996) draws on the concept of strong and weak situations, and argues that, when a situation weakens, people redraw boundaries to create a different strong situation. For those who live in a world in which organizational boundaries become permeable and no longer provide a strong definition for the self—as, for example, 'an IBMer'—other ways are needed. Knowing why, how, and who may provide these alternatives (Arthur *et al.* 1995): why am I doing what I'm doing, how do I do it, and with whom do I interact to do it?

But for many other people, this view of boundaries leads us to believe that they do not disappear as organizations lose their interest in providing long-term employment; they are reshaped in ways that make sense to the career-owners and selectors. Indeed, Parker and Arthur (in Chapter 5) elaborate on this thought with their idea of 'career communities'. In labor-market terms, people might define themselves by their membership of a category defined by a labor-market boundary of the kind that might surround a firm, a division of a firm, an occupation, a geographical area, or several of these co-terminously, and express this identity by their reluctance to consider moving outside the boundary. Their identity is reinforced by the decisions of selectors who consider them for jobs inside the boundary and reject them for jobs outside the boundary. In other words, we are proposing, not a world of boundaryless careers, but one of careers that are bounded in ways that emerge from the striving of actors to make sense of their place in the world.

At present, the boundaryless-career argument is eerily reminiscent of the quest for the 'one best way' that dominated management and organizational writing for the first half of the twentieth century. Boundaryless careers, goes the argument, are the way of the future, and the only question is learning how to live in a world of boundarylessness. But we have argued here that pure boundarylessness is perhaps better seen as a special case, a limiting condition that works well under certain very special circumstances, but not in others. There is no necessary shame in recognizing that there are boundaries that shape one's career, and there may be a great deal to be gained from understanding the forces that create these boundaries.

Notes

1. This frame is used extensively in the current volume (Parker and Arthur in Chapter 5, Jones and Lichtenstein in Chapter 8, Cadin *et al.* in Chapter 11). However, it is not a theme we will explore in this chapter. It is one that we shall explore in further empirical work.
2. We endorse Alvarez's (Chapter 6) call for more qualitative research. It was an ethnographic research process that led Gunz to identify these different career patterns, only one of which exemplifies the traditional 'Russian Doll' type career.
3. One counter-force to this process is the way in which some firms or, in Japan, central agencies place their employees in client firms (Chapter 7).
4. Several authors have suggested this as a problem in terms of: sense of self (Baker and Aldrich 1996; Ellig and Thatchenkery 1996), explicit statements about cumulation of knowledge (Baker and Aldrich 1996; Bird 1996), and implicit concern about cumulation of knowledge (DeFillippi and Arthur 1996).
5. We make no assumptions about the nature of the contractual relationship between the manager and the organization with which he or she is associated.
6. See Chapter 9 for an intensive study of managers and scientists in two biotechnology firms in the Route 128 area.
7. The roles are listed as President, Manager (i.e. Chief Operating Officer (COO) or equivalent), and the heads of Marketing, R&D, and Purchasing. This raises an interesting question about whether people in different roles might have, or perceive, different boundaries. The most obvious distinction might be between people in technical roles (R&D) and those in managerial roles (President/Manager); alternatively people with technical backgrounds (Master's or Ph.D.) in the technical field(s) within which the firm operates might have different boundaries from those with more generalist backgrounds (Bachelor's degree or MBA). It might be, for example, that people in managerial roles feel more obligated, especially if they have an ownership stake in the company, to stay with the firm than do technical specialists. If so, the sample may underrepresent mobility in the industry. Similar observations might hold for managers at different levels of authority (Jones 1996; De Fillippi and Arthur 1998). Analyses exploring these differences are beyond the scope of this chapter.
8. Initially we examined the simple linear effect of size. However, a reviewer suggested that executives might choose to remain with a firm because of 'golden shackles'. This might be the situation in larger firms. Alternatively, managers might stay with a firm because they are the founders and owners and have considerable equity stakes in the firm. This is likely to be the case for the smaller firms. Accordingly, we undertook a curvilinear analysis to see whether stayers predominated at the extremes of size. Again, no differences were found.
9. We used the parametric one-way analysis of variance and the non-parametric Friedman test. The non-parametric test is probably the most appropriate here as the data showed considerable non-normality with many firms having no alliances

and there being a long tail to the maximum number (fifty-four alliances). Ninety % of the firms had fewer than ten alliances.

10. The Herfindahl–Hirschman Index (HHI) is a measure of concentration defined as the sum of the squares of the proportions of all the alliances in each type of alliance in each firm. It ranges from 0 when the firm just has a single alliance to 1 when the firm has a large number of alliances spread equally over a variety of alliance types.

11. The standard deviation has high skew and kurtosis, so differences should be evaluated by the non-parametric test; the more powerful parametric test is suitable for the normally distributed HHI.

12. We plan to undertake a more broad-based investigation of the people listed in the database in a subsequent analysis.

13. One colleague suggested that in very mature industries where decline was setting in there might be increased mobility as 'turnaround' managers were brought in to revitalize the business.

References

Abell, D. F. (1980), *Defining the Business* (Hemel Hempstead: Prentice-Hall).

Arthur, M. B., and Rousseau, D. M. (1996) (eds.), *The Boundaryless Career: A New Employment Principle for a New Organizational Era* (New York: Oxford University Press).

—— Claman, P. H., and DeFillippi, R. J. (1995), 'Intelligent Enterprise, Intelligent Careers', *Academy of Management Executive*, 9: 7–20.

Baker, T., and Aldrich, H. E. (1996), 'Prometheus Stretches: Building Identity and Cumulative Knowledge in Multiemployer Careers', in M. B. Arthur and D. M. Rousseau (eds.), *The Boundaryless Career: A New Employment Principle for a New Organizational Era* (New York: Oxford University Press).

Baum, J. A. C., and Silverman, B. S. (1998), 'Alliance- and Patent-Based Competitive Dynamics in the Canadian Biotechnology Industry', unpublished working paper.

Bergman, E., Maier, G., and Todtling, T. (1991), *Regions Reconsidered: Economic Networks, Innovation, and Local Development in Industrialized Countries* (London: Mansell).

Bird, A. (1996), 'Careers as Repositories of Knowledge: Considerations for Boundaryless Careers', in M. B. Arthur and D. M. Rousseau (eds.), *The Boundaryless Career: A New Employment Principle for a New Organizational Era* (New York: Oxford University Press).

DeFillippi, R. J., and Arthur, M. B. (1996), 'Boundaryless Contexts and Careers: A Competency-Based Perspective', in M. B. Arthur and D. M. Rousseau (eds.), *The Boundaryless Career: A New Employment Principle for a New Organizational Era* (New York: Oxford University Press).

—— —— (1998), 'Paradox in Project-Based Enterprise: The Case of Film Making', *California Management Review*, 40/2: 125–39.

Ellig, J., and Thatchenkery, T. J. (1996), 'Subjectivism, Discovery, and Boundaryless Careers: An Austrian Perspective', in M. B. Arthur and D. M. Rousseau (eds.), *The Boundaryless Career: A New Employment Principle for a New Organizational Era* (New York: Oxford University Press).

Garud, R., Jain, S., and Phelps, C. (1997), 'Linking Mechanisms and Transient Advantages in Network Industries: A Tale of Two Browsers', paper presented at INFORMS conference, Dallas.

Gouldner, A. W. (1957), 'Cosmopolitans and Locals: Toward an Analysis of Latent Social Roles', *Administrative Science Quarterly*, 281–306.

Gunz, H. P. (1989), *Careers and Corporate Cultures: Managerial Mobility in Large Corporations* (Oxford: Basil Blackwell).

—— and Jalland, R. M. (1996), 'Managerial Careers and Business Strategies', *Academy of Management Review*, 21: 718–56.

Hall, D. T. (1976), *Careers in Organizations* (Pacific Palisades, Calif.: Goodyear).

Jones, C. (1996), 'Careers in Project Networks: The Case of the Film Industry', in M. B. Arthur and D. M. Rousseau (eds.), *The Boundaryless Career: A New Employment Principle for a New Organizational Era* (New York: Oxford University Press).

Keating, M., and Loughlin, J. (1997), *The Political Economy of Regionalism* (London: Frank Cass).

Markoff, J. (1996), 'The Microprocessor's Impact on Society', *IEEE Micro*, 16: 54.

Ohmae, K. (1995), *The End of the Nation State: The Rise of Regional Economies* (New York: Free Press).

Perrow, C. (1996), 'The Bounded Career and the Demise of the Civil Society', in M. B. Arthur and D. M. Rousseau (eds.), *The Boundaryless Career: A New Employment Principle for a New Organizational Era* (New York: Oxford University Press).

Pfeffer, J., and Leblebici, H. (1973), 'Executive Recruitment and the Development of Interfirm Organizations', *Administrative Science Quarterly*, 18: 449–61.

Rogers, E. M., and Larson, J. K. (1984), *Silicon Valley Fever: Growth of High-Technology Culture* (New York: Basic Books).

Rosenbaum, J. E., and Rafiullah Miller, S. (1996), 'Moving In, Up, or Out: Tournaments and Other Institutional Signals of Career Attainments', in M. B. Arthur and D. M. Rousseau (eds.), *The Boundaryless Career: A New Employment Principle for a New Organizational Era* (New York: Oxford University Press).

Saxenian, A. (1989), 'The Cheshire Cat's Grin: Innovation, Regional Development and the Cambridge Case', *Economy and Society*, 18: 448–77.

—— (1996), 'Beyond Boundaries: Open Labor Markets and Learning in Silicon Valley', in M. B. Arthur and D. M. Rousseau (eds.), *The Boundaryless Career: A New Employment Principle for a New Organizational Era* (New York: Oxford University Press).

Sonnenfeld, J. A., and Peiperl, M. A. (1988), 'Staffing Policy as a Strategic Response: A Typology of Career Systems', *Academy of Management Review*, 13: 588–600.

Storper, M. (1997), *Perspectives on Economic Change. The Regional World: Territorial Development in a Global Economy* (New York: Guilford Press).

Tolbert, P. S. (1996), 'Occupations, Organizations and Boundaryless Careers', in M. B. Arthur and D. M. Rousseau (eds.), *The Boundaryless Career: A New Employment Principle for a New Organizational Era* (New York: Oxford University Press).

Weick, K. E. (1996), 'Enactment and the Boundaryless Career: Organizing as We Work.', in M. B. Arthur and D. M. Rousseau (eds.), *The Boundaryless Career: A New Employment Principle for a New Organizational Era* (New York: Oxford University Press).

Motivation–Selection–Connection: An Evolutionary Model of Career Development

Nigel Nicholson

Careers research has lately been much absorbed with the radical changes to employment we have been witnessing, wrought by the information revolution and the globalizing of the economy. Writers have sought, successfully in the main, to reinvigorate the concept of career itself in the face of potentially dissolving forces, by a renewed emphasis upon aspects of career identity and contractual relationships in employment. At the same time both traditional and new themes have enjoyed enhanced attention: career decision-making processes, determinants of mobility, workplace socialization and mentoring, commitment dynamics, race and gender issues, and lifespan development (Arnold 1997). Career-development interventions—counseling and educational for the individual, structural and contractual for the organization—have also figured strongly.

The danger for the field seems not that the concept will evaporate in the new context of employment, but that it will become fragmented as research develops in a multitude of centrifugal directions—that 'careers' will become a vehicle for almost any work on employment experience. This vitality is healthy, but it raises the question of what lies at the center from which these interests spin off. Integrating theoretical perspectives have become unfashionable in this diffuse but fertile field, but perhaps there is value in trying to establish some guiding principles for individual career development and the systems that shape it. Until recently, there has been no theoretical foundation on which to build such a consensus. In this chapter I wish to argue that one is now emerging, through the new perspective of evolutionary psychology, and I shall attempt to show how it might do so.

The Principles of Evolutionary Psychology

The integrating perspective offered by evolutionary psychology (EP) is a normative model, which can provide a framework for an integrated account of career interests and how these are conditioned by social contexts. I shall not here attempt a full exposition of this rapidly developing theory (for a fuller account see Nicholson 1997; Pinker 1997), but aim only to articulate its main principles and how they may be relevant to careers.

EP's thesis is that we are the possessors of a defined human nature, genetically encoded and structurally embedded in the physical systems of brain and body, which evolution has shaped over millions of years of hominid evolution. Drawing upon neuroscience, comparative anthropology, primatology, and other sources, it contends that far more of our nature is biogenetically encoded than it has been fashionable to assume in twentieth-century social science. Its normative thesis is that evolution has shaped the human mind for the hunter-gatherer clan life that predominated for over 99 per cent of our historical existence and that no further evolution has occurred, or indeed been possible, during the very brief interval since the invention of agriculture. In other words, our essential human nature is untouched by the post-agrarian features of civilization: communal dwelling in city-sized settlements, the nation state, and organizational structures for warfare, work, or worship.

The key corollary theme of EP that widens its revolutionary implications and integrating potential is the idea of co-evolution. This holds that culture and social forms unfold under the twin forces of an essentially unchanging human nature and a changing matrix of environmental contingencies. Critics of EP raise two objections to this idea—namely, that cultural evolution has supplanted biological evolution and that human nature is now under the control of socially constructive processes. However, the underlying argument that we are effectively reinventing ourselves through cultural media is problematic. Difficulties arise from the dualistic separation of humans from nature. How are we to reconcile the constructionists' promise of a seemingly limitless capacity for development through culture with the awkward fact of a fundamental human biogenetic identity?

The EP position of this chapter is a form of 'hard' interactionism, which asserts the non-arbitrariness of social constructions (Sperber 1996). Cultural evolution operates under the continual guiding hand of our biologically evolved human purposes. This determinism is open-ended and diverse in its products, (a) because of adaptation to local environmental conditions (including current social structures and population characteristics), and (b) because more than one social form may seek to achieve compromise between human nature and human environments. Thus social forms are experiments in accommodation between these forces. It follows that, as we no longer inhabit the world for which we were designed, our new cultural designs will exhibit points of misfit or tension with our nature, with visible consequences in various social ills and disorders. It also follows that EP suggests which elements may require attention for these tensions to be ameliorated.

An EP Model of Careers: Motivation–Selection–Connection

EP's central insight is that human psychology bears all the marks of elaborated design for survival and reproduction under the conditions that prevailed for most of the 4 million years of our species evolution—the clan life of hunter-foragers. Part of our design is a capacity for learning and adaptation, but how we use this capacity is guided by our evolved toolkit of 'hardwired' emotional and cognitive systems (Nicholson 1998).

In this framework career development can be seen as an adaptive challenge for humans. Individuals have enduring motive structures that they seek to satisfy through their occupational development and have to do so via social structures that in a non-arbitrary selective manner act upon us.

This construction of career dynamics is illustrated schematically in the Motivation–Selection–Connection (MSC) model of Fig. 3.1, which portrays career development processes, issues, and outcomes as the product of three interacting sets of forces: (1) Motivation: innate goals, action modules, and cognitive attributes—species-general and individually differentiated—of which careers are the principal means of expression; (2) Selection: selective forces embedded in organizations and cultures that govern career opportunities; and (3) Connection: perceptions and behavioral strategies through which individuals make sense of their situations and seek reconciliations between motivation and opportunity structures. In the figure the solid arrows represent the dominant causal flows, and the outline arrows what are, in general, rather weaker feedback processes. Arrow 1 represents the co-evolutionary path of how career structures contain the imprint of human drives in their design. Arrow 2 represents selection—how individual characteristics are differentially valued for opportunities and positions by career structures, plus the interactionist proposition that motives can be amplified or dampened by these forces (for example, by selective education). Arrow 3 represents the proactive force of career drives—individuals seeking and making connections that satisfy their goals. Arrow 4 represents the constraining influence on the Connection process of local opportunity structures—that is, which subsets of resources and linkages are accessible. The feedback Arrow 5 represents how success or failure in career aspirations moderates perceptions and motives, and Arrow 6 how achieved Connections open the door to new opportunity structures, or how failures to satisfy career motives can narrow the range.

One outcome of the latter process is mobility and change—for example,

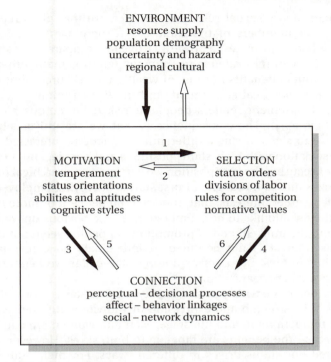

Fig. 3.1. The Motivation–Selection–Connection Model

frustration stimulates migration from one set of opportunity structures to another where selective forces are more favorable to the individual. The system overall thus operates with what evolutionists call a selectionist logic (production, variation, and selection) (Cziko 1995), driven at the center by identity self-regulation (the building blocks of control loops through which perceptions, goals, and actions find internal consistency) from a core of stable individual attributes. The whole system is embedded in environmental contingencies, such as population demography, resource supply, environmental uncertainty and threat, and established sociocultural forms. I will shortly illustrate how the model can be applied to some familiar themes in the careers literature. First, let us briefly consider the content of its terms in a little more detail.

Motivation

An EP perspective draws attention to human universals in drives and other psychological attributes, and how they are subject to individual differences. Of primary relevance to careers is our abiding interest in status attainment.

In Darwinian theory sexual selection—any feature that gives reproductive advantage over members of the same sex (Cronin 1991)—has created in humans (and other primates) a powerful drive for comparative status advantage. There is plentiful evidence for humans (and for many other species) that status confers benefits not just of wealth and resources, but of health, happiness, psychological adjustment, and the like (Brunner 1997). Conversely, status debasement renders people at risk to numerous hazards and ailments (Ellis 1994). The consequence is that we are universally attuned and sensitive to signs of status differentiation, acutely interested in attainment or association with high-status positions and people, and motivated to seek ways of securing the best position we can in any hierarchical order. It no longer amazes me, as it did when I first started surveying employee populations on their career interests, that, routinely, 80 per cent or more of respondents say they would like to be promoted. Even the obvious unavailability of positions and the unlikelihood of promotion happening seem not to dim the desire. This interest is not confined to individuals on career ladders in corporate hierarchies, but persists among blue-collar workers and people in flatter or smaller organizations.

When we look more widely across society, we find status motivation is also moderated in its strength and expression by individual differences, of three kinds: sex, temperament, and life stage. Men and women are equally interested in status—the benefits are tangible to both sexes. However, evolution has gendered our status drives in different ways. For men, status is associated with competitive dominance—proving you are better than others and being rewarded via power and position. Women's psychology is more oriented to status through relationships, via networks and friendships. The point is controversial, but under conditions of near universal patriarchy (Smuts 1995) the structures of employment are more geared to male than female status orientation. More on this later, but one consequence is the glass ceiling (Lyness and Thompson 1997). This persists not just because men block women's opportunities (which they do) but because many women are just not prepared to act out status competition by male game rules.

The nature of temperament—the physical basis of personality—is being unraveled by research into innate differences in endocrine and neural functioning. Personality—what is measurable in terms of individual motives and dispositions—grows out of this matrix of response potentialities. Although the structure of personality has a universal architecture (Wiggins and Trapnell 1997), there is no single preferred individual personality profile for reproductive advantage. In the absence of consistent selective forces to value one character over another, we differ from one another on the principle of frequency dependent selection—being different from others offers unique opportunities for status and reproductive advantage in a complex and variegated human community. Behavior geneticists estimate upwards of 40 per cent of personality is heritable, and indeed genes for specific aspects of temperament and personality are being discovered (Cloninger *et al.* 1996;

Rowe 1997). This still leaves a large proportion of variance unaccounted for, though attempts to identify reliable predictors from shared environmental features (for example, social class) have generally failed. The rest, it seems, is due to a mix of measurement error and non-shared environmental influences—the unique experiences of the growing child. But even here research is suggesting that aspects of this experience are more determined by personality than vice versa—life events, parental warmth, peer relations all exhibit significant heritabilities (Plomin 1994). The implication is that much of the careers literature has tended to underestimate how much of career development is determined by personality and other stable attributes, though this theme has been a consistent feature of the vocational-choice literature. Holland's six-factor model of career interests has been the most successful and widely used framework for analyzing how individuals 'fit' with work environments, and there is every reason to believe that these dimensions of career interests are closely linked with personality, and strongly underpinned by heritable traits (Loehin *et al.* 1998). Other individual differences—in physique, abilities, and cognitive capacities—similarly shape career orientations and behavior. Individuals seek to maximize their fitness through choices.

It is apparent that life stage moderates the expression of these drives (Cohen 1991; see also Chapter 4). Maturation effects on temperament and personality, beyond adolescence, seem quite minimal on the genotype, but not the phenotype. Although we retain our individual profiles, powerful selective forces discriminate between us on the basis of age, while experience continually reshapes the matrix of Connections we forge over the lifespan. Thus, career life-cycle models are as much, if not more, reflective of our environments than our unique identities. The Super (1953) model correctly identifies youth as a time of exploration of environmental alternatives for our best 'fitness landscapes' (to borrow a term from complexity theory (see Kaufman 1995)), adulthood as the refinement and embedding of connections, and later life as progressive disengagement. If career interests change over this period, it is more likely to reflect how the expression of interests is filtered rather than any more fundamental reshaping of underlying drives through feedback from experience. It should also be remembered that work and careers are not the only domain for the achievement of fitness. Family, voluntary associations, recreational activities, and the like offer alternative paths for fulfilment to those offered by employment. Apparent changes in career motivation may only represent their deflection from the work to the non-work sphere, as in Scase and Goffee's 'reluctant managers' (1989).

Selection

It is known that cultural forms—mating systems, family structures, vertical and horizontal stratification by status and function, norms and social contracts, and symbolic systems (of art, display, and ritual)—are adaptive to environmental contingencies of food supply, population density, and hazard. Despite the enormous diversity of cultural forms, it is increasingly being pointed out by evolutionists that they exhibit numerous universal themes, reflecting the persistent imprint of the invariances of human nature (Brown 1991). Thus it is that career systems the world over have to accommodate the search of individuals for opportunities for betterment and fitness optimization (see Chapter 2). The ability of the corporate hierarchy to provide this is part of the reason for its enduring popularity in post-industrial culture, benefits outweighing the human and other costs that it imposes, especially when it also offers economies of scope and scale to buffer the corporation from environmental turbulence, and the control efficiencies delivered by hierarchy and divisions of labor. Now we find commentators predicting its demise, on the basis of mounting fixed costs coupled with rigidities and slowness in response to increasingly dynamic environments. For these reasons many predict a bright future for boundaryless and virtual organizations. However, a countervailing view is that the corporate hierarchy not only continues to retain advantages of market power and operational control, but also offers, in a single institutional microcosm, a superb array of differentiated fitness niches for its members. This view predicts, as we are observing, not only the persistence of the corporate form, but also longevity of employment with relatively few external flows to middle- and senior-ranking positions, since these tend to undermine the aspirations of current members. It is noticeable that, contrary to the confident predictions of the death of the corporate career system, many leading companies remain firmly dedicated to methods that select, nurture, and bring to maturity their managerial cohorts (Nicholson 1996).

However, the forms of hierarchy that can be found, and the value that attaches to specific roles within them, do vary cross-culturally. One likely reason, unmentioned in the organizational literature (for fear of political incorrectness, perhaps), is that cultural differences are not purely environmental adaptations, but reflect genetic differences in the temperamental profiles of global regions, for such differences have been reported (Kagan et al. 1995). These, combined with more local forces, help to determine which are the time-honored pathways to positions of wealth and respect within a society, what value attaches to different occupations and professions, and thereby what individual attributes are subject to favorable or unfavorable selective processes. Far too little is known empirically about these cultural differences and how they function.

At the organizational level, selective forces primarily serve the purposes of role allocation. Among these one can distinguish between those that set up competitive tournaments from those that use more formalistic criteria, such as length of service or qualifications (Sheridan et al. 1990). As Rosenbaum (1989) points out, the competitive model is more ubiquitous than appears on the surface, because many tournaments take place covertly or in disguised form. Employees seem to recognize this when they express the widely held view that the politics of impression management are a major driver of opportunity. The tournament model is one that seems especially suited to the competitive impulses and strategic preferences of males.

There are alternative models. Two merit special mention: the family and the team. The family model accounts for much more of total employment in most economies than the corporate form. Selection operates firstly on the basis of kinship ties, and, at levels below the leading group, on quasi-kinship 'tribal' principles. Interestingly, kinship is relatively blind to individual differences, which ensures diversity among the leading members of the firm (because of the near zero-correlation of personality attributes between family members, apart from identical twins (see Lykken *et al.* 1992)). This does not apply to non-kin managers, who must attain advancement through the selective filter of attraction and trust in relation to the leading family group. Perceived similarity with the agents of Selection is likely to matter in this, for personal congruence is a selective principle around which loyalty and trust can be forged. This is not unique to family firms, but applies to any firm or subunit in which communal/tribal rather than bureaucratic or meritocratic values operate. The consequence of this principle is a sympathetic mutuality between selection and self-selection into organizational units on the 'cloning' principle, creating communities of similarity, especially among key managerial incumbents. Evidence for inter-company personality differences points to this cause (Jordan *et al.* 1991), as Schneider (1987) has argued in his 'the people make the place' theory of how attraction, selection, and attrition result in firms developing distinctive psychological profiles.

The team model offers a viable alternative, though in reality it remains a scarce paradigm. Its features are egalitarian values, informal status distinctions rather than rigid hierarchy, fluid division of labor based upon mutual adjustment and high interdependence, and self-determination of roles and goals. Interestingly, this looks close to the ancestral model of hunter-gatherer existence for which we were designed (Erdal and Whiten 1996), and therefore should be where people feel most effective, protected, and satisfied. If this is true, why are team-based structures not more common? There are a number of obstacles. One is that it restrains male competitive striving, and has not been preferred by the male power-holders in society. Secondly, it is a form particularly adapted to conditions of relative isolation, diffuse resource supply (Pierce and White, in press), low accumulation of assets, and a dynamic environment of changing goals. These conditions have not predominated in organizational society, where high social embeddedness, contested and centralized resource supply, high asset accumulation, and niche specialization have favored more stable mechanistic forms. Some consultancy organizations probably come closest to exhibiting the features and preconditions for the team model, though they quickly transmute into less organic forms as they grow. In some cases team-based structures may be spun off from the center, on the 'starburst' model (Quinn 1992), or following conglomerate acquisition be allowed to function with a high degree of autonomy (such as happened in the early days of the Virgin organization, or as seems to have been so successful in the Swedish-based conglomerate ABB). So, although the model may be close to an ideal type in terms of fit with human dispositions and capabilities, it will not become common because of economic and environmental constraints.

Just as it is difficult for egalitarian team forms embedded within conventional structures to resist the contrary forces surrounding them, so it is also difficult for team-based structures to prosper in an organizational world founded on other principles. Selective and self-selective processes will lure away from them individuals for whom the conventional hierarchy offers more rewards and better psychological fit (for example, individuals with low tolerance of uncertainty or high needs for autonomy). This selective assortment can be self-defeating for all types of organization by truncating the diversity that helps adaptiveness. A key feature of the ancestral community was that there was no alternative to membership, and therefore they exhibited a normal (in the statistical sense) diversity of individual member characteristics. Modern society allows, encourages indeed, the assortment of individuals to organizations that suit them. This is fine for the individual but is it healthy for the organization? Team-based organizations that contain too many like-minded people may become functionally maladaptive and unable to cope with change.

Connection

As argued elsewhere (Nicholson and West 1989) the individual career stands at the intersection between the forces of identity and social structure, recast here as Motivation and Selection. In fact, the present analysis suggests identity is an outcome rather than an input to the process, or rather that it represents how these interactive forces resolve. Here I am drawing a distinction between what I have called Motivation—the enduring goals states of the individual—and identity—how the individual conceives of herself as a social actor. The latter is more plastic than the former, and, for career theory, represents the connectedness of the self-concept with work experience, opportunities, and constraints—past, present, and future. Let us look at this in three ways: perceptual/decisional processes, affect–behavior linkages, and social dynamics.

Perceptual/decisional processes

Perceptual control theory (Powers 1973) and its successors in self-regulation theory (Kuhl 1992; Lord and Levy 1994) accord a central role to the framing of percepts, under the guidance of goal states, in how we act and choose. This reasoning has important implications. It suggests that socialization affects careers more by the reframing of perceptions than by the reshaping of underlying deep motive structures. These effects can be powerful—deflecting the individual's attention from one set of proximal goals to another as vehicles for the expression of motives. Evolutionary theory suggests that perceptual/cognitive systems are not designed for veridicality, probabilistic accuracy, or analytical completeness (Pinker 1997). Despite its extraordinary computing power the brain is inferior to even the most primitive computers in its calculative ability. Rather it is an organ for action—a superbly complex control system, designed for hyper-awareness of threat and opportunity, empathy and inference about the motives of others, mobilization and focusing of energy for action states, discourse and display to attract and manipulate relationships, the power to imagine and visualize future states, the ability to categorize and memorize novel stimuli, and to maintain states of self-consciousness for integrated goal-directed behavior. The so-called perceptual biases documented by behavioral decision theorists (Bazerman 1994) are the fallout from these gifts—illusions of control, over-attention to prominent stimuli, asymmetrical positive and negative value judgments, distorted estimates of improbable and highly probable events, and the over weighting of interpersonal information sources.

In this context career perceptions are socially mediated sensemaking with an eye to possible action (Feldman 1988). An aspiring manager does not coolly analyze the probability of vacancies occurring at higher levels, the number of possible candidates, and a rational assessment of how others' qualities compare with her own. Rather she will listen to the rumor mill, form an image of what it takes to get noticed, evaluate the personal payoffs of possible scenarios, orient toward a preferred strategy, and selectively accrue information that supports her orientation. This purposive pathfinding makes informal socialization processes all-important in guiding perceptions and actions. Management's attempts to eradicate employee cynicism about career opportunities become akin to trying to clear a rational path in an unabating blizzard of cultural snow.

How the perceptual guidance system operates 'irrationally' can be seen at every stage of career development. During the career exploration stage individuals match self-perceptions with idealized images of personally prominent models rather than objective appraisals of a wide array of career paths (Power and Aldag 1985) and escalating commitment to a limited set of opportunities leads to a circumscribed set of behavioral strategies. One of the chief functions of vocational guidance is to help counteract this bias. During the stage of selection/recruitment, self-presentation is calculated to manipulate received perceptions rather than accurate self-disclosure. Assessment centers and other measurement methods are designed to overcome this bias. The candidate judges employers on the basis of their interview experience and attraction to the interviewer rather than reliable information about the employer or job demands (Rynes *et al.* 1991). Realistic job previews aim to reduce this effect. During and after the induction phase, formal training and management attempts to control learning are supplanted by informal peer-mediated attitudes and beliefs. During the career establishment and maintenance stages, external and internal career opportunities are misperceived according to subjective payoff values of risk and reward—for example, fear of loss in a competitive tournament leads an individual to create a set of self-justifying beliefs for resigned adaptation. The accumulated side-bets of long tenure similarly underpin false perceptions of low external labor-market opportunities. Careers counseling is designed to counteract these tendencies.

Affect–behavior linkages

The unfolding nature of the career is thus very much under the control of changing perceptual frames, and the continual rematching of goals with apprehended fitness landscapes. This cognitive connectedness is driven by two additional processes: affective responses to experience, and social/interpersonal influences. The first is the outcome of feedback cues from the selective environment, which reinforce positive or negatively. Recent work at London Business School on 'failure' (Cannon and Nicholson 1996) indicates these are asymmetrical in their impact. Positive reactions are very readily overwhelmed by negative affect. Appraisal systems frequently fall foul of this problem, coming into disrepute with employees as regimes of tasteless carrot and clumsily wielded stick. The smart of the stick instantly supplants any gratification from the taste of the carrot. Failures and setbacks tend not to stimulate analytical insight or rational search, as popular theories of organizational learning optimistically advocate, but much cruder more categorical avoidance learning (Argyris 1992). This model suggests that many people's career motives do not become steadily enriched into a matrix of synthesized insights, but are more akin to a trim and salvage operation, where discouraging paths are blanked out of consciousness. A mixture of superstition and hopeful vigilance are adopted as defenses against further negation, while affirming experiences are pursued, away from the danger zone. Goal focus can thus easily become deflected from organizationally prescribed career paths into the alternative economies of non-work life, professional association, and arenas for games of insurgency, social dominance, and the like. This resembles closely the selectionist paradigm of evolutionary processes, in which, when the environment suddenly changes, extinction and 'habitat tracking' (migrating to seek out one's familiar landscape) are more common outcomes than successful mutation of the motivational profile genotype (Eldredge 1995). This argument suggests that career change is a much more difficult and serendipitous process than the new orthodoxy of the portmanteau career would have us believe.

To break out of this pattern and find genuine transformation requires 'double loop learning' (Argyris 1993). Argyris's writings illustrate why defensive routines of the sort we have been describing are so prevalent. They are much less threatening and effortful than a more far-reaching review of goals, for the latter course entails honest and potentially painful career introspection that not only questions the fundamentals of career identity, but also requires a critical re-evaluation of many past decisions and commitments. Individual differences, especially in emotionality, play an important part here. The response of many individuals to experienced failure is fundamental self-questioning, in some cases resulting in chronically impaired self-esteem. Here the MSC logic can work in a negative spiral, with the person becoming insensitive to positive feedback, and locking into the only available cognitively consistent frame of self-identity—self-derogation (LaRonde and Swann 1993), which in extreme cases culminates in depressive states of 'learned helplessness'.

Social dynamics

The social forces governing Connection operate on the same principles. The social construction of career meaning is highly selective and purposive, geared toward maintaining consistency between goals and perceptions of the environment. Communities and networks mediate shared meaning, and membership of them is non-arbitrary. Evolutionary theory suggests access is impeded by tendencies for people to make discriminatory in-group/out-group distinctions, and to relate to psychological communities of cognitively manageable proportions. Members of networks by these devices build linkages of similarity and proximity with each other, and thereby help each other to maintain consistent self-identity perceptions. Thus do people become locked into occupational subcultures and discouraged from radical change. In the organizational hierarchy, these subcultures are often associated with vertical strata. One of the most striking features of Hill's (1992) longitudinal study of people stepping into managerial roles was how difficult it was for them to make the shift to adopting the new perceptual frame of their former superiors, even though they had been close observers of their bosses' behavior over a prolonged period.

Themes in the Careers Literature

Let us now examine how this analytical frame reconstructs some familiar and topical themes in the careers literature: how career opportunities differ across populations, the determinants of mobility and immobility, the development of leaders, and new forms of organization and career.

The structure of advantage and disadvantage

Sociologists used to talk about the inheritance of careers. This has become unfashionable with the demise of social class as a predominant focus of scholarship, due to increasing affluence, a burgeoning middle class, and a proliferation of new occupations and organizational types. However, as I have argued, it would be mistaken to discount the pervasive influence of social stratification on life and career chances. Social inequality is greater now than ever before (Wilkinson 1997), as free-market capitalism has extended its dominance as the economic paradigm of our times. The consequences can be analyzed in terms of the MSC model. The first is a widening separation between three broad groupings: a professional educated elite, a large and varied middle mass of employment, and a substantial underclass, comprising ethnic minorities, casualized and migrant labor, and manual workers with low levels of literacy and resources (for example, property). Available evidence shows that the forces of career inheritance act continually to discriminate to a very high degree between these groupings, even under conditions of (relative) equality of state education provision. The fact is that the MSC process has much deeper biases than state provision can ameliorate. Career motives need to be equipped with psychological mechanisms for their transmission into achievement—positive self-images, self-efficacy beliefs, and a repertoire of social and cultural skills. Connection is also aided by the communities in which people are reared, the networks they activate, and the expectations they foster. Even when individuals, by virtue of native talents, aspire to escape these constraints, they may still be deflected by rejection from the structural forces of Selection.

In short, much career advantage and disadvantage comes out of the Selection domain of the model. But variations in Motivation are also important. The chances of many are impaired by heritable individual difference factors: limited intellectual gifts, low stamina, emotional instabilities, and physical attributes. It has been politically incorrect to suggest that some of these may be social-class linked, though, in the case of intelligence, some assortment does appear to occur on this basis (Loehlin 1997). However, even if there are proportionately more constitutionally disadvantaged in underclass groupings, it is also true that similarly impaired individuals born into high status are typically immunized from the negative consequences by the connections their wealth can give them. They might not find their way into the professions with the ease that the dim-witted offspring of the gentry in Victorian times were guaranteed commissions in the army or the church, but they will still prosper with the aid of the best that money can buy in education, property rights, and family connections. The net of Selection has a graded mesh, which allows easy Connection to even small fish of the right class. The market mechanism is driving the MSC model in the direction of a widening gulf between the strata of advantage and disadvantage, with negative consequences for us all, in terms of health, longevity, and the quality of life (Wilkinson 1997). The commitment of democracies to provide access to education and health care for the most disadvantaged groups only partially mitigates these effects.

Career exploration and mobility

Across all social strata, but perhaps especially in the middle mass, the increased variety and diversity of employment do offer more opportunities for change and mobility than ever before. But there are two countervailing obstacles to this. One is that higher levels of structural unemployment—a feature of the widening wealth inqualities in Western societies—provide a powerful incentive toward security of employment. The second is that sunk costs in technical skills and extended education argue against career change, especially in mid-career when property debt and family dependencies place a premium upon a reliable disposable income. This is somewhat ameliorated by dual careerism (partners buffering each other's changes), but in general there is no reason to suppose that barriers to movement are, for most, falling away significantly.

The MSC model is conservative about radical career change. The three elements reinforce one another in most people's lives, yet rates of inter-organizational mobility have increased over the past thirty years (Nicholson and West 1988; Inkson 1995). Four categories of career changer can be identified. First are the young, for whom the impeding circumstances described are often absent, and whose change is exploration among fitness landscapes to choose where to invest their Motivation. Second are the lifelong explorers—individuals whose personality is restless, entrepreneurial, and driven by high openness. My own current work is revealing this and other personality dimensions to be key predictors of career risk taking and radical change, and twin studies strongly suggest that this motivational propensity is genotypical (McCall et al. 1997). The rate of change has risen for these individuals as opportunities have widened, but they remain a small proportion of the population overall (Judge and Watanabe 1995). Third are people whose fitness landscapes change abruptly, as the forces of Selection expel them from settled employment. The increasing rate of business restructuring is responsible for much mobility of this kind, and the search for 'employability', especially among longer-tenure staff in declining industries, is designed primarily to defend against this eventuality. The fourth and largest group are those in more gradually changing environments, where many perceive a potential progressive degrading of the fitness landscape. Two subgroups are identifiable: those who perceive a climate of instability and threat and jump ship before they are pushed, and those who enact a strategy of moving regularly between employers to stay ahead of change waves and to avoid the risks of dependence on a single long-term employer. Many career movers in the fourth category thus look like explorers (even to themselves), but in reality their mobility is largely defensive. Most of them are 'habitat tracking' rather than evolving—the switches they make are within familiar domains rather than to genuinely new ones—for example, switching between sectors but maintaining their functional identities. The reported shift of emphasis from organizational to occupational careers reflects this trend (Tolbert 1996).

According to this analysis, a substantial proportion of mobility (groups three and four above) is driven more by the forces of Selection than by Motivation. In this context varieties of immobility bear some examination. Many individuals are plateaued or in routine careers. The former include managers without opportunities for further promotion in their professions and a heterogeneous population of manual workers, semi-skilled white-collar employees, craftspeople, technically skilled workers, and many professionals. Almost everyone's career eventually plateaus—it is just a question of how early. In MSC terms this is the point at which there is diminished utility in searching for enhanced Connection. Selection and Motivation conspire in many cases to this end (also Connection, in so far as individuals misperceive opportunities to be consistent with their motives). Every individual has to consider the payoff matrix attached to choices and challenges. In a hierarchical society, the higher the aspirational target, the more status seeking becomes risky, effortful to enact, and likely to be thwarted. Plateau points come when 'satisficing' is the best option—forgoing the right to compete in exchange for the benefits of a secure position of subordination—or when the criteria of Selection signal the person has reached the end of a particular aspirational road (e.g. by age and qualifications) (Nicholson 1993). Individual differences are important here, and the ranks of the plateaued contain many with low drives for achievement. The comfortable trade of non-contest for a peaceful life is, however, increasingly denied to people in corporate life where contracts have become insecure and where performance management systems enforce a competitive-achievement ethos at every level. The result, as commentators on business trends have been pointing out, is obsessive and defensive hard work and long hours.

Leaders and professionals

Schein's (1975) career-anchor concept (security, autonomy, technical competence, general management, entrepreneurship, service, and challenge) embodies a synthesis of Motivation and Selection—that is, they are a model of varieties of Connection. His categories are in part a schema of individual differences—genetic- and childhood-founded preferences for different kinds of activity, and in part a map of the structure of roles in organizational society—the Selection landscape. Interestingly, they remain as relevant at the end of the twentieth century as when Schein proposed them (in the 1970s), and probably have wide cross-cultural and historical relevance as a reflection of the enduring evolutionary order of working communities the world over (Schein 1996).

Leadership cuts across these categories—read head of household for security, creative celebrity for autonomy, unique craftsperson for technical competence, appointed authority for general management, wealthy trader for entrepreneurship, politician or high priest for service, and sporting hero for challenge. Writings about leadership are usually concerned with only a fraction of this range, and still fail to bring clarity to the subject. The MSC model offers two ways of thinking about the careers of leaders. The Motivational path to all these positions shares the unifying feature of the desire for prominence—the status aspiration to be a leader—and the successful are those who marry this drive with a developed skill set, plus the good fortune of a propitious selective environment. In general, people with talent in one or other of these domains, aspirational drive, and a sound constitution do rise to prominence. The career development of such individuals is unproblematic—they make their own luck, as the saying goes—though much of the literature on the subject seems absorbed with finding an elixir that can create them.

In some cases it is possible to identify, select, and nurture talent, but what many career systems for the development of leaders are really doing is manipulating a second theme—the selective environment. The guardians of career management systems see their role as enhancing the Motivation–Connection linkage, by identifying talent, fostering the practice of skills, supporting self-belief, and opening up networks. More often though, talent is unreliably detected, and consequently career management systems are devoted to controlling elements of post-entry Selection—establishing hierarchical criteria, supervising tournaments, and distributing payoffs. This has two consequences. One is that leader development becomes a self-fulfilling engine. Early success or advantage—for example, placement with an influential boss—sets the MSC processes on a cycle of progressive endowment. The agents of Selection have a powerful interest in having their judgments validated, and the objects of Selection a powerful interest in conforming with and confirming with the criteria of Selection. Thus do we see the justified cynicism of the Dilbert® comic strip in which mediocrity is rewarded, impression management triumphs over dedication, and self-cloning guides the patronage of top management. 'High Potential' schemes court the danger of refining this process into a fast-track caste system disguised as a meritocracy (Thompson et al. 1985), much as elite socialization/education institutions have done in just about every society throughout history. The second consequence is that leader development becomes culturally localized. Research indicates that the demographic characteristics of CEOs is highly dependent upon the local power arrangements of the firm (Zajac and

Westphal 1996), as in like manner the personality of leaders reflects the normative values of the local elite.

The career development of professionals conforms to these patterns, but within the domain of occupations rather than organizations (see Chapter 9). Motivated excellence provides one source of supply, and in general talented professionals do find their economic value. But alongside them, and often in authority over them, are many more who have been advanced on conveyer belts of networks of influence. Leading roles in professionalized occupations are more readily gained by those who gain high visibility on the conference circuit, the professional association, and by the trading of favors than by mere professional competence (see Chapter 7). This is because, in all occupational and organizational communities, much of the most instrumental tacit knowledge is social intelligence about networks, not the store of functional expertise that most hold in common, and the more one gossips and grooms—talents for which we have highly evolved capacities (Dunbar 1996)—the richer becomes one's social identity and network access for further advantage.

Virtual organizations and boundaryless careers

How much is the organizational world changing? Much recent writing on careers has an uplifting millennial and evangelical spirit to it. Organizations will cease to be monolithic hierarchies and become empowering decentralized matrices of opportunity. Employees will become protean venturers, building knowledge-based competencies for creative and flexible lives. This model owes much to the experience and aspirations of people from the worlds of consultancy, the media, and academia, as is apparent from contributions to Arthur and Rousseau's (1996) collection on *The Boundaryless Career*. It does indeed point a way forward to significant new possibilities for organizing, though the MSC model suggests that, for all but a minority, careers will continue to be heavily bounded by needs, structures, and opportunities. What is genuinely new in the present era is the information-based organization, in which physical proximity, bricks and mortar, fixed technology, and the like are no longer required. The Internet is the new paradigm—a self-organizing network of opportunity. Virtual organizations are part of the new reality as mechanisms for instrumental wealth creation, but where are the people within them and what are they doing? At their nodes are small numbers of information and network managers, and attached to their axons are armies of suppliers, intermediaries, advisers, and independents. Many of these will be in conventional work organizations holding what I have termed routine careers within their functional specialism. The virtual organization might provide a new channel for their outputs but one doubts the extent to which it can resist the consequences of the MSC dynamic. First, electronic communication has significant insufficiencies in its ability to satisfy people's need for contextual framing and elaborated meaning in decision-making. Secondly, many features of operations and decision-making cannot be conducted remotely without inefficiencies, moral hazard, or costly controls. Thirdly, for emotional gratification, access to influence, and legitimacy of action, people have a strong need for face-to-face interaction and visible display. It is part of the human design that we desire to be close to the center of the field, interact in common space, and have time for casual exchange. Home-working is a case in point (Baruch and Nicholson 1997). It has increased dramatically, but there appear to be severe limitations on its potential for growth as a way of working. These stem from the functional separation of work and family that persists in most employment domains, and the desire of individuals to maintain strong links into the networks of Selection.

The MSC model similarly places limitations on the extent to which peripatetic, portfolio, and other exotic hybrids will replace the more conventional paradigms of hierarchical, professionalized, or routine careers we have discussed. As more than one contributor to the Arthur and Rousseau volume acknowledge, much employment remains locked into more traditional forms (Perrow 1996), while the boundaryless alternatives have oversold benefits (Hirsch and Shanley 1996).

However, there is a sense in which a new (old) model for careers is becoming more attainable—the communal model (Goffee and Jones 1996; see also Chapters 5 and 12). It is old in the sense that it resembles the model of clan living that seems likely to have characterized the ancestral hunter-gatherer groupings which predominated throughout our long pre-agrarian evolutionary history. Comparative anthropology and palaeobiology suggest the following characteristics: size no more than 150; status order fluid and dynamic; division of labor flexible and pragmatic by project and skill base; leadership specific to tasks and circumstances; work and non-work heavily intersecting; kinship and friendship networks governing sub-group–community bonds. This is less a boundaryless than an organic model, for which we are arguably well fitted in our psychological design. The information age could be seen to offer the prospect of this model as increasingly accessible. On trading floors, in consultancies, media firms, agricultural communities, craft enterprises, academies, and the like, elements of it are to be found. Evolutionary psychology suggests it is a model to which we may consciously aspire to restore career fulfilment to many whom mechanistic forms have dispossessed. But, as discussed above in relation to team-design structures, the interdependencies of the modern economy, and the divisions within it by function, sector, and power, restrict the scope for the communal model to spread enough to become a dominant paradigm.

Conclusion: Implications of the MSC Model for Intervention and Change

I have argued that a coherent set of processes continue to govern career development, and are reworked rather than suspended in the new climate of employment that the information revolution and global economy are creating. Intervention is needed to ensure that the MSC processes we have discussed enhance rather than diminish the dignity of individuals, and deliver the benefits of creative and productive commitment to work and occupation.

Career intervention in the realm of Motivation is fundamentally psychological, for which techniques and models are already well developed and, in some areas, practiced. Insight, reflection, and skill development can be aided by psychometry, which helps individuals to appreciate and build upon their uniqueness. The aim here should be to equip people with the repertoires of skills that enable them to capitalize on their profile of dispositions and aptitudes, not to try to reform them. The latter folly is a latent implication of the new career orthodoxy that people can reinvent career identities without limitation.

In the domain of Selection, intervention is already proceeding apace, but often without any clear sense of the consequences. Delayering without regard for implicit status orders and downsizing without awareness of the fragility of contractual trust have been hallmarks of the 1990s (Nicholson 1996). Within traditional organizations, above all an understanding is needed of how selective processes operate implicitly and consideration given to how they can be reformed towards transparency, non-discrimination, and goal focuses with which individuals can meaningfully identify. Evolutionary theory suggests that the more radical alternatives to this reside in the design of 'organic' business forms—that is, varieties of occupational and organizational community, rather than the more fantastical worlds of virtual careers in virtual organizations.

In the sphere of Connection, anyone who has any responsibility for someone else's career development—managers, counselors, educators—can contribute in two ways. One is to help individuals toward a true appreciation of network dynamics and how to access them. The second is to support career resilience and identity integrity, by counteracting perceptual biases and facilitating constructive responses to emotion-laden outcomes of career processes.

Finally, the MSC model underlines the continuing relevance of many traditional themes in theory and research, and suggests where future efforts may bear fruit. Specifically, in each of the three MSC domains, this draws attention, respectively, to the need for better understanding of the psychological drivers of occupational choice, the consequences of implicit career structures, and the biases affecting career identity and decision making.

References

Argyris, C. (1992), *On Organizational Learning* (Oxford: Blackwell).

—— (1993), *Knowledge for Action* (San Francisco: Jossey-Bass).

Arnold, J. (1997), 'The Psychology of Careers in Organizations', in C. L. Cooper and I. T. Robertson (eds.), *International Review of Industrial and Organizational Psychology*, vol. 12 (Chichester: Wiley).

Arthur, M. B., and Rousseau, D. M. (1996) (eds.), *The Boundaryless Career: A New Employment Principle for a New Organizational Era* (New York: Oxford University Press).

Baruch, Y., and Nicholson, N. (1997), 'Home, Sweet Work', *Journal of General Management*, 23/2: 15–30.

Bazerman, M. H. (1994), *Judgement in Managerial Decision Making* (3rd edn., New York: Wiley).

Brown, D. E. (1991), *Human Universals* (New York: McGraw Hill).

Brunner, E. J. (1997), 'Stress and the Biology of Inequality', *British Medical Journal*, 314: 472–6.

Cannon, D. A., and Nicholson, N. (1996), 'Making Sense of Failure: Memory, Motive and Self-regulation', unpublished working paper, Centre for Organisational Research, London Business School.

Cloninger, C. R., Adolfsson, R., and Svrakic, N. M. (1996), 'Mapping Genes for Human Personality', *Nature Genetics*, 12: 3–4.

Cohen, A. (1991), 'Career Stage as a Moderator of the Relationships between Organizational Commitment and its Outcomes: A Meta-Analysis', *Journal of Occupational Psychology*, 64: 253–68.

Cronin, H. (1991), *The Ant and the Peacock* (Cambridge: Cambridge University Press).

Cziko, G. (1995), *Without Miracles: Universal Selection Theory and the Second Darwinian Revolution* (Cambridge, Mass.: MIT Press).

Dunbar, R. (1996), *Gossip, Grooming and Evolution of Language* (London: Faber & Faber).

Eldredge, N. (1995), *Reinventing Darwin: The Great Evolutionary Debate* (New York: Wiley).

Ellis, L. (1994), 'Social Status and Health in Humans: The Nature of the Relationship and its Possible Causes', in L. Ellis (ed.), *Social Stratification and Socio-Economic Inequality*, ii. *Reproductive and Interpersonal Aspects of Dominance and Status* (New York: Praeger).

Erdal, D., and Whiten, A. (1996), 'Egalitarianism and Machiavellian Intelligence in Human Evolution', in P. Mellars and K. Gibson (eds.), *Modelling the Early Human Mind* (Oxford: Oxbow Books).

Feldman, D. C. (1988), *Managing Careers in Organizations* (Glenview, Ill.: Scott Foreman).

Goffee, R., and Jones, G. (1996), 'What Holds the Modern Company Together', *Harvard Business Review* (Nov.–Dec.), 133–48.

—— and Scase, R. (1992), 'Organizational Change and the Corporate Career: The Restructuring of Managers' Job Aspirations', *Human Relations*, 45: 363–85.

Gunz, H. (1989), *Careers and Corporate Cultures* (Oxford: Blackwell).

Hill, L. A. (1992), *Becoming a Manager: Mastery of a New Identity* (Cambridge, Mass.: Harvard Business School Press).

Hirsch, P. M., and Shanley, M. (1996), 'The Rhetoric of Boundaryless—Or, how the Newly Empowered Managerial Class Bought into its own Marginalization', in M. B. Arthur and D. M. Rousseau (eds.), *The Boundaryless Career: A New Employment Principle for a New Organizational Era* (New York: Oxford University Press).

Holland, J. L. (1973), *Making Vocational Choices* (Englewood Cliffs, NJ: Prentice Hall).

Inkson, K. (1995), 'Effects of Changing Economic Conditions on Managerial Job Changes and Careers', *British Journal of Management*, 6: 183–94.

Jordan, M., Herriot, P., and Chalmers, C. (1991), 'Testing Schneider's ASA Theory', *Applied Psychology: An International Review*, 40: 47–53.

Judge, T. A., and Watanabe, S. (1995), 'Is the Past Prologue?: A Test of Ghiselli's Hobo Syndrome', *Journal of Management*, 21: 211–230.

Kagan, J., Snidman, N., Arcus, D., and Reznick, J. S. (1995), *Galen's Prophesy: Temperament in Human Nature* (New York: Basic Books).

Kaufman, S. (1995), *At Home in the Universe: The Search for Laws of Complexity* (New York: Oxford University Press).

Kuhl, J. (1992), 'A Theory of Self-Regulation: Action versus State Orientation, Self-Discrimination and some Applications', *Applied Psychology: An International Review*, 41: 97–129.

LaRonde, C., and Swann, W. B. (1993), 'Caught in the Crossfire: Positivity and Self-Verification Strivings among People with Low Self-Esteem', in R. F. Baumeister (ed.), *Self-Esteem: The Puzzle of Low Self-Regard* (New York: Plenum).

Loehlin, J. C. (1997), 'Dysgenesis and IQ: What Evidence is Relevant?', *American Psychologist*, 52: 1236–9.

—— McCrae, R. R., Costa, P. J., and John, O. J. (1998), 'Heritabilities of Common and Measure-Specific Components of the Big Five Personality Factors', *Journal of Research in Personality*, 32: 431–53.

Lord, R. G., and Levy, P. E. (1994), 'Moving from Cognition to Action: A Control Theory Perspective', *Applied Psychology: An International Review*, 43: 335–66.

Lykken, D. T., McGue, M., Tellegen, A., and Bouchard, T. J. (1992), 'Emergenesis: Genetic Traits that may not Run in Families', *American Psychologist*, 47: 1565–77.

Lyness, K. S., and Thompson, D. E. (1997), 'Above the Glass Ceiling? A Comparison of Matched Samples of Female and Male Executives', *Journal of Applied Psychology*, 82: 359–75.

McCall, B. P., Cavanaugh, M. A., Arvey, R. D., and Taubman, P. (1997), 'Genetic Influences on Job and Occupational Switching', *Journal of Vocational Behavior*, 50: 60–77.

Nicholson, N. (1993), 'Purgatory or Place of Safety? The Managerial Plateau and Organizational Agegrading', *Human Relations*, 46: 1369–89.

—— (1996), 'Career Systems in Crisis: Change and Opportunity in the Information Age', *Academy of Management Executive*, 10: 40–51.

—— (1997), 'Evolutionary Psychology: Toward a New View of Human Nature and Organizational Society', *Human Relations*, 50: 1053–78.

—— (1998), 'How Hardwired is Human Behavior?', *Harvard Business Review*, 76/4: 134–47.

—— and West, M. A. (1988), *Managerial Job Change* (Cambridge: Cambridge University Press).

—— —— (1989), 'Transitions, Work Histories, and Careers', in M. B. Arthur, D. T. Hall, and B. S. Lawrence (eds.), *The Handbook of Career Theory* (Cambridge: Cambridge University Press).

Perrow, C. (1996), 'The Bounded Career and the Demise of the Civil Society', in M. B. Arthur and D. M. Rousseau (eds.), *The Boundaryless Career: A New Employment Principle for a New Organizational Era* (New York: Oxford University Press).

Pierce, B. D., and White, R. (in press), 'The Evolution of Social Structure: Why Biology Matters', *Academy of Management Review.*

Pinker, S. (1997), *How the Mind Works* (New York: Norton).

Plomin, R. (1994), *Genetics and Experience: The Interplay between Nature and Nurture* (Thousand Oaks, Calif.: Sage).

Power, D. J., and Aldag, R. J. (1985), 'Soelberg's Job Search and Choice Model: A Clarification, Review, and Critique', *Academy of Management Review*, 10: 48–58.

Powers, W. T. (1973), *Behavior: The control of perception* (New York: Aldine/de Gruyter).

Quinn, J. B. (1992), *Intelligent Enterprise* (New York: Free Press).

Rosenbaum, J. E. (1989), 'Organizational Career Systems and Employee Misperceptions', in M. B. Arthur, D. T. Hall, and B. S. Lawrence (eds.), *The Handbook of Career Theory* (Cambridge: Cambridge University Press).

Rowe, D. C. (1997), 'Genetics, Temperament and Personality', in R. Hogan, J. Johnson, and S. Briggs (eds.), *Handbook of Personality Psychology* (New York: Academic Press).

Rynes, S., Bretz, R., and Gerhart, B. (1991), 'The Importance of Recruitment in Job Choice: A Different Way of Looking', *Personnel Psychology*, 44: 13–35.

Scase, R., and Goffee, R. (1989), *Reluctant Managers: Their Work and Lifestyles* (London: Routledge).

Schein, E. H. (1975), 'How Career Anchors Hold Executives to their Career Paths', *Personnel*, 52/3: 11–24.

—— (1996), 'Career Anchors Revisited: Implications for Career Development in the 21st Century', *Academy of Management Executive*, 10: 80–8.

Sheridan, J. E., Slocum, J. W., Buda, R., and Thompson, R. C. (1990), 'Effects of Corporate Sponsorship and Departmental Power on Career Tournaments', *Academy of Management Journal*, 4: 578–602.

Schneider, B. W. (1987), 'The People Make the Place', *Personnel Psychology*, 40: 437–53.

Smuts, B. (1995), 'The Evolutionary Origins of Patriarchy', *Human Nature*, 6: 1–32.

Sperber, D. (1996), *Explaining Culture: A Naturalistic Approach* (Oxford: Blackwell).

Super, D. E. (1953), 'A Theory of Vocational Development', *American Psychologist*, 8: 185–90.

Thompson, P. H., Kirkham, K. L., and Dixon, J. (1985), 'Warning: The Fast Track may be Hazardous to Organizational Health', *Organizational Dynamics*, 13: 21–33.

Tolbert, P. S. (1996), 'Occupations, Organizations, and Boundaryless Careers', in M. B. Arthur and D. M. Rousseau (eds.), *The Boundaryless Career: A New Employment Principle for a New Organizational Era* (New York: Oxford University Press).

Wiggins, J. S., and Trapnell, P. D. (1997), 'Personality Structure: The Return of the Big Five', in R. Hogan, J. Johnson, and S. Briggs (eds.), *Handbook of Personality Psychology* (New York: Academic Press).

Wilkinson, R. G. (1997), *Unhealthy Societies: From Inequality to Well-Being* (London: Routledge).

Zajac, E. J., and Westphal, J. D. (1996), 'Who shall Succeed? How CEO/Board Preferences and Power Affect the Choice of New CEOs', *Academy of Management Journal*, 39: 64–90.

4

Performance, Learning, and Development as Modes of Growth and Adaptation throughout our Lives and Careers

Richard E. Boyatzis and David A. Kolb

Growth occurs throughout our jobs and careers in many forms. The elimination of mandatory retirement in some countries, the flattening of organizations, global competition, the changing composition of the workforce, the complexity of balancing work and family roles, and the shifting values of the workforce are among the many forces contributing to a changing landscape of jobs and careers. This drives a need to understand what excites and stimulates an individual toward growth and adaptation throughout his or her life. In the current economic and social milieu, people are changing careers at an increasing rate (Arthur and Rousseau 1996). Different definitions of career that trace a person's progression through several defined stages, such as those of Dalton and Thompson (1986), are not sufficient to provide insight into the complexity of the paths through multiple careers. To address this need, a general model of growth and adaptation is presented in this chapter, as applied to life and career development.

Related to our model is a broad conception of management. If people enter management from jobs as individual contributors, such as being a salesperson, an engineer, a physician, or a student, the challenge of continuous growth appears dramatic. The manager's degree of growth, excitement, comportment, and performance affects other people's careers and lives. This multiplier effect perpetuates a preoccupation with exploring continuous growth of those who engage in management, but the underlying challenges of adaptation and continuous growth are the same for people in all jobs. In addition, because people enter management at many points in their life and careers, development of managerial competencies is needed and should be available for people throughout their lives and careers.

In the past, contemplation of career-long, or lifelong, growth has often led to models in which growth is a function of experience and time. The more experience a person has, the more developed we believe him or her to be. The more time a person is in a job, or alive, the more learning we believe is gained. *But experience does not imply learning or adaptation.* People can be performing jobs and not growing or adapting. If this were not the case, we would seldom see people repeat a mistake or confound one by continuing to act as if the earlier error had not occurred. Hindsight, reflection, and the study of history provide an overwhelming set of examples of individuals (even organizations and nations) that do not appear to learn from experience.

It has been noted that often people who have abilities or competencies do not use them in certain settings. Competencies are defined here as those characteristics of the person (for example, skills, values, motives, traits, social roles, and so on) that lead to or cause effective or superior perfor-mance in specific jobs (Boyatzis 1982); others refer to these characteristics as 'abilities' (Boyatzis *et al.* 1995) or 'capabilities' (Stevenson 1994). Over twenty years, competency studies in organizations, especially on middle-management and executive jobs, have focused on the top 3 per cent of the job-holders in any organization, who appeared truly outstanding in all aspects of the job (Boyatzis 1982; Spencer and Spencer 1993). Frequently, the observation has been made that many individuals in management jobs had these competencies (that is, abilities or capabilities) but did not use them at work (Boyatzis 1993, 1996). The confusion increased when it was often discovered that the same people *did use* these competencies in volun-teer work, small businesses, professional, and avocational activities outside their 'main' job.

Over twenty years of managing hundreds of consultants and dozens of professors in several consulting companies and university departments, we have been puzzled by a Jekyll-and-Hyde phenomenon. Many of these con-sultants or professors would demonstrate all of the competencies character-istic of outstanding and effective managers and leaders while interacting with their clients or students but then seemed to 'check them at the door' when they entered the consulting company offices or faculty meetings. The same people who could demonstrate competencies involving collaboration, empowerment, sensitivity, and inspired motivation with clients and students turned into individualistic martinets who avoided people, or sometimes treated their colleagues like furniture. Colleagues in other professional ser-vice organizations, such as hospitals and law firms, have reported observing a similar process.

These puzzles haunted us. Assuming that the current models had missed some vital ingredient, we looked for yet another competency. When that search proved futile, we looked for other levels of the competencies. This search also failed to account for these differences in behavior. The answer was far simpler than we thought at first: *these people were choosing not to use their abilities (that is, their competencies or capabilities).* This was particularly evident in advanced professionals and executives, and helped to explain the absence of leadership felt in a number of organizations. The misleading concept in this search was the assumption that everyone would want to use their abilities and capability whenever they had the opportunity. Career-long or lifelong theories of growth must take into account and explain such choices and dynamics.

Frustrations with Existing Theories

Many theories and models of growth are hierarchical and time dependent: with the passage of time, one is expected to progress along the path, rising higher in the sequence of stages. Time may be good as a model for physical growth, but it is inappropriate as a model for intellectual, emotional, or spiritual growth. Hierarchical theories do not appear to explain many of the dynamics people experience in their careers and lives regarding growth. Alexander, Druker, and Langer (1990) identified four characteristics of hierarchical, developmental theories, based on their analysis of Piaget's theory. They were: (1) each successive stage integrates schemata of the previous stages; (2) the end points are the logical culmination of stages preceding them; (3) there is an inevitable movement through the stages; and (4) movement to the next stage is an attempt to attain equilibrium. The last point of such theories assumes that: (*a*) attempts to assimilate experiences and challenges characteristic of a stage often (*b*) result in an imperfect fit, which (*c*) leads to realization of a conflict, which (*d*) leads to attempts to accommodate the conflict, which (*e*) leads to a new equilibrium.

As a person who has changed careers is observed or interviewed, it is often noted that he or she seems energized, revitalized, and excited by the challenge of the new career. The same observation can often be made of people changing organizations, industries, or becoming 'boundaryless' (Arthur and Rousseau 1996). In this new arena, they demonstrate many of the behaviors they showed much earlier during a former career or in a former organization. They identify where they can make a difference, identify standards of performance, and seek ways to meet or exceed the standards, to be sensitive to others, to build relationships, and to find ways to innovate or approach the issues in a new manner. These conditions do not appear to incorporate all prior moods about their former job, career, or organization, but in fact replace the mood in which they found themselves immediately prior to the change. Instead of being bored, or feeling underutilized, they show spirit and excitement.

The movement from one career to another (or the less dramatic change of organizations or industries), although often associated with 'mid-life crisis' or the loss of a job, appears most often to be associated with a growing restlessness inside the person. He or she may express it as boredom, fatigue, a loss of purpose, direction, or meaning, and so forth. At these times, a person appears to be making both conscious and unconscious choices to change, or at least to look for something different. The impetus for these changes is not logical, as hierarchical stage theories would predict, but appears non-rational, often discontinuous. The new condition sought is often not a 'new equilibrium' but in fact a disequilibrium and stimulation of novelty. Csikszentmihalyi and Csikszentmihalyi (1988) described that a person out of the 'flow' experience will seek the stimulation of being in it—not the comfort of being in it. Hall and Mirvis' (1996) concept of protean careers, Arthur and Rousseau's (1996) concept of the 'boundaryless career' and Nicholson's (1990) work on transitions and transition cycles assume career changes are discontinuous and people seek stimulation when seeking career changes.

Historically, models, or theories, of career development were hierarchical stage models. The imbedded hierarchy might have been based on time or age, as in Miller and Form's (1951) and Super's (1957) models. They may have been based on a sequential hierarchy, such as maturity within a career, but not necessarily age related, as in Dalton and Thompson's (1986) model or Schein's (1978) concept of progressive movement toward integration. Other models, including Driver's (1982) career concepts and Schein's (1978) career anchors, provide non-hierarchical, individual difference models (Dalton 1989).

Not all life-developmental theories are hierarchical, as Alexander, Druker, and Langer (1990) reviewed. Levinson *et al.* (1978, 1996) and Sheehy (1995) conceptualized a life-cycle concept for adulthood, in which the person proceeds through a number of stages or phases. Although these are considered non-hierarchical because they do not conform to the Piagetian criteria, they usually describe a sequence through which a person passes. This non-recursive characteristic of 'sequential' developmental theories, such as Levinson *et al.*'s (1978, 1996), Sheehy's (1995), Kolhberg's (Colby and Kolhberg 1987), or Loevinger's (Loevinger and Wessler 1983), imposes a type of value-based hierarchy: it is more mature (and therefore better) to be at the later stages or phases. This conceptualization would label re-entry into a former stage/phase as regression, and not as a natural evolution through one's life or careers.

These developmental theories typically offer a positive image of the ideal (that is, the good) and a negative image belittling to many individuals (that is, the bad). The difficulties arising from attempts to apply or use these theories emerge as conflicts between the empirically driven aspects of the theories and the ideologically driven aspects. This often occurs when the theorists depart from their descriptive efforts and move into prescriptions based upon justifications of the ideal stage they offer.

It appears, therefore, that, to understand the dynamics of lifelong career development in today's world, we must entertain a non-hierarchical theory in which a specific stage or set of value-based conditions does not dictate the 'best' or most mature place to be. We must entertain a recursive theory that allows for people to enter new careers with the enthusiasm, excitement, and the 'wide-eyed naivety' that was characteristic of our entrance into our first career of interest (to differentiate this experience from entering a career or job for survival reasons and without excitement). Hall and Mirvis (1996: 34) described a cycle of change in today's protean careers: 'people's careers increasingly will become a succession of "ministages" (or short-cycle learning stages) of exploration–trial–mastery–exit, as they move in and out of various products areas, technologies, functions, organizations, and other work environments'. We must entertain a non-linear theory to accommodate the pace and timing differences of individuals making jobs and career shifts at various ages (like people entering a doctoral program at 45, facing an eight-year growth process, or rite of passage before entering a new career).

The career transitions literature often incorporates a recursive model in the process of change described. Nicholson's (1984) earlier work on work role transitions postulated a cycle of Replication–Absorption–Determination–Exploration, which he later (1990) simplified into Replication–Gradation–Mutation when expanding the application of transition cycles beyond individuals to organizations. His recent Motivation–Selection–Connection model from evolutionary psychology (Chapter 3) may also be a recursive model. These models appear similar to Hall and Mirvis' (1996) conceptualization of the 'mastery to learning to mastery to learning and so forth' cycle evident in people's careers today. Transition theories of adult development tend to be process models and cite life events as markers of key changes (Schlossberg *et al.* 1995). Although the career transition theories such as Hall and Mirvis' (1996) and Nicholson's (1990) focus on the person's experience of the transitions, the adult development transition theories acknowledge the importance of the person's transitions but often stop short of classifying them.

While earlier theorists (e.g. Schein 1978) may have accounted for life and career transitions separately, an increasing number of people in industrialized and post-industrial societies do not experience compartmentalization of their personal life and jobs. The struggle of balancing different roles experienced by women in management and professional jobs may be an expression of the dissatisfaction with attempts at compartmentalization. The integration and balance sought in one's life among all of our competing interests, responsibilities, and pressures seem to be an increasing part of our lives (Latack 1984; Bailyn 1993; Marshall 1995; see also Chapter 9) and precludes compartmentalization. Once we acknowledge and view our lives and careers in terms of our relationships, the mental game of separating one's work and family or personal life seems an elusive pursuit with little utility. A relational approach to our careers leads us into a more holistic view of our lives (Kram 1996). Therefore, career and life developmental theories should address these arenas of our life in an integrated, or at least contextual, manner. This does not obviate the need for clarification of the syndrome of 'overwork' or 'workaholics'. As pointed out by Peiperl and Jones (1998) and Brett, Medvec, and Stroh (1998), balance in life and the definition of 'working a lot or too much' have different meanings to various people.

Elements of the Theory

The proposed theory (Boyatzis and Kolb 1991, 1994, 1995) has three modes of adaptation and growth: (1) the Performance Mode as the quest for mastery; (2) the Learning Mode as the quest for novelty; and (3) the Development Mode as the quest for meaning. The purpose of the theory is to elaborate and reconstruct experiential learning theory explained by Kolb (1984) as it is applied to lifelong adaptation and integrate the competency acquisition and development process explained by Boyatzis (1982). Exploration of these three modes in the context of each other has been difficult, because the validation research within each of these modes is found predominantly in different bodies of literature.

The Performance Mode

A person's growth and adaptation in the Performance Mode is understood through a focus on effective job performance, as shown in Table 4.1. The person in this mode is preoccupied with success and his or her intent is mastery of a job or arena of his or her life. This mode represents an attempt to establish self-validation—proving yourself worthy (Hall and Mirvis 1996). The key abilities, or capabilities, are situationally specific, behavioral skills. These are related to job and organizational demands, and in this sense are specific to a context of performance—that is, the context to which the person aspires to attain mastery. Since the focus of validation research in this mode has been effective job performance, the typical methods of measurement of competencies in the literature concerning this mode are methods of behavioral observation, such as critical incident interviews (Flanagan 1954; Boyatzis 1982; Spencer and Spencer 1993), simulations, assessment centers (Thornton and Byham 1982), and so forth.

A person often has some desire to change the condition of his or her job, life, or some degree of engagement with work. Routine acts performed with the intent of coping or in the pursuit of survival are in this mode. While in this mode, people may be in one of several sub-modes. In one sub-mode, they are coping. In another sub-mode, they are attempting to change or improve within the current job or career, or a major aspect of their life. Another sub-mode—attempting to change or improve with regard to a future job, career, or life aspiration—may be characteristic of a person on the cusp between the Performance and Learning modes. Throughout the time spent

Table 4.1. *Three modes of growth*

Themes	Performance Mode: The Quest for Mastery	Learning Mode: The Quest for Novelty	Development Mode: The Quest for Meaning
Intent and preoccupation	Job and situational mastery and success	Novelty, variety, and generalizability	Fulfillment of purpose (e.g. holistic sense of self; a value-based vision of the future; selfless contribution; connectedness for men and autonomy for women)
Orientation	Self-validation	Self-improvement	Self-fulfillment
Key abilities	Situationally specific, behavioral skills	Learning skills, self-image, contingent values	Traits, motives, and core values
Sub-modes	• Doing (i.e. coping) • Doing better within job/career	• Exploring other settings for skill application • Discovering underlying constructs of learning	• Personal integration • Social integration • Different ways of being
Scope of awareness and extension of time	Discrete settings and limited time (e.g. weeks)	Generalizing, extending, and extrapolating	Time elongation
Focus of validation research	Effective job performance	Learning	Adult development
Typical measurement in literature	Behavioral observation (e.g. critical incident interviews or simulations)	Self-report (e.g. questionnaires or card sorts)	Interactive and interpretive
Prerequisite to entry	Desire to survive, change, or improve one's life	Success or mastery in work or other activity	Life events provoking discovery or search for purpose or calling

in this mode, a person is focused on discrete settings. Time perspectives are also discrete in the sense of being limited. For example, when absorbed in the present, a person loses temporal context.

Two examples of people predominantly in the Performance Mode will illustrate some of the characteristics discussed. Mark is 25 years old. He is a former journalism major who worked on a set of business magazines following graduation. He had felt he had learned about as much as he was going to learn about writing and editing a magazine on his former job and began looking for other kinds of business reporting assignments. After applying to several major newspapers and media companies, he heard their feedback that he did not have enough experience in business or television to get the types of jobs of interest to him. He wanted to get ahead and as a journalist was tired of living like a pauper. So he enrolled in an MBA program as a major step in his growth. He describes this choice as career enhancement. He wants to be more marketable and get the education (and degree) so that he will be more attractive in the job market. Although enjoying some of his courses, classmates, and school activities, he is excited about the several internships and part-time job he has obtained during his graduate years because they are directly related to enhancing his job-related skills and experience for the specific career he wishes to pursue upon graduation. Mark's growth activities are directed at job and career success and enhancing his marketability to potential employers.

Another example is Barbara, who is President of a consulting company specializing in education. As head of a small, but influential, not-for-profit consulting company, she and others pursue the mission of the organization with enthusiasm and dedication. Barbara is in her mid-40s and has worked in higher education (i.e. colleges and universities), as well as creating innovative programs in secondary and collegiate education. Within several months of becoming President of the company, Barbara found herself focused on helping the company survive and grow. She began reading books on marketing, seeking meetings with consultants on pricing of services, attending conferences on strategic planning, asking for help in reviewing accounting systems, and developing company information systems. While continuing to promote the company's services and working with clients, her primary objective was the health of the company. As she reflected on the changes in how she spends her time and the growth activities she is currently selecting, Barbara says she is clearly predominantly in the Performance Mode focused on doing well as President. She wants to lead the company in growth and innovation, and has left past endeavors she described as being more characteristic of the other modes.

In both cases, Mark and Barbara not only select growth activities specifically focused on job, career, and company mastery and success, but their evaluation of the benefit of an activity is typically measured in terms of how clearly the activity will advance their capability to succeed. This is not to say that occasionally either one of them will not engage in actions for another purpose, but such 'divergences' are viewed as distractions from their direction.

The Learning Mode

Growth and adaptation in the Learning Mode is understood through a focus on learning, as shown in Table 4.1. The person in this mode is preoccupied with novelty, variety, and generalizability. The emphasis is on self-improvement, but appears different than the self-improvement in the Performance Mode, which is focused on improvement toward some standard of excellence or goal. The key abilities, or competencies, are learning skills, self-image, and contingent values (that is, those values adopted from reference groups). Since the focus of validation research on this mode has been learning, the typical methods of measurement of competencies in the literature concerning this mode are self-report methods (such as the card-sort Learning Skills Profile (Boyatzis and Kolb 1991, 1995) and the Myers–Briggs Indicators (Myers and McCaulley 1985)). People do not appear ready or eager to enter this mode until they have achieved, attained, and recognized a degree of success, or validation.

While in this mode, a person may be in the sub-mode of exploring other settings for application of skills already being used in a particular setting. Another sub-mode is discovering underlying constructs to explain learning. The person in this mode often looks for generalizing, extending, and extrapolating from the current and present situations into new, different, and possibly future ones. This mode is similar to Hall and Mirvis' (1996) 'learning mini-stage'. Although it appears similar to Nicholson's (1984) 'exploration' phase, his theory requires high discretion and high novelty at work to enact this phase of transition. In contrast, we suggest that people in routine jobs may enter the Learning Mode and find their adaptation, growth, and excitement outside work.

Examples of people predominantly in the Learning Mode are Frank and Giovanni. Frank is in his early 50s. He is Controller of a billion-dollar-a-year division of a Fortune 500 US company, and is considered a vital member of the executive staff of the division and corporation. The workshops he has selected to attend during the past several years have all involved extending his skills and perspective into new settings. For example, he has become interested in cross-functional teams and cross-functional staffing. As Frank discusses his excitement about these activities, he describes the potential for applying skills and perspective from one type of function (for example, manufacturing) to another function (for example, marketing). In addition, the vague restlessness he reports with merely continuing to do the current job, which he does exceedingly well, hints at his desire for a different type of challenge. He has even wondered about the possibility of becoming the President of a division or company as a next career step. He then moves to become the Chief Financial Officer of a European corporation, relocating to Brussels. This represents less of a 'promotion' and more of a 'different' type of organization and setting in which to work—he has the novelty of living in Brussels and the experiment of generalizing his capability in working for a European company with global operations.

Giovanni is in his mid-30s. He is in public relations at a major chemical manufacturer in Italy. His former jobs had been as Executive Director of two professional and industrial associations. Describing his current challenges, Giovanni gets excited at the examples of incidents in which he has been able to apply skills, experience, methods, and networks developed in his former career into the new setting. His choices of growth activities include projects to experiment with new methods of performing the public-relations function by defining the company as an industry leader in its field, and conducting events typically characteristic of a trade association.

In both examples, Frank and Giovanni appear to be predominantly in the Learning Mode. Their excitement and growth activities are directed at transferring skills, expertise, and knowledge from one setting into another setting. They want to experiment with new methods or new jobs. They are fascinated by the potential for generalization. They are both committed to their organizations and want to be effective, but neither is choosing growth activities that would maximize success or job mastery in his current job, or career path, such as attending courses directed at improving his 'job performance'. They are stretching into new areas, taking risks that may endanger the certainty of success. In these ways, they appear to be primarily in the Learning Mode. It is important to note that each will, at times, return briefly to the Performance Mode for growth activities related to a specific task or project, but the excitement and interest is not sustained, and they return to the Learning Mode.

The Development Mode

Growth and adaptation in the Development Mode is understood through a focus on adult development, as shown in Table 4.1. A person in this mode is preoccupied with perpetual human and social dilemmas, typically in the form of a 'calling'. The person's intent is focused on fulfillment of his or her purpose, or calling, in terms of a specific agenda. The heart of the Development Mode is the articulation of current meaning in one's life and attempted behavioral consistency with this meaning. The person's awareness of being in this mode may have a fuzzy, or emergent quality.

So far in our understanding, there appear to be four basic types of human and social dilemmas characteristic of this mode, called challenges by Kolb (1991). One dilemma is developing a holistic sense of self. In this quest, the person is seeking integration of the emotional, intellectual, behavioral, spiritual, and physical aspects of oneself. This may emerge as seeking a balance in life, but within this mode the desired distribution of time and attention will be dramatically different from other modes. For someone in the Performance Mode, 'overwork' generates appropriate rewards of evidence of progress toward mastery, despite occasional lip service to the need for balance in one's life. Individuals in the Development Mode would not care about the rewards of 'overwork' and are less likely to appear as workaholics (Brett *et al.* 1998; Peiperl and Jones 1998).

A second dilemma is seeking understanding in the context of values and/ or a vision of the future (that is, wisdom). The person is attempting to understand how the world works for the sake of insight or because it is believed to help on the path toward an ideal vision of the future. This does not necessarily involve, and is certainly not driven by, social activism, which could be characteristic of the Performance Mode.

A third dilemma is seeking connectedness in a global context. This may emerge as wanting to re-establish contact with 'long-lost' friends or relatives, a search for 'roots', or a desire to get to know others. Given the relational world of women, this dilemma may emerge as seeking autonomy for women in the Development Mode.

A fourth dilemma is finding the courage to make selfless contributions (that is to be generative). The person may seek to make a personal contribution of time or effort, but the selfless aspect of the desire is critical. This should not be confused with mentoring or wanting to help others, which may be a concern of a person in any of the modes. Someone in the Performance Mode might mentor someone to stimulate better performance. Someone in the Learning Mode might do it to provoke innovation. Someone in the Development Mode and pursuing selfless contribution would view mentoring as a desirable objective, without further instrumentality. A person in any of these modes could be self-centered, and be providing mentoring or coaching in pursuit of other objectives.

The pursuit of one's calling in the Development Mode is embedded in the pursuit of one's own agenda, and in this sense self-fulfillment is the primary orientation, rather than a responsiveness to the expectations of others. The key abilities related to this mode are mostly unconscious (that is, below our daily awareness) dispositions or capabilities, such as motives, traits, and core values. Since the focus of validation research in this mode has been adult development, the typical methods of measurement of competencies in the literature that seem most fruitful concerning this mode are interactive and interpretive, such as the Thematic Apperception Test (McClelland 1985), the Career Appreciation Interview (Stamp 1981, 1989), or the use of narrative life histories (see Chapter 10).

While in this mode, a person experiences time elongation, almost a sense of time slowing. Urgency and expediency lose importance. Although not always associated with advanced age, an example of the shift in time and perspective characteristic of this mode is found in a quote from Nancy Astor, on her eightieth birthday in 1959. She said, 'I used to dread getting older, because I thought I would not be able to do all the things I wanted to do. But now that I am older, I find I do not want to do them.' Time elongation occurs when a person adopts a perspective dramatically opposite to a 'just-in-time' orientation based on the proposition that saving the precious commodity of time is an important goal.

The prerequisite to entry into this mode is typically an event in life that provokes the search for purpose or calling. An event that precipitates a questioning of the meaning of life may develop into the discovery of one's purpose or calling. Too often, denial, repression, and avoidance replace the reflection and introspection needed for this discovery.

There are various sub-modes within the Development Mode. One is the search for personal integration. Another is probably the search for social integration, although the latter is questioned by women, who contend that their lives have been spent within the Performance Mode focused on the success and mastery of social responsibilities and expectations of others (that is, they were immersed in social connectedness). For them, the quest for autonomy (not merely rebellion or reaction formation to earlier roles and demands) may represent a sub-mode. It is possible, therefore, that sub-modes within the Development Mode may reflect different ways of being and knowing.

There are many examples of people in the Development Mode making choices about their careers that do not make sense to others. For example, when a successful executive decides to 'step off the ladder' of success and follow a different path, the media, people in the organization, and others often attribute the move to being removed from office or a terminal illness. Peter Lynch, formerly head of the Fidelity Magellan Fund, moved into philanthropic activities (Fierman 1990). Bill Phillips, former CEO of Ogilvy & Mather, moved on to pursue personal physical fitness and other hobbies; John Macomber, former CEO of Celanese, moved on to take a government position as head of the Export–Import bank; Andrall Pearson and Ralph Sørenson, former heads of PepsicCo and Barry Wright respectively, moved on to teach at the Harvard Business School (Fromson 1990). The concept of executive 'sabbaticals' is becoming increasingly acceptable in some corporate circles as a vehicle for people to take a 'moratorium' from their current activities (Erikson 1985) and find or pursue a calling (Hong 1990). These people appear to have been in the Development Mode, and chosen to follow their 'calling, or purpose' in a way that clearly was not aimed at job mastery or success (the primary intent in the Performance Mode). The changes appear more dramatic than extending their abilities into new arenas to explore generalizability (the primary intent in the Learning Mode) (Knecht 1995; Stevens 1995).

Two examples of people in the Development Mode are Paolo and Sandy. Paolo is in his late 40s and is head of the research unit at an Italian, biomedical engineering company. Although he has several advanced degrees (an MD and a Ph.D.), Paolo talks about his growth activities readily. He has been reading philosophy. He began with the philosophy of science because he was intrigued with how scientists and engineers create meaning, and has expanded his quest into philosophy of knowledge, and even general philosophy. Paolo is a dedicated professional and executive, who reads and attends meetings to keep abreast of developments in his technical field and management, but his heart follows a different path. His pursuit of wisdom through the study of philosophy does not preclude his effectiveness in his current job. But his growth activities appear to be primarily in the Development Mode.

Sandy is in her early 50s and has retired from a career in teaching. She has devoted a great deal of time to learning about and understanding the aging process and the elderly. What began as an attempt to understand what was occurring to her parents, and herself (the emotional, physical, mental, and spiritual changes in herself), led to broader areas such as quality of life. She has chosen to attend a few seminars and has read several books, but mostly she has sought growth in these areas through volunteering in various 'elderly housing' and other related projects. When asked, Sandy will explain that it seems the best way for her to learn about the phenomena of aging, seek preparation for changes within herself and in her future, and contribute to addressing some social needs. The selection of activities has no connection to job mastery, or event–career transfer (Sandy having turned down the opportunity to study gerontology at the graduate level). It is a personal journey filled with the desire for self-insight, caring for others close to her (her parents), and others less fortunate (those without close family). She appears to be operating in the Development Mode.

Postulates and questions

There are four major aspects of this theory that offer a different structure to growth and adaptation throughout life and careers from other theories. We can, at this time, offer two as postulates and the other two as questions, which we will propose as postulates still in the formative stage.

Postulate 1. There are three modes describing a person's growth or adaptation in his or her career and life, as explained earlier.

Postulate 2. This is a recursive theory. People may enter the Performance Mode after having been in the Development Mode. This may be associated with a major life change, career change, new opportunity, or some other event. The Development Mode is not the 'most advanced' or 'best' mode. It does not represent the highest state of being, nor the most complex. Each mode is a different orientation to growth and adaptation. A person is expected to revisit, recycle, or 'loop' through these modes throughout life.

Question 1. We believe at any one point in a person's life or career, he or she will be predominantly in one mode. This mode will function as an umbrella. Once through the cycle, a person may have momentary, or episodic, excursions into the other modes for specific tasks or goals. For example, a person in the Learning Mode may want to develop skills in making oral presentations. She may place herself in the Performance Mode in seeking growth activities, feedback, and change specifically to improve her oral presentation skills (seeking job mastery or success), but then revert to her predominant mode, in this case the Learning Mode, to continue in her life and career. This also means that the preoccupation, focus, and motivating forces of one mode divert a person from the benefits of the forces and focus of the other modes. In this way, the limitations of each mode can be found in the description of the other two modes. A person in transition between two modes will demonstrate a mixture of the characteristics of both modes.

Question 2. We believe that a person's dominant mode will affect his or her adaptation, growth, and excitement in both personal life and career. Similar to the umbrella notion described above, people will be approaching adaptation and growth in their lives with the same preoccupation, concerns, and perspectives as their careers, or vice versa. A person may function in multiple modes, but not seek adaptation, growth, or excitement in multiple modes at the same time. For example, a person may be in a job demanding the Performance Mode, but be in the Development Mode in other aspects of life. The job will either be refined and redesigned to suit his or her interests or he or she will decrease the amount of energy and discretionary effort utilized at work; such a person will not engage in adaptive or growth activities to seek mastery!

People will seek those reference groups, communities (Chapter 5), or social architecture (Chapter 11) that value the same incentives and focus in life and/or work as they do in their current mode. People in transition to another mode will find their reference groups, communities, or the social architecture of their organizations decreasingly exciting. Conscious recognition of this change will probably follow a prolonged period of emotional or unconscious arousal of the conflicted feelings.

People's dominant mode is independent of their personal level of initiative or efficacy. People may take action to engage in activities, even growth activities in any of the modes. The basic question that allows insight into the mode is not the choice of activity but what people are doing with the experience. What does the experience and activity mean to them? The intent and source of excitement about the experience will reveal that an activity could be used by people in each of the three modes.

Identification of a person's 'dominant mode' relies upon understanding the person's focus of attention. It involves investment of energy into activities with an intention characteristic of predominantly one mode. The dominant mode is *not* reflected in the time a person spends in one activity or another. For example, a person may spend most of his or her working hours in the Performance Mode, but find energy, excitement, and growth in pursuit of novelty and experimentation (that is, in the Learning Mode). Although we believe a person is 'in' one, dominant mode, the anomalies or aberrations from what is expected in that mode may shed light on an emerging mode (a new focus of attention). Of course, it could also reveal a dissatisfaction or psychic disruption with the person's current job or activities in life.

Applications and Implications for Lifelong Growth

There are many levels of implications for this theory. Each has its own applications for education and human resource development. One level concerns ideas for helping individuals grow and adapt throughout their careers and life. Another level addresses the potential conflicts between an individual in each of these modes and the organization in which he or she is currently studying or working (or the organizations through which he or she is pursuing a 'boundaryless career'). The third level of implication concerns human resource management (HRM) and development systems, and their design and use in organizations.

Helping individuals grow and adapt

Individuals' desire to continue their growth and adaptation emerges for several reasons. Some people may not be using competencies they possess, and, therefore, are not using their full resources or talent. Some people may be losing interest, vitality, productivity, commitment, or innovativeness, and there is a desire to stimulate or provoke them into regaining the excitement they once showed. Some people may not have certain competencies important for their current job, and there is the desire to help them find a path for the development of these competencies.

The ultimate reason may be conceptual or philosophical—that is, a belief that people *must* continue to grow throughout life or they atrophy. Like unused muscles losing strength, elasticity, and eventually tissue, unused capability eventually extinguishes itself. Unused or lost emotional, intellectual, or spiritual excitement eventually leads to boredom, apathy, or disconnectedness—anomie. Stimulation of lifelong growth does not assume that people should be 'moving into the next mode'. Such thinking reveals an underlying hierarchical concept (some modes are seen as better than other modes) and will nullify the benefits of using this theory.

If a person is in the Performance Mode, the appeal to stimulate growth and adaptation activities would be to his or her desire for success or mastery, as shown in Table 4.2. Publicly, the appeal would be made in terms of increased personal, job, or organizational performance and success. The best developmental opportunities would be those projects or jobs where there was a maximum 'fit' or harmony between the skills needed to maximize success in the job and the individual's skills.

Table 4.2. *Growth activities appropriate for each mode*

Themes	Performance Mode	Learning Mode	Development Mode
Effective appeal	Success or mastery	Experimentation	Listen to your inner voice; back to basics
Legitimate public appeal	Improve personal, job, or organizational performance	Personal or organizational innovation	Contribute to and arouse nobility of human spirit; appeal to greatness
Assessment feedback	With normative standards: • Where am I with regard to others? • Where should I be? • How do superior performers act?	Self-referent: • Where are my flat sides? • What do I do often? • What do I do seldom?	Stimulation to awareness
Outcome orientation	Provides goals	Provides benchmarks	Not applicable
Major frustrations with activities in a different mode	Lack of relevance	Boring	Trivial pursuit
Best change activities	Practice through iteration	• Experimentation with new ideas, acts, and styles • Conversion of skills to new settings	• Legitimizing exploration of personal agenda • Reflection
Setting of change activities	a) Place to practice b) Place to apply it on the job	Place to explore and experiment	a) Begin out of usual context b) Continue in context
Best developmental opportunities	Job/person 'fit' with regard to skills needed to maximize success	Job with some 'fit' but sufficient lack of 'fit' to provide opportunity for expansion	Job with 'fit' in terms of calling, purpose, values, and traits

An outcome orientation to the activities helps by providing goals for the effort. The best type of activities involve practice through iteration. Whenever possible, assessment feedback should be provided with normative standards. That is, the person receiving the feedback will want to know: Where am I with regard to others? Where should I be? Where do I stand with regard to superior performers or excellent companies? It is the comparison to normative information that provides some of the energy and drive to pursue the growth activities. The best settings for these change activities should first be a place to practice outside the consequences to his or her job and organization. Then, the person should be encouraged to practice the activities on the job, or within the organization.

The major frustration voiced by people in the Performance Mode when engaged in activities presented from the Learning or Development mode perspective (that is, appealing to people in the Learning or Development Modes) is the 'lack of relevance'. For example, senior faculty in a graduate management program in a university often get into disputes with students, who are typically in their twenties and have interrupted their early career to return to school. When students claim the material or perspective is not relevant, they want the faculty member to work on concepts and use materials more relevant to their potential job and organizational setting. They ask faculty, 'How will this help me get a job or do it well once obtained?' The faculty member's response might be a condemnation of their crass, pragmatic, utilitarian orientation. The faculty might be heard to say, 'How can you be so preoccupied with jobs and success when you have the opportunity to explore, learn, and question the philosophical roots of our society?' In such a situation, it is likely that the faculty member is in the Learning or Development Mode, and is presenting material and using teaching methods appropriate to that mode. Meanwhile, the students' comments suggest that they are in the Performance Mode. The issue of lack of relevance is true—but not in the way either is saying or hearing it. The students and faculty are missing each other's mode and, therefore, *the experience is not relevant*.

If a person is in the Learning Mode, the appeal to stimulate growth and adaptation activities would be to his or her desire for experimentation and novelty, as shown in Table 4.2. Publicly, the appeal would be made in terms of increased personal, job, or organizational innovation or change. The best developmental opportunities would be those projects or jobs where there is some 'fit' or harmony between the knowledge, skills, and experience needed for effectiveness in the job and the individual. But there should be sufficient 'lack of fit' or lack of harmony to provide opportunity for expansion into new arenas and what the person would view as their 'flat sides'.

An outcome orientation to the activities helps by providing benchmarks against which to mark movement or change. The best types of activities include: (*a*) experimentation with new ideas, behaviors, and styles; and (*b*) transfer of skills to new settings. Whenever possible, assessment feedback should be provided in a self-referent format. That is, the person receiving the feedback will want to know: Where are my strengths and weaknesses relative to each other? What do I do most often? What do I do seldom? Does it matter to me? It is the comparison within the self that provides some of the energy and drive to pursue the growth activities. The best setting for these change activities should be a place to explore and experiment.

The major frustration voiced by people in the Learning Mode when engaged in activities presented from the Performance or Development mode perspective is, 'This is boring!' For example, people who do not demonstrate certain specific job-related skills, such as planning, are often sent on a training program. The objective is to help them improve their performance by using the target skill more frequently once back on the job. The most common criticism of management training workshops is that the targeted behaviors or skills are seldom applied once the participant returns to work. The response to this observation has been to develop even more training programs, often called reinforcement sessions, to help the person remember the skill and support its use. But if the participant is in the Learning Mode, and he has used his planning skill throughout his career, the excitement and commitment to use this skill are absent. The training program, emphasizing improved efficiency and effectiveness in the job, is playing a song to someone who is listening to a different rhythm. Such people will not demonstrate more planning at work because they are bored with planning and its consequences. Additional training, performance feedback about lack of its use, and reinforcement sessions become nagging reminders of why they are not feeling excited about their current job.

If a person is in the Development Mode, the appeal to stimulate growth and adaptation activities would be to ask a person to listen to his or her inner voice, a form of personal 'back to basics', as shown in Table 4.2. Publicly, the appeal could be made in terms of a contribution to and arousal of the nobility of the human spirit, an appeal to greatness. The best developmental opportunities would be those projects or jobs where there is a maximum 'fit' or harmony between the person's calling, sense of purpose, values, and traits (not necessarily skills) and the needs and opportunities of the project or job. An outcome orientation to the activities is not useful or even appropriate.

The best types of activities include: (a) activities legitimizing exploration of personal agendas; and (b) activities that provide time, space, and catalysts for reflection. Whenever possible, assessment feedback should be used as a stimulation to awareness, and not as a source of information to shape change goals oriented at reducing the real-ideal discrepancy. It is the comparison of current thoughts, behavior, feelings, and so forth to the inner voice, purpose, and calling that provides some of the energy and drive to pursue the growth activities. These change activities should best begin out of the context of usual cues (that is, away from work and home), and then move into the work and home setting to continue the growth in a holistic manner.

The major frustration voiced by people in the Development Mode when engaged in activities presented from the Performance or Learning mode perspective is, 'This is a trivial pursuit!' The previous example of a manager sent to a management training program and not applying the material back on the job is even more dramatic when the participant is in the Development Mode and the training is delivered in the Performance Mode, with behavioral objectives, performance-oriented feedback, and the like.

Addressing individual and organization conflict

Conflicts may arise when the organization has developed a culture (a belief system, norms, and values) predominantly characteristic of one mode and a person is in another mode. In such a situation, the people around this individual expect and need him or her to be functioning in another mode than the one that is natural. For example, a professional may be in the Learning Mode, but the organization is in the Performance Mode, and wants her to be in the Performance Mode as well. In this situation, she can keep her excitement to herself, following the separation of internal sensations and thoughts and those revealed to others characteristic of the Japanese concept of public thoughts and private thoughts. In time, she will seek opportunities for growth and adaptation outside the work organization. When a person is shifting modes, and his or her organization has not changed its culture and climate, the person's evolving change may be relatively unnoticeable to others in the organization. As the person's interests are changing, he or she will often attempt to change jobs or priorities, redesign the job, or shift the use of his or her talent to more satisfying opportunities outside the work organization. This may result in a shift in reference groups and communities of interest (Chapter 5). This is similar to a change in the type of community, or social architecture, which would be desired by the person as described by Goffee and Jones (Chapter 11). Using their terms, a person may have been excited and a high performer while in the Performance Mode in a *mercenary* organization. As the person shifts into a Learning Mode, he or she may seek the flexibility of a *fragmented* or *networked* organization to allow the freedom of experimentation. If the primary work organization does not shift, which it often does not, then the person devotes increasing energy and attention to another organization offering the appropriate social architecture (which may be a work organization or not).

A method to avoid such a waste of human resources would be for organizations, including educational institutions, to create opportunities for people to discover their current mode. Then the organization can structure or provide a variety of choices to the individual from which he or she can choose appropriate growth activities.

This may be complicated by the observation that even within organizations, the culture or atmosphere of specific functions may have a bias toward particular modes. For example, in many organizations the sales and marketing function may have a bias toward the Performance Mode; the information systems and technology function may have a bias toward the Learning Mode; and the HRM function may have a bias toward the Development Mode.

Implications for education and human resource development

The major implication of this theory for education and human resource development is a challenge to drop simplistic notions of 'a competency', and build a complex map of types of competencies or abilities. The different types of competencies that are of most interest to a person in each of the growth modes are related to stimulation, growth, and adaptation, as well as to the mode itself. The conceptual maps, guides, or desired outcomes provided by competency models must, therefore, incorporate all of these types of characteristics.

Another challenge to education and human resource development is to drop the job mastery and Performance Mode as the universal goal. If we accept people, knowing the diversity within the workforce, we will undertake to stimulate growth activities for people in whatever mode they currently find themselves.

In designing education or training programs, analysis of the dominant mode of the students or participants will assist in the construction of courses. Often, with mixed mode groups, universities and organizations will be forced to drop universal behavioral objectives and 'single' structure courses. New designs with variation in appeal, methods, and expectations should emerge. Graduate education and lifelong learning programs can be designed with this desired pluralism, addressing the structure and process of the learning experiences to suit the needs and interests of people in each mode (Boyatzis et al. 1995; Boyatzis and Kram, in press).

Lastly, hierarchical, or even time-based models of development do not appear to be as valuable guides as they may have been in the past for understanding and stimulating growth in careers. Organizations and managers must develop perspectives and theories of lifelong growth and adaptation reflecting different notions of development.

Concluding Comment

Growth and adaptation begin within the person. He or she must choose to grow. Therefore, efforts to 'help' people grow and adapt must begin with recognition, appreciation, and acceptance of their individuality. The mode of growth is but one of many aspects of a person's uniqueness. Integration of this perspective and related methods will allow people to grow in their own way, and not oppress the human spirit with one 'best' or prescribed path.

References

Alexander, C. N., Druker, S. M., and Langer, E. J. (1990), 'Introduction: Major Issues in the Exploration of Adult Growth', in C. N. Alexander and E. J. Langer (eds), *Higher Stages of Human Development* (New York: Oxford University Press).

Arthur, M. B. and Rousseau, D. M. (1996) (eds.), *The Boundaryless Career: A New Employment Principle for a New Organizational Era* (New York: Oxford University Press).

—— Hall, D. T., and Lawrence, B. S. (1989), *Handbook of Career Theory* (New York: Cambridge University Press).

Bailyn, L. (1993), *Breaking the Mold: Women, Men, and Time in the New Corporate World* (New York: Free Press).

Ballou, R., Bowers, D., Boyatzis, R. E., and Kolb, D. A. (1999), 'Fellowship in Lifelong Learning: An Executive Development Program for Advanced Professionals', *Journal of Management Education*, 23/4: 338–54.

Boyatzis, R. E. (1982), *The Competent Manager: A Model for Effective Performance* (New York: John Wiley).

—— (1993), 'Beyond Competence: The Choice to be a Leader', *Human Resource Management Review*, 3/1: 1–14.

—— (1996), 'Consequences and Rejuvenation of Competency-Based Human Resource and Organization Development', in R. W. Woodman and W. A. Pasmore (eds.), *Research in Organizational Change and Development*, ix (Greenwich, Conn.: JAI Press).

—— and Kolb, D. A. (1991), 'Assessing Individuality in Learning: The Learning Skills Profile', *Educational Psychology*, 11/3–4: 279–95.

—— —— (1994), 'Performance, Learning, and Development as Modes of Growth and Adaptation', in M. T. Keeton (ed.), *Perspectives on Experiential Learning: Prelude to a Global Conversation about Learning* (Chicago: Council on Adult and Experiential Learning).

—— —— (1995), 'Beyond Learning Styles to Learning Skills: The Executive Skills Profile', *Journal of Managerial Psychology*, 10/5: 3–17.

—— and Kram, K. E. (in press), 'Reconstructing Management Education as a Lifelong Process', *Selections*.

—— Cowen, S. C., and Kolb, D. A. (1995), 'A Learning Perspective on Executive Education', *Selections*, 11/3: 47–55.

Brett, J., Medvec, V., and Stroh, L. (1998), 'The Overworked American Manager', paper presented at Career Realities Conference, London Business School.

Colby, A., and Kohlberg, L. (1987), *The Measurement of Moral Judgement*, i, ii (New York: Cambridge University Press).

Csikszentmihalyi, M., and Csikszentmihalyi, I. S. (1988), *Optimal Experience: Psychological Studies of Flow in Consciousness* (New York: Cambridge University Press).

Dalton, G. (1989), 'Developmental Views of Careers in Organizations', in M. B. Arthur, D. T. Hall, and B. S. Lawrence (eds.), *Handbook of Career Theory* (New York: Cambridge University Press).

—— and Thompson, P. (1986), *Novations: Strategies for Career Development* (Glenview, Ill.: Scott Foresman).

Driver, M. J. (1982), 'Career Concepts—A New Approach to Career Research', in R. Katz (ed.), *Career Issues in Human Resource Management* (Englewood Cliffs, NJ: Prentice Hall).

Erikson, E. H. (1985), *The Life Cycle Completed: A Review* (New York: W. W. Norton).

Fierman, J. (1990), 'Peter Lynch on the Meaning of Life', *Fortune*, 23 Apr., 197–200.

Flanagan, J. C. (1954), 'The Critical Incident Technique', *Psychological Bulletin*, 51/4: 327–58.

Fromson, B. D. (1990), 'Second Acts for the Top Guys', *Fortune*, 23 Apr., 251–62.

Gladly Wolde he Lerne, and Gladly Teche: Festschrift for Morris Keaton (San Francisco: Jossey-Bass).

Hall, D. T., and Mirvis, P. H. (1996), 'The New Protean Career: Psychological Success and the Path with a Heart', in D.T. Hall and Associates, *The Career is Dead: Long Live the Career* (San Francisco: Jossey-Bass).

Hong, P. (1990), 'Taking Time Out for Fellowship', *Business Week*, 15 Oct., 127.

Knecht, G. B. (1995), 'Do you Know me? As American Express Loses its President, his Kids Gain a Dad', *Wall Street Journal*, 77/28, 22 Nov. 1995, A11.

Kolb, D. A. (1984), *Experiential Learning: Experience as the Source of Learning and Development* (Englewood Cliffs, NJ: Prentice Hall).

—— (1991), 'The Challenges of Advanced Professional Development', in L. Lambden (ed.), *Roads to the Learning Society* (Chicago: Council on Adult and Experiential Learning).

Kram, K. E. (1996), 'A Relational Approach to Careers', in D. T. Hall and Associates, *The Career is Dead: Long Live the Career* (San Francisco: Jossey-Bass).

Latack, J. C. (1984), 'Career Transitions within Organizations: An Exploratory Study of Work, Nonwork, and Coping Strategies', *Organizational Behavior and Human Performance*, 34: 296–322.

Levinson, D. J., in collaboration with Levinson, J. D. (1996), *Season's of a Woman's Life* (New York: Knopf).

—— with Darrow, C. N., Klein, E. B., Levinson, M. H., and McKee, B. (1978), *The Seasons of a Man's Life* (New York: Knopf).

Loevinger, J., and Wessler, R. (1983), *Measuring Ego Development*, i, ii (San Francisco: Jossey-Bass).

McClelland, D. C. (1976), *A Guide to Job Competency Assessment* (Boston: McBer).

—— (1985), *Human Motivation* (Glenview, Ill.: Scott, Foresman and Co.).

Marshall, J. (1995), *Women Managers Moving On: Exploring Career and Life Choices* (London: Routledge).

Miller, D. C., and Form, W. H. (1951), *Industrial Sociology* (New York: Harper & Row).

Myers, I. B., and McCaulley, M. H. (1985), *Manual: A Guide to the Development and Use of the Myers–Briggs Type Indicator* (Palo Alto, Calif.: Consulting Psychologists Press).

Nicholson, N. (1984), 'A Theory of Work Role Transitions', *Administrative Science Quarterly*, 29/2: 172–91.

—— (1990), 'The Transition Cycle: A Conceptual Framework for the Analysis of Change and Human Resources Management', in G. R. Ferris and K. M. Rowland (eds.), *Career and Human Resources Development* (Greenwich, Conn.: JAI Press).

Peiperl, M.A., and Jones, B. C. (1998), 'Workaholics and Overworkers: Productivity or Pathology?', paper presented at Career Realities Conference, London Business School.

Schein, E. H. (1978), *Career Dynamics: Matching Individual and Organization Needs* (Reading, Mass.: Addison-Wesley).

Schlossberg, N. K., Waters, E. B., and Goodman, J. (1995), *Counseling Adults in Transition: Linking Practice with Theory* (2nd edn., New York: Springer).

Sheehy, G. (1995), *New Passages: Mapping your Life across Time* (New York: Random House).

Spencer, L. M., Jr., and Spencer, S. M. (1993), *Competence at Work: Models for Superior Performance* (New York: John Wiley).

Stamp, G. (1981), 'Levels and Types of Managerial Capability', *Journal of Management Studies*, 18/3: 277–97.

—— (1989), 'Career Path Appreciation: A Key to Well-Being for the Individual and the Organization', *IPM* (July).

Stevens, A. (1995), 'More Firms Let Partners Work Only Part Time', *Wall Street Journal*, 10 July, p. B1.

Stevenson, J. (1994), 'Capability and Competence: Are they the Same and Does it Matter?', *Capability*, 1/1: 3–4.

Super, D. E. (1957), *The Psychology of Careers* (New York: Harper & Row).

Thornton, G. C., and Byham, W. C. (1982), *Assessment Centers and Managerial Performance* (New York: Academic Press).

5

Careers, Organizing, and Community

Polly Parker and Michael B. Arthur

In Fritjof Capra's book *The Web of Life* (1996) there is an illustration. On the left-hand side of the illustration are several circles, meant to represent life's phenomena as we usually understand them. The phenomena may be any commonly recognized units: parts of the human anatomy, collectives of people, members of other biological species, rivers, forests, oceans, and so on. From each circle, and connecting it to other circles, flow multiple lines. The representation concurs with how we usually think in social science, in viewing the world as relationships among similar phenomena or units of analysis. For instance, individuals, groups, social classes, institutions, governments, countries, and—not least—private or public companies, are popular units of analysis in psychology, social psychology, sociology, political science, economics, and organizational and management science.

On the right side of the illustration the circles are shown more faintly, and their boundaries are crossed by the connecting lines. The lines join together at common points, or nodes, within each circle, so that the new representation appears as a network of internal nodes rather than a network of larger units. The emphasis is now on what Capra (1996: 37) calls the underlying 'web of relationships' through which more traditional units or levels of analysis may appear or reappear. The second side of the illustration, entitled 'figure-ground shift', challenges much of what we have customarily assumed about social science.

Works like Capra's reflect the shift from 'old' to 'new' frameworks being adopted in the natural sciences. Moreover, such new-science approaches (Wheatley 1992) are being increasingly found in the management and

We are grateful to Kerr Inkson, Regina O'Neill, and Maury Peiperl, as well as to several other contributors to this volume, for their comments on an earlier draft of this chapter.

organizational science arenas. However, their form of presentation frequently takes the boundaries of the employer company as given. For example, the popular discipline of Organizational Behavior typically focuses on human behavior within single company settings. At a more macro-level, the disciplines of economics and strategic management typically assume the company as their basic unit of analysis. In accordance with these assumptions, the management and organizational realm of new-science work has so far concentrated most on what happens within a company (e.g. Wheatley 1992; Stacey 1996) or what happens between companies (e.g. Sanchez 1997). In this chapter we adopt a different point of departure, viewing the person as a node to a 'web of relationships', and, after Capra's (1996) inspiration, anticipating how the web is likely to span company boundaries (see Fig. 5.1).

An objection sometimes raised to the boundaryless-career perspective—which argues that employment mobility is becoming more likely in an increasingly uncertain world (Arthur and Rousseau 1996)—is that people need a sense of community in their lives. However, this kind of objection can overlook the possibility of more enduring community attachments developing outside the employer company—for example through shared industrial or occupational affiliations (Saxenian 1996; Tolbert 1996). Communities can also form within the company but be detached from its purpose, as has been reported, for example, about technicians (Zabusky and Barley 1996). Or, communities can be formed for a temporary project-based purpose but have long-term effects on network arrangements, as occurs in independent film-making (Jones 1996). In this chapter we emphasize the multiple forms that community attachments can take. Put another way, we not only explore people's 'webs of relationships'; we also

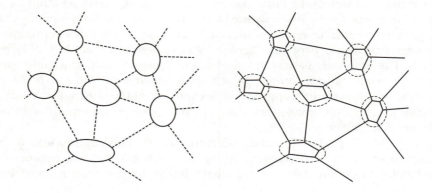

A focus on companies   A focus on relationships

Fig. 5.1. Figure-ground shift from companies to relationships
Source: from Capra (1996: 38).

explore how multiple webs can intersect to create shared community attachments.

The 'Intelligent' Subjective Career

From the standpoint of the career, our point of departure is the concept of the 'intelligent career' (Arthur *et al.* 1995). This approach to careers emphasizes the subjective component of career behavior through which community-building might be expected to evolve. The approach also responds to ideas about 'intelligent enterprise' (Quinn 1992) or, more broadly, about 'core competencies' (e.g. D'Aveni 1994; Prahalad and Hamel 1994) associated with the successful contemporary firm.

The core competencies of any firm can be broadly categorized in three distinct groups concerned respectively with a firm's culture, know-how, and networks. Briefly, culture encompasses the values and beliefs supporting strategic behavior, know-how involves accumulated skill and knowledge capabilities, and networks represent the relationships through which a firm participates in the economic marketplace (Hall 1992). The intelligent career perspective responds to these categories by suggesting three corresponding categories of career competency for individuals (Arthur *et al.* 1995).

Knowing-why career competencies relate to company culture, and incorporate individual values, motivation, and identification. Despite the potential of company culture to bind people together, responses to it will vary from individual dispositions, as well from differences in the balancing between work and family or other non-work arrangements. The interplay between people's *knowing-why* competencies and company culture will affect not only the company's future, but also people's future career choices, adaptability, and commitment.

Knowing-how career competencies relate to overall company know-how, and reflect an individual's career-relevant skills and understanding. These individual competencies underlie people's current work behavior. However, people may also have, or may wish to develop, a broader set of competencies than their present job demands. The interplay between *knowing-how* competencies and company know-how will reflect people's attempts to expand or change their work arrangements, to enhance future career opportunities and employability.

Knowing-whom career competencies relate to company networks, and include the relationships people maintain on the company's behalf. These include internal company contacts, as well as supplier, customer, and further industry contacts. People also have personal connections through family, friends, fellow alumni, and professional and social acquaintances. The interplay between *knowing-whom* competencies and company networks will reflect people's pursuit of personal support, access to information, and reputation building in their careers.

The intelligent-career framework stands in marked contrast to traditional and widely held organizational-career views that relate careers to hierarchical, institutional, or status-driven assumptions (Inkson 1997). Instead, the framework emphasizes the importance of people knowing their aspirations and strengths, maintaining a reflective posture and adapting successfully to a changing environment. De-emphasizing external or objective measures of success, the intelligent career instead focuses on internal or subjective measures relating to personal adaptation, growth, and learning. Engaging the subjective career calls, in turn, for people to consider development of their own career competencies and to assume responsibility for their future employability (Parker 1996).

The intelligent-career framework may also be related to various behavioral-science perspectives that concur with new science in emphasizing a non-linear, self-organizing, and interdependent world (Parker and Arthur 1997). Such approaches involve seeing the person as an 'active agent at the grounding point for all human and human-impacted activity' (Loye 1995: 26), as well as seeing 'the non-linear dimensions of social life lying just below the surface of seemingly staid, equilibrated institutions and groups' (Harvey and Reed 1996: 321). We emphasize, though, that, in looking below the surface of institutions and groups, we are also looking beyond their boundaries. We are interested, like Capra (1996), in the larger 'web of relationships' that shapes the world, or more particularly the world of work. This interest also connects to a relational view of careers, which sees personal growth involving 'movement through increasingly complex states of interdependence' (Kram 1996: 140), as well as to a view of organizing that sees work arrangements evolving from consensual processes rather than from administrative authority (Weick 1979).

Eliciting Subjective Career Data

An 'Intelligent Career Card Sort' exercise, originally conceived by the first author, was developed specifically to elicit subjective career information (Parker 1996; Parker and Arthur 1997). In contrast to traditional career-assessment instruments, the card-sort methodology makes no direct assumptions about the items that people select. Rather, the items provide a starting point for further investigation and elaboration about subjective career phenomena. The three comparisons below illustrate the kind of elaboration that can occur. Since its inception the card sort has been further developed and piloted as an instrument for career counseling and awareness-raising in both individual and group settings. Clients are asked to select and rank three sets of seven cards, one set each from three groups of up to forty cards arranged in *knowing-why, knowing-how* and *knowing-whom* categories. The three comparisons below illustrate the kind of elaboration that can occur. They also illustrate how different two people's responses can be to the same card-sort item.

Rachael, a 25-year-old management consultant, selected the *knowing-why* card 'I like to gain a sense of achievement from my work'. She described how this stemmed from the completion of work assignments, and in particular from feedback she received from colleagues about the quality of her work. Rachael's sense of achievement was closely tied to the external recognition she received. In contrast, Tom, an experienced partner in an accounting firm, used the identical card to describe how he enjoyed the freedom that he has to choose his own directions. He was critical of authoritarian managers in his past who had denied him feedback. Tom had learned to measure achievement against his own standards rather than other people's expectations.

Annabelle, a young primary school teacher, selected the *knowing-how* card 'I enjoy working in job situations from which I can learn'. She worked in an open-plan classroom, aware of her own shyness, but in close physical proximity to more experienced teachers. Annabelle learned from quietly observing other teaching techniques and then integrating them into her own repertoire. Staff nurse Jane's reflections on the same card were different. An extrovert with management responsibilities, Jane was at the center of continuing dialogue between the nursing and medical staff. Her learning stemmed from her active engagement in this dialogue, as well as from her willingness to experiment with previously untried methods.

Jenny had recently shifted from a public sector position in health education to a private-sector job in a large corporation. She chose the *knowing-whom* card 'I work with people from whom I can learn', and explained that she was in a beginner's role again. She therefore placed a high value on working with colleagues who would act as positive role models as well as accepting her mistakes with good grace. Psychotherapist Katie had remained in the non-profit sector, and was confident in her own abilities. Katie felt that the 'people from whom I can learn' were other therapists with whom she participated in co-counseling arrangements. Katie felt that the two-way learning process was essential to her and other therapists' continuing professional development.

In each of the above examples we see two markedly different career responses to the same card-sort item. Each respondent sees the item as important, but each interprets its meaning in a different way. These differences in meaning are brought out by encouraging people to explore and express their own, inherently subjective, interpretations about why the items were selected. The differences also extend to connections people make across the three *knowing-why, knowing-how,* and *knowing-whom* arenas, when they relate, for example, the connections between their personal values, their current learning agendas, and their networking and mentoring attachments.

Communities of Practice

Other social-science perspectives support the importance of relationships in career behavior, but also emphasize the collective settings in which relationships are concentrated. For example, Weick (1996: 54) suggests that careers will function less through fixed levels in a hierarchy, and more through fluid positions 'in a heterarchy organized around *collective* learning' (emphasis added). The suggestion is reminiscent of work by Van Maanen and Barley (1984: 347) on occupational communities, where careers are 'defined in terms of member-perceived boundaries' and where within such boundaries members claim 'a distinctive and valued [*knowing-why*] social identity, share a common perspective toward the [*knowing-why*] mission and [*knowing-how*] practices of the occupation, and take part in a sort of interactive [*knowing-whom*] fellowship that transcends the workplace'.

However, the concept of occupational community focuses on a predominant aspect of identity (that is, occupation) rather than on the multiple aspects of identity that the intelligent-career framework suggests. A broader view stems from the literature on 'communities of practice' (Brown and Duguid 1991; Lave and Wenger 1991; Wenger 1998), in which—as in occupational communities—learning is viewed as fundamental, and as a social activity rather than merely an individual endeavor. Communities of practice can extend beyond both the workplace and the occupation, and thereby beyond the constraints that have traditionally been applied to thinking about careers. Thus, Brown and Duguid (1991: 49) observe that communities of practice can be discerned to be 'often crossing the restrictive boundaries of the organization to incorporate people from outside'. Wenger (1998: 149) emphasizes that we usually participate in a number of communities of practice simultaneously. We experience participation differently within different communities and we 'reconcile our various forms of membership into one identity'.

Ideas on communities of practice relate closely to the intelligent-career framework. For example, Sergiovanni (1994: 217) describes that 'communities are defined by their centers of values, sentiments, and beliefs'—all *knowing-why* attributes—'that provide the necessary conditions for creating a sense of We from a collection of Is'. Lave and Wenger (1991) describe how *knowing-how* skills and knowledge within different communities may reflect our varying levels of expertise or experience in different fields. In some communities we may be central members, respected and valued for our expertise, whereas in others we may be on the periphery, still learning how to speak as 'insiders' of the practice. Wenger (1998) describes how learning is in turn a socially organized activity revolving around *knowing-whom* relationships. Individual constellations of networks give rise to communities united by a shared sense of purpose to which people voluntarily commit (and in so doing further construct their *knowing-why* identities).

Career Communities—a Typology

Drawing from both the intelligent-career and the communities-of-practice frameworks, we suggest that 'career communities' are member-defined communities from which people draw career support. Career communities are different from configurations of personal networks. Career communities are subjectively defined, self-organizing, informal entities that provide a social structure for engagement in (*knowing-how*) practice, and a shared sense of (*knowing-whom*) belonging that reinforces a personal sense of (*knowing-why*) identity. As such, career communities closely follow the principles of communities of practice, while offering a non-traditional approach to exploring how the organizing of work unfolds. It is an approach that sees careers unfolding in a larger, less bounded, context than any single company or occupational setting.

The above conception of the career community was applied to a literature search for the various forms that such a community might take. The search covered contemporary ideas about changing forms of organizing, including ideas from the behavioral sciences, organizational studies, and strategic management. The results of that search suggest ten kinds of career community, as summarized in Table 5.1. The table also indicates that each kind of community can provide a basis for members' overlapping *knowing-why* identities and motivation, *knowing-how* skill and knowledge investments, and *knowing-whom* work relationships. The discussion below elaborates on Table 5.1 by providing capsule descriptions of each of the ten 'pure types' of career community identified. The discussion also makes connections to examples of work that promote each community perspective described.

Industry communities. These are communities centered around a particular industry such as construction, retailing or high technology. Industry has long been an assumed basis for classifying economic activity, and for studying the activities of employer firms (e.g. Porter 1985). Industries also often have their own 'recipes' (Spender 1989) both reflecting and influencing a sense of participation within them, and may also have their own training or employment boards influencing collective career arrangements. A sense of industry participation may be transmitted by firms and industry and trade associations to their members, or it may be nurtured within an industry as a whole through trade publications, annual conferences, and exhibitions. One such publication is the *Canadian Biotechnology Yearbook*, used by Gunz, Evans, and Jalland (Chapter 2) to explore industry career mobility.

Occupational communities. Overlapping with, but more precise than, industry communities are occupational communities. We include the traditional professions, such as law, as well as more manual or technical pursuits, such

Table 5.1. *Career communities and related ways of knowing*

Types of community	Ways of knowing		
	Knowing-why	*Knowing-how*	*Knowing-whom*
Industry	Identities are shaped by people's industry affiliation. Motivation is influenced by the industry's norms and its new developmental directions.	New learning is informed by industry measures of expertise, where available, or by industry norms or recognized lines of industry development.	Relationships are centered around a particular industry—for example, retailing, construction, boatbuilding, winemaking, etc.
Occupational	Identities are developed through an implicit social structure of belonging with similarly qualified people—often tied to the prestige associated with professional roles.	Explicit and tacit knowledge are increased through participation with occupational peers, ideally in a process of continuous learning.	Colleagues are connected and relationships sustained through occupational or professional associations. Entry into these networks is typically qualification- or experience-based.
Regional	Individual identities are largely 'local', but attach value to the collective prosperity of the host geographic region. Entrepreneurial activities are likely to be regionally focused.	Informal exchange of information occurs through regional networks. Experimentation may be encouraged to advance learning across the geographical area.	Social support emanates from a regional network of relationships producing loyalty to a larger group, and a shared interest in regional reputation and success.

Ideological	People are driven by their internal beliefs and values or by a desire to make a contribution to society. Personal ideologies underlie choice of and commitment to work.	Personal values underlie learning agendas. These in turn seek skills and knowledge allowing for greater inclusion or expression of ideological beliefs.	Key relationships and support stem from others with overlapping interests or values. Mutual support in turn reinforces a collective sense of purpose.
Project	Short-term identification is with a specific project and its outcomes. People are also motivated to use current projects to enhance their employability on future projects.	Short-term skill investments relate to project success. Longer-term investments involve exchange of current expertise for new learning, both tacit and explicit, among project group members.	Relationships unfold through time-bound work arrangements that provide information regarding future work possibilities and also transmit reputation.
Alumni	Identification with a particular shared experience—for example, through high school, university, the military, or joint participation in a memorable training program.	Learning builds from a shared life or educational experience, perhaps supplemented by overlapping subsequent application of shared learning through work.	The sustaining of relationships stems from past shared experiences. Social networks are also maintained to increase 'social capital' for future career contacts and mobility
Support	Identifying with, seeking approval from, and being motivated both to support and to find support through others experiencing a similar life situation.	The nature of the support situation shapes the learning agenda. Also, the process of learning with others may be given primacy over the content of the learning itself.	Involves the active encouragement and approval of colleagues. Relationships sustain a loyalty to one another and to shared overlapping interests.

Table 5.1. *Continued*

Family	Shared identification through family membership is a critical driver for learning, support, and security. Loyalty to the family serves to shape its members' career directions.	Role and learning direction defined by family agendas. Stretches from traditional homemakers to broader participation in family structures, family business, and inter-generational dynamics.	Relationships sustain an immediate or extended family structure. A strong emphasis is placed on trust, loyalty, reciprocity, and sensitivity within the overall family group.
Virtual	Identification with and the maintenance of career-relevant connections with others, but without direct interpersonal interaction.	Involving knowledge or knowledge-acquisition activities in the absence of face-to-face interaction. Includes remote membership of professional societies, or participation in the World Wide Web.	Incorporates people who are not physically present, but with whom interaction occurs through mail, telephone, or (increasingly) e-mail connections.
Company	Identity and psychological well-being are linked to continuing participation in the company, and motivation is harnessed toward pursuit of company-specific goals.	Learning agendas are guided by the company's career paths and its training programs. Markets and competition, and the company's strategic response, also shape learning opportunities.	Involving fellow members of the same employer company, and often extending to social support through company employment benefits and company-sponsored leisure activities.

as carpentry, and their representing unions, in this broad category. An industry (such as construction) can have multiple occupations within it (architecture, civil engineering, the building trades) or an occupation (such as computer programming) can have application in multiple industries. Occupations typically have their own associations and membership arrangements, often involving credentialing through examination and continuing education. Occupational communities also support themselves through regional and national conferences, as well as perhaps increasingly through emergent informal arrangements at work (Zabusky and Barley 1996).

Regional communities. This kind of community is centered around a particular geographic location, such as a city, a harbor area, or a valley. Regional communities, and so 'regional labor markets', may be sustained by people's desire to stay in the location where their social life has become established (Piore and Sabel 1984). Regional career communities may also be sponsored by, for example, chambers of commerce, or any other kind of regional economic institution. Many regional communities reflect professional association or trade-union chapters, again presumably to promote the benefits of direct member interaction. Other kinds of regional community can evolve through government initiatives, or from people's propensity to organize in their own economic self-interests (Best and Forrant 1996).

Ideological communities. These communities are centered around a particular ideological belief or goal. Perhaps most prominent among them are religious congregations, through which people share a common faith, as well as a convenient means for social interaction, mutual support, and networking about matters of personal or mutual significance. Other communities can form around a particular cause, such as helping the aged, relieving hunger, or counseling people in distress. Charitable institutions cultivate or spring from people's ideological beliefs providing a shared outlet for expressing those beliefs and putting them into action. The tasks and training of charitable institutions can also have a direct impact on work careers—for example, when training for book-keeping or counseling transfers into usable skills at work (Richardson 1996).

Project communities. Project communities occur where there is a distinct point of closure to the work, such as in a construction project, the delivery of a suite of computer programs, the making of a film, the development of a new drug, or the conclusion of a particular research activity. What typically binds such communities together is a shared sense of purpose in the project's completion or success (Heckscher 1995). In such project-based organizing, careers are interdependent with project arrangements, and commonly move—or reflect people's attempts to move—from one employment situation to another as old projects terminate and new ones come into being (DeFillippi and Arthur 1998). Both Gunz *et al.* (Chapter 2) and Jones and Lichtenstein (Chapter 8) indicate the importance of project communities underlying biotechnology and architectural employment practice (respectively).

Alumni communities. Alumni communities evolve from a shared experience, notably that of graduating from the same high school, boot camp, training program, or college or university experience. Such communities are often the basis for long-term friendships, or for the exploitation of 'weak ties' whereby it is common to call on people who share the same background experience for occasional career assistance (Granovetter 1985). Even when connections are not directly made, shared experiences can still be the basis for overlapping identities and skill sets. People may find tacit support or enjoy particular status from being a member of the same alumni group, even if they make no active investments to sustain relationships (Litchfield 1993).

Support communities. These kinds of communities evolve out of people's needs for social support and include such arrangements as parent–teacher associations, women's or men's support groups, people of shared ethnic origins, and groups that share common interests or recreational activities. Some support communities promote specific skills, such as public speaking, while others, like alcoholics anonymous, offer new coping skills in the face of past personal difficulties. Other support communities are more concerned with situational factors, and provide understanding in the face of particular forms of hardship or discrimination (Ibarra 1995). The broad intention of a support community is to bring together people with common interests and both to affirm and to promote those interests.

Family communities. These are communities that derive their underlying logic from family or extended-family work arrangements. Careers are inseparable from the larger lives, including the home lives, that people pursue. Families influence the identities people assume in their careers, and make what may be competing demands for people's time and energy. Families also engage directly with careers, most obviously through the widespread family business activities that contribute to the world's economic arrangements (as Nicholson describes in Chapter 3). These family communities often maintain full or partial private control, and in turn control the opportunities for members' careers (Neuberger and Lank 1998). Family communities can also reach well beyond the single firm, as reflected, for example, in the sprawling international family networks behind much of South-East Asia's developed countries' commercial activities (Granrose and Chua 1996).

Virtual communities. These are communities that exist without their members being in direct contact. Early forms of virtual community were encouraged by the arrival of the mail service, which allowed professional and trade associations to organize and identify with one another even when their members did not directly meet. Today, advances in information technology mean that traditional 'physical proximity, bricks and mortar, fixed technology and the like' are no longer essential to the organizing of work (Chapter 3). The presence of the World Wide Web means that today's virtual communities commonly straddle traditional country boundaries. The further emergence of technology that 'can bring anyone into anyone else's office' (Peiperl and Baruch 1997) adds to the depth of virtual-community building that can be attained. As e-mail evolves to incorporate voicemail, and in turn videomail, the lines between what is a virtual and what is a real community are becoming increasingly blurred.

Company communities. We end with the employing company itself. This is the kind of community promoted in the widespread literature on employee participation and involvement that has been accumulated in the post-war years. This kind of community has been promoted through multiple attempts to satisfy what Maslow (1987) influentially called 'social needs' through company employment arrangements, as well as by more recent initiatives concerning company-wide teamwork (Hackman 1990), gainsharing (Case 1995), shared values (Senge 1990), or unifying culture (Chapter 12). In larger companies, the business unit, department, or work group are often targets for the same kind of thinking at a more local level of analysis. In sum, the employer company is one, but far from the only, mechanism through which people may gain a sense of community through their work.

Although we have a made a point to describe all ten of the above types in pure form, most career-community situations are likely to be hybrids of the above types of one kind or another. For example, Porter's (1990) evidence of globally distributed 'industry regions' suggests a common combination of industry and regional types, and therefore a related combination of career investments. Saxenian's (1994) work on Silicon Valley lays a further occupational (electronic engineering) theme onto the regional (valley) and industry (high-technology) themes, and suggests alternative occupational community connections for others, such as complementary venture capital specialists. People working for charitable institutions commonly combine both ideological investments to serve the charitable cause and support for one another's devotion to that cause. Construction workers join together in overlapping industry and project community investments while also sustaining separate occupational subgroups. Political campaign workers combine ideological, project, and support community arrangements. Alumni of nursing programs retain connections with their educational past while practicing their craft in different employment settings. Participants in family business may also have overlapping religious (ideological), geographic (regional), and extended-family (support) community investments.

Hybrid community arrangements may also create tensions—for example, between occupational and family communities (Chapter 9) or between company and support communities, especially in cases where people—more commonly women than men—seek balance between their work and non-work lives (Chapter 10). Reports of French career behavior point to a widespread tension between company communities—inspired by an 'honor-based' national cultural tradition—and support communities sanctioning more autonomous career activity (Chapter 11).

An Example: The Rose Foundation

Our most basic proposition is that people's career situations may be understood through the types of career-community investments that they make. Our further general proposition is that people's career investments are interdependent with their particular combination of career communities, shaping and being shaped by multiple community attachments over time. We anticipate that these two propositions will underlie the particular combination of career community types active in any situation. For example, we recently gathered preliminary evidence from MBA alumni in the same graduating class, where focus groups revealed a strong 'community of practice' orientation emerging from group members. Further evidence offered some support for the proposition that alumni, occupational, and to a lesser extent regional community investments appeared to be influencing and supporting people's current career behavior (Parker *et al.* 1998).

The first author recently worked with a group of nineteen psychotherapists and counselors employed by the Rose Foundation (a pseudonym), a not-for-profit institution providing specialized counseling to victims of sexual abuse. All nineteen participants first completed the 'intelligent career card sort' and used their selections as a basis for reflecting on their own career situations. The participants were then brought together in two successive focus-group sessions, in which the most popular card-sort selections in each of the *knowing-why, knowing-how,* and *knowing-whom* categories were highlighted as a basis for group discussion. The focus groups provided an opportunity for field-testing the card-sort in a new way—namely, as a vehicle for eliciting collective rather than individual interpretations of shared career circumstances. The adopted protocol encouraged participants to talk directly with one another to determine their level of intersubjective agreement (Morgan and Krueger 1993).

The Rose Foundation's leaders saw the focus-group sessions as providing an opportunity for shared convergence on the foundation's mission and values. In the language of our typology, the leaders' hope was to emphasize company community attachments. However, the participants' previous selection and explanation of card-sort items suggested other kinds of community attachment were in play. For example, several participants indicated a communal focus on their occupation, consistent with the previously cited literature on occupational communities (Van Maanen and Barley 1984). The focus-groups' sessions were facilitated with an openness to different kinds of community attachment, and the transcripts of the sessions were subsequently examined for evidence of each of the ten 'pure types' of career community summarized in Table 5.1. In the paragraphs below we will briefly illustrate each of the *knowing-why, knowing-how,* and *knowing-whom* focus-group discussions, and then turn to more systematic analysis of the data generated.

The most popular *knowing-why* card-sort items covered *wanting to work in an industry that matters* and *seeking to make a contribution to society.* These evoked personal ideologies that had drawn people to work for the foundation in the first place. One participant saw 'crisis work as being fundamental to social change'. Another asked rhetorically 'how do you support a girl who has been assaulted and [at the same time] cut down on the [larger social] problem of historical assault?' Similarly, comments on gaining *a feeling of achievement* from work also indicated a shared sense of the work's importance. One participant, for example, described her 'huge sense of achievement in being political, being able to respond'. In addition, *working in a supportive environment* was a key aspect of personal motivation. Citing a process that paralleled their work with clients, members believed that the quality of their conversations deepened their understanding of how colleagues were feeling, and in turn how best to help each other.

Turning to the *knowing-how* cards, participants emphasized investing in *skills particular to their chosen occupations* (that is, in counseling and psychotherapy). Work colleagues were seen as participants in a two-way learning process. One participant offered that 'I have a lot to learn and a lot to offer, [this] is my passion'. Another said, 'knowing-how is about what I get and I can reciprocate that and then give'. Participants sought *job situations from which they could learn* but worried about internal competition over insufficient resources and support. One participant characterized this as an '"I" and "We" dilemma', while another feared 'get[ting] into competition about which aspect of our work has the most impact'. A related card selection was to *develop knowledge about one's own abilities,* which triggered concerns about the opportunity for subsequent utilization of these abilities while working for the foundation.

The most popular *knowing-whom* card selections covered *maintaining relationships within one's occupation* and exercising those relationships *to make a contribution to other people's lives.* As one member reflected, 'What would be the healthy practices that we would need to have collectively . . . in order to actually work effectively and meet our collective values?' Others reaffirmed a previously expressed sentiment that the sharing of information and knowledge increased personal *knowing-how* through *knowing-whom* interpersonal relations. Another popular card selection was about *maintaining relationships to receive social support*. This elicited the observation that participants relied on their colleagues' support to reinforce their separate professional activities. One participant reflected that 'integrating [my role as a therapist] with my relationships is fundamental and reciprocal'.

When participants thought further about the interplay among the three ways of knowing, they focused again on how to effect meaningful social change. They emphasized the need for congruence between personal agendas and actions and those of the foundation. There was a related tension between a shared ideological focus and the need jointly to survive through the revenues the foundation generated. As one speaker expressed it, 'trying to bridge those two things [counseling services and revenue generation] is when we get into trouble. My value base is flat but the structure is two-leveled. How can we make that work in a feminist organization?'

Our brief review of the focus-group sessions suggests what more systematic transcript analysis confirmed: that the group was characterized by four 'pure types' of career-community attachment. The four types were support community, ideological community, occupational community, and finally the company community that the leaders of the Rose Foundation sought to encourage.

Support-community attachments are evidenced by expressions of the *knowing-why* importance of peer support, in turn reflected in *knowing-how* learning influences, and reinforced through *knowing-whom* mutual loyalties. Signs of these kinds of attachments were prominent, perhaps in part because of the foundation's leaders' expressed purpose behind the focus-group activities. However, the participants made a distinction between their commitment to support one another and what they saw as the separate, often conflicting, demands of their employer.

Ideological-community attachments are indicated in expressions of a *knowing-why* desire to contribute to society, in turn enhanced through new *knowing-how* learning, and affirmed through *knowing-whom* interactions. These kind of expressions were also prominent, and appeared interdependent with the level of support people gave or sought from one another. Ideological attachments stem from people's underlying values, and the opportunity to self-organize around shared values can be a powerful driver behind people's subjective career behavior. This suggests shared ideology may be a cause of people working together, rather than a company-inspired effect (as some management literature would suggest).

Occupational-community attachments are related to the *knowing-why* identification people share with similarly qualified people, and the related honing of new *knowing-how* occupational skills through further *knowing-whom* professional attachments. The focus groups brought out a strong current of shared expertise, and of giving and receiving learning in support of one another's professional interests. Consistent with an occupational focus, these interests were expressed as ends in themselves, rather than merely as vehicles for the foundation's own ends.

Finally, *company-community* attachments are indicated in people's *knowing-why* motivation to support the company's mission, *knowing-how* investments that respond to the company's needs, and *knowing-whom* social involvement with other company members. Again, there was considerable evidence for this kind of community attachment, which was encouraged in this case by the leaders' exhortations to support the company's agenda. However, the focus group data suggest that the leaders' level of success was contingent on the values and professionalism people brought to the work. In other words, company-community attachments appeared to rest on the coexistence of ideological and occupational community connections.

Table 5.2 provides selected data in support of the four kinds of career community identified above. However, it would be misleading to suggest that all of the data could be cleanly separated according to one community attachment or another. Some of the evidence clearly indicates connection with more than one career community. The previous observation that company-community attachments were linked to broader professional attachments is one example. Similarly, evidence about support-community attachments appears to link with further ideological- and occupational-community themes. Some of the quotations in Table 5.2 reflect these interconnections, and—we submit—provide a more complete picture of the subjective careers that they represent.

The evidence provided is limited by the focus of the study. For example, there were certain individual references made during the study to support- or family- or occupational-community attachments beyond the workplace. However, the nature and announced purpose of the focus groups did not allow for these to be fully explored. The strength of the case study is that it shows the multiple career-community attachments underlying what could otherwise be seen as a simple company-community situation. What is needed next is to apply the same methodology to other career situations so that the nature of career communities—and the subjective career behavior that underlies them—may be more completely understood.

In sum, our theoretical framework and preliminary evidence suggest a further refinement to Capra's 'figure-ground reversal' previously illustrated in Fig. 5.1. The suggestion is that people's 'webs of relationships' may self-organize into multiple clusters, with each cluster representing a career community held together by overlapping *knowing-why, knowing-how,* and *knowing-whom* attachments of its members. The new figures that emerge, and the new threads of continuity in subjective career behavior, stem not just from interpersonal relationships but from the larger community attachments that people form and re-form as they act out their careers.

Table 5.2. *The Rose Foundation: Support-, ideological-, occupational-, and company-community evidence*

Types of community	Ways of knowing		
	Knowing-why	*Knowing-how*	*Knowing-whom*
Support	'This feels like such a good place to be—support is offered in so many ways. [It's good] knowing there is a range of support I can connect to.'	'When there is a gap, people will come forward here—that is how people learn about the work, supporting the work.'	'When I think of our team I know that if anyone asks for support that will be responded to.'
	'Collectively I feel support here—it just happens and is quite reassuring.'	'We have peer support that is separate from the whole group—so there is an overlapping of process and content.'	'We are caught between individual knowing [knowing each other as individuals] and the context in which we work.'
	'We extend to each other with warmth, [and that] carries forward the work we do.'		
Ideological	'I get a huge sense of achievement in being political—being able to respond.'	'A value base is multi-roled as well. We need to be explicit [about our separate roles] so we can address the issues with integrity.'	'There is a ripple effect when you are supported, you achieve and then you can contribute. The ripple effect goes wider and wider to a political effect. All under one umbrella.'
	'Social change happens through healing and has ripple effects through the whole of society.'	'Let's be creative about how we manage and share our work to increase visibility [in society].'	'We have a collective focus and it's emerged from individual needs. It's the 'I' and 'We' dilemma—how do we be both simultaneously?'
	'My own values are always embedded in my work.'		

Occupational	'It is important to keep reviewing myself—I am a healer in an holistic sense—emotional, spiritual and physical.' 'We need to acknowledge the multiplicity of roles here and the reality around that.'	'When I think of support I think of the work—for example, the after-hours team. People come on board to help fill gaps in the roster and that's actually how they learn about the work.' 'The [foundation's professional] forum needs to be used to ensure there is learning across the groups—the forum is much wider than clinical and we all need to be a part of it.'	'I need role models from many different sources. The relationships are fundamental.' 'Within the therapeutic team we have collegial relationships and feel appreciated.' 'In my therapeutic team we speak the same language and can share the personal and the professional process.'
Company	'In this [foundation] we all have multiple roles. So that affects how I view these items.' 'There are multiple roles played in here. I think there are a lot of constraints.' 'We need to accept the fundamental philosophy—we need agreement on this and then we can move to integrate our various subfields.'	'Do we have to get into competition about which of us has the most impact?' 'We are experiencing competition and we want to take responsibility for integration.' 'There needs to be more of an integration between individual needs and agency needs.'	'The reason I am here [in this foundation] is because I can be supported as I contribute.' 'I used to think I would get all of my support from here [this foundation], but [support needs to be seen from] a much broader perspective.'

Conclusion

This chapter has explored the notion that people's 'webs of relationships' in the workplace are supported by career-community attachments that may include, but are far from restricted to, a sense of community within the employer company. A framework has been presented linking the development of *knowing-why, knowing-how,* and *knowing-whom* career competencies to the consideration of what we propose as a typology of 'career-community' attachments. A typology of ten career communities has been proposed as a basis for interpreting the diversity of contemporary career arrangements. An example has been provided from focus-group data generated through the Rose Foundation's sexual abuse counselors and therapists. That example provided initial support for the argument that career situations can be interpreted as involving multiple career-community attachments.

The next step is to apply the typology and research method to a broader and more diverse group of careers and career settings. We are not saying that company career communities are unimportant, but that such communities will be better understood beside a more complete picture of related and potentially more enduring career-community attachments. To improve our understanding, the figures of such attachments need to be set clearly against the ground of changing company employment arrangements. This chapter represents a start in highlighting those figures.

References

Arthur, M. B., and Rousseau, D. M. (1996) (eds.), *The Boundaryless Career: A New Employment Principle for a New Organizational Era* (New York: Oxford University Press).

—— Claman, P. H., and DeFillippi, R. J. (1995), 'Intelligent Enterprise, Intelligent Careers', *Academy of Management Executive,* 9/4: 7– 20.

Baker, P. L. (1993), 'Chaos, Order and Sociological Theory', *Sociological Inquiry,* 63/2: 123–49.

Barley, S. R. (1989), 'Careers, Identities and Institutions: The Legacy of the Chicago School of Sociology', in M. B. Arthur, D. T. Hall, and B. S. Lawrence (eds.), *Handbook of Career Theory* (New York: Cambridge University Press).

Best, M. H., and Forrant, R. (1996), 'Community-Based Careers and Economic Virtue: Arming, Disarming, and Rearming the Springfield, Western Massachusetts, Metalworking Region', in M. B. Arthur and D. M. Rousseau (eds.), *The Boundaryless Career: A New Employment Principle for a New Organizational Era* (New York: Oxford University Press).

Brown, J. S., and Duguid, P. (1991). 'Organizational Learning and Communities of Practice: Toward a Unified View of Work, Learning and Innovation', *Organization Science,* 2/1: 40–57.

Capra, F. (1996), *The Web of Life* (New York: Anchor Books).

Case, J. (1995), *Open Book Management* (New York: HarperBusiness).

D'Aveni, R. (1994), *Hypercompetition* (New York: Free Press).

DeFillippi, R. J., and Arthur, M. B. (1994), 'The Boundaryless Career: A Competency-Based Perspective', *Journal of Organizational Behavior*, 15: 307–24.

—— —— (1996), 'Boundaryless Contexts and Careers: A Competency-Based Perspective', in M. B. Arthur and D.M Rousseau (eds.), *The Boundaryless Career: A New Employment Principle for a New Organizational Era* (New York: Oxford University Press).

—— —— (1998), 'Paradox in Project-Based Enterprise: The Case of Film-Making', *California Management Review* 40/2: 125–39.

Goerner, S. J. (1995), 'Chaos, Evolution, and Deep Ecology', in R. Robertson and A. Combs (eds.), *Chaos Theory in Psychology and Life Sciences* (Mahwah, NJ: Lawrence Erlbaum).

Granrose, C. S., and Chua, B. L. (1996), 'Global Boundaryless Careers: Lessons from Chinese Family Business', in M. B. Arthur and D. M. Rousseau (eds.), *The Boundaryless Career: A New Employment Principle for a New Organizational Era* (New York: Oxford University Press).

Granovetter, M. (1985), 'Economic Action and Social Structure: The Problem of Embeddedness', *American Journal of Sociology*, 91: 481–510.

Hackman, J. R. (1990) (ed.), *Groups That Work (and Those That Don't)* (San Francisco: Jossey-Bass).

Hall, R. (1992), 'The Strategic Analysis of Intangible Resources', *Strategic Management Journal*, 13: 135–44.

Harvey, D. L., and Reed, M. (1996), 'Social Science as the Study of Complex Systems', in L. D. Kiel and E. Elliott (eds.), *Chaos Theory in the Social Sciences* (Ann Arbor: University of Michigan Press).

Heckscher, C. (1995), *White-Collar Blues: Management Loyalties in an Age of Corporate Restructuring* (New York: Basic Books).

Ibarra, H. (1995), 'Race, Opportunity, and Diversity of Social Roles in Managerial Networks', *Academy of Management Journal*, 38/3: 673–703.

Inkson, K. (1997), 'Organization Structure and the Transformation of Careers', in P. Clark (ed.), *Advancements in Organization Behaviour* (Aldershot, UK: Ashgate Publishers).

Jones, C. (1996), 'Careers in Project Networks: The Case of the Film Industry', in M. B. Arthur and D. M. Rousseau (eds.), *The Boundaryless Career: A New Employment Principle for a New Organizational Era* (New York: Oxford University Press).

Kram, K. E. (1996), 'A Relational Approach to Career Development', in D. T. Hall and Associates, *The Career is Dead, Long Live the Career: A Relational Approach to Careers* (San Francisco: Jossey-Bass).

Lave, J., and Wenger, E. (1991), *Situated Learning: Legitimate Peripheral Participation* (Cambridge, UK: Cambridge University Press).

Litchfield, R. (1993), 'Forget the Diploma, Get me a Rolodex', *Canadian Business* (Apr.), 20–6.

Loye, D. (1995), 'Prediction in Chaotic Social, Economic, and Political Conditions: The Conflict Between Traditional Chaos Theory and the Psychology of Prediction, and some Implications for General Theory', *World Futures*, 44: 15–31.

Maslow, A. (1987), *Motivation and Personality* (3rd edn., New York: Harper & Row).

Morgan, D. L., and Kreuger, R. A. (1993), 'When to Use Focus Groups and Why', in

D. L. Morgan (ed.), *Successful Focus Groups: Advancing the State of the Art* (Thousand Oaks, Calif.: Sage).

Neuberger, F., and Lank, A. G. (1998), *The Family Business: Its Governance and Sustainability* (London: Routledge).

Parker, H. L. (1996), 'The New Career Paradigm: An Exploration of Intelligent Career Behaviour among MBA Graduates and Students', unpublished master's thesis, University of Auckland, New Zealand.

Parker, P., and Arthur, M. B. (1997), 'Applying "New Science" to Careers Research Methods', paper presented to the Academy of Management Meeting, Boston.

—— Inkson, K., Stewart, A., and Arthur, M. B. (1998), 'Looking beyond the Firm: The Role of Boundaryless Careers in Strategic Management Practice', working paper, Department of Management and Employment Relations, University of Auckland.

Peiperl, M., and Baruch, Y. (1997), 'Back to Square Zero: The Post-Corporate Career', *Organizational Dynamics* (Spring), 7–22.

Piore, M. J., and Sabel, C. F. (1984), *The Second Industrial Divide* (New York: Basic Books).

Porter, M. E (1985), *Competitive Advantage* (New York: Free Press).

—— (1990), *The Competitive Advantage of Nations* (New York: Free Press).

Prahalad, C. K., and Hamel, G. (1994), *Competing for the Future* (Boston, Mass.: Harvard Business School Press).

Quinn, J. B. (1992), *Intelligent Enterprise* (New York: Free Press).

Richardson, M. S. (1996), 'From Career Counseling to Counseling/Psychotherapy and Work, Jobs and Career', in Mark L. Savickas and W. Bruce Walsh (eds.), *Handbook of Career Counseling Theory and Practice* (Palo Alto, Calif.: Davis-Black Publishing).

Robertson, R. (1995), 'Introduction: Chaos Theory and the Relationship between Psychology and Science', in R. Robertson and A. Combs (eds.), *Chaos Theory in Psychology and Life Sciences* (Mahwah, NJ: Lawrence Erlbaum).

Sanchez, R. (1997), 'Strategic Management at the Point of Inflection: Systems, Complexity and Competence Theory', *Long Range Planning*, 30: 939–46.

Saxenian, A. L. (1994), *Regional Advantage: Culture and Competition in Silicon Valley and Route 128* (Cambridge, Mass.: Harvard University Press).

—— (1996), 'Beyond Boundaries: Open Labor Markets and Learning in Silicon Valley', in M. B. Arthur and D. M. Rousseau (eds.), *The Boundaryless Career: A New Employment Principle for a New Organizational Era* (New York: Oxford University Press).

Senge, P. M. (1990), *The Fifth Discipline* (New York: Doubleday).

Sergiovanni, T. J. (1994), 'Organizations or Communities? Changing the Metaphor Changes the Theory', *Education Administration Quarterly*, 30/2: 214–26.

Spender, J. C. (1989), *Industry Recipes* (Oxford: Basil Blackwell).

Stacey, R. D. (1996), *Complexity and Creativity in Organizations* (San Francisco: Berrett-Koehler).

Tolbert, P. (1996), 'Occupations, Organizations and Boundaryless Careers', in M. B. Arthur and D. M. Rousseau (eds.), *The Boundaryless Career: A New Employment Principle for a New Organizational Era* (New York: Oxford University Press).

Van Maanen, J., and Barley, S. R. (1984), 'Occupational Communities: Culture and Control in Organizations', in B. Staw and L. Cummings (eds.), *Research In Organizational Behavior* (Greenwich, Conn.: JAI Press).

Weick, K. E. (1979), *The Social Psychology of Organizing* (2nd edn., Reading, Mass.: Addison-Wesley).

—— (1996), 'Enactment and the Boundaryless Career', in M. B. Arthur and D. M.

Rousseau (eds.), *The Boundaryless Career: A New Employment Principle for a New Organizational Era* (New York: Oxford University Press).

Wenger, E. (1998), *Communities of Practice: Learning, Meaning, and Identity* (New York: Cambridge University Press).

Wheatley, M. J. (1992), *Leadership and the New Science: Learning about Organization from an Orderly Universe* (San Francisco: Berrett–Koehler Publishers).

Young, T. R. (1996), 'Chaos Theory and Social Dynamics: Foundations of Postmodern Social Science', in R. Robertson and A. Combs (eds.), *Chaos Theory in Psychology and Life Sciences* (Mahwah, NJ: Lawrence Erlbaum).

Zabusky, S. E., and Barley, S. R. (1996), 'Redefining Success: Ethnographic Observations on the Careers of Technicians', in P. Osterman (ed.), *Broken Ladders: Managerial Careers in the New Economy* (New York: Oxford University Press).

II

KNOWLEDGE WORKERS: PROFESSIONALS IN THE POST-CORPORATE AGE

The focus of this section is on those knowledge workers whose expertise, valued by organizations as a source of competitive advantage, offers them access to rewarding jobs and careers. The chapters that follow deal with the context of organizational change in which the careers of these professionals are enacted, with the sorts of policies firms may adopt to manage careers (while stressing that highly planned or programmatic systems are unrealistic, even in the largest bureaucratic organizations), and with the career concerns of individuals themselves. Throughout, they focus on the ways in which individual knowledge may create and sustain the strategy and structure of the organizations for which they work. Thus, careers shape organizations as well as being shaped by them.

The title of this section deliberately links knowledge and professionals. Where professionals have high power and status in the labor market, their privileged position is built on the expert knowledge of products, processes, and markets that forms the basis for complex problem solving of client problems. Thus, know-how gained through practical experience extends the purely technical knowledge on which formal professional qualification is grounded. The chapters define professional status broadly to include those occupations that have formally organized as professions, with supporting institutions and a defined statement of ethics, and other, newer occupations that display many of the same characteristics. Crucially, as well, the majority of professionals are salaried employees or owner-producers in professional firms and their careers are enacted in organizational settings.

None the less, the complexities of professionals' careers reflect the multiple allegiances or commitments that many of them have. They are not purely 'locals', to use Gouldner's term. Their work values are shaped in a broader institutional setting and they identify with peers outside their employing organization. While the pure professional model of careers, shaped by occupational boundaries within which individuals may freely move across organizations over their working life, is clearly inappropriate for understanding the career experience of many professional employees, the notion of a career tied up with the fortunes of a single employer is also inappropriate and, arguably, becoming more so.

At the level of the nation state as well as the firm, the quality and performance of those with expert knowledge have been seen as critical sources of competitive advantage in the future. As a result, organizations increasingly define what is uniquely known about products or services, the production process, and their client markets as their knowledge base. Seeing this as a strategic asset, they then develop policies to manage it. These developments provoke important theoretical questions and policy issues around the arena of careers that are considered below and in Parker and Arthur's piece on occupational values and career perceptions (Chapter 5). For instance, how far and in what ways can organizations provide the context in which professionals can operate productively, not least by sharing their knowledge with others? In what ways do organizations actually build successful strategies on the basis of talented individuals or teams? Where individuals identify with a set of values formed by institutions other than their employer, or seek to balance concerns that extend beyond the workplace, how does this affect career expectations and choices?

Although they have distinct research subjects and methods, the chapters that follow are linked by the broad theme of interest in the career issues facing key organizational actors. The locus of research in the chapters is mainly smaller professional firms, but the issues addressed clearly have relevance for larger public- and private-sector concerns, many of which have begun to be defined as knowledge-based organizations. Aerospace engineering, health care, and financial services are sectors where this sort of redefinition is occurring and it is no coincidence that, at the same time, changes in the boundaries of these industries and forms of work organization are taking place. Thus, studying professionals raises interesting organizational issues about the way people-intensive units are directed, whether in newer, smaller firms or in mature industries populated by large bureaucracies.

The chapters also show that, even with valued expertise, the career choices of individuals are far from being unrestricted. The 'portfolio' model of careers popularized in recent years ostensibly fits the needs of professionals perfectly, but has arguably overemphasized the discretion individuals can exercise in selecting which projects they undertake and how much control they have over the pace and quality of their work. The reality of contemporary careers is a long way from this. As the fieldwork reported in this section reminds us, professionals frequently face severe commercial uncertainties and operate within the constraints of organizational controls. They may have relatively high task discretion, but they have to deliver results on the basis of their expertise: knowledge on its own is not enough.

Building on the issues of autonomy and constraints, the first chapter in the section is Alvarez' thought-provoking theoretical discussion of theories of action. Reviewing these theories, Alvarez develops the argument that they can provide us with important insights into the challenges facing those in the de-layered and more loosely structured organization. Theories of action offer a contrast to the strong, structurally determined models of organization on which traditional career models have been erected. Instead of seeing career and role requirements being determined by hierarchy, with middle managers having, for instance, distinct responsibilities and opportunities from senior ones, theories of action focus upon the scope for individuals to define their roles more: to enact structures to a greater or lesser degree in their own interests. In this sense, they present an optimistic contrast to accounts that see relatively limited career opportunities in the contemporary 'downsized' organization and Alvarez discusses some of the entrepreneurial management skills likely to be associated with career success in these looser environments.

Morris' chapter reassesses existing promotion models in the light of the argument that much new knowledge in the professional firm is generated by those in the operating core, rather than being concentrated at the top level of the firm. Surveying explanations for the conventional model of promotion using up-or-out rules, he argues this model is likely to be inappropriate for firms seeking to exploit organization-specific knowledge competitively by concentrating on familiar markets, but more appropriate for those firms where knowledge is codified and public or where they compete in unfamiliar markets. It is also incompatible with broader changes in careers brought about by the growth of dual careers and the desire to balance work and family commitments, discussed in the following chapters, particularly Chapter 9 by Eaton and Bailyn. Morris provides the basis for further research into promotion systems in professional firms by suggesting that different knowledge strategies as well as the preferences of individuals may affect the extent to which firms retain and develop 'home-grown' talent or rely on external sources.

Jones and Lichtenstein present data from research in small professional firms, in this case architecture practices. Using the career categorization of De Fillipi and Arthur in terms of three types of competencies for success— *knowing-why, knowing-how,* and *knowing-whom*—they show how the skills, values, and actions of partners in these practices shape organization strategies. They suggest this occurs because partners select projects on the basis of their expertise and, collectively, these become the substance of a firm's strategy. Over time, these choices also influence the skills and knowledge of the staff required to carry out these projects. Echoing Alvarez' chapter, the authors suggest that there are important links between the career choices individuals take and the evolution of organization structures in which they are enacted. This is well illustrated through the case studies reported in the chapter where a fine-grained analysis of the partners in these firms reveals not just the sort of work they like to do (and how they define professional practice) but also how they maintain or build client knowledge and cultivate networks of contacts to aid this, as well as how new skills are created. Their conclusion that firms create different *dominant logics* or modes of competing based on career competencies is an exciting proposition that offers potential for further comparative analysis of professional firms in different sectors and countries.

In contrast to the other three chapters (but echoing Chapter 2 in Part I and Chapters 10 and 11 in Part III), the piece by Eaton and Bailyn is a detailed empirical study of careers from the perspective of individuals. Focusing on employees in small biotechnology firms in the USA, their chapter looks at how professionals seek to integrate career with other issues—family, professional interests, and lifestyle. Starting from the premise that existing theory has taken insufficient note of the non-career domain in individuals' choices about their careers, it shows how these are actually an outcome of numerous external factors, especially for women, as well as formal policies. What is also striking is the importance of informal deals that are struck by these professionals with their managers to balance competing demands. As the authors show, the reality of careers is that they are constructed in response to the myriad ongoing demands facing actors as much as they are determined by human-capital considerations.

6

Theories of Managerial Action and their Impact on the Conceptualization of Executive Careers

José Luis Alvarez

In this chapter I intend to show how the diffusion of new organizational forms makes theories of action a fruitful perspective to address the challenges presented by the careers of executives in contemporary organizations.

The chapter has affinities with Weick's (1996) argument that trends towards the softening and fragmentation of organizational structures favor the impact on social systems of enactment attempts by career actors. In other words, in the absence or lesser salience of external cues provided by strong, hierarchical structures, such as clear lines of command or detailed instructions for performance, actors such as managers ought to rely more on internal guides. Psychological dispositions will be more important than external organizational scripts.

I focus on the organizational context, tasks, and careers of top managers. This is not an ideological preference but partly reflects my own previous work on the subject of top-management teams and chief executives. Additionally, top management has usually been more subject to the ambiguous effects of uncertain contexts and weak structures than lower-level managers or employees, and more often. In this regard, top management is a good target group for examining trends that are rapidly becoming more widespread.

The Changing Social Settings

Managerial careers are undergoing a transformation probably without parallel since the spread of the divisional form in large organizations and the establishment of a professional management model around the set of executive tasks and careers required by capital-allocation processes, such as planning and budgeting, organizing and staffing, controlling and problem solving (Kotter 1982).

Ghoshal and Bartlett (1997) argue that the old management model is no longer valid in complex organizations. They categorize managerial work and careers in today's leading corporations, where the scarce resource is now knowledge rather than capital, into three types. First is the entrepreneurial work performed by front-line managers, such as heads of strategic business units. This is dominated by an external orientation, and focused on results, by which managers are evaluated. Second is an integrative function, focused primarily on people development, carried out by experienced managers who are the middle management of the firm, although their responsibilities are likely to have changed as organizations have downsized. Thirdly, there is institutional work aimed at holding the corporation together through mechanisms such as values, distinctive competencies, and strategic priorities or intent. This task is carried out by the top management of the corporation. Since these different tasks demand highly specialized competencies that cannot be either quickly developed or readily transferred, they lead to distinct executive career paths.

Another consequence of the corporate revolution described by Ghoshal and Bartlett concerns the attachment between the individual and the organization. It has been widely noted that a social contract based upon a 'loyalty model', characterized by a strong and enduring relationship, where commitment was rewarded with employment security, is being substituted by a new type of attachment. This is the 'flexibility model', with shorter and more tenuous relationships between organizations and individuals. In this model, employees build their careers across organizations, displaying loyalty to themselves, their competencies, and their professions, and, temporarily, to project teams, rather than to single organizations. This centering of professional careers around individuals' competencies, and the shortened length of time people are attached to organizations, has led Peiperl and Baruch (1997) to reflect on the apparent return to a sort of guild organization of some professional labor markets. To put it differently, external labor markets are taking over domains previously held by internal labor markets.

Thus a great deal of contemporary work on executives' careers starts from the idea that shifts in the environment require highly adaptive, non-hierarchical organizations, capable of transforming structures, competencies, and activities. These organizations in turn demand flexible managers, capable of learning and displaying new skills for the performance of a wide and changing range of tasks. Changes in managers' careers, therefore, come from new forms of organizing.

While the foregoing model of changing careers is fruitful, a complementary perspective is based on theories of managerial action. This refers to the ways in which the motives, purposes, and skills of the actors themselves (in this case, managers) help to construct or maintain organizational forms, such as large corporations. It is concerned with the interface between executive actions, professional interests, and personal identities, on the one side, and organizational strategies and structures, on the other. Theories of action assume some degree of autonomy for individual actors (such as managers) and recognize the impact they can have on the social system, or their capability for 'enactment', to use Weick's (1996) term.

Indeed, changes in the ways organizations work, so that there is less reliance on formal structures and systems, make managerial action more important. As Burt (1997: 359) summarizes:

The shift away from bureaucracy means that managers cannot rely as much on directives from the firm. They are more than ever the authors of their own work. Firms gain by being able to identify, and adapt more readily to, needed production changes and market shifts. There are new opportunities for managers, but there are also new costs . . . a corresponding increase in uncertainty, stress, and potentially disruptive conflict.

It is in this situation that the managerial action perspective could be fruitful.

The Elusive Phenomenon: Managerial Action

The role of top managers, their competencies, and their professional trajectories has had a limited presence in theories of organizations, which have traditionally been focused on structural topics and dominated by structural arguments. Contributions in the domain of strategy, such as the work of Finkelstein and Hambrick (1996), do recognize the impact of top-management teams' decisions and actions on the performance of firms. However, the prominent use of demographic variables and the scant attention to processes of decision making and implementation impede a true action perspective, as I shall describe below.

Network approaches have rebalanced organization theory by noticing the internal and external openness of organizations, by paying special attention to social rather then formal structures, and by emphasizing a process of structuring. This has led to a positive acknowledgment of the behaviors and roles of those structuring agents actively involved in the process of shaping organizations, and in particular of top managers, the more autonomous action-takers in organizational settings. For example, Jones and Lichtenstein (Chapter 8) provide an illuminating example of how senior architects influence the strategies of their firms.

Fortunately, there have been several efforts at theorizing managerial action. They are built upon the notion that managers do not have clear or consistent notions about what it is they are trying to do (problematic preferences), how it is they are supposed to do it (unclear technology), or who it is that should make the decisions (fluid participation). Peters (1980) provides an early summary of the practical implications of this sort of analysis, but a more recent formulation in the managerial action tradition is that of Eccles and Nohria (1992). They react against the overflow into management education in the 1980s and 1990s of business fads and fashions that obscured the essentials of management, and pushed executives into a frantic search for the acquisition and implementation of the latest 'how-to' techniques (on these dynamics, see also Alvarez 1997).

Eccles and Nohria identify the essence of management not in technical procedures that can be standardized or translated into formulas, but in some pragmatic and highly tactical competencies that help in 'getting things done'—that is, accomplishing goals in complex social settings. Eccles and Nohria express the pragmatic essence of the managerial job in the notion of 'robust action'—that is, in arranging the mix of organizational elements (from systems and formal structures to shared values and styles) in ways that facilitate the accomplishment of short-term objectives while preserving long-term flexibility. 'Robust action' involves, first, acting without certainty; secondly, constantly preserving flexibility; thirdly, being politically savvy; fourthly, having a keen sense of timing; fifthly, judging the situation at hand; sixthly, using rhetoric effectively; and, seventhly, working multiple agendas. The principles of 'robust action' give us more evidence that what managers do—that is, taking action—springs from a set of competencies that are not dependent on formalized knowledge. Thus robust action is not easily conducive to standardization nor to professionalization.

The current fragmentation of organizations into many semi-autonomous business units favors 'robust action', in what Leifer (1988) calls 'local games'. Understanding organizational action as local events is in timely accordance with generalized processes of organizational decentralization into highly autonomous structures, or with trends towards the so-called 'commodification' of organizations (the partition of corporations into smaller, highly focused business units, easily exchangeable in the market with other corporations), along with the high differentiation of managerial tasks and careers noted by Ghoshal and Bartlett (1997). Moreover, localization adds to the characterization of managerial action as being highly political in nature. As the saying goes: 'all politics is local'. Inspiration for Leifer, Eccles and others cited here stems from the seminal work of White (1992). He argues that organizations arise out of control efforts that produce structure, social order, stability, routines, and responsibilities. Action is a reverse social phenomenon of organizations, an attempt at change. A paradox emerges from the fact that agents in their quest for action, and in their 'decoupling' of extant rigidities, create new connections and structures of control, which in turn generate attainment differentiation and consolidate new inequalities.

An inspiration for Eccles and Nohria could be the classic piece aimed at practitioners, Wrapp's 'Good Managers Don't Make Policy Decisions' (1984). Going against the conventional portrayal of executives as primarily setting policies, communicating precise goals and objectives, and making clear-cut decisions, Wrapp's recommendations to general managers coincided with the familiar 'robust-action' features: develop a network of information sources; concentrate energies and time on priorities; play the power game; cultivate a sense of timing; press on cautiously; appear imprecise; maintain viable options; avoid policy straitjackets; muddle with a purpose; exploit change. The following lines from his article became an often reproduced quote in many later works on the topic:

The good manager can function effectively only in an environment of continual change. . . . Only with many changes in the works can the manager discover new combinations of opportunities and open up new corridors of comparative indifference. . . . In the day-to-day operation of a going concern, they find the milieu to maneuver and conceptualize.   (Wrapp 1984: 14)

Another recent contribution to a theory of action is that of Fligstein (1997), who proposes that such a theory should conceptualize organizational actors as 'specialists' in obtaining desired social outcomes by working through others, as skilled agents in motivating cooperation from other parties. The paramount competency of these actors is 'empathy'—that is, being capable of relating to the constituencies operating in particular situations, and developing those constituencies' identity (both interests and world views) in ways that are coherent with the strategy of the actors themselves. These actors have a repertoire of tactics available for the implementation of their strategies that are similar to those mentioned above, including: setting the agenda for other actors; understanding and exploiting the ambiguities and uncertainties of organizational settings; using the resources available at any moment; framing action by linking broader interpretations of reality to groups' existing conceptions of interest; brokering or being highly active at networking; asking for more and accepting less; building alliances and coalitions through the aggregation of interests; and initiating several courses of action in the hope that some will succeed.

The many coincidences of all these lists really suggest that scholars are zeroing in on a bundle of behaviors that embody the fundamentals of managerial action. Executive tasks are primarily conceived of as 'unobtrusive'. Managing the context is seen as more appropriate in uncertain and changing environments than managing the content. To put it another way, managing organizing (or the *process* of organizing) is more appropriate than managing organizations; that is, setting up structures and systems. Put yet another way, what Weick (1995) calls 'sensemaking' is at least as relevant as controlling.

Top managers as politicians

The tasks described lead us to a basic view of top managerial action as highly political, and of managers as experts in long-term strategic action through playing short-term local games. This political model of top managers' roles is similar to that of March (1988), who saw executives as political brokers, negotiating the composition of the firm and bargaining its goals.

This political, pragmatic notion of executives' work, derived from theories of action, fits contemporary corporate realities and professional tracks particularly well. For one thing, the 'revolt' of shareholders and other stakeholders against managerial prerogatives pushes top executives to be more responsive to a variety of external constituencies, as well as to balance internal groups (Uyterhoeven 1991). Further augmenting the political content of managerial work is the 'commodification' of organizations already alluded to in this chapter. All these features are pushing managers to become more like mobilizers of collective action, leaders of social movements created around specific and transitory issues, or coordinators of a number of small or middle-size cells or teams enacted around projects.

The impact of psychological make-up on managerial action and careers

The political nature of management action requires of executives a peculiar set of dispositions or attitudes and even predisposition or a particular psychological profile, which has implications for managerial careers. In this regard, Athos' (1975) work on executives' personal and professional development stands out. He discusses the multidimensionality of the 'managerial experience', one that cuts simultaneously across cognitive levels and what are called realms of experience: ideals, purpose, social, psychological, learning. The implications are that managers cannot comprehend everything that is going on at all those levels and realms; that managers inevitably face ambiguity, for even the things and events available as data are not clear in their meaning; and, finally, that there is uncertainty, because, although executives are supposed to act, they will never be sure of the outcomes of their decisions and actions. Being able to develop professionally in a context of imperfection, ambiguity, and uncertainty demands strong personal balance. As Athos suggests, this requires personal growth based first upon flexibility, as well as the ability to recognize mistakes and to learn.

Over forty years ago Argyris (1957) argued that bureaucratic organizations with a strict division of labor and high power differentials do not facilitate healthy personal and professional developments. Changes in organizations towards less hierarchical structures and more decentralized decision making have, therefore, been welcomed by some. For example, there are those that see in the new forms of work organization, characterized by flexible and highly skilled employees, engaged in lifelong learning, working in entrepreneurial structures, an opportunity for more organizational productivity and richer and more autonomous lives (Mirvis and Hall 1994). However, new organizational arrangements, even for white-collar and executive groups, have also been criticized for being intensified, decentered, and destabilized (Smith 1997). Intensified, because the blurring of boundaries between personal and professional realms, as well as the demands on managers by high performing organizations, usually mean more work time. Decentered, because the subcontracting of work, which is increasingly important, requires, in the absence of the superior's presence, self-monitoring—that is, self-administered control. Destabilized, because the job instability and insecurity traditionally reserved to non-management groups have also reached executives.

Thus new organizational forms may create psychological difficulties. This is evidenced by the study by Pucik *et al.* (1995) of the executive temperament and of careers better suited to manage and go through change processes. The characteristics that Pucik and colleagues studied in managers were tolerance for ambiguity, risk aversion, self-efficacy, self-esteem, affective disposition, and openness to experience. Another feature was the previous type of career of the executives: linear, spiral, expert, and transitory (Driver 1979). They confirmed that, as expected, being able to cope with change facilitates personal and career adjustment. More significantly, successful coping was found to be predicted above all by three features of the managerial character: high tolerance for ambiguity, positive affectivity (a tendency to respond positively to the environment), and low risk aversion. However, only a minority of the managers in the sites studied by Pucik *et al.* exhibited those psychological characteristics.

This reinforces one of the insights provided by theories of action. Managerial tasks and careers are not only highly contingent on a variety of heterogeneous social forces coalescing locally. They are also dependent on individual characters. Moreover, the capabilities required for being a pragmatic, efficient manager in the context of widespread change and in 'soft', highly politicized structures are not likely to be widely distributed in the population. In fact, as Nicholson implies in Chapter 3, those capabilities go against some of the features of the common genetic heritage, such as status aspiration, risk aversion, and maximization of fitness with the environment.

In summary, the reality of managerial work is rapidly becoming extremely varied and diverse, both objectively—in terms of tasks—and subjectively—in terms of predisposition and felt experience. Theories of action, with their situational focus and their acknowledgment of organizations as political arenas, could then provide a fruitful perspective for the study of the careers of managers operating in increasingly diffused weak structures. These theories assume that executives operate within highly local contexts, constrained by their firms' strategies and dependent upon their own skills, especially tactical ones. Executives are oriented in their actions by their interests and their perception of their own professional identities (Ibarra 1996). Moreover, theories of managerial action recognize that the political maneuvering of actors has impact in unpredictable ways beyond local domains on larger systems. The theories therefore complement and re-inforce Weick's (1996) assertion that careers cannot be considered any more simply as dependent variables whose outcomes are the result of particular organizational characteristics, such as structure or strategy.

Concluding Reflections

The adoption of practices of organizing based upon less clearly defined structures is leading to high levels of differentiation in executives' tasks and, as a consequence, in careers. These practices make the application of theories of action to understanding career trajectories especially timely.

I have detailed in the previous pages several sets of behaviors that a group of authors have presented as representing the themes of managerial action. These show obvious and significant similarities around a political understanding of management tasks. This political analogy has been labeled by authors such as Eccles and Nohria (1992) as 'pragmatist', because of its alignment with contemporary developments in social and political philosophy.

While theories of action do not imply radically different ways for conceptualizing career trajectories, they may complement or reinforce some of the perspectives already in place, especially in the domain of executive careers.

An example of the potential contribution that theories of action could provide relates to Ghoshal and Bartlett's (1997) rejection of what they call the 'Russian Doll Syndrome' (the assumption that performing well in a managerial position is the best predictor of success in a hierarchically superior assignment). Ghoshal and Bartlett argue against the supposition that managerial positions are essentially similar, and against the view that there is something like a generalist career for top managers. Rather, managerial work is becoming diversified and fragmented (Leicht and Fennell 1997). Diversified, because one of the characteristics of new organizational forms is that they are more heterogeneous than the old dominant model. Organizational models are going to proliferate, and, with them, templates for structures, combinations of organizational tasks, and types of managerial careers. Fragmented, because, even in single organizations, as Ghoshal and Bartlett describe, managerial roles are increasingly differentiated, implying again different tasks, behaviors, orientations, and careers, and, consequently, very difficult work transitions. This argument by Ghoshal and Bartlett is consistent with what theories of action would have to say of managerial work.

The diversification and fragmentation of managerial work pose difficult challenges, both theoretical and methodological. The tenets of theories of action, of the 'localization' and idiosyncrasy of managerial tasks, converge with other chapters in this volume (particularly Chapters 5, 9, and 10) on the need for modifying the basic image of the notion of careers. An analogy of careers as predictable trajectories along an upward path of hierarchical positions, essentially equivalent and therefore comparable across organizations, is increasingly unable to capture the essentials of the managerial experience at the beginning of the twenty-first century. However, this established image is still the underlying hypothesis of a good deal of existing research on careers, which argues that structures determine tasks and positions, and the sequence of these determine careers. Theories of action echo other contributions in this volume in suggesting that new managerial careers could perhaps be better grasped by a more blurred, impressionistic, and subjective basic analogy: a succession of work experiences only loosely related to an organizational architecture, that cannot be easily plotted along a line of hierarchical advancement. Probably, the criterion for the assessment of these experiences, and of the professional identity they provide, is no longer the objective metric of level within a hierarchy. Instead, several measures, individual, social, and professional, are needed. Even more relevant, and difficult to grasp academically, these measures are no longer external, but internal to the individuals being studied and fundamentally subjective.

This leads me to a second reflection stimulated by an action perspective. The heterogeneity of the trajectories of professional careers demands special academic work, and this requires innovative research methodologies.

In-depth case studies have traditionally been recommended for the first stages of exploration of an uncharted subject, or one where substantial change is occurring. To an important degree, managerial careers now constitute a qualitatively distinct phenomenon and, therefore, they warrant qualitative methodologies, such as ethnographies, and then grounded theories, which would provide rich, 'thick' descriptions of the phenomenon as well as the constructs for looking at it.

Although qualitative research in the field of careers is not novel, there are two more factors that invite a more widespread use of what are generally called ideographic research approaches. First, because the architecture of organizations is no longer the dominant dimension in ordering the professional career, field methodologies, which are more apt to capture local and idiosyncratic combinations of variables in different social settings, seem better fitted than quantitative methods. A second reason lies in the basic research hypothesis. Theories of action allow us to conceive of managers as being more autonomous—that is, not merely the occupants of pre-established domains, but significant shapers through their actions of their tasks and positions in the structure, and, through these, of their organizations. In order to capture the decision-making processes of those managers, their subjective strategies, and their orientation to action, ethnographic research strategies are very well suited.

Breiger (1995), in a review of research on social structures and their effects on inequality and individual opportunities—what has been called the sociology of the life course—describes how this field is drifting increasingly away from over-encompassing and abstract variables such as class, status, structures, and the like; that is, from basic general characterizations of the social system. Breiger argues, for instance, that social or organizational, opportunities are embedded in intersections of local networks of personal, social, organizational, and institutional relations. Sometimes these relations become communities, such as the Canadian biotechnology industry described in Chapter 2. Concern is also being directed by this emerging perspective to the subjective views of the individuals, to whom the capability to act purposively and pragmatically, and to make tactical use of the available resources, is assigned. While the traditional approach to organization theories is usually labeled 'structuralist', the second, because of the attention to the strategies and subjective positioning towards action of actors within systems, such as managers, is being called 'phenomenologist'.

On the topic of careers, there are two interesting points in these developments in the sociology of the life course. First is the acknowledgment that socio-economic attainment is derived from specific positions at the firm and organizational level that, in turn, are structured 'far less along the lines of routine promotion and more around circles of affiliated networks' (Breiger 1995). Because of the extent that these networks of mutual acquaintance, obligation, and information channeling are idiosyncratic and local, this perspective fits the diversification of tasks, actions, and careers that has been repeatedly noted in this chapter. Secondly, because of the extent that careers are intertwined with personal and social variables, the field of careers should overlap to an important degree with the field of the life course.

There is, therefore, an opportunity for cross-fertilization of the fields of managerial careers and life course. This would see managers' careers more as a life-course matter; that is, their study should include personal and social variables, such as networks of friendship and acquaintances, and not limit itself to strictly professional variables such as intellectual capital.

In sum, in this chapter I have tried to approach the field of careers from the viewpoint of a scholar educated in macro-theories. I have proposed that theories of action could enrich the approaches used in addressing new career realities, and increase the overall level of understanding already developed through research on careers.

References

Alvarez, J. L. (1997), 'The Sociological Tradition and the Spread and Institutionalization of Knowledge for Action', in J. L. Alvarez (ed.), *The Production and Consumption of Business Knowledge in Europe* (London: Macmillan).
Athos, A. (1975), *Behavior in Organizations: A Multidimensional View* (Englewood Cliffs, NJ: Prentice Hall).

Argyris, C. (1957), *Personality and Organization: The Conflict Between the System and Individual* (New York: Harper & Row).

Breiger, R. L. (1995), 'Social Structure and the Phenomenology of Attainment', *Annual Review of Sociology*, 21: 115–36.

Burt, R. S. (1997), 'The Contingent Value of Social Capital', *Administrative Science Quarterly*, 42/2: 339–65.

Driver, M. (1979), 'Career Concepts and Career Management in Organizations', *Behavior Problems in Organizations* (London: Prentice Hall International).

Eccles, R., and Nohria N. (1992), *Beyond the Hype: Rediscovering the Essence of Management* (Boston, Mass.: Harvard Business School Press).

Finkelstein, S., and Hambrick, D. C. (1996), *Strategic Leadership: Top Executives and their Effects on Organizations* (Minneapolis/St Paul: West Publishing).

Fligstein, N. (1997), 'Social Skill and Institutional Theory', *American Behavioral Scientist*, 40/4: 397–405.

Ghoshal, S., and Barlett, C. A. (1997), *The Individualized Corporation: A Fundamentally New Approach to Management* New York: Harper Business.

Ibarra, H. (1996), 'Inauthentic Selves: Image, Identity and Social Network in Professional Adaptation', working paper, Harvard Business School.

Kotter, J. P. (1982), *The General Managers* (New York: Free Press).

Leicht, K. T., and Fennell, M. L. (1997), 'The Changing Organizational Context of Professional Work', *Annual Review of Sociology*, 23: 215–31.

Leifer, E. M. (1988), 'Interaction Preludes to Role Setting: Exploratory Local Action', *American Sociological Review*, 53 (Dec.), 865–78.

March, J. G. (1988), 'The Business Firm as a Political Coalition', in J. G. March (ed.), *Decisions and Organizations* (Oxford, UK: Basil Blackwell).

Mirvis, P. H., and Hall, D. T. (1994), 'Psychological Success and the Boundaryless Career', *Journal of Organizational Behavior*, 15: 365–80.

Peiperl, M. A., and Baruch, Y. (1997), 'Back to Square Zero: The Post-Corporate Career', *Organizational Dynamics* (Spring), 7–23.

Peters, T. (1980), 'Symbols, Patterns and Settings: An Optimistic Case for Getting Things Done', *Organizational Dynamics* (Autumn), 3–23.

Pucik, V., Judge, T., and Welbourne, T. (1995), *Organizational Transformations: Implications for Career Management and Executive Development in the US, Europe and Asia* (Lexington, Mass.: International Consortium for Executive Development Research).

Smith, V. (1997), 'New Forms of Work Organization', *Annual Review of Sociology*, 23: 315–39.

Uyterhoeven, H. (1991), 'General Managers in the Middle', in J. Bower (ed.), *The Craft of General Management* (Boston, Mass.: Harvard Business School Publications).

Weick, K. E. (1995), *Sensemaking in Organizations* (Thousand Oaks, Calif.: Sage).

—— (1996), 'Enactment and the Boundaryless Career: Organizing as we Work', in M. B. Arthur and D. M. Rousseau (eds.), *The Boundaryless Career: A New Employment Principle for a New Organizational Era* (New York: Oxford University Press).

White, H. C. (1992), *Identity and Control: A Structural Theory of Social Action* (Princeton, NJ: Princeton University Press).

Wrapp, H. E. (1984), 'Good Managers Don't Make Policy Secisions', *Harvard Business Review*, 62/4: 8–21.

Promotion Policies and Knowledge Bases in the Professional Service Firm

Timothy Morris

The professional service firm (PSF) is a classic example of the knowledge-based or knowledge-intensive organization. In spite of this, the role that knowledge plays has received little research attention. It has been treated as a basic building block of the firm but in a somewhat oversimplified fashion with the result that our models of organization and careers are of limited use in describing or explaining practices inside the PSF. This short-coming has been highlighted by the fact that those managing PSFs (and other organizations, too) have become preoccupied with defining and managing their knowledge base: believing every other asset is susceptible to replication, they have turned to their stock of proprietary knowledge in the search for uniqueness and competitive advantage. Theory has lagged changes in policy and practice.

In this chapter I aim to develop a model of the PSF in which the role and diversity of knowledge are recognized and then explore some of the implications for promotion policies. To do this, I argue that theory has been built around a model of professional knowledge that, being codified and transferable, is not the basis for uniqueness. I also suggest knowledge is assumed to be concentrated at the center and to form the basis of leveraging labor. Existing models of promotion in the PSF follow from these assumptions. My general aim is, therefore, to advance the conceptualization of promotion systems in the PSF by developing a fuller understanding of the role of knowledge within it.

Definitions and Existing Theories of the PSF

The professional service firm (PSF) is a term describing organizations involved in a variety of activities from consulting, law, civil engineering, and architecture to software production (Maister 1993; Greenwood and Lachman 1996). The term has been used interchangeably with the knowledge intensive firm (Starbuck 1992), human asset intensive firm (Coff 1995), and knowledge-based organization (Alvesson 1993; Winch and Schneider 1993), although all of these terms are used in relatively imprecise ways. Some of these firms, such as architecture practices, have formally accredited employees as professionals; others, such as consulting firms, do not. None the less, their employees are in occupations that are similar to the professionals in claiming relatively high status and expertise (Freidson 1986).

The term PSF here refers to an organization that trades mainly on the knowledge of its human capital—that is, its employees and the producer-owners—to develop and deliver solutions to client problems. Like other service organizations, the outputs of the PSF are intangible, but a distinction can be drawn between the outputs of the PSF and those of mass service firms, such as retail banks. The latter trade on relatively standardized and simple products through a large fixed asset base of buildings and information technologies (Bowen and Schneider 1988), whereas the products of the PSF are generally more complex and, crucially, can be bundled in a variety of ways to customize solutions to the client's specific circumstances. Customization involves the application of different types of expertise contained within the firm and close involvement of professional staff in delivering the product, often in conjunction with the client and over an extended time period. This produces task uncertainty, requiring professionals to create their roles to some extent as they go along through mutual adjustment (Mills *et al.* 1983). The result is that product knowledge and process knowledge—that is, knowledge of the way the firm's services are delivered to the client over time—are closely interlinked.

Because of these characteristics, the PSF basically has to manage two markets: the client market, where the objective is to produce profitable solutions to client problems, and the labor market, where it seeks staff of appropriate quality (Maister 1993). The client market is managed through the generation and maintenance of demand for the firm's services. The market for professional labor is managed through the provision of intrinsic incentives, such as the opportunity to pursue interesting work (see Chapter 8) and extrinsic factors, notably pay and promotion opportunities, and to attract, retain, and motivate staff once they are in the firm. Other factors of production are less important and do not strongly influence the PSF's internal form or working. Frequently, but not invariably, the ownership form of the PSF is the partnership. In this form, the owners are actively involved in the day-to-day running of the business and, typically, claim governance rights including information about the performance of the firm and consultation over major decisions, as well as their rights to a share of the profits (Greenwood *et al.* 1990). A key decision for the existing owners is promotion to partner, because of the implications for the reputation of the firm as well as its future direction, given how much professional firms' strategies reflect the individual interests and preferences of their partners (Nelson 1988; Morris and Pinnington 1998*a*; see also Chapter 8). These, in turn, are bound to affect its revenues.

Knowledge and the PSF

In the main areas of research on the PSF, the expert knowledge of the core producers has been recognized as a source of distinctiveness in organization form and functioning (Mintzberg 1987), but has not been treated as a variable that is independent from the labor that embodies it. I have argued elsewhere (Morris and Empson 1998) that this is because interest in the PSF arose originally out of the broader concern with the consequences of growing expertise in society organized around occupational groups or professions (e.g. Mills 1951). Subsequently research focused on the reasons for, and consequences of, its distinctiveness from the orthodox firm (Morris and Empson 1998). While expert knowledge has always been seen as the basis for the claimed distinctiveness of the PSF, the nature of this knowledge and its influence on organizational form and performance have not been fully addressed.

Thus, explanations of why PSFs are formed treat knowledge as part of the larger problem of obtaining efficient co-production with other professionals. Generally, it has been argued that firms are able to form where one or more producer has sufficient expertise or reputation to employ other staff, extracting profit from the surplus of fees over employment costs (Leibowitz and Tollison 1980; Malos and Campion 1995). Leveraging the knowledge and experience of the owner-producer, which is central to profit generation (Fama and Jensen 1983), is achieved by deploying on client assignments relatively inexperienced staff who are able to resolve complex problems by calling on the wisdom of their senior colleagues. Firms then grow as individuals pool their expertise to share risks, allowing the production of a range of services around different combinations of knowledge (Gilson and Mnookin 1985). Growth is facilitated by the powerful incentives firms can use in the form of career advancement to partner and profit-sharing prospects which allow them to economize on monitoring costs and obtain exceptional effort from aspiring candidates (Landers *et al.* 1996). Clearly, these theories accept that the interests of professional staff and owners may diverge, but assume knowledge transfer is unproblematic because labor embodies expert knowledge. The analytical assumption is essentially Marxian: profit is generated from the efforts (rather than the knowledge) of junior labor (Marx 1959; Boisot 1998).

A critical problem for those who own and manage the PSF concerns the consequences for performance of the organization where the most valuable asset is not owned by the shareholder and is mobile. As product knowledge and client contacts are transferred around employees, the risk of one or more leaving and taking this with them can be serious. When this occurs, not only may specialist knowledge be lost to the firm, but those who were colleagues one day are competitors the next, as has been seen in numerous cases in investment banking. This sort of problem has particularly been the focus of agency and transaction cost analyses that concentrate on the utility of rewards in the form of promotion and profit-sharing to retain knowledge in the firm (Gilson and Mnookin 1985; Morris and Pinnington 1998b). Again, the analysis works from the premise that labor embodies expertise and that knowledge management is indistinct from the management of professionals.

Knowledge has been treated this way because existing models have assumed it is organized on the professional model. That is to say, professional knowledge has a predominantly technical-rational base codified in general principles or rules. These offer cause-and-effect linkages or ways of reasoning that are designed to explain phenomena in a systemic way (such as medical knowledge of human anatomy) and provide guidance for interpreting specific problems (such as what a client's position may be in a legal dispute) (Parsons 1954; Torstendahl 1990). Clearly, this sort of knowledge is not owned or exclusive to one firm, although it may be possible to patent the applications that follow from particular advances in it for a time period. Such knowledge is formally codified and regulated by the institutions of an occupational group external to the firm. It is the professional institute that controls entry to the profession and acts as the repository of extant knowledge (Abbot 1991).

A second assumption is that expertise increases with seniority and forms the basis of career progress. Typically, in the PSF, new hires are brought in at junior levels to serve a period of apprenticeship. This may include acquiring formal qualifications while they gain experience of the firm's clients and methods of working, thereby linking theory and practice. In this period, they are involved in what is sometimes known as 'grunt' work, carrying out routine tasks under the guidance of more senior professionals. On formal qualification, they are allocated to a department and begin to specialize. This enables the firm to balance the supply of labor with client demand, keeping only those staff of appropriate quality at this juncture (Malos and Campion 1995) and replacing the rest with a new crop of juniors. For the employees, motivation comes through the opportunity to specialize and work on the most challenging assignments as well as competition for more senior positions (Gilson and Mnookin 1985; Landers et al. 1996). Personal professional knowledge, satisfaction, and productivity increase concomitantly.

In other sorts of PSF, such as management consulting, the employees are not formally accredited professionals and their expertise is more organizationally specific. None the less, the induction and career paths follow a similar route of learning-by-doing—experiencing client problems and the skills of client handling under the guidance of a senior—and specialization. In these firms, the formal knowledge base is exclusively controlled by the organization and may be legally protected as intellectual property (although knowledge leakage to other firms may still occur through employees leaving to work elsewhere). But the assumption that knowledge concentrates at the center of the firm and is transferred outwards is the same as in other PSFs. Juniors can be charged at rates far in excess of their earnings, because they are applying the knowledge of others embodied in proprietary products, or 'service offerings', as they are called by practitioners. These are usually techniques or 'methodologies' that significantly increase consultants' marginal productivity by providing standardized ways of defining and then tackling clients' problems.

Rethinking Knowledge in the PSF

In practice, knowledge in the firm is more than the existing professional knowledge base. For those who manage knowledge in the PSF, knowledge is information that it can organize and apply to earn revenues from clients. Thus, knowledge is not limited to technical or product based expertise (professional know-how, as Sveiby and Lloyd (1987) call it) but may also be knowledge of clients or industries and how they operate (*knowing-whom*, as it is referred to in Chapters 2, 5, and 8). In turn, knowledge takes particular forms as it accumulates over time depending on the historical development of the firm (Dodgson 1993). How problems are defined, and how new solutions evolve and are either discarded or promoted, reflect values and experiences about the right or appropriate ways to act. In effect, then, the knowledge base represents the core technology of the organization (Thompson 1967) and is an input and an output of the PSF. It is an input in terms of the expertise residing in the firm and an output in the form of products or services generated to solve client problems (Conner 1991; Grant 1996).

Knowledge created inside the firm is more likely to be 'situated and local', as MacKenzie and Spinardi (1995) put it. That is to say, knowledge that seems to offer generalized cause-and-effect linkages typical of much scientific reasoning is actually highly context specific, making its relevance to other circumstances and transfer to other organizations more problematic. Knowledge is also informal and 'tacit' (Polanyi 1966; Nonaka 1994). That is to say, knowledge is generated from everyday practice and resides in the minds of operators without necessarily being made explicit or documented. This knowledge has been described as 'know-how', being procedural and problem solving in many cases rather than content based. Indeed, what is defined as knowledge in an organizational setting is not simply based on 'objective facts' but is socially constructed. It is particularly affected by beliefs about that which is *useful* or will *add value* (Alvesson 1993).

Applied knowledge is frequently developed experientially in response to current client problems. This happens in an *ad hoc* fashion, away from the center of the firm, where employees are exposed to demands that cannot be resolved by the existing menu of solutions or where experience provides the key to new, more effective ones. The need to interact with clients in the process of delivering the product further reinforces the locus of new knowledge in the PSF in the operating core. Firms may seek to standardize their products, making the technologies more routine (Perrow 1967), in order to achieve leverage, but extensive process standardization is very difficult (Mills and Moberg 1982). Applying even relatively standardized services such as auditing requires some appreciation of the client's idiosyncracies and interaction with the client's staff. Indeed, some professionals may well spend more of their working life inside the client organization than their own (Grey 1994). In more highly customized services, such as merger and acquisition work in corporate law firms, the client even collaborates in defining what the final product will be as well as the process by which this is achieved.

It is in the firm's interest to appropriate new, firm-specific knowledge and extend its application. Not only does this create new revenue streams, but, if the knowledge base is not updated, the firm runs the risk of offering yesterday's solutions to new problems. Appropriation, through the codification of informal knowledge by documentation and transfer to other parts of the firm, requires knowledge transfer to some form of knowledge bank. Recognizing the importance of this, some of the large consulting firms have created specialist knowledge management positions to coordinate the process of knowledge transfer and storage. Contrary to the assumptions of the leverage principle, based on a top-down model of knowledge deployment, this means knowledge flows from the client-facing periphery inwards and across the firm (Quinn 1992).

Drawing on Spender (1996), Fig. 7.1 sets out a model that incorporates the main types of knowledge used within the PSF. Along the vertical axis, it distinguishes between knowledge held by one person and that held by a group or collectively. Individuals working alone can create knowledge, but knowledge creation often occurs by collaboration between colleagues. For instance, in a large audit and financial advisory firm there may be one person with great expertise in the area of corporate tax or pensions, or an individual who has expertise about one particular client area, including an unrivalled range of personal contacts. Collectively, there may be a body of knowledge about change management or business process redesign if these are general products offered by the firm. Thus, following the resource-based models of the firm, organizational knowledge or learning can be found in the relationships and routines shared by groups of co-workers.

Along the other dimension, the nature of the knowledge is divided between codified and tacit. Taxation knowledge exemplifies codified knowledge, as it is based in well-documented and organized systems of information with a set of generalizable principles underlying actual tax provisions. Knowledge of a client group and the way a group of individuals thinks and interacts is more tacit, being based on experience and without formal

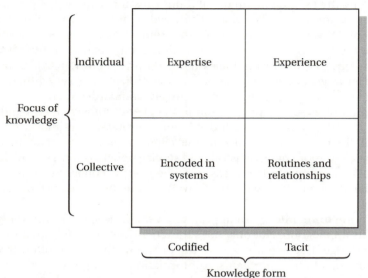

Fig. 7.1. **Types of knowledge in organizations**

models, which can help others to understand the network easily. Collective tacit knowledge is embedded in the routines of groups of people as they carry out everyday assignments or is encultured in 'the way that people (in an organization) do things around here'. By individual tacit knowledge I refer to the experience and know-how of one person.

Implications for Promotion in the PSF

PSFs conventionally use up-or-out promotion policies, excluding from permanent tenure all but those offered partnership (Gilson and Mnookin 1985). If employees fail to obtain promotion within a certain time period, they are expected to quit or are dismissed (Wholey 1985; Galanter and Palay 1991). Up-or-out has been described as being like a tournament career system, but in the PSF it usually differs from the strict tournament model (see Rosenbaum 1989) in at least two respects: losers do not stay at the existing level but leave, and the tournament does not operate over several rounds early in the candidates' careers, up-or-out only becoming critical at the point at which selection to partner or senior director occurs (Nelson 1992; Malos and Campion 1995).

The attraction of up-or-out for the owners of the firm is that it creates a strong incentive for aspiring juniors to perform, reducing supervision or monitoring costs. It also leaves the career paths inside the firm relatively clear by exiting those not elected to the top jobs, thereby helping to attract ambitious entrants who do not want to be stuck in a promotion logjam. However, up-or-out involves losing talented and knowledgeable staff in whom the firm will have invested not only formal training (and possibly signing bonuses) but also the time and effort associated with mentoring and development (Baker *et al.* 1988). Agency theorists argue that these losses have to be borne, because unsuccessful candidates cannot be retained. In the absence of the incentive of promotion to partner in the future to maintain their commitment, the firm runs the risk that they will shirk, or grab clients and leave, once they have been passed over (Gilson and Mnookin 1989).

From the employee's point of view, up-or-out presents a career risk, but it has been argued that it also has benefits. In particular, the *quid pro quo* for a tournament loss is that employees are found or can find alternative employment because of the strength of the networks between firms and clients. Some firms, such as McKinsey, make a virtue out of a necessity by seeking out alternative employment for those it exits and maintaining strong links with these 'alumni', who then frequently become the most loyal buyers of the firm's services. Further, it has been argued that up-or-out eliminates uncertainty for the aspiring employee because the implicit rule that the firm has to make a promotion decision within a limited time period means candidates are not left hanging around indefinitely (Gilson and Mnookin 1985). This argument rests on the somewhat heroic assumption that employees would prefer to move out if they cannot move up.

More generally, up-or-out appears to be increasingly incompatible with changes in the wider labor market prominently discussed in the career literature (e.g. Arthur and Rousseau 1996). Up-or-out has worked on the assumption that employees want or can have careers that are uninterrupted, linear, and mainly, if not exclusively, with one employer. Minimal inter-firm mobility is necessary to allow a reliable assessment of candidates against other members of the cohort; it also means candidates have demonstrated the sort of commitment firms think is appropriate before being appointed to senior positions for which their real money-making ability is hard to judge *ex ante* (Landers *et al.* 1996). Such a prerequisite does not fit well with those in the labor market who cannot or do not wish to have full-time employment, for example, because of family commitments, or who move around the labor market to accommodate dual-career demands (Chapter 9). Nor does it suit those who seek 'employability' and the opportunity to switch employers to advance their careers (Quinn 1992), or those whose values mean they wish to concentrate on a particular type of professional work rather than move up a firm's hierarchy (Chapter 5). To these groups, up-or-out may act as a disincentive to joining a firm or remaining with it. Thus, the more that predictions of portable careers and employer switching by professionals actually occur, the less likely that the strong internal labor market on which up-or-out is based can be maintained.

Up-or-out also has to be applied within the constraints of demand for the firm's services. Market demand has to be sufficient to justify promotion without reducing the leverage ratio of the firm, otherwise this would *ceteris paribus* dilute firm profits (Malos and Campion 1995). This implies up-or-out works best where firms face solid long-term growth in demand for their existing services, so that they can maintain a target leverage ratio and offer promotion prospects to ambitious young staff. And, because promotion decisions tend to have long-term consequences for the direction and performance of the firm (Chapter 8), judgments about the effects on leverage and profits have to be taken with some care. In contrast, the more that firms face periods of flat or declining demand for their existing services or the sort of marked variations in client demand many have experienced since the mid-1980s and therefore choose to import new knowledge from outside the firm, the less likely up-or-out will continue to be used.

How PSFs react in terms of promotion system will also depend on how knowledge is conceived. Where the profession is formally organized, such as law, knowledge is more likely to be seen as collective and codified (Freidson 1986; Abbott 1988). By contrast, where there is no identifiable occupational knowledge base and practice is not based on a common set of underlying abstract principles, such as in consulting, knowledge is likely to be specific to the firm (and held by either an individual or a group) and more tacit, being based on experience.

Consider, then, the implications for careers in relation to the model illustrated in Fig. 7.2. Where knowledge is codified and collectively shared, functional career paths are likely to exist, as specialization occurs in

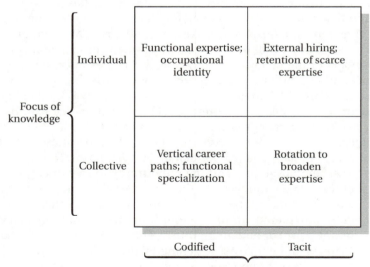

Fig. 7.2. Careers and types of knowledge

response to market demand. Up-or-out will work where knowledge is not regarded as firm specific and career progress will be based on the development of know-how (applying the formal knowledge base to client problems) and know-whom (networks inside the firm and in the client market).

Where knowledge is collective but largely tacit, career paths will be more likely to reflect the value of accumulating firm-specific knowledge through team and job rotation. The dynamic is lateral development rather than vertical movement and the incentive will be fresh challenges broadening knowledge, consistent with the boundaryless-career model (DeFillippi and Arthur 1994). More emphasis will be placed on team-based and collaborative skills. The lateral dynamic of this sort of career makes the up-or-out model less appropriate.

Where knowledge is individual and tacit, the logic of knowledge management is to place employees alongside others to learn by doing. New knowledge can be generated by lateral hiring (for example, at partner level), and to this extent up-or-out policies come under strain. Further, where knowledge is difficult to articulate and transfer, that is highly tacit, the retention of valued staff in permanent positions, even if they are not promotable, is likely to occur. Finally, where knowledge inside a firm is held by an individual but codified, it is likely that the codification is based on an occupational training and that the holder of the knowledge is a member of a formal profession, such as an actuary. Career paths are likely to be occupationally organized so that the individual can move between firms to practice his or her profession. The codified nature of the knowledge is amenable to up-or-out, but the relative rarity of the expertise and its importance to the firm's activities will also influence policy. Where expertise is scarce or valuable to the organization, firms will seek to retain individuals, even if they are not promotable. Such individuals are likely to concentrate on professional practice even in very senior positions rather than on fee generation like other senior staff. Know-how is the critical resource.

Thus, the more that firms value their knowledge base and see it as a source of comparative advantage, the greater the costs in knowledge loss of exiting unsuccessful candidates through up-or-out. Adaptations in career systems to avoid this knowledge loss are likely to occur in those firms that see their knowledge as a competitive resource or where knowledge loss represents a competitive threat. Where firms change and introduce permanent career positions, agency theories would lead to the prediction that monitoring costs will rise and they will adjust their compensation policies (Eisenhardt 1989). Hence, higher-powered incentives linked to firm performance can be expected for those in permanent career positions below partner in order to minimize the shirking risk. In addition, where the probability of achieving partnership is reduced by the retention of staff in career positions below partner, the firm is likely to have to compensate by paying a premium on its current salaries to attract and retain good-quality staff.

A second implication is that, where firms are concerned about the costs of knowledge loss, but wish to retain up-or-out, policies to capture knowledge will be important. These firms are more likely than others to introduce codification mechanisms such as databases and manuals or seek to transfer knowledge by training staff alongside experienced employees and through job and team rotation.

However, there are constraints on codification as a general strategy. One is that it requires the willingness of an employee to transfer to the firm a revenue stream he or she has developed. Why should an individual do this without the proper incentive in firms where an important basis of power is expertise (Larson 1977) and when knowledge forms the basis of his or her employability?

A second constraint may be the nature of the knowledge itself. Codification is worthwhile to a firm only if knowledge can be captured and then used by others in ways that add value. Yet there may be circumstances when the form of knowledge is codified but, because the context is not properly documented, replication of the knowledge is inappropriate. This is particularly a problem when knowledge is changing fast, as in computer software. Codified knowledge still requires human judgment to be reapplied elsewhere. There may also be important limits to codification because some knowledge may be so utterly reflexive and automatic that is it used without being recognized.

Where firms recognize that valuable knowledge is generated in the operating core of the organization, a further impact is likely to be on the roles associated with different career stages. Because the existing organization of the PSF is based on the leveraging of experience, employees are progressively drawn away from this operating core as their experience rises, to concentrate on business generation (Nelson 1988). Policies to maximize knowledge transfer and avoid what might be called knowledge starvation by emphasizing continuing professional practice are likely to be used. The more that firms value firm-specific knowledge, the more likely they are to adopt the sort of fluid division of labor on projects that ensures senior as well as junior staff are exposed to current client problems and share their work experiences.

More broadly, I would argue that there is a relationship between the knowledge base and the internal structure of the firm that mediates the above analysis. Consider, for example, the three different types of PSF identified by Maister (1993): the routine firm, with high leverage, and the 'brains' and 'greyhair' models, which have less scope for high leverage. Routine firms require standardized forms of knowledge that have been codified and widely distributed. Those *without* the potential for high leverage have to concentrate on higher billing rates, which require relatively high proportions of experienced staff in the middle ranks of the organization. The career systems in these different types of firms will vary because of basic differences in structure. For example, the systematic codification and transfer of knowledge has enabled Andersen Consulting to develop a highly leveraged organization structure. This means it can provide a series of structured career steps and be relatively ruthless in promotion policies at partner level (approximately 90 per cent of professional staff are said to leave before reaching partner), because the ability to replace leavers with new trainees and achieve high productivity from them quickly is achieved through routin-ization. Careers involve a series of steps up a steep ladder during which expertise is measured against the firm's competencies, to the point where the critical promotion decision is made.

Where firms compete more on expertise or experience, they are less likely to have been able to codify so completely the knowledge of their staff or routinize their activities. These firms need to retain experienced staff in the firm, even if they are not promotable. The promotion system is, therefore, likely to incorporate permanent positions below partner. Where they find market demand cannot be matched to the existing staff skill set, they are also more likely than routine firms to recruit from the external labor market right up to the most senior levels. Routine firms, in contrast, will cover holes in their knowledge by developing solutions inside the firm, which will fit with the existing knowledge base.

Conclusions

Analyses of the PSF suggest that they are formed to exploit the expertise of seniors by lending it to less-experienced juniors. These firms then grow by bringing together different types of expertise, not least to spread risk. The conventional promotion system, up-or-out, has been explained as a means by which the best people can be attracted and selected for the top jobs, a particularly important issue in organizations that depend so heavily on the quality of their human assets. This chapter has argued that, while knowledge *loss* has been recognized as a cost of such a system, existing theories have none the less underestimated the value of this knowledge, because they have assumed it is codified and public. It also means that they have failed to establish when up-or-out may be appropriate for a professional firm and when it may not.

Much knowledge in these firms is, in reality, tacit and contextual. It is often formed by interaction with clients and it may be collectively or individually held. Where firms perceive of their knowledge base as distinctive and a source of competitive advantage, a promotion system like up-or-out is less likely to prove appropriate; where it is assumed to be codified and publicly available along the lines of the professional model, firms are more likely to retain up-or-out.

While this sort of proposition can form the basis for empirical inquiry within and between sectors or professions, there may well be important intervening variables that affect how firms behave. In particular, up-or-out has resonance as a professional norm, reflecting a strong meritocratic ideology. It may be retained not because it is efficient but because it is seen as the appropriate way to organize decisions about promotion based on the predominant values in the profession, or what Weber (1978) called value rationality (see also DiMaggio 1991). Further research could also usefully pay more attention to the interaction between firm policies and the preferences or constraints facing aspiring professionals. Quite how employee demands are affecting policy making is not well understood, but clearly firms do not have a free hand to devise what they want. As other contributions to this volume show, in a period when more portable careers are required and partnership offers higher risks with uncertain rewards, for many employees up-or-out may no longer be the powerful incentive it was assumed to be.

References

Abbott, A. (1988), *The System of Professions* (Chicago: University of Chicago Press).
—— (1991), 'The Future of the Professions: Occupations and Expertise in the Age of Organization', in P. Tolbert and S. Barley (eds.), *Research in the Sociology of Organizations: Organizations and Professions* (Greenwich, Conn.: JAI Press).
Alvesson, M. (1993), 'Organizations as Rhetoric: Knowledge Intensive Firms and the Struggle with Ambiguity', *Journal of Management Studies*, 30/6: 997–1015.
Arthur, M. B., and Rousseau D. M. (1996) (eds.), *The Boundaryless Career: A New Employment Principle for a New Organizational Era* (New York: Oxford University Press).
Baker, G., Jensen, M., and Murphy, K. (1988), 'Compensation and Incentives: Practice vs. Theory', *Journal of Finance*, 63/3: 593–616.
Barney, J. B. (1991), 'Firm Resources and Sustained Competitive Advantage', *Journal of Management*, 17/1: 99–120.
Boisot, M. (1998), *Knowledge Assets* (Oxford: Oxford University Press).
Bowen, D. E., and Schneider, B. (1988), 'Services Marketing and Management: Implications for Organizational Behavior', in B. M. Staw and L. L. Cummings (eds.), *Research in Organizational Behavior*, vol. 10 (Greenwich, Conn.: JAI Press).
Coff, R.W. (1995), 'Adapting to Control Dilemma when Acquiring Human-Asset-Intensive Firms: Implications of the Resource-Based View', paper presented at the Academy of Management Conference, Vancouver, BC.
Conner, K. R. (1991), 'An Historical Comparison of Resource-Based Theory and Five Schools of Thought within Industrial Organization Economics: Do We Have a New Theory of the Firm?', *Journal of Management*, 17: 121–54.
DeFillippi, R. J., and Arthur M. B. (1994), 'The Boundaryless Career: A Competency-Based Perspective', *Journal of Organizational Behavior*, 15: 307–24.
DiMaggio, P. (1991), 'Introduction', in W. W. Powell and P. J. DiMaggio (eds.), *The New Institutionalism in Organizational Analysis* (Chicago: University of Chicago Press).
Dodgson, M. (1993), 'Organizational Learning: A Review of Some of the Literature', *Organization Studies*, 14/3: 375–94.
Eisenhardt, K. (1989), 'Agency Theory: An Assessment and Review', *Academy of Management Review*, 14/1: 57–74.

Fama, E., and Jensen, M. (1983), 'Separation of Ownership and Control', *Journal of Law and Economics* 26: 301–25.

Ferner, A., Edwards, P., and Sisson, K. (1995), 'Coming Unstuck? In Search of the Corporate Glue in an International Professional Service Firm', *Human Resource Management* 34/3: 343–61.

Freidson, E. (1986), *Professional Powers* (Chicago: University of Chicago Press).

Galanter, M., and Palay, T. (1991), *Tournament of Lawyers: The Transformation of the Big Law Firm* (Chicago: University of Chicago Press).

Gilson, R., and Mnookin, R. (1985), 'Sharing Among the Human Capitalists: An Economic Enquiry into the Corporate Law Firm and How Partners Split Profits', *Stanford Law Review*, 37: 313–92.

—— —— (1989), 'Coming of Age in a Corporate Law Firm: The Economics of Associate Career Patterns', *Stanford Law Review*, 41: 567–95.

Grant, R. (1996), 'Towards a Knowledge-Based Theory of the Firm', *Strategic Management Journal*, 17, Special Issue: 109–23.

Greenwood, R., and Lachman, R. (1996), 'Change as an Underlying Theme in Professional Service Organizations: An Introduction', *Organization Studies*, 17/4: 563–72.

—— Hinings, C. R., and Brown, J. (1990), 'P2 Form Strategic Management: Corporate Practices in Professional Partnerships', *Academy of Management Journal*, 33/4: 725–55.

Grey, C. (1994), 'Career as a Project of the Self and Labor Process Discipline', *Sociology*, 28/2: 479–97.

Gunz, H. P., and Jalland, R. M. (1996), 'Managerial Careers and Business Strategies', *Academy of Management Review*, 21/3: 718–56.

Hinings, C. R., Brown, J., and Greenwood, R. (1991), 'Change in an Autonomous Professional Organization', *Journal of Management Studies*, 28/4: 375–93.

Lam, A. (1997), 'Embedded Firms, Embedded Knowledge: Problems of Collaboration and Knowledge Transfer in Global Co-operative Ventures', *Organization Studies*, 18/6: 973–96.

Landers, R., Rebitzer, J., and Taylor, L. (1996), 'Rat Race Redux: Adverse Selection in the Determination of Work Hours in Law Firms', *American Economic Review*, 86: 329–48.

Larson, M. S. (1977), *The Rise of Professionalism: A Sociological Analysis* (London: University of California Press).

Leibowitz, A., and Tollison, R. (1980), 'Freeriding, Shirking and Team Production in Legal Partnerships', *Economic Inquiry*, 18: 380–90.

MacKenzie, D., and Spinardi G. (1995), 'Tacit Knowledge, Weapons Design and the Uninvention of Nuclear Weapons', *American Journal of Sociology*, 101/1: 44–99.

Maister, D. (1993), *Managing the Professional Service Firm* (New York: Free Press).

Malos, S. B., and Campion, M. A. (1995), 'An Options-Based Model of Career Mobility in Professional Service Firms', *Academy of Management Review*, 20: 611–45.

Marx, K. (1959), *Capital*, i–iii (London: Lawrence & Wishart).

Mills, C. W. (1951), *White Collar: The American Middle Classes* (Oxford: Oxford University Press).

Mills, P., and Moberg, D. (1982), 'Perspectives on the Technology of Service Organizations', *Academy of Management Review*, 7: 467–82.

——Hall, J., Leidecker, J., and Margulies, N. (1983), 'Flexiform: A Model for Professional Service Organizations', *Academy of Management Review*, 8/1: 118–31.

Mintzberg, H. (1987), 'Crafting Strategy', *Harvard Business Review* (July-Aug.), 66–75.

Montagna, P. (1968), 'Professionalization and Bureaucratization in Large Professional Organizations', *American Journal of Sociology*, 74 (Sept.), 138–45.

Morris, T., and Empson, L. (1998), 'Organization and Expertise: An Exploration of Knowledge Bases and the Management of Accounting and Consulting Firms', *Accounting Organizations and Society*, 23/5: 609–24.

—— and Pinnington, A. (1998*a*), 'Promotion to Partner in Professional Firms', *Human Relations*, 51/1: 3–25.

—— —— (1998*b*), 'Patterns of Profit Sharing in Professional Firms', *British Journal of Management*, 9/1: 23–39.

Nelson, R. (1988), *Partners with Power: The Social Transformation of the Large Law Firm* (Berkeley and Los Angeles: University of California Press).

—— (1992), 'Of Tournaments and Transformations: Explaining the Growth of Large Law Firms', *Wisconsin Law Review*, 38: 733–50.

Nonaka, I. (1994), 'A Dynamic Theory of Knowledge Creation', *Organization Science*, 5/1: 14–37.

Parsons, T. (1954), *Essays in Sociological Theory* (Glencoe, Ill.: Free Press).

Perrow, C. (1967), 'A Framework for Comparative Organizational Analysis', *American Sociological Review*, 32/2: 194–208.

Polanyi, M. (1966), *The Tacit Dimension* (London: Routledge & Kegan Paul).

Quinn, J. B. (1992), *Intelligent Enterprise* (New York: Free Press).

Rosenbaum, J. (1989), 'Organization Career Systems and Employee Misperceptions', in M. B. Arthur, D. T. Hall, and B. S. Lawrence (eds.), *Handbook of Career Theory* (Cambridge: Cambridge University Press).

Schein, E. (1988), *Process Consultation* (2nd edn., London: Addison-Wesley).

Spender J.-C. (1996), 'Making Knowledge the Basis of a Dynamic Theory of the Firm', *Strategic Management Journal*, 17 (Special Issue), 45–62.

Starbuck, W. R. (1992), 'Learning by Knowledge Intensive Firms', *Journal of Management Studies*, 29/6: 713–40.

Sveiby, K. and Lloyd, T. (1987), *Managing Know-How* (London: Bloomsbury).

Thompson J. (1967), *Organizations in Action* (New York: McGraw Hill).

Tolbert, P., and Stern, R. (1991), 'Organizations of Professionals: Governance Structures in Large Law Firms', in P. Tolbert and S. Barley (eds.), *Research in the Sociology of Organizations*, vol. 8 (London: JAI Press).

Torstendahl, R. (1990), 'Introduction: Promotion and Strategies of Knowledge Based Groups', in R. Torstendahl and M. Burrage (eds.), *The Formation of Professions: Knowledge, State and Strategy* (London: Sage).

Weber, M. (1978), *Economy and Society* (Berkeley and Los Angeles: University of California Press).

Wholey, D. (1985), 'Determinants of Firm Internal Labor Markets in Large Law Firms', *Administrative Science Quarterly*, 30: 318–35.

Winch, G., and Schneider, E. (1993), 'Managing the Knowledge-Based Organization: The Case of Architectural Practice', *Journal of Management Studies*, 30/6: 923–37.

The 'Architecture' of Careers: How Career Competencies Reveal Firm Dominant Logic in Professional Services

Candace Jones and
Benyamin M. Bergmann Lichtenstein

Careers are the process by which 'information and knowledge embodied in skills, expertise, and relationship networks are acquired through an evolving sequence of work experiences' (Bird 1994: 326). In this way, the careers of key firm members, especially partners in small to mid-size professional service firms (PSFs) and other knowledge-based industries, are the means by which a firm accumulates and develops its capabilities: a set of differentiated skills, complex routines, and complementary assets (Teece *et al.* 1997). The possession of capabilities that are difficult to imitate, substitute, or replicate is seen as an important source of competitive advantage (Barney 1991; Collis 1994). Yet, few studies have examined empirically the strategies for and processes by which firms gain and develop these capabilities.

A careers perspective provides insight into strategies that partners in PSFs use to acquire and hone the distinctive capabilities in their profession, and thus in their organization. There are three ways in which the career goals of a partner in a PSF directly influence the strategies developed and used within the firm over time. First, partners' values, passions, and interests guide the selection of the projects they choose to undertake; over time these choices enact a firm-level strategy (Greenwood *et al.* 1990). Secondly, partners' professional expertise is an anchor for the strategy of their firm (Mintzberg and McHugh 1985). Thus, as partners hone or alter their expertise through the projects they pursue, they also hone or alter the knowledge, skills, and routines that are required by associates and staff to execute these projects. Thirdly, as Greenwood, Hinings, and Brown (1990: 730) suggest, 'ownership, management and operations are all fused. A partner is an owner of the firm, is involved in its overall management, and is a key production worker.' In this way professional partnerships 'craft strategy through the intimate connection between thought and action' (Mintzberg 1987: 68). Thus, the career development of a partner in a PSF provides a strategic map of that firm's strategies for developing its capabilities.

Some scholars argue that careers as work histories are 'individual-level characteristics' whereas 'strategy choice and strategic outcomes are organizational-level' (Gunz and Jalland 1996: 737). This individual/organizational distinction taps into the problems and challenges of multi-level research. While important and vexing, this apparent distinction focuses on assessing the attributes of individuals and organizations rather than the processes by which relationships between individuals and organizations unfold.

However, a careers perspective may also be claimed to provide 'access to the empirical *relation* between social action and social structure' (Barley 1989: 52; emphasis added). Careers provide a link between individual actions and social structures in two ways. First, partners in PSFs have high degrees of autonomy, often choosing and pursuing distinct areas of expertise (Maister 1993). In this sense, partners enact not only their individual careers, but also their firms' strategies and structures. Secondly, role motivation theories explicitly link individual action to organizational systems (Miner *et al.* 1994). Role motivation theory suggests that staffing is absolutely critical to a PSF, and that staffing generates a congruence between individual motivations and necessary role behaviors (Miner *et al.* 1994). Thus, the hiring decisions of a partner reflect the interdependence between micro-level behaviors and meso-level organizational activity (Arthur *et al.* 1989). Individual careers are the conduit by which organizational systems are both enacted and maintained (Jones 1996). By examining partners' careers, we can gain insight into the strategies by which partners acquire and develop their own and their firms' capabilities.

The goal of this chapter is to explore this relationship between the career choices of partners in PSFs and the development of capabilities in those firms. We analyze interviews with partners in architectural firms to examine empirically how individual career choices influence the development of firm capabilities. The chapter makes three contributions. First, we show that a careers lens provides important insights into how competencies are acquired and developed within PSFs. Secondly, we provide a simplified framework for exploring key capabilities within professional services. Thirdly, we show how career competencies provide important insights into firm dominant logic.

The chapter is organized as follows. First, we provide a brief literature review on three areas of competency development within the careers research—*knowing-why, knowing-how,* and *knowing-whom*—that relate to developing expertise and relational assets in a PSF. Secondly, we provide background on the sample and research methods employed. Thirdly, we provide the results of our interviews in two sections. We first show how partners' career competencies in terms of values and beliefs (*knowing-why*), skills (*knowing-how*) and networks (*knowing-whom*) are enacted in their firms. Then we show how specific combinations of these competencies form coherent patterns that reveal a dominant logic in these firms: 'ways in which partners conceptualize the business and make critical resource allocations' (Prahalad and Bettis 1986: 490). Finally, we offer some concluding remarks and suggestions for future directions.

Career Competencies in Professional Service Firms

Insights from organizational-capability and resource-based perspectives (Prahalad and Hamel 1990; Barney 1991; Collis 1994) have recently been applied to career theory in the context of boundaryless careers (DeFillippi and Arthur 1994, 1996, 1998; Bird 1996; Jones and DeFillippi 1996). These authors suggest that boundaryless careers initiate a shift in focus from careers within organizations to individual competencies that are developed through ongoing and changing work experiences. In project-based industries such as film and architecture, individual skills and resources are constructed through a series of projects within the industry network. These cumulative career competencies are embodied in three key career qualities. The competency of *knowing-why* relates to values, beliefs, and identities; the competency of *knowing-how* relates to skills and knowledge; and the competency of *knowing-whom* relates to the networks of relationships and social contacts in an industry (DeFillippi and Arthur 1994: 320). Next we briefly review how these three competencies of *knowing-why*, *knowing-how*, and *knowing-whom* generate a PSF's capabilities. These competencies work together to generate a firm's 'dominant logic': its overall identity and competitive strategy. Understanding a firm's dominant logic, especially as it emerges out of the motivations and values of a partner in a PSF, provides a useful method for linking partner careers and firm strategies. Making this link is the goal of the following analysis.

Knowing-why: Motives and identities in project selection

Knowing-why refers to values, meanings, and interests that shape what activities are pursued in a career (DeFillippi and Arthur 1994, 1996). Career scholars have called these passions and values career anchors (Schein 1987), career orientations (Derr 1986), and career roles (Chandler and Jansen 1992); together they comprise a self-image that 'guide[s] and constrain[s] career decisions' (Schein 1987: 155).

These scholars identify several common career motivations: entrepreneurial, autonomy, challenge, managerial, technical/functional, balance/lifestyle, service, and security. The career motivations most relevant to partners in PSFs are those most widely found and most likely to have variance in professionals—namely, technical, managerial, and service. A *technical career motivation* is based on the need for challenging work, to be recognized as a crafts person (Schein 1987: 164), and the desire to be an 'expert in the tools, techniques and procedures of a specialized field' (Chandler and Jansen 1992). A *managerial career orientation* refers to the desire and capacity to organize people and resources to accomplish goals (Schein 1987; Chandler and Jansen 1992) and to gain recognition from one's peers and rewards from critical others (Derr 1986; Schein 1987). A *service career orientation* refers to a relational or interpersonal motivation and was initially seen in doctors, consultants, and financial analysts (Schein 1987). Chandler and Jansen (1992) identify a distinct component of interpersonal relations—the ability to make connections with those who hold key resources.

Founders' motivations and values have a profound influence in shaping firm culture (Selznick 1958; Schein 1985). These firm-specific shared meanings influence professional practice and strategy by defining 'how professional standards should be applied' (Greenwood *et al.* 1994: 252). Firm culture is seen as a critical source of competitive advantage because it is based on specific events in a firm's history and its development is not well understood; hence it is not easily imitated (Barney 1991). The internal career is important, because different career orientations appear to align systematically with firm-level strategy. For example, small business-owners who are higher in managerial or technical orientations are associated with more profitable but lower-growth firms, whereas founders higher in service orientations are associated with high-growth firms (both more and less profitable) (Chandler and Jansen 1992). Consequently, partners' motivations and values should influence not only firm strategy but also the knowledge, skills, and routines necessary to implement this strategy.

Knowing-how: Knowledge, skills, and routines in distinctive expertise

Knowing-how reflects career-relevant skills and job-related knowledge needed for competent performance in one's work roles and job assignments (DeFillippi and Arthur 1994: 309; Jones and DeFillippi 1996). In professional services, *knowing-how* is captured by one's distinctive expertise in a given domain. Distinctive expertise refers to the technical knowledge, creative skills, and complex routines that firm members use to codify tacit understandings into organizational systems (Jones *et al.* 1998). For architects, it involves explicit knowledge such as building codes, schematics, and blueprints, as well as tacit knowledge gained through experience, such as the process by which a particular building comes together, the problems encountered with certain materials, and what constitutes 'good design'.

We expect that partners' current expertise shapes not only their future expertise but also their strategies for pursuing this expertise. For example, do partners generate or exploit current areas of expertise internally, or do they tap into new areas of expertise from external sources? Central to the enactment of these different strategies are staffing issues (Sonnenfeld and Peiperl 1988), specifically whether expertise is bought, made, or transferred. By their choice of projects, partners in PSFs explicitly hone or alter their present skills, knowledge, and routines. By their choice of staffing, partners in PSFs explicitly implement their make, buy, or align strategies for developing this expertise.

Knowing-whom: Developing client relationships and identifying key social contacts

Knowing-whom, derived from work on social capital (Coleman 1988; Burt 1992), refers to relationships and social contacts that involve proximity to others who provide opportunities and important resources (DeFillippi and Arthur 1994; Jones and DeFillippi 1996). In professional services, client relationships are 'the bonds and specialized knowledge that develop from the intense, reciprocal, and repeated interactions between clients and providers during the creation and delivery of a professional service' (Jones *et al.* 1998: 401). Developing these relationships creates a commitment between client and provider (Levinthal and Fichman 1988), and prior studies show that professionals are willing to invest significant time and energy in maintaining these relationships (Fichman and Goodman 1995).

In contrast to these intense personal relationships, broader social contacts are more generic, instrumental, and infrequent (Jones and DeFillippi 1996). Prior research has shown that managers with greater numbers of external ties (for example, through membership in clubs and professional organizations) make more money (Boxman *et al.* 1991; Belliveau *et al.* 1996), and secure jobs more easily (Granovetter 1974). This ability to generate and exploit social contacts may require career motivations and skills that are different from those necessary for building intensely personal client relations.

Although client relationships and social contacts are widely viewed as important, little empirical research exists on the strategies parties use to identify and develop these contacts and relationships. An important corollary is whether a partner's focus on either exploiting diverse social contacts or developing intense client relations has an influence on firm strategy and the competencies developed within the firm.

Career competencies reveal firm-dominant logic

Over time, a partner's career strategies of *knowing-why, knowing-how,* and *knowing-whom* combine in unique ways to generate specific goals and firm-level strategies to achieve them. This combination can be described in terms of a dominant logic. Dominant logic is characterized by implicit views about not only the goals and tactics that define an actor's strategic action, but also the relationship between the actor's goals and tactics. Prahalad and Bettis (1986: 491) defined dominant logic as 'a mind set or world view or conceptualization of the business and the administrative tools to accomplish goals and make decisions in that business'. These tools may be decisions about compensation, career management, organization structure, and planning (ibid.: 490). This conceptualization, while focusing on top managers and how they handle firm diversification, can be applied to all actors who pursue a set of goals and make decisions about how to accomplish their goals. Dominant logic is similar to Bacharach, Bamberger, and Sonnenstuhl's (1996: 479) concept of logics of action: 'the implicit relationship between means and ends underlying the specific actions, policies, and activities of organizational members.' Gunz and Jalland (1996) refer to these as managerial rationalities and Gunz (1989) has applied these ideas to career systems showing how organizational careers have distinct logics related to business strategy.

The content of dominant logics is an under-explored area. Much of the career research has focused on identifying the structure of dominant logic as reflected in distinct career patterns within large firms, and the structure of industry-level career systems (Sonnenfeld and Peiperl 1988; Gunz and Jalland 1996). However, we have little understanding of the content of these career systems and how this content influences the competencies and strategies developed within the firm (Bird 1994). Organizational theory—primarily network and transaction-cost theories—provides insight about different types of dominant logics.

Two dominant logics have been identified in research in inter-organizational relations using network or transaction-cost theories. One, derived from network theory, is a 'relational' logic that is founded in recurring relations. This is described as a 'logic of embeddedness' by Uzzi (1996), who characterizes it in terms of trust, fine-grain information transfer, and joint problem solving. Rousseau (1995), using transaction-cost theory as a base, describes the qualities of a 'relational' psychological contract in terms of socio-emotional content, open-ended commitments, and a long-term perspective. In contrast to a relational logic is a market-based, 'transactional' logic that is characterized by frequent switching among partners, specific and bounded commitments to one another, and short-term interactions that allow for easy exit from relations. Parties who share a transactional logic also share low levels of partner-specific learning and high levels of explicit knowledge (Hirschman 1970; Williamson 1985; Rousseau 1995; Uzzi 1996).

The source of these two distinct dominant logics is open to question. In one view, prior experience and organizational power struggles explain how a dominant logic is created and enacted (Prahalad and Bettis 1986; Gunz and Jalland 1996). However, prior firm experience does not explain why individuals chose these particular experiences in the first place. In a PSF, partners' choice of project motivations and strategies for enactment can be traced to the creation of their dominant logic. These choices constitute their professional career identity and motivation (*knowing-why*). The tactics used to achieve their goals are expressed in the competencies they develop in their firm (*knowing-how*) and in their particular network composition (*knowing-whom*). Through the examination of partners' career motivations, their decisions about competencies, and their industry networks, the dominant logic of their firms can be empirically uncovered. We explored empirically PSF partners' dominant logics, and how these are uncovered, by examining their career motives and decisions about their capabilities and networks.

Research Methods

Architectural firms in a western state of the USA that participated in public-sector work during 1993–5 were the sampling population from which our interviews are drawn. There were 51 firms participating in public work during these years. We interviewed 23 members of 20 firms (19 architectural firms and 1 architectural/engineering firm). Of these 23 interviewees 12 were founding partners of their firms, 5 partners, 2 associates (mid-level architects), 1 business manager, and 3 marketing directors. The data for the preliminary analysis presented in this chapter were derived from six founding partners and one partner for firms that ranged in size: two small, two medium, and two large PSFs. Demographic data for these seven firms are provided in Table 8.1.

The sampling of firms was random, stratified according to the frequency that they submitted Statements of Qualification for State work. Three categories emerged for work submitted for between 1993 and 1995: six or more projects, two to five projects, and one project. We sampled more heavily from firms that submitted six or more times for State projects. These firms were larger and more successful within this regional commercial building industry.

A semi-structured interview protocol was employed. Interviews lasted from 45 minutes to $3\frac{1}{2}$ hours and averaged $1\frac{1}{2}$ hours. Table 8.2 identifies the questions used in this analysis. These questions were used to elicit insight about parties' motivation for project selection (*knowing-why*), the skills and competencies required and how they were acquired for these projects (*knowing-how*), and the relationships and social contacts important for gaining work (*knowing-whom*), as well as how these competencies and contacts

Table 8.1. *Partner and firm characteristics*

Firm name	Partners	Firm size	Partner ratio
OMB	4	32	1:8
HMO	7	29	1:4.1
XYZ	3	25	1:8.3
G&Q	2	12	1:6
NCB	3	12	1:4
GPA	2	8	1:4
DEF	2	6	1:3

Table 8.2. *Interview questions*

Career competencies and strategies	Interview questions
Knowing-why: identities, motives, and meanings	What attributes of a project motivate you to propose for it? What do you hope to gain from a project?
Knowing-how: knowledge, skills, and routines	What skills and competencies does your present mix of projects require? What do you see as your competitive strengths?
Strategies for developing know-how	How do you acquire new skills and competencies?
Knowing-whom: social contacts and relationships	Who is critical for you to know to gain projects in commercial architecture?
Strategies for developing know-whom	How did you get to know your key contacts?
Closing comments	What words of advice would you give to a newcomer to commercial architecture?

were developed. Several other questions about partner selection were asked during the interview. These questions are not relevant or used in the analysis of issues in this chapter. All interviews were transcribed, coded, and content analyzed using FolioBuilder®, a content analysis computer program.

Findings: Career Competencies and Dominant Logics

As described above, the strategies in PSFs are likely to be generated out of the career competencies of their partners. First, the career competencies of *knowing-why* would result in a strategy of projects selected for their technical orientation, their managerial motivation, or their service focus. Secondly, the career competencies of *knowing-how* would result in a strategy to develop a distinctive expertise in a PSF, whether internally by developing neophytes, externally by hiring from the outside, or by partnering with other firms. Thirdly, the career competencies of *knowing-whom* would result in a particular strategy of relationship building, either building intense, specific client relationships over time, or wooing a diverse set of social contacts within the industry.

Our data suggest that these three competencies, and the strategies they generate, were expressed in the architectural firms we studied. In addition, partners' choices and decisions about developing competencies in their careers and their firms were expressed in coherent patterns. These patterns are the dominant logics in these firms, reflecting partners' assumptions and tactics for what goals to pursue and how they should be accomplished. These are described more fully below.

Career competencies and firm strategy

Knowing-why: *the basis for project selection.* Our interviewees were asked what attributes of a project motivated them to pursue it and what they hoped to gain from the project. Earlier, we identified three career motivations potentially important in professional services: (1) *technical* is defined by the desire for challenging projects and developing expertise, (2) *managerial* thrives on organizing people and resources, and (3) *service* involves identifying and developing relationships with key decision-makers and helping clients. In our interviews these three orientations were all found.

Technical orientation corresponds to Schein's (1987) notion of challenge and Derr's (1986) 'getting high' career orientation. A technical project motivation was seen in partners' descriptions of how the aesthetic or technical challenges motivated them to pursue a project. 'We are doing a visitors center that's very unique architecturally. It's a once-in-a-lifetime building, truly an architectural piece,' explained one partner from firm HMO. Another partner in firm G&Q also described this in terms of projects he hates: 'I did a jail. . . . I have the skills for it . . . but jails are not a real fun project, they're terrible. It's the worst job I've ever done. . . . They're so dreary . . . so depressing . . . the materials are just real basic, [the environment] is real sterile. . . . not a fun job.'

In contrast, a managerial motive was seen primarily in those who were challenged by the business rather than by the technical or design issues, and thus geared their firms and projects around business issues and project management skills. The founding partner in OMB described this difference: 'We're more business than design oriented. It's hard to be both. It's a whole different mentality. We're working on a project with another architecture firm. Our motivation is budget and schedule and theirs is let's make it neat. They don't coincide very well.' Another partner at DEF described his firm's 'main strength [a]s our ability to take a job and really carefully see it through'.

A service orientation was seen in architects who liked to help people, empathize with clients, and interact socially with industry contacts. A partner from GPA who 'likes people' describes the firm's focus on developing their social contacts by 'getting to know the people in the industry' and by 'concentrating on service to the clients. We have done quite a bit of repeat work. We want the client to continue to use us when they build other schools.' At NCB a partner explains how his motivation is to 'help people out' by doing projects when needed and by empathizing with and understanding the client's needs.

Our data show that project motivations in PSFs operate in two dimensions. At the individual level they can be seen as career anchors for the partners in these firms (Schein 1987). These motivations provide the 'reason why' certain projects are chosen over others, being based on a certain set of identities and goals that the individual has developed over a period of time. At the organizational level, these motivations shape the strategic choices of the firm, as they become realized in practice through specific tactics that develop distinct firm capabilities. These tactics for developing knowledge and skills are described next.

Knowing-how: *developing distinctive expertise.* An essential source of competitive advantage for a PSF is developing distinctive expertise (Jones *et al.* 1998). The strategies for building distinctive expertise ranged from internal development, to hiring experienced professionals, to partnering with more experienced firms. Perhaps the most important determinant of strategies for developing distinctive expertise was the current level of experience a firm had. PSFs that started with some experience were more likely to build on it internally, whereas those with limited or no experience needed to gain this experience externally, either through alliances or hiring expertise.

These strategies can be understood as learning through absorptive capacity (Cohen and Levinthal 1990) or transformative capacity (Garud and Nayyar 1994). Absorptive capacity is the ability of the organization to recognize, pull in, and make use of resources that are external to it. For example, a firm with high absorptive capacity would be likely to hire in new talent, or partner with others to bring in needed resources. In contrast, transformative capacity is the ability of an organization to identify already existing resources within it and transform them to another level of effectiveness. Firms with high transformative capacity would be likely to mentor and train internally, or build up expertise through working on more challenging and larger projects. We identified how firms generated capabilities by examining their degree of external to internal sourcing of expertise.

One strategy was to build firm expertise and reputation internally through projects of increasing size. As one partner at DEF said, 'The State agency is a tough place to break into. We did it by going after little projects—little by little we got larger and larger projects.' Securing these projects is critical, because they provide the opportunity for training staff and extending not only the partners' but the staff's skills as well. As one partner at HMO said, 'quality people aren't necessarily "at-the-top-of-the-rung" [*sic*] people—principals—it's people that know how to produce a drawing and have the experience. [You need] to have the people on board that have the expertise—not necessarily on the cutting edge but have the ability to push that envelope. You continue to have to push them to expand their focus. I think that's critical to be able to keep them on board but push them forward.'

A different strategy for developing expertise is to hire experts into the firm from the outside to further the development of current expertise. As the partner from OMB said, 'We need to bring in others that are high in design. We recruit from around the West to build our specialty.' These specialists become an important element of the firm's strategy. A third strategy, the most external form of sourcing, was partnering with more experienced firms. This partnering process generated knowledge transfer between firms. A partner from G&Q explains: 'I think anybody starting into the business cannot be successful in the business unless they do teaming. I mean that's the only way to break in. . . . We would never have got that [project] on our own but we got that by finding someone that had enough background in it that brought us to the top of the pile, so to speak, and we got the job.' According to this architect, partnering helps develop a range of project strengths and skills. 'Teaming brings new skills and a new understanding of how to do projects.'

Knowing-whom: *strategies for developing relational assets.* The choices partners make about how to develop firm expertise are influenced by whom they know and how they choose to develop relationships in the industry over time. Thus an important asset that PSFs must develop is relational (Jones *et al.* 1998). We found two primary strategies for expanding a firm's relational assets: specific client relationships, which involve intense and reciprocal bonds, versus social contacts with key institutional decision-makers, which are more generic, politically skilled, and less intense inter-personal relationships.

A number of firms focused on the client as being the end-user, and developed specific skills to help understand, empathize with, and sometimes educate the end-user. For example, emphasizing the close client relation-ships at XYZ, the partner there said, 'they feel that you are on their side on the job and that if there is a question or a situation that you're available and anxious to talk about [it]. . . . If the client calls you up with a question or a situation that could become a problem. . . . you get back to them soon and quickly with an explanation . . . that solves the problem.' This strategy of close client relations also comes across in the interview with HMO: 'You talk to the end-user and make sure that they understand who you are and get a face-to-face relationship going—talk about their needs, follow up with them in terms of what is going on. . . . 75 to 85% of what you do is take care of the client and make sure that their needs are met.'

In contrast to the client-intensive approach is a strategy that focuses on developing contacts with key institutional decision-makers for projects, such as State agency personnel, financial institutions, real-estate developers, and contractors. This strategy is exemplified by the principal at MCB: 'It's important to know all the coordinators (at the State office), as many as you can. It's important to know the Director; it is probably more important to know the Assistant Directors because they make more of the decisions than the Director does. We let them know that we are a resource they can tap into. That's something that has worked.' Another partner at PGA concurred with the importance of making political connections: 'Public relations is very, very important . . . You have to get to know the people in the industry, the State for example. You really need to know the Director and maybe his assistant director and their staff. You need to get to know institutions, their people and the people who finance a building, and building people [e.g. contractors].'

Knowing-whom is a critical competency, because client relations and social contacts provide the lifeline to repeat projects with clients and to new projects within the community and for institutions. Yet it may be difficult to have both sets of skills. Client relations involve empathy, intense communication, and problem-solving skills to identify and understand client needs. On the other hand, maintaining diverse social contacts and political connections requires tactical skills of identifying key decision-makers and image management skills for wooing these key decision-makers.

These three career competencies—*knowing-why, knowing-how,* and *knowing-whom*—revealed coherent patterns within each firm and distinct-ive strategies between firms. We describe this more fully next.

The interaction of career competencies: evidence of firm level dominant logics

These coherent patterns of career competencies uncovered three rather than the two dominant logics recognized by organizational scholars. These are a competence logic, a relational logic, and a calculative logic (see Table 8.3). The differences in these dominant logics are ones of emphasis rather than mutual exclusivity. For example, a partner may acknowledge the need for both client relations and social contacts but emphasize developing client relations more than social contacts in conjunction with selecting projects providing technical or aesthetic challenges. We describe these three domi-nant logics in some detail below.

Table 8.3. *Dominant logics: The interaction of career competencies*

Dominant Logic	Knowing-why		Knowing-how			Knowing-whom	
	Orientation	Focus	Expertise	Learning	Staffing	Client relations	Social contacts
Competence	*Technical*	*Professional*	Be state-of-the-art	*Transformative:* Develop internally through smaller projects, OR	Hire novices and train them	Solve client's problems	Identify key clients and institutional decision-makers
	Push the technical or aesthetic envelope Develop unique solutions Solve complex problems		Do good design	*Absorptive:* Partner with experts to move into new areas and develop skills		Exceed client expectations	Focus on end-user as client
						Educate client	Invest in long-term relationship primarily through performance
Relational	*Service*	*Client and network*	Identify and understand client needs	*Transformative:* Train staff in client relations and expand with clients into new areas	Hire novices and mentor	Listen to client	Identify key institutional decision-makers
	Help clients					Empathize with client	
	Like people		Develop intense relations			Engender reciprocity through smaller, less profitable jobs to aid client	Fraternize
							Provide insights and help
Calculative	*Managerial*	*Market*	Project management and delivery	*Absorptive:* Hire experts to advance skills	Buy expertise	Learn contractors' systems	Promote image through location and managing perceptions
	Meet business challenges		Bargaining skills	*Absorptive:* Partner with experts to move into new areas and develop skills		Switch around among clients (contractors)	

Competence dominant logic. Competence as a dominant logic was shaped by several congruent themes. When partners' career motivation derived from meeting technical or aesthetic challenges, their firm competence was shaped by developing expertise internally (transformative capacity) *or* gaining expertise through external alliances with specialized firms (absorptive capacity). Additionally, in firms displaying competence logic, a distinctive expertise in client relations was developed by solving client problems or exceeding their expectations. We describe two firms in depth to show the congruence among these career competencies and how they form a dominant logic distinct from other firms in the sample.

Our partner at XYZ described his project motivation (*knowing-why*) as meeting technical and interpersonal challenges. 'When people I've worked with in the past call me up and say: "I've got a tough client, a rigorous program, and we'd like you to help us on it," I'm flattered. I like to do it.' He pursues projects in which he has a great deal of experience and his 'personal résumé [CV] is strong.' 'Clients', he explains, 'expect of us some critical mass of experience that can be brought to bear on any project and to identify and resolve its difficulties.'

Knowing-how in this firm was developed by gaining experience in desired areas, which could be used later on in unknown ways to move into new markets or hone skills. Essentially, this is transformative capacity (Garud and Nayyar 1994). This tactic was seen in XYZ's venture into institutional housing.

We were recommended at *X* University because of our science building expertise. . . . Later they invited us to propose on a housing project. So we put together the experience we had in housing . . . And because we work well with the housing people on campus—that got us into doing new housing down there. . . . We hope that it's a spring board to put us in competition for the [major] housing project at *Z* university. Now with our experience in housing coming together we think that's going to be important.

These projects were staffed by hiring younger architects with a 'general architecture background', many of whom were top students from the regional architectural school. In these new hires, they look for 'somebody who will fit in and work hard'.

Knowing-whom at XYZ involves a concerted focus on providing 'personal service' to clients. This emphasis on developing in-depth client relations rather than on generic social contacts is seen in their marketing tactics. 'When we market a project we don't send our special marketers out, we send the people they will be working with and we always suggest that they call our previous clients and talk to them about how we've provided service.' He goes on to describe how client relations involve 'the capacity to get in the trench and solve their problems' and suggests that 'you network with those people best by performing on the projects that you've had previously versus any social interaction'.

G&Q is another firm whose partner had a technical motivation that also focused on developing competence and expertise. His goal is to 'try to leave something with that project that is unique'. His firm's 'track record' shows their 'unique uses of materials or unique approaches to problems that a client might have'. Through technical competence, the partners endeavor to create 'something above the benchmark, something that is really somewhat unique, something that he [the client] would have never thought of, something that we have brought to his attention that is beyond his expectations'.

Like the partner at XYZ, this partner described his concern for building on existing skills, but he also augments those skills through the strategic use of specialists. 'Usually we feel we . . . have to have a strong background ourselves, [but] if it had some peculiar or unique aspect . . . we might bring in a specialist and we work with specialists . . . in achieving where we are at now.' In this context, the partner at G&Q emphasized the value of teaming with more experienced firms: 'We really focus on team.' He explained, 'The first jail, the first parking structure we did, we did it with an architect from in state, but the second one we got on our own. But we would never have got that second one if we hadn't done the first one.' He continues, 'We have never had an unsuccessful experience [with partnering]. We learn something from every one of them; you can kind of pick up your own skills.' Thus, he employs external sources as the means for honing and altering firm expertise, essentially learning through absorptive capacity.

This extensive use of partnering at G&Q seems to be driven by an implicit belief that their choices are partnering and developing talent internally. For example, the partner described how 'You either have to have an excellent consultant, specialist, to at least break into the industry, or you have to have staff people that have a tremendous background. Well, at this point we don't have staff people, so we have to work with a specialist.' The option of hiring expertise to augment the firm's skills did not seem to occur to him. He suggested that they 'have lots of students on our staff. We think they are a little more adaptable, more interested in seeking out information; they are always a little more curious.'

G&Q, like XYZ, puts emphasis on the relationships it has with clients, especially on how it educates the client: 'Lots of clients, especially on the private side, are not really aware of what they are getting into. They are novices and so you have to kind of bring them along, help them understand what they are doing and why you are doing this.' Equally, XYZ takes a long-term developmental orientation to relationships with key decision-makers: 'You want to know who the people are who make those decisions because it takes a long time to grow a reasonable relationship; you can't do that quickly.'

Both of these interviews show a coherent relationship between career–firm strategies and goals, and how these are anchored in a concern for competence. The two partners described their desire for technical challenges, the use of firm or partner experience to gain access to new projects and extend competence, the ability to educate the client and develop in-depth relations, and the use of their competence to solve client problems. Their successful performance allows the firm further to enhance its experience through expanded project opportunities with clients.

Relational dominant logic. Two firms appeared to have a relational dominant logic. A service motive was seen in the partners in these firms who liked interacting with others, either specifically with a client or with diverse decision-makers. The partner at NCB described how he 'like[s] [University] clients—intelligent and quasi-rational . . . people who appreciate that you did a nice building for them'. Although providing good design expertise was mentioned by him, 'helping people out' was a key motivator. These firms seemed less focused on systematically developing their design or technical expertise and more focused on developing relational skills. He said, 'I think the biggest skill you could have is to listen to the client. Listen to what they have to say and seriously consider their views. These are smart people . . . intelligent, well-educated people and they are worthwhile. . . . You don't always do what they want you to do but I think they respond to being listened to.' The focus was on empathy with the client to understand the client's needs and concerns. This relational skill is what wins future projects. 'We started doing some [public work] and people were pleased and came back to us.'

A relational dominant logic extends beyond specific client interactions to include networks of decision-makers in the industry. 'You work through the networks of people you know,' he explained. 'We have just heard about [a new project] from a former employee who now works . . . as an architect for a large private company.' In addition, he described the process by which relations with building managers, primarily those at the State agency, were cultivated.

You go up there [State agency], you hang around; you go to every meeting they have. Every time they have a seminar, you go. You introduce yourself to them. You don't get pushy but you just get to meet them. We try to get to know them by helping them out and let them know that we are a resource they can tap into. They call us and ask us what we've thought about certain ideas. You make yourself available, put yourself in front of them, and let them know you've got something.

Once these '*knowing-whom*' relationships are cultivated, they become linked to and must be supported by the '*knowing-how*' in the firm, because technical or aesthetic incompetence can result in lost jobs. The partner affirmed this as he continued, 'When they ask, you've got to deliver. You can't be all PR. We did a nice job. We won a design award; everybody paid attention.'

A relational logic can be seen in the desire to establish conditions for reciprocity. The NCB partner explained how with another set of institutional clients he took on a small but not profitable job 'to help people out, to try and keep this network of friendly people going. We just finished a job at the University, a tiny little job and actually we never would have agreed to do it but we like the people, we worked with them before on bigger jobs. They needed some help and we helped them. You hope that the next time a big job comes they will think of you.'

The strategic focus on learning is on developing skills to discern, enter into, and maintain relationships. This relational learning is a transformative capacity in that the firm does not know in what ways the investment in learning about and with the client will pay off in future projects. Yet, these relationships provide the basis for taking the firm in unanticipated future directions. In this case, the client relations led to cultivating an experience base in public-sector work (primarily university buildings) that had not been consciously planned. The staffing and development of their relational expertise was internally driven and based on mentoring of younger architects by more senior architects. The partner described their process: 'our architects are part of the [client] process. Generally we always have at least two of us in the client meetings—one to avoid having to repeat information but also so that that younger architect learns the process that we want them to learn.' He explains the importance of mentoring for gaining the tacit knowledge involved in being a good architect: 'I don't know if you can teach someone how to do it. I think you can show them how to do it. I think architecture, when it does work . . . works because it's one of the few businesses that still have an apprentice system. I don't know anybody who's a good architect who didn't learn from another good architect.'

A relational dominant logic is quite distinct from a competence dominant logic. Even though both require competent professional and interpersonal skills, they differ in the emphasis on reciprocity and liking people rather than on technical challenges and educating the client. In addition, the implied logics of what provides opportunities are quite different. In a relational logic, the goal is to establish relations through helping behaviors with key decision-makers. These decision-makers provide opportunities for competent performance, gaining the firm more opportunities. In contrast, a competence logic sees expertise as the basis for opportunities: clients come to you because you can do technically competent work with rigorous requirements. Both dominant logics are similar, however, in their emphasis on internal staffing or aligning with, but not hiring, experts. Both of these contrast with a calculative dominant logic, which we discuss next.

Calculative dominant logic. A calculative dominant logic employs an economic rationality (Williamson 1993). Rather than emphasizing professional or technical aspects of one's business and work, the focus is on business issues and positioning within a competitive environment, and on using a cost-benefit approach to decision making. Partners using a calculative dominant logic employed a managerial rather than a technical or service career orientation. The founding partner in OMB talked about the difference in mentality between being more business oriented versus more design oriented. This difference was well expressed above: 'We're more business than design oriented. It's hard to be both. It's a whole different mentality. Our motivation is budget and schedule and theirs is let's make it neat. They don't coincide very well.' This connects to his emphasis on developing organizational processes and systems within the firm. He describes the firm's expertise as business oriented: 'Our highest skill is project management. They teach you in school to fuss around with details. Nothing about business. I do both. Design is fun but I can't sit at the boards all day.'

This firm also focused more on competitive and marketing strategies than did other firms with different dominant logics. 'My head is focused on marketing. It's part of the success of the firm. I'm thinking what's gonna help me get the job—number one.' He also asserted the importance of competitive qualities, such as having the right location and managing perceptions. 'I set up an office in [the city] to get a job. . . . The day I opened we got a job from a university there.' He explained there were two things involved. 'The first is the perception of being in town and the second is the perception of [being in a] big town. It's all perception.'

This firm's strategy is to 'dominate the market in XX specialty' and 'become a regional' player. To achieve this strategy, it plans on hiring expertise: 'We think we have to hire it. We have good design people but need to be better. We recruit from around the West to build our XX specialty.' This learning strategy is one of absorptive capacity (Cohen and Levinthal 1990), tapping into external sources of expertise to propel one's own learning. When this learning becomes internalized, the hope is that it becomes the basis for transformative capacity by allowing the firm to develop staff in this expertise and by expanding opportunities to become a regional player. The staffing strategy involves an external sourcing of talent at high levels within the firm, since it would be difficult to attract such skilled talent at an entry-level position.

In terms of social contacts and client relations, the partner at OMB pursued a very different means for developing clients than did firms with either the relational or the competence dominant logic. In essence, he formed strategic relationships with contractors, who are typically seen as architects' adversaries. Emphasizing how they can be used for his advantage, the partner at OMB described a design/build strategy: 'In design/build, you are a team. The architect and contractor are friends. Some firms don't get this.' He developed these strategic relations through negotiation and bargaining leverage among contractors.

I went into the three biggest contractors and developed relationships with them. I said to one contractor, and this was a deliberate strategy: you teach us what you want us to do and we'll listen. The next one saw me with the first guy and decided he wanted to work with me so on the next project we did. Then maybe I worked with the first guy again. We all switch. It's like . . . pick-up basketball. You can be on a project with a firm and simultaneously be bidding against them on another one. It's all friendship and competition.

This competitive attitude and business focus marks the calculative dominant logic.

Summary. Our analysis presents three rather distinct combinations of career competencies, each of which generates a firm-level 'dominant logic' in these PSFs. A competence dominant logic, found in three of our firms, is shaped by a technical orientation that focuses on meeting technical and interpersonal challenges. *Knowing-how* is developed through either absorptive capacity or transformative capacity. Additionally, relationships with clients are designed to educate, solve problems, and build long-term relationships.

A relational dominant logic, found in two firms, has a strong service orientation. *Knowing-why* competencies emphasize developing and utilizing interpersonal skills such as empathy, listening to systematically build *knowing-whom*. A relational logic focuses on creating both intense client relationships and diverse social contacts with institutional decision-makers. New skills are developed primarily through transformative capacity. Tactics for transformative capacity include strong mentoring relations and intense use of apprenticeship. These skills of client relations and good performance combine to allow the firm to expand in new areas.

A calculative dominant logic, also found in two firms, emphasizes business challenges, market share, and project management. New skills are developed through absorptive capacity, in which experts are hired to extend current skill sets. *Knowing-whom* is focused on key institutional decision-makers, which can provide large-scale or lucrative projects. These relationships involve bargaining and strategic skills, strategic deciphering, and responding to competitive moves by various parties.

Although this analysis compares these three dominant logics against one other, a more complex, in-depth reporting (which is impossible given space constraints) would show that some elements of all three logics are found in each firm, albeit in differing degrees. For example, the partner at OMB acknowledged that the firm was 'trying to become more design oriented' and not simply relying on project management skills. Similarly, although G&Q emphasized aesthetic challenges, the partner there mentioned that they were upgrading their computer systems to improve project delivery. These differences are degrees of emphasis rather than mutually exclusive relations. Nevertheless, a careful reading of the full transcripts of these interviews does reveal an underlying logic these partners employ to conceptualize their business and make resource allocations. In large part this logic is an interaction of the partner's career competencies. Thus, the career perspective provides a useful lens for understanding firm-level strategies and operational tactics for achieving goals in the firm's industry.

Conclusion

We extend current careers research by linking the career strategies of partners in PSFs with a competency base perspective from the strategy and learning literatures. Specifically, we identify how career staffing, types of firm expertise, and learning strategies for extending or exploiting these competencies create an integrated system of career competencies. The patterns of these systems are quite distinct and can be identified by their different dominant logics. A second contribution is integrating the strategy and organization theory literature with careers research to identify different logics underlying goals, means, and the exchanges among parties employed to attain firm goals. This integration allows us to take some initial steps toward identifying the content of dominant logics.

Clearly, our study has several important limitations. First the sample size is very small and our analysis uses only a portion of the data. The next step is to analyze the remaining architect interviews to see whether these patterns hold across a much larger set of firms. An additional next step would be to perform a more systematic quantitative analysis on the data, such as multi-dimensional scaling of firms based on key attributes, to see if these three dominant logics are consistently identifiable. Finally, given that the data are cross-sectional, we cannot disentangle whether a partner's career motives caused PSFs to pursue specific capabilities or whether the successful development of capabilities influenced partners' career motives.

Our research points out several useful directions for future research. First, an important issue is the implication of these dominant logics. Do they make any difference in firm performance, growth patterns, or profitability? Performing cross-level research that assesses partners' career competencies with firm performance relative to competitors would enlighten us about the pragmatic importance of career competencies for firm competitive advantage.

A number of future research directions are also implied by the other chapters in this volume. One such direction is examining the viability of this model in different national contexts. For example, Cadin *et al.* (Chapter 11) suggest that important differences in *knowing-why, knowing-how,* and *knowing-whom* are based on national culture. Their research shows that French culture is more likely to embody a 'feudal' model. This may create a very distinct type of dominant logic not seen, for example, in the USA. This is especially relevant given the rapid expansion of national professional service firms into international markets.

A second future research direction is the relationship between various kinds of community described by Parker and Arthur (Chapter 5) and the development of dominant logics. Professionals in some firms may overlap in membership across several communities—for example, they may be deeply involved in professional, regional, and ideological communities. Essentially, this is akin to the social-network notion of multiplexity—the overlap of several multiple-role contents across one interaction (as often takes place, for instance, in family businesses). Do firms with members having greater overlap among communities develop different kinds of dominant logics? Are PSFs with fewer memberships freer to pursue more competitive and bargaining-oriented dominant logics, while those who share overlap across multiple communities, creating social embeddedness, are more likely to develop relational dominant logics?

A third direction is suggested by Morris' (Chapter 7) research on up-or-out policies in PSFs. Morris examines exit of professionals (for example, up-or-out policies), whereas we examine acquisition and development. An important avenue for research is combining these two perspectives. For example, are PSFs employing transformative capacity less likely to have up-or-out policies, whereas those using absorptive capacity are more likely to do so? If these firms employ both absorptive capacity and up-or-out policies, are they more likely to enter into highly competitive arenas dominated by a few large firms? In contrast, do those employing transformative capacity and less likely to use up-or-out policies enter into specialty niches? Continued investigation of these and related questions may further enlighten us about the relationship between human resource and competitive strategies in professional services.

References

Arthur, M. B., Hall, D. T., and Lawrence, B. S. (1989), 'Generating New Directions in Career Theory: The Case for a Transdisciplinary Approach', in M. B Arthur, D. T. Hall, and B. S. Lawrence (eds.), *Handbook of Career Theory* (Cambridge: Cambridge University Press).

Bacharach, S., Bamberger, P., and Sonnenstuhl, W. J. (1996), 'The Organizational Transformation Process: The Micropolitics of Dissonance Reduction and the Alignment of Logics of Action', *Administrative Science Quarterly*, 41: 477–506.

Barley, S. R. (1989), 'Careers, Identities, and Institutions: The Legacy of the Chicago School of Sociology', in M. B. Arthur, D. T. Hall, and B. S. Lawrence (eds.), *Handbook of Career Theory* (Cambridge: Cambridge University Press).

Barney, J. B. (1991), 'Firm Resources and Sustained Competitive Advantage', *Journal of Management* 17: 99–120.

Belliveau, M. A., O'Reilly, C., III, and Wade, J. B. (1996), 'Social Capital at the Top: Effects of Social Similarity and Status on CEO Compensation', *Academy of Management Journal*, 39: 1568–93.

Bird, A. (1994), 'Careers as Repositories of Knowledge: A New Perspective on Boundaryless Careers', *Journal of Organizational Behavior* 15: 325–44.

—— (1996), 'Careers as Repositories of Knowledge: Considerations for Boundaryless Careers', in M. B. Arthur and D. M. Rousseau (eds.), *The Boundaryless Career: A New Employment Principle for a New Organizational Era* (New York: Oxford University Press).

Boxman, E. A., De Graaf, P. M., and Flap, H. D. (1991), 'The Impact of Social and Human Capital on the Income Attainment of Dutch Managers', *Social Networks*, 13: 51–73.

Burt, R. S. (1992), *Structural Holes: The Social Structure of Competition* (Cambridge, Mass.: Harvard University Press).

Chandler, G. N., and Jansen, E. (1992), 'The Founder's Self-Assessed Competence and Venture Performance', *Journal of Business Venturing*, 7: 223–6.

Cohen, W., and Levinthal, M. (1990), 'Absorptive Capacity: A New Perspective on Learning and Innovation', *Administrative Science Quarterly*, 35: 128–52.

Coleman, J. S. (1988), 'Social Capital in the Creation of Human Capital', *American Journal of Sociology*, 94 (supplement), S95–S120.

Collis, D. J. (1994). 'How Valuable are Organizational Capabilities?', *Strategic Management Journal* 15 (Winter Special Issue), 143–52.

DeFillippi, R. J., and Arthur, M. B. (1994), 'The Boundaryless Career: A Competency-Based Perspective', *Journal of Organizational Behavior* 15: 307–24.

—— (1996), 'Boundaryless Contexts and Careers: A Competency-Based Perspective', in M. B. Arthur and D. M. Rousseau (eds.), *The Boundaryless Career: A New Employment Principle for a New Organizational Era* (New York: Oxford University Press).

—— (1998), 'Paradox in Project-Based Enterprise: The Case of Film Making', *California Management Review*, 40/2: 125–39.

Derr, C. B. (1986), *Managing the New Careerists* (San Francisco: Jossey-Bass).

—— and Laurent, A. (1989), 'The Internal and External Career: A Theoretical and Cross-Cultural Perspective', in M. B. Arthur, D. T. Hall, and B. S. Lawrence (eds.), *Handbook of Career Theory* (Cambridge: Cambridge University Press).

Fichman, M., and Goodman, P. (1995), 'Customer-Supplier Ties in Interorganizational Relations', in *Research in Organizational Behavior*, vol. 18 (Greenwich, Conn.: JAI Press).

Fladmoe-Lindquist, K., and Van Dyne, L. (1993), 'Professional Services and International Strategic Human Resources: Interfirm Teams and Ongoing Relationships with Free Agents', in *Research in Personnel and Human Resources Management*, supplement 3 (Greenwich, Conn.: JAI Press).

Garud, R., and Nayyar, P. (1994), 'Transformative Capacity: Continual Structuring by Intertemporal Technology Transfer', *Strategic Management Journal* 15: 365–85.

Granovetter, M. (1973), 'The Strength of Weak Ties', *American Journal of Sociology*, 78: 1360–80.

—— (1974), *Getting a Job: A Study of Contacts and Careers* (Cambridge, Mass.: Harvard University Press).

Greenwood, R., Hinings, C. R., and Brown, J. (1990), 'P2–Form Strategic Management: Corporate Practices in Professional Partnerships', *Academy of Management Journal*, 33/4: 725–55.

—— —— —— (1994), 'Merging Professional Service Firms', *Organization Science*, 5: 239–57.

Gunz, H. P. (1989), *Careers and Corporate Cultures: Managerial Mobility in Large Corporations* (Oxford: Basil Blackwell).

—— and Jalland, R. M. (1996), 'Managerial Careers and Business Strategies', *Academy of Management Review*, 21/3: 718–56.

Hirschman, A. O. (1970), *Exit, Voice, and Loyalty: Responses to Decline in Firms, Organizations, and States* (Cambridge, Mass.: Harvard University Press).

Jones, C. (1996), 'Careers in Project Networks: The Case of the Film Industry', in M. B. Arthur and D. M. Rousseau (eds.), *The Boundaryless Career: A New Employment Principle for a New Organizational Era* (New York: Oxford University Press).

—— and DeFillippi, R. J. (1996), 'Back to the Future in Film: Combining Industry- and Self-Knowledge to Meet Career Challenges of the 21st Century', *Academy of Management Executive* 10/4: 89–104.

—— Borgatti, S. P., and Walsh, K. (1997a), 'Career Competencies in a Cultural Industry: Resources for Influence and Structure', paper presented at Cultural Industries conference, New York University, May.

—— Hesterly, W. S., and Borgatti, S. P. (1997b), 'A General Theory of Network Governance', *Academy of Management Review*, 22: 911–45.

—— —— Fladmoe-Lindquist, K., and Borgatti, S. P. (1998), 'Professional Service Constellations: How Strategies and Capabilities Influence Collaborative Stability and Change', *Organization Science*, 9: 396–410.

Krackhardt, D. (1992), 'The Strength of Strong Ties: The Importance of *philos* in Organizations', in N. Nohria and R. G. Eccles (eds.), *Networks and Organizations: Structure, Form, and Action* (Boston: Harvard Business School Press).

Larsson, R., Bengtsson, L., Henriksson, K., and Sparks, J. (1998), 'The Interorganizational Learning Dilemma: Collective Knowledge Development in Strategic Alliances', *Organization Science*, 9/3: 285–305.

Levinthal, D., and Fichman, M. (1988), 'Dynamics of Interorganizational Attachments: Auditor-Client Relationships', *Administrative Science Quarterly*, 33/3: 345–69.

Maister, D. (1993), *Managing the Professional Service Firm* (New York: Free Press).

Miner, J. B., Crane, D. P., and Vandenberg, R. J. (1994), 'Congruence and Fit in Professional Role Motivation Theory', *Organization Science*, 5: 86–97.

Mintzberg, H. (1987), 'Crafting Strategy', *Harvard Business Review* (July-Aug.), 66–75.

—— and McHugh, A. (1985), 'Strategy Formation in an Adhocracy', *Administrative Science Quarterly*, 30/2: 160–97.

Prahalad, C. K., and Bettis, R. A. (1986), 'The Dominant Logic: A New Linkage between Diversity and Performance', *Strategic Management Journal*, 7: 485–501.

—— and Hamel, G. (1990), 'The Core Competence of the Corporation', *Harvard Business Review*, 68/3: 79–91.

Rousseau, D. M. (1995), *Psychological Contracts in Organizations* (Thousand Oaks, Calif.: Sage).

Schein, E. H. (1985), *Organizational Culture and Leadership* (San Francisco: Jossey-Bass).

—— (1987), 'Individual and Careers', in J. Lorsch (ed.), *Handbook of Organizational Behavior* (Englewood Cliffs, NJ: Prentice Hall).

Selznick, P. (1958), *Leadership in Administration* (Evanston, Ill.: Row, Peterson).

Sonnenfeld, J. A., and Peiperl, M. A. (1988), 'Staffing Policy as a Strategic Response: A Typology of Career Systems', *Academy of Management Review* 13: 588–600.

Teece, D., Pisano, G., and Shuen, A. (1997), 'Dynamic Capabilities and Strategic Management', *Strategic Management Journal* 18/7: 509–33.

Uzzi, B. (1997), 'Social Structure and Competition in Interfirm Networks: The Paradox of Embeddedness', *Administrative Science Quarterly*, 42: 35–67.

—— (1996), 'The Sources and Consequences of Embeddedness for the Economic Performance of Organizations: The Nework Effect', *American Sociological Review*, 41: 674–98.

Williamson, O. E. (1985), *The Economic Institutions of Capitalism: Firms, Markets and Relational Contracting* (New York: Free Press).

—— (1993), 'Calculativeness, Trust, and Economic Organization', *Journal of Law and Economics*, 36: 453–502.

Winch, G., and Schneider, E. (1993), 'Managing the Knowledge-Based Organization: The Case of Architectural Practice', *Journal of Management Studies*, 30/6: 923–37.

9

Career as Life Path: Tracing Work and Life Strategies of Biotech Professionals

Susan C. Eaton and Lotte Bailyn

Contrary to traditional depiction, professional careers are not purely individual, linear, and primarily determined by human capital. Rather, they are profoundly shaped by family and other extra-work relationships in which individual employees are embedded, are anything but linear over the lifespan, and are determined partly by circumstance, luck, and the actions of others as well as by one's education and training. In this chapter, we argue that, at least in the industry we examine, an individualistic, linear, human-capital intensive view does not explain work experiences well. We propose a more complex, textured explanation of factors influencing work outcomes, along with a more fluid, evolving conception of career.

Careers are changing rapidly, especially in knowledge-based professions. Established expectations for long-term employment in a single firm with regular upward progression appear under serious challenge. Some authors have suggested that the implicit social and employment contract of the post-war period is breaking down, and being replaced by a much less clear, less mutual, and less binding set of expectations between employers and employees (e.g. Kanter 1990; Kochan 1997). Other scholars note the fraying of the psychological contract that used to bind employers and employees together (De Meuse and Tornow 1990; Rousseau and Parks 1993; Robinson and Rousseau 1994; Rousseau 1995).

Careers in the future may look much more like the boundaryless careers described in recent years (Arthur and Rousseau 1996).[1] Many managerial and professional careers have been transformed, at least in the public mind, from relatively protected to newly vulnerable to economic pressures (see e.g. Heckscher 1995). While the popular image of the entrepreneurial professional who is principally concerned about employability may be overstated, the evidence remains ambiguous (Swinnerton and Wial 1995; Herzenberg *et al.* 1998). For example, a recent Harris poll showed that a majority of all US employees expect to leave their jobs voluntarily within the next five years, and one in six expects to be fired or laid off (Louis Harris and Associates 1997).

More than in the past, an individual's life choices are complicated by the career and life choices of his or her partner, and by children and/or elders who need care, time, and attention at unpredictable times (Fletcher and Bailyn 1996). Families are also changing, and have been, in a consistent direction in both Europe and the USA, for several decades. The most dramatic indicator of this is the shift in the employment patterns of women, so that two-job or two-career families are now the majority, while single-earner, two-adult households comprise less than 15 per cent of US households. Because divorce is increasing (currently between half and two-thirds of new marriages are expected to end in divorce), single-headed households are also on the rise. Demographic changes in industrialized countries mean that parents are living longer, sometimes well past their children's planned retirement age, while childbearing is being delayed into the thirties or even forties by more and more couples (Ferber and O'Farrell 1991).

In this rapidly changing context, what can one say about the nature of careers in firms that are themselves changing? Despite the popular image of dominant large companies, most people labor in workplaces that are small; fully 51 per cent of employees in the USA work in establishments employing less than fifty people.[2] And with the shift from production to knowledge work, it seems likely that small, entrepreneurial firms will be more typical of future workplaces than the old industrial corporations are. Thus, what happens to employees of these firms is important to help us understand the challenges ahead for careers and individuals. Firms in the future are also more likely to be in strategic and communicative alliances and networks with other similar and related firms (Powell *et al.* 1996). The present study is based within such firms of the future—a set of biotechnology firms that, according to Powell, epitomize the new, networked, entrepreneurial, collaborative, and small environments where many professionals of the future will work.

The Biotechnology Industry

Biotechnology is a rapidly growing industry, which includes companies that engage in the research, development, production, and commercialization of products using recombinant DNA, cell fusion, and novel bioprocessing techniques (Office of Technology Assessment 1991).[3] The national population of biotechnology firms in the USA is about 1,300, and they employ 153,000 people. Most biotechnology firms are small. A biotech firm of 50 to 150 employees is a medium-sized firm in the industry. Most firms are less than fifteen years old, and are networked in one form or another via partnerships, alliances, formal and informal collaborations and agreements, and so on. (Powell *et al.* 1996). These firms rely on a combination of venture capital, initial public offerings of stock, and alliances or contracts to provide working capital for many years. On average, a new drug requires fifteen years and more than $304 million in 1996 dollars to be brought from conception to market (DiMasi *et al.* 1991; Hewitt 1997).

Uncertainty is the watchword of the industry. 'Job insecurity goes with the business,' one scientist told us. 'There is no such thing as a secure job.' Pharmaceutical researchers estimate that only three of ten drugs introduced from 1980 to 1984 had returns higher than their average after-tax research and development cost (Grabowski and Vernon 1994). The regulatory process, especially in the USA, adds another layer of uncertainty, in cost and time.

It is in this setting that we studied thirty professionals in two biotech firms, in an attempt to understand how they experience their work, the strategies they use to integrate this work with the rest of their lives, and what this tells us about the shape of their careers.

Subject Profile

The data[4] are based on in-depth case studies in two typical biotechnology firms drawn from the population of 130 biotech firms in one US state. They stem from focused interviews, observations, and group discussions. The employees were selected to represent a range of occupations, ages, family status, and lengths of service. While not chosen as a representative sample, they included more than 50 per cent of the professional scientific employees in each firm, and these employees were not significantly different in their family and professional status from the firms' research employee population as a whole.[5] We explored in detail the work and personal life experiences of these men and women as they pursued their careers in this setting.

For a profile of the sample of professional employees interviewed, see Table 9.1, which includes sex, highest degree obtained, position in company, full- or part-time status, length of service, estimated age, and family status.

In this sample, as in the industry as a whole, fully half the employees held a Ph.D. or equivalent degree, and half of these were women. Men and women were nearly equally represented in managerial, scientific, and professional administrative jobs. Almost all the managers had doctorates, whereas the scientists split about equally between doctorate and bachelor's degrees. Only two scientists had a master's degree. All the administrators had masters degrees, mainly MBAs.

While three of the fifteen women, or 20 per cent of this small sample, worked part-time (one worked twenty hours, one worked twenty-four hours, and one worked thirty hours per week), none of the men did. The women's median length of service was longer (7.5 years) than the men's (5.8 years),[6]

Table 9.1. *Characteristics of professional employee sample* (*n* = 30)

Characteristic	Female	Male	Total
Sex	15	15	30
Highest degree obtained			
Ph.D. or equivalent	7	8	15
Master's	3	4	7
BA/BS	5	3	8
Less than BS	0	0	0
Position in company			
Manager (scientific)	4	4	8
Scientist[a]	10	9	19
Administrative	1	2	3
Status			
Full-time	12	15	27
Part-time	3	0	3
Length of service			
Median	7.5	5.8	7
Shortest	1	2	1
Longest	11	13	13
Age (est.)			
Oldest	57	54	57
Youngest	30	28	28
Median	39	38	39
Family status			
Single			
no children	1	1	2
with children	3	0	3
Married			
no children, 2 full-time jobs/careers	0	2	2
with children, spouse at home	0	1	1
with children, spouse works part time	0	5	5
with children, 2 full-time jobs/careers	10	5	15
Partner			
no children, 2 full-time jobs/careers	1	1	2

[a] Many scientists have at least one employee to manage.

and the seniority of the sample ranged from one to thirteen years. The men's and women's median age was nearly the same, at 38 and 39 years respectively; this was a young workforce, since most people came to work in their late twenties or early thirties after a postdoctorate or another short-term job or two. Only a few employees were in their fifties, and none was near the traditional US retirement age of 65.

In the sample as a whole, twenty-four of the thirty employees had children (most of whom were pre-school or school-aged, with a few college-aged or adult children), and twenty-two were either in two-career families or were single parents. But there were important gender differences in the potential impact of family status on these scientists. While three women were single mothers, no men were single fathers. Also, the men had more family support from their partners. One man had a non-working spouse, and five of the eleven men with children had partners who were working part-time. None of the fifteen women had such support. In contrast, ten women were married with children and had partners working full-time, compared to only five of the men. Thus, of the eleven men with children, more than half ($n = 6$) had the support of either a non-working or a part-time working spouse. In contrast, all thirteen women with children either had no partners or had partners working full-time.

These data suggest that the issues of work and family (including but not limited to dependent care) were highly salient to this group, but not equally by gender. The women were nearly three times as likely as the men (13 versus 5) to be in the high-stress situation of being either single parents, or parents with a full-time working partner. And yet, as we will show, the careers of both are responsive to their family situations.

Career Choices and Work Motivations

Professional employees in biotech have career options, also, in academe, as faculty members or full-time researchers in a non-profit institution like a university hospital, or in large pharmaceutical firms. We did not find many people who had worked in pharmaceutical companies. But the sentiment was expressed by several of the biotech employees we interviewed that such jobs constrain their intellectual freedom or make them into 'just a number' because of the large size of typical pharmaceutical companies. As one science manager said, 'the concept of a small company had appeal. At Company X [a large pharmaceutical firm], there was great security, but I didn't feel like I was making a difference.'

Many, however, had academic experience as a point of direct comparison. All the Ph.D. scientists in our sample had completed at least one post-doctoral fellowship at a university before coming to industry, and several had completed two. The master's level scientists also commonly had university lab experience, though their paths into academic teaching would have required completing a doctoral degree. Even the bachelor's degree scientists had often begun their paid employment in a university lab as undergraduates, and some had continued working in such a lab before coming to work at a biotechnology firm.

Careers in a university setting are typically well defined; employment contracts are most often explicit, rather than implicit. Scientists are usually required to raise their own research funds, whether or not they have tenure, sometimes including their own salaries and lab costs. If untenured, they often have a term-limited contract. To acquire tenure, at least in the USA, requires long years of teaching, research, and publishing. As one male Ph.D. scientist said, 'you have to bring in grant money, teach, advise, get a lab up and going. You have to put a huge amount of effort in, with little return. In biotech, they seem to compensate well and do neat things, though you have to give up some independence.' So biotech seems to be a career setting between the more bureaucratic pharmaceutical and the more autonomous university setting with its accompanying multiple responsibilities.

Nor is the burden of attaining tenure an issue in biotech companies. And this appeals, particularly, to women. Women achieve tenure less frequently than men, particularly in the hard sciences, even accounting for their smaller numbers in junior faculty ranks (Aisenberg and Harrington 1988; Valian 1998). To them, even the uncertain environment of biotechnology seemed to have advantages over the academic setting. 'It's too tough for a woman to get tenure in academe,' said one successful female Ph.D. biochemist. 'I had friends in academe, and friends in industry. I didn't want to work 80-hour weeks in academe and then not get tenure.' This perception may explain, in part, why biotechnology employs nearly 50 per cent women scientists,[7] a much higher proportion than is true in universities (see Eaton 1999). For people trained and interested in science, biotech firms thus offer career possibilities that have advantages over both the large corporation and the university setting. And at least half the scientists, both men and women, said that they came to biotech companies in part because of the excitement of being able to do applied science. They felt it was an environment where 'I get to keep doing new things. Things are always changing in this industry. . . . I want work that is challenging, not boring.' Part of this reasoning depended on the small size of most biotechnology firms, which appealed to many.

Many scientists also mentioned that they had personal, family, or lifestyle reasons for choosing or staying with their particular company. One bio-chemist, for example, joined his biotech firm because his wife had an academic job offer in the local area, his only academic offer was out of state, and they wanted to stay together in the area. The three women working part-time (as well as the expectant mother hoping to become the fourth) each explained independently that the opportunity to work part-time was the key reason they were still working at their firm, and that their commitment to their jobs had increased because of the chance to meet both their family and work commitments in this way.

Though most research on careers, particularly that focused on the inte-gration of work and family concerns, has been conducted in large firms (see e.g. Bailyn *et al.* 1996), what research does exist on smaller firms suggests that they provide a more flexible work environment, with fewer formal rules and more social support (MacDermid *et al.* 1994; MacDermid and Williams 1997). Our work confirms this overall conclusion. These small biotechnology firms appear to provide something important, related to size and scope of work, that draws multiple levels of scientists to seek work in them, and they seem to be a particularly hospitable environment for women scientists.

In summary, the scientists we interviewed worked in biotechnology because of the attraction of exciting, remunerative, and innovative science conducted in a small, flexible environment, despite its potential instability. Many left an academic setting to work in biotechnology because they perceived even greater uncertainty in pursuing a scientific career in the university, and because they were attracted to the financial and advancement possibilities available in industry. Careers in such firms seem to fit the needs of highly educated employees whose life priorities extend beyond the confines of their occupational identities.

Careers and Internal Mobility in Smaller Biotechnology Firms

Promotion and internal mobility within biotechnology firms do not reflect the linear career pattern that characterized internal labor markets in larger more traditional firms in the past (Doeringer and Piore 1985). In these small firms, Ph.D.s were usually hired in the position of Scientist (at an entry grade 1 or a higher grade 2), and could then become full or associate Directors, managing projects or departments. Without a Ph.D., employees tended to be called a Research Associate or an Associate Scientist or to have a title associated with a specialized technician job. But apart from the distinction between directors and non-directors (which itself can evaporate when projects change or the company's focus shifts), limited formal hierarchy exists. Further, as the research changes, and sometimes as the administrative apparatus changes (for example, human resource (HR) people come or go), department names and codes change, and scientists move around from one to another. The fact that a number of scientists were unsure of their current job titles or grades and the researchers had to check with the HR department to find out for certain, confirms this fluidity.

Positional changes, which sometimes occurred in the context of a promotion and sometimes not, did not seem to be overly dependent on degree level, another difference between biotechnology and the university environment. Academic degrees were important, but not wholly determinative of status in the firm, though Ph.D. scientists clearly began at higher rates of pay and were more often eligible for advancement. While Ph.D. scientists generally supervised employees with bachelor's degrees, a few BS and MS scientists also supervised other scientists with similar degrees, and were considered to be members of full scientific grades. This could be a double-edged sword, however, serving as an advantage to some individuals without doctorates, but also keeping them tied to the firm where their skills and abilities were well known, because they possessed, in essence, firm-specific knowledge not easily marketable on the outside. These issues are familiar from the literature on internal labor markets (see Osterman 1984, 1993, 1996; Doeringer and Piore 1985), but the degree of fluidity we saw in these firms was unusual.

None the less, nearly all the scientists in the sample had been promoted since their arrival at the firms, though not all on the same timeline. Most of the Ph.D. scientists who had been hired at the entry level of Senior Scientist 1 had advanced during their first two to three years to Senior Scientist 2. Three women and three men had also become Directors. On the whole, however, the men seemed to have done better than the women, which fits generally established conclusions (see e.g. Valian 1998). Men were promoted to higher positions than women in five of the six cases where they had started at the same levels as the women. Of those who were promoted furthest and fastest, two single men without children and three fathers with home support did the best. Though one male scientist with a full-time working spouse and two children also fell into this group, his wife's job was secretarial and he reported that she handled the greater part of their home responsibilities. Again we see that, even for the men, careers seem to respond to their family situations.

What is particularly interesting about the biotech setting is that non-Ph.D. scientists advanced even further, as a group, though their careers were more uneven and idiosyncratic. One BS scientist became an Associate Director. Though he did not manage a group, he was recognized as the source of many creative ideas by everyone in the firm. But his career path was defined by all as unique. One other BS employee, who entered as a temporary Quality Control Analyst, basically a technician's job, was not only hired on a permanent basis but was promoted to Research Associate during his seven years with the company. Finally, in one firm, two male BS Research Associates advanced through the ranks to Scientist, and, in the other firm, two women BS Associate Scientists became Senior Scientists 1. Thus, at both firms, the scientific jobs were not only for Ph.D.s, but could be earned by those with bachelor's or master's degrees who performed well over the years.

These mobility patterns suggest that internal labor markets (in whatever modified form) are alive and well in these small firms, even with limited room for mobility at the top. While advancement does not follow a single track, or a single set of job titles, or even a predictable degree-based order, promotion still occurs for the majority of employees.[8] This finding is somewhat surprising in the insecure environments of the biopharmaceutical companies, but perhaps not so surprising when we realize that promotions are one of the few means to reward employees in this setting. Giving them bonuses is difficult in tight financial times (always), giving them stock options is of limited value if the stock is hovering at a low value (as it was in both firms here), and interesting or luxurious travel and time off are both limited by the rigorous time requirements of the work. The particular character of these firms and the needs of these employees require new thinking about the standard view of career incentives (see e.g. Schein 1990).

In summary, careers in biotechnology are not linear, but they do as a rule appear to provide opportunity for growth and movement up a shifting hierarchy of job titles and responsibilities. This seems to occur in some cases unpredictably, because of vacancies left by departing managers or senior staff. While degrees and training do count in hire-in grade and doing the work, they are not definitive in determining who can be a scientist or who can lead a project—if someone with a bachelor's degree has creative ideas and good scientific skills, that person can become a project director or associate director.

It is clear, also, that career success and family duties (or support) and gender are interlinked in this professional workforce; employees' careers are embedded in the jobs and commitments of their partners and spouses. These issues are at the core of the questions raised in this chapter, so we describe, in the next sections, how employees integrate family responsibilities with their work demands and career goals, and what differences firm practices make.

Integration of Work and Family

The classic view of careers assumes professionals are predominantly acting as individuals, making maximizing choices. Yet people are embedded in relationships outside work. Though 'work and family' have been the subject of much recent attention (e.g. Ferber and O'Farrell 1991; Vanderkolk and Young 1991; Hood 1993; Nippert-Eng 1995; Hochschild 1997), there has been little research that systematically tries to link employees' family needs and concerns to work structure (some exceptions are Rapoport, Bailyn, *et al.* 1996 and RPPI 1998). In order to understand better how these issues affect careers, we tried to discover how professional employees sought to integrate work and family in these biotechnology settings, and how companies responded.

The biotech industry, with its insecurity and long hours, made full engagement with both work and family difficult for many scientists in the sample, particularly the women who were more likely to be in families where both partners had full careers and, in the presence of children, had less support for their parental responsibilities. Several women and one man in the sample became parents for the first time in their late thirties or early forties, which changed their circumstances and their pattern of involvements. Other couples, in contrast, reluctantly postponed having children because of the uncertainty of their jobs and/or work demands on the partners. One male scientist explained that he and his wife had not had children because she too is a scientist, working in the medical research industry; she had in fact recently changed jobs because women in her previous company who had had children were not permitted to return to work by the lab director, who felt they could no longer put in the long hours required. Another phenomenon we found was commuting marriages, which meant that two of the employees saw their spouses only once a week or once a month.

The women tended to be more explicit in voicing the difficulties and stress of these integration issues—perhaps because all the women with children were either single mothers or had full-time working spouses with their own demanding careers (none of their husbands was a blue-collar worker or a lower-level white-collar worker equivalent to the secretary mentioned above, for instance). But it may also reflect what Marshall (Chapter 10) describes as the push to find a context in which one can experience one's whole self. One woman explained that she was thinking of an alternative career. She wanted to work, and knew she would have 'no trouble getting a job [in biotechnology]'. But, she said, 'the work is not as challenging as it used to be. It's not the focus of my life and I do not want it to be.' None the less, the pragmatics of life also play a role, and she continued:

I would prefer to have a job with better hours, more like school hours. For instance, when the nursery wants parents to participate, I can never do it. I have to be at work. I do not want my daughter to go to kindergarten and then after-school care every day, and rarely see me except for a couple hours every night![9]

This theme was echoed by a woman Ph.D. scientist, mother of an 18-month-old, who said that, since she had become a parent, 'my days are more defined in terms of time. I have to be slightly more organized. Before the baby, I used to work 'til 6 or 6.30 at night. Now I take work home if there is a real push, but I leave at 5 to pick my daughter up at day care.'

These examples make clear how closely family and work conditions intersect in deciding the shape of careers. To understand the contours of this intersection, we looked at the barriers to full engagement in both work and family.

One barrier for many was a long commute, which usually resulted from their spouses' jobs or careers, a preference for schools in a specific community, or firm or industry uncertainty. One scientist said he had a 'horrible commute, at least 40 minutes each way, and more in traffic'. When asked why he did not consider moving (since his wife's job location was not an issue), he said, 'With the kind of situation we're in, the company's [lack of] stability . . . it would make no sense to move. Who knows what will happen?' In this case, the employee had to choose between spending nearly two hours a day driving to work and back, or moving his family nearer an indefinite work situation.

A second barrier was the individualistic way in which flexible arrangements were frequently negotiated. Even in a company where the Chief Executive Officer and HR Director agreed in principle to be flexible, the actual decision on alternative scheduling was up to the person's immediate manager, usually a senior director or vice-president. In one company, a request for a four-day work week was rejected flatly, indicating that flexibility was defined extremely narrowly. In another, two women scientists worked out their own part-time arrangements with their director, and everyone involved expressed satisfaction. But, at the same company, a new mother was denied her request to return to work three days a week by a different director, and her employment was officially terminated when she was unwilling to return full-time. All she could do was to accept the company's offer to rehire her part-time as a consultant, which meant no benefits or permanent status. The arrangement seemed partially satisfactory, because it was extended indefinitely, but the practice for new parents within a single company seemed inconsistent and *ad hoc*. If each person has to arrange his or her own exceptions to the standard schedule, a barrier is created by concerns about precedent, and by the constraints of individual supervisors' personalities and beliefs, which can (and do) limit fruitful experimentation.

When one person who had briefly experimented with a four-day, full time schedule that worked well for her was asked why she was not permitted to continue it, she said her manager told her: 'I want you on site. I do not want to deal with your job. I can only rely on you if you are here.' She explained that she could be available on the fifth day via computer, phone, or fax, but that was not sufficient for him, even though she described herself as working with '100% autonomy' and rarely seeing her manager. When he was asked about this, he agreed that he was a 'hands-off' manager, but said he 'preferred' to have her there for five days. This is an example where traditional assumptions about what is a standard or normal schedule create a formidable barrier to integration. Moreover, it seems that this expected schedule fits neither the actual needs of the job nor those of the employee.[10]

Thus, some scientists were expected to be present in person, whether that was necessary for their particular kind of work or not. And employees were responsive to this unstated belief. One noted that he stayed until 6 p.m. 'at least two or three days a week', and that he came in 'by 8.30, which is earlier than most people here', so that people would observe him working long hours at least some of the time. He was clearly aware he was staying for appearances' sake, and not because he was engaged with the work or the work required it.

The specific work organization patterns and demands in biotech can themselves be a barrier to full integration, if no one with authority is attending to these issues. 'I have no predictability,' said one Ph.D. senior director. 'I could be in the lab [at 5 p.m.] and get caught up, and not be able to leave. We are understaffed now, so I am in the lab a lot. I am writing memos, reports, and making phone calls. I have multiple projects and project meetings. I have minimal secretarial support.' This successful woman felt she had to make terrible choices to succeed in her work. 'I gave up a lot of family time to get work done,' she said. 'To get ahead, you have to make a decision. And I have moved farther ahead than women who did not make the same decision. But I am not sure I should have done it.' She found that, when she tried working fewer hours for a period, to spend more time with a seriously ill child, 'it took several months to get back the same level of authority and respect' that she had had before the shorter work days.

Her view is confirmed by another Ph.D. scientist, who found that 'I had to come in one day a week during my maternity leave because of the politics, and to keep my influence. I hired in absentia. I worked on the phone at least two hours a day. When the baby went down for his nap, I got on the phone.' She explained that she had to be there because 'I do all the interactive work for our group, so people want to talk to me. They come looking for me every 10 minutes.' This comment is reminiscent of Joyce Fletcher's (1999) research on the importance of 'relational work', which her study found is often performed by women engineers.

One senior director explained how poor work organization of projects exacerbates the problem. 'There is always a crisis, something that needs to be resolved "right now". Once when my younger daughter was two months old, I worked twenty-one straight days. I was trying to breastfeed, and it was impossible. I do not usually work eighty-hour weeks, but when there are crises, I do. Management is not shy about asking people to "put their personal lives on hold".'

Working at home is a solution that might help some employees, especially for work such as writing reports, which can often best be done uninterrupted. Some portion of biotechnology work cannot be done at home, either because it is based in the lab, or because of regulatory or confidentiality concerns. But some scientists estimated that up to half the work could be done elsewhere, particularly report writing, data analysis, and reading. Despite this generally shared perception, one HR director explained that 'only the top eight people in the company are allowed to work at home. Below that, it is not permitted.' Here hierarchy served as a literal barrier, for the bottom 80 per cent of employees, to use this way to integrate work and family. Working at home would not solve all problems, of course. To the extent that work actually requires eighty-hour weeks, doing it at home does not provide much relief. But most front-line managers did not see such long hours as necessary, though some high-level managers did.

Industry and firm status also have an effect. The industry, described as well by Gunz *et al.* (Chapter 2), is still immature. Thus firms grow and decline in size subject to financial vagaries. For example, half the scientists in this sample joined the companies at least seven years ago, when both companies were smaller than they are now; each then grew larger, and then smaller again. Each situation represents a different context for work–family integration.

Similarly, different life stages present different issues. During this period of time, many scientists became parents of small children, so their personal needs changed.[11] It is clear, therefore, that family status interacts with firm status in shaping employees' careers. And this is true for male as well as female employees. No conception of career that ignores this intersection can reflect the realities of modern life.

Company Responses

Careers, thus, are not only forged from individual need or through individual choice. They also reflect the organizational context—the values, norms, and practices of the company in which they occur (Van Maanen 1977; Barley 1989). It is important, therefore, to see how these companies respond to professional employees' efforts to integrate the work and non-work portions of their lives. Following are some examples of ways the companies made it easier, in some cases, or harder, in others, for employees to live fully engaged lives at work and at home. Some of these are generic, not specific to biotechnology, and we start with those.

One positive company response that emerged in the study occurred when a flexible or creative supervisor was willing to bend the rules or traditions to provide the support that employees needed to integrate their work and family lives. For example, part-time schedules negotiated at one of the companies (individually) were described as very satisfactory to both the affected employees and their supervisors. One employee worked twenty hours weekly during two days, coming in one weekend day and working one long day during the week. This allowed her to monitor cell cultures and experiments at odd hours so that others did not have to check them then, and enabled her family members to care for her children. Another woman worked thirty hours weekly, the minimum for benefit eligibility, but would have preferred to work fewer hours if she could have had access to health insurance. All the part-time employees (and their managers) were pleased with the amount of work they were doing on these schedules, and said they were even more productive as part-timers than they were as full-timers, because they could focus intently on what they had to get done in more limited time.

However, one company had a policy against part-time work, and the other depended on a case-by-case negotiation, which was not always successful. What was clear was that, in the absence of a sympathetic supervisor, company statements or policies concerning 'family-friendly' practices did not seem to result in major changes in traditional cultural assumptions (such as the importance of face time or employees' physical presence at work).

These tacit beliefs about the relation of presence and time to work effectiveness are general barriers to work–personal life integration (see also Bailyn 1993; Perlow 1997). In biotechnology, as in many other industries, productivity or effectiveness is not actually linked directly to hours worked. One thoughtful manager, a female Ph.D. scientist, said, 'People have very different work styles. Some people work full out and can get more done in seven hours than some other people who work ten hours a day.' One is not necessarily a better worker than the other, she said, but 'most people's work is not set up where number of (assay) plates done per day is important as a measure or a real indicator of productivity'. She thinks 'slower people tend to be good at more analytical kinds of work, compared with faster people who are more data churning people. So the trick is to try to get people to do things they are the best at. You can't make everybody into one thing.' When asked how she managed people's work, she said, 'I try to deal with content, not time. . . . Most people probably can do their jobs in a forty-hour week. I used to think about work more at home, but now with the baby, I find that I do not.' However, she was worried that her boss would 'probably die' if the CEO found out what she had said about forty hours. 'But I just don't believe that more hours is more productivity. If you expect sixty hours a week of people, I find that they burn out. Once they burn out, they can't do much of anything well.'

Another more general barrier, confirmed by our data, relates to gender roles, which seem to prevent an equitable integration (cf. Hochschild 1989; Bailyn 1993; Rapoport *et al.*, in press). Though, as we saw, women preferred this environment to academia and some women were able to arrange satisfactory part-time schedules, their careers were adversely affected by the differential support they had at home. Men moved further and faster on the promotion track: even though women were 50 per cent of the bench scientists, they were only 5 per cent of top management in these firms. Further, most examples of people without Ph.D.s who had moved up were men, particularly in one of the firms; nor were any of the Ph.D. women allowed a part-time schedule in either firm. It seems as if women needed the Ph.D. more than men did, that their work alone was not sufficient for recognition by advancement. All in all, women were given some help in managing their lives outside work by these firms, but this also had some inequitable career consequences for them. Some of these stemmed from the difficulties, already detailed, that occur when negotiations for flexibility have to be individual, rather than systemic or collective.

And yet there are aspects of biotechnology work that could facilitate an integration with personal life, and these may differ from the pressures existing in other settings. The first one is the long product cycle. This is one of the main differences that Gunz *et al.* (Chapter 2) outline between the Canadian biotech industry and Silicon Valley. With product cycles of ten years or more—compared, for example, to nine months in software design—pressures are not as intense and options for flexibility are greater. In biological work one cannot force certain kinds of processes: things take time to grow. Hence more hours are even less likely to mean more results in this industry than in others.

Secondly, despite the popular image of lab science, some of the work *can* be done in different places and at different times. Data analyses and reports need not be done in a lab. And in some cases we heard it was even possible to reset a lab computer and monitor it from home. So people could do their own work at hours (and sometimes places) that made sense to them—as long as they were permitted to do so by the firm.

Finally, the project nature of work in biotechnology means that work is both autonomous as well as interdependent. The autonomy of our subjects' work meant that there was always independent work to do, which helps in the control of one's schedule. And strong co-worker relationships resulted from the interdependence, even when loyalty to the firm was shaky. We found scientific employees unfailingly willing to help each other when asked. In some respects, other project-oriented work—even in fast-paced high technology—may share this characteristic.

In summary, our study found that work and family integration is an active issue for both male and female scientists in biotechnology firms. Company responses to this issue in the two firms varied from quite unresponsive to relatively flexible, as long as negotiations were individually conducted with direct supervisors. Though aspects of biotechnology work would seem to permit incorporating employees' personal needs into work design, we saw no evidence that this was done systematically at either firm. The situation was thus one of unrealized potential. The structure of the work would seem to permit creative and flexible arrangements, but we found few actual examples. Our preliminary evidence suggests that the work of these technical professionals would be amenable to being designed with employees' personal needs in mind, which would allow both men and women to incorporate, over time, flexibility in both work and home commitments. Though this would seem to be desirable for long-term retention and development of professional staff in today's small and medium-sized biotechnology firms, traditional assumptions still precluded serious effort in this direction.

Conclusion

So what does all of this mean for the understanding of careers? Clearly the old human-capital view of careers is no longer viable, as much recent work has shown (e.g. Arthur and Rousseau 1996; Hall 1996). It is obvious that we need a more nuanced, more contextual understanding of this concept. The notion of the 'protean career' (Hall 1976; Hall and Mirvis 1996) or the 'intelligent career' (Arthur *et al.* 1995) or the 'relational career' (Kram 1996) all begin to fill this void. In many ways, these concepts apply to one aspect of our data—that is, what the individual brings. But we are trying to position the concept of career at an intersection of domains. Some previous work has done this, by conceptualizing career as residing between the individual and the organization (Schein 1978; Bailyn 1989). This view, based on the sociology of work, sees a career as a series of work experiences (Hughes 1958) within an occupational or organizational context (Van Maanen and Barley 1984). The data presented here indicate that the situation (and the concept needed to understand and analyze it) is even more complex.

First, based on the professionals participating in this study, we can no longer think of the individual component of career as separate from workers' personal lives. Most people must respond to the career needs of their partners as well as their own. And, although some researchers have long been aware that family and community are important contexts (e.g. Rapoport and Rapoport 1965; Kanter 1977; Fletcher and Bailyn 1996), this awareness is only slowly entering mainstream thinking about careers. We suggest that an individual's career cannot be understood outside the person's relationship with one or more other persons, and their occupational concerns, as well as their personal needs and relationships. It is not easy to map these inter-connections, though we make a first attempt in Fig. 9.1. Future work in career theory could specify these multiple influences more exactly, and develop more dynamic models for understanding the intersections.

Secondly, the character of the organization in which any part of a career plays out is also critical. To these scientists, apparently insecure firms seemed secure enough if their own skills were developing, and their work fitted in with their overall life situation. While firm boundaries are not rigid and permanent as proposed in older 'bounded' career models, they are still important to the specific day-to-day learning, opportunities, and experi-ences, and to the relationships and networks these professionals develop. Moreover, the nature of the products being developed and the particular task to which one is assigned, and their rhythms and requirements, are also relevant for the careers of these people, because they may limit, define, suggest, or create the next opportunity.

Finally, time plays a role in this understanding. We have seen that the careers studied and the motivations attached to them change with circum-stance and over time. Clearly, one's family stage (e.g. presence or absence of children or occupational involvement of partner) plays a significant role. But so does the character of the industry (whether mature or immature (see Chapter 2)) or the stage of the firm (e.g. whether developing or producing a drug, and the length of financial viability). Even if people change organiza-tions only on average every six years, they are likely to be in another stage of life in the new organization. In other words, it seems that what is important about these careers is that they are embedded in a number of intersecting cycles: a family and life cycle, a firm and industry cycle, and a task/project/ product cycle.

For this reason, we argue for a conception of career as life path: a series of initiatives and adaptations to employment, family, and community, and evolving not only with changes in individual interests or skills or the characteristics and requirements of one's employment context, but with the life experiences of oneself and of the people central to one's personal space. Marshall (Chapter 10) gives a vivid picture, from the individual side, of such paths.

Most conceptualizations of career put work in the foreground and use occupation and organization as context. Personal life—what anthropologists (e.g. Rosaldo and Lamphere, 1974) call the private sphere—is clearly in the background. We envision a shift of figure and ground.[12] In our case, the data we have presented imply that life (encompassing stages of work, family, community, and other aspects of personal life) becomes the figure, a life

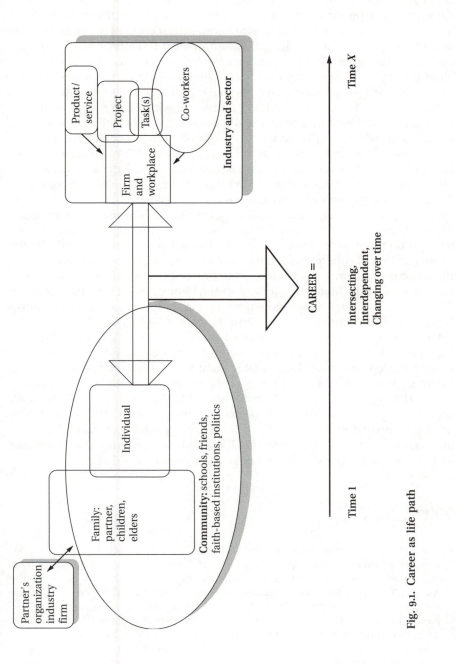

Product/
service

Project

Task(s)

Co-workers

Firm
and
workplace

Industry and sector

Individual

Family:
partner,
children,
elders

Community: schools, friends,
faith-based institutions, politics

Partner's
organization
industry
firm

CAREER =

Intersecting,
Interdependent,
Changing over time

Time 1

Time X

Fig. 9.1. Career as life path

that evolves in intersection with economic or public-sphere characteristics (industry, firm, products, tasks), which are themselves continuously evolving and changing. Our conception resembles an intersection of the communities described by Parker and Arthur (Chapter 5), even though we would change the emphasis somewhat in one respect. We believe, based on these data, that what they call 'family communities', and limit to specific kinds of organizations and linkages, actually play a 'figure' role under all conditions.

No longer do we have an isolated individual with human capital, but an individual embedded in a family and a community, and often in a primary relationship with another adult also engaged with organization, industry, firm, project, and task aspects of occupational work. Though we recognize the limits of our small sample, we suggest that these intersections should move to the front of our vision. Rather than viewing boundaries as practical limitations to theoretically free labor markets (Chapter 2), we view them as creative spaces for negotiation and opportunity, both at work and at home. These boundaries may not be the same on average for men and women; our data, as do many other studies, suggest that women are more likely to seek an integration of spheres, which may involve less single-focused attention to their occupations at certain times, while men are more likely to be able to put work concerns first and still have strong family ties. At the same time, we find men to be much more influenced by circumstances outside the workplace than is reflected in the literature on careers.

We are left, thus, with a complicated set of intersections among domains that are themselves continuously changing. The career is the evolving path among these domains, which interact and mutually affect each other (cf. Chapter 4). Very few paths can be forecast in today's world. As the educator Myles Horton (1990) said, 'We make the road by walking.' This in itself creates both uncertainty (and accompanying anxiety) and opportunity (and accompanying excitement). To look at careers without taking all these intersections into account across the lifespan is to miss what is experienced by the professionals we interviewed as most central to them.

Notes

1. Gunz *et al.* (Chapter 2), in arguing for a contingency theory of careers, propose 'not a world of boundaryless careers, but one of careers that are bounded in ways that emerge from the striving of actors to make sense of their place in the world' (p. 50). We agree with this proposition, but emphasize, as they do not, the role of non-occupational and non-organizational factors in this process.
2. Laubacher and Malone (1997) note that one in five persons (in the USA) worked for a Fortune 500 firm in 1970, while one in ten persons does in the 1990s.
3. Some of the industry characteristics in this section are drawn from work done by Sandra Resnick (1996, 1997). See also Gunz *et al.* (Chapter 2) for more description of this industry.

4. The data used in this chapter are part of a larger study of the biotechnology industry conducted under a grant from the Alfred P. Sloan Foundation to the Radcliffe Public Policy Institute at Radcliffe College. The Sloan Foundation project team at the time of writing includes: Françoise Carré (Co-Principal Investigator), Paula Rayman (Co-Principal Investigator), Lotte Bailyn (Study Director), Ann Bookman (Study Director), Constance Perin (Study Director), Susan C. Eaton (Senior Research Associate), Wendy-Jade Hernandez (Research Associate), and Sandra Resnick (Research Associate).

5. This conclusion is based on interviews with the firms' human resource personnel.

6. This length of service, longer than one might expect from the precariousness of these firms, matches data of Gunz *et al.* (Chapter 2) from the Canadian biotech industry.

7. This number is confirmed by data from the biotech industry around San Diego (DeHaan 1997).

8. Morris (Chapter 7) analyzes the up-or-out system of professional service firms, and speculates that, in firms where a knowledge base is the source of competitive advantage, such a system may not be optimal. Our data seem to support this conjecture.

9. The men and women interviewed generally reflected a different standard of what they felt was a reasonable amount of time for themselves as parents to spend with their children. While Ms Q, above, did not want her child to see her for only 'a couple hours every night', a male science manager in her firm described himself as quite pleased with spending 'two hours a night' with his sons, one of whom was the same age as Q's daughter, before they went to bed. In his case, his wife worked part-time and handled 'all the communication' with their childcare provider, unless she was out of town, and all the coordination of household schedules and chores. Such was not the case with Q's husband, who worked full-time and was also stressed by the demands of getting a child to and from a childcare center at certain times. The male manager also made more money and could purchase more flexible childcare than the female science employee and her husband. Gender equity was not evident in household labor, or in individuals' expectations of themselves as parents, which confirms the findings of other studies (e.g. Hochschild 1989).

10. For more examples and a fuller argument about the role of traditional assumptions on people's careers, see Bailyn (1993).

11. One male scientist noted that he spent more time with 'the younger two children' because 'I realized what I missed with the older ones'. Another Ph.D. scientist noted that 'stability is becoming more important to me; having a child did that. And we are building a new house.' Thus, he needed to spend more time at home than he did before.

12. Cf. Capra's notion as discussed by Parker and Arthur (Chapter 5).

References

Aisenberg, N., and Harrington, M. (1988), *Women of Academe: Outsiders in the Sacred Grove* (Amherst, Mass.: University of Massachusetts Press).

Arthur, M. B., and Rousseau, D. M. (1996) (eds.), *The Boundaryless Career: A New*

Employment Principle for a New Organizational Era (New York: Oxford University Press).

—— Hall, D. T., and Lawrence, B. S. (1989), *Handbook of Career Theory* (Cambridge: Cambridge University Press).

—— Claman, P. H., and De Filippi, R. J. (1995), 'Intelligent Enterprise, Intelligent Careers', *Academy of Management Executive*, 9/4: 7–20.

Bailyn, L. (1989), 'Understanding Individual Experience at Work: Comments on the Theory and Practice of Careers', in M. B. Arthur, D. T. Hall, and B. S. Lawrence (eds.), *Handbook of Career Theory* (Cambridge: Cambridge University Press).

—— (1993), *Breaking the Mold: Women, Men, and Time in the New Corporate World* (New York: Free Press).

—— Rapoport, R., Fletcher, J. K., and Kolb, D. (1996), 'Relinking Work and Family: A Catalyst for Organizational Change', Working Paper WP No. 3892–96, MIT Sloan School of Management, Apr.

Barley, S. R. (1989), 'Careers, Identities, and Institutions: The Legacy of the Chicago School of Sociology', in M. B. Arthur, D. T. Hall, and B. S. Lawrence (eds.), *Handbook of Career Theory* (Cambridge: Cambridge University Press).

DeHaan, H. A. (1997), 'Demographics of Women in the San Diego Biopharmaceutical Industry', *BioPharm* (Feb.), 8–10.

De Meuse, K. P., and Tornow, W. W. (1990), 'The Tie that Binds—has Become Very, Very Frayed', *Human Resource Planning*, 13/2: 203–13.

DiMasi, J. A., Hansen, R. W., Grabowski, H. G., and Lasagna, L. (1991), 'Cost of Innovation in the Phamaceutical Industry', *Journal of Health Economics*, 10: 107–42.

Doeringer, P. B., and Piore, M. (1985; first published 1971), *Internal Labor Markets and Manpower Analysis* (Lexington, Mass.: D. C. Heath).

Eaton, S. C. (1999), 'Surprising Opportunities: Gender and the Structure of Work in Biotechnology', *Annals of the NY Academy of Sciences*, 869 (Apr.), 175–89.

Ferber, M. A., and O'Farrell, B. (with Allen, La Rue) (1991), *Work and Family: Policies for a Changing Work Force* (Washington: National Academy Press).

Fletcher, J. K. (1999), *Disappearing Acts: Gender, Power, and Relational Practice at Work* (Cambridge, Mass.: MIT Press).

—— and Bailyn, L. (1996), 'Challenging the Last Boundary: Reconnecting Work and Family', in M. B. Arthur and D. M. Rousseau (eds.), *The Boundaryless Career: A New Employment Principle for a New Organizational Era* (New York: Oxford University Press).

Grabowski, H., and Vernon, J. (1994), 'Returns to R and D on New Drug Introductions in the 1980s', *Journal of Health Economics*, 13: fig. 2–8. http://www.phrma.org./.

Hall, D. T. (1976), *Careers in Organizations* (Pacific Palisades, Calif.: Goodyear).

—— (1996), 'Long Live the Career—A Relational Approach', in D. T. Hall and Associates, *The Career is Dead: Long Live the Career* (San Francisco: Jossey-Bass).

—— and Mirvis, P. H. (1996), 'The New Protean Career: Psychological Success and the Path with a Heart', in D. T. Hall and Associates, *The Career is Dead: Long Live the Career* (San Francisco: Jossey-Bass).

Heckscher, C. (1995). *White Collar Blues* (New York: Basic Books).

Herzenberg, S. A., Alic, J. A., and Wial, H. (1998), *New Rules for a New Economy: Achieving Postindustrial Prosperity* (Ithaca, NY: Cornell University Press).

Hewitt, P. (1997), 'Tufts Center for the Study of Drug Development', personal interview with Sandra Resnick.

Hochschild, A. (1997), *The Time Bind: When Work Becomes Home and Home Becomes Work* (New York: Metropolitan).

—— (with Machung, A.) (1989), *The Second Shift: Working Parents and the Revolution at Home* (New York: Viking).

Hood, J. C. (1993), *Men, Work, and Family* (Newbury Park, Calif.: Sage).

Horton, M. (1990), *We Make the Road by Walking: Conversations on Education and Social Action* (Philadelphia: Temple University Press).

Hughes, E. C. (1958), *Men and their Work* (Glencoe, Ill.: Free Press).

Kanter, R. M. (1977), *Work and Family in the United States: A Critical Review and Agenda for Research and Policy* (New York: Russell Sage Foundation).

—— (1990), *When Giants Learn to Dance: Mastering the Challenge of Strategy, Management, and Careers in the 1990s* (New York: Simon & Schuster).

Kochan, T. A. (1997), 'Back to Basics: Creating the Analytical Foundation for the Next Industrial Relations System', paper presented at the IRRA 50th Anniversary Meeting in Chicago, MIT Institute for Work and Employment Research, 3–5 Jan.

Kram, K. E. (1996), 'A Relational Approach to Careers', in D. T. Hall and Associates, *The Career is Dead: Long Live the Career* (San Francisco: Jossey-Bass).

Laubacher, R. J., and Malone, T. (1997) 'Flexible Work Arrangements and 21st Century Worker's Guilds', Working Paper 004, Initiative on Inventing the Organizations of the 21st Century, MIT Sloan School of Management, Oct.

Louis Harris and Associates, Inc. (1997), Harris Survey at Work, unpublished summary, Louis Harris and Associates, Inc., 111 Fifth Ave., New York, 10003.

MacDermid, S. M., and Williams, M. L. (1997), 'A Within-Industry Comparison of Employed Mothers' Experiences in Small and Large Workplaces', *Journal of Family Issues*, 18/5: 545–67.

—— —— Marks, S., and Heilbrun, G. (1994), 'Is Small Beautiful? (Influence of Workplace Size on Work–Family Tension)', *Family Relations*, 43/2: 159–67.

Nippert-Eng, C. (1995), *Home and Work: Negotiating Boundaries through Everyday Life* (Chicago: University of Chicago Press).

Office of Technology Assessment (1991), *Biotechnology in a Global Economy* (Washington: Government Printing Office).

Osterman, P. (1984), 'White Collar Internal Labor Markets', in P. Osterman (ed.), *Internal Labor Markets* (Cambridge, Mass.: MIT Press).

—— (1993), 'Internal Labor Markets: Theory and Change', in C. Kerr and P. Staudohar (eds.), *Labor Economics, Institutions and Markets* (Palo Alto, Calif.: Stanford University Press).

—— (1996), *Broken Ladders: Managerial Careers in the New Economy* (New York: Oxford University Press).

Perlow, L. (1997), *Finding Time: How Corporations, Individuals, and Families can Benefit from New Work Practices* (Ithaca, NY: ILR Press).

Powell, W., Koput, K. W., and Smith-Doerr, L. (1996), 'Interorganizational Collaboration and the Locus of Innovation: Networks of Learning in Biotechnology', *Administrative Science Quarterly*, 41: 116–45.

Rapoport, R. and Rapoport, R. N. (1965), 'Work and Family in Contemporary Society', *American Sociological Review*, 30: 381–94.

—— Bailyn, L. *et al.* (1996), *Relinking Life and Work: Toward a Better Future* (New York: Ford Foundation).

—— —— and Fletcher, J. K. (in press), 'Moving Organizations toward Gender Equity: A Cautionary Tale', in L. Haas (ed.), *Organizational Change and Gender Equity:*

International Perspectives on Fathers and Mothers at the Workplace (Newbury Park, Calif.: Sage).

Resnick, S. (1996), 'Appendix to the Proposal: Biotechnology Industry Information', in P. Rayman and F. Carre (eds.), *Opportunities for Work and Family Integration for Professionals: A Study in Small and Medium-Sized Biotechnology Firms* (Cambridge, Mass.: Radcliffe Public Policy Institute).

—— (1997), 'Background Information on the Biotechnology Industry—Profiles', unpublished memorandum.

Robinson, S. L., and Rousseau, D. M. (1994), 'Violating the Psychological Contract: Not the Exception but the Norm', *Journal of Organizational Behavior*, 45: 245–59.

Rosaldo, M. Z., and Lamphere, L. (1974), *Women, Culture and Society* (Stanford, Calif.: Stanford University Press).

Rousseau, D. M. (1995), *Psychological Contracts in Organizations: Understanding Written and Unwritten Agreements* (Thousand Oaks, Calif.: Sage Publications).

—— and Parks, J. M. (1993), 'The Contracts of Individuals and Organizations', *Research in Organizational Behavior*, 15: 1–43.

RPPI (1998), *Creating Work and Life Integration Solutions* (Report of the Radcliffe–Fleet Project; Cambridge, Mass.: Radcliffe Public Policy Institute).

Schein, E. H. (1978), *Career Dynamics: Matching Individual and Organization Needs* (Reading, Mass.: Addison-Wesley).

—— (1990), *Career Anchors* (rev. edn.; San Diego, Calif.: Pfeiffer).

Schwartz, F. N., with Zimmerman, J. (1992), *Breaking with Tradition: Women and Work, the New Facts of Life* (New York: Time Warner).

Swinnerton, K. A., and Wial, H. (1995), 'Is Job Stability Declining in the US Economy?', *Industrial and Labor Relations Review*, 48/2: 293–304.

Valian, V. (1998), *Why So Slow? The Advancement of Women* (Cambridge, Mass.: MIT Press).

Vanderkolk, B. S., and Young, A. A. (1991), *The Work and Family Revolution: How Companies Can Keep Employees Happy and Business Profitable* (New York: Facts on File).

Van Maanen, J. (1977), *Organizational Careers: Some New Perspectives* (New York: Wiley International).

—— and Barley, S. R. (1984), 'Occupational Communities: Culture and Control in Organizations', in B. Staw and L. Cummings (eds.), *Research in Organizational Behavior*, vol. 6 (Greenwich, Conn.: JAI Press).

III

WORK AND NON-WORK, BOUNDARIES AND CULTURES

Each of the contributions in Part III is concerned with the fundamentals of career theory: with individuals, their work, the social context of their work, and how their experiences unfold over time. Start points vary: Marshall begins with individuals—the stories of sixteen women; Cadin and colleagues with broad context—institutional and cultural features of French society; Goffee and Jones with a conceptual discussion of the social architecture within which career experiences may be embedded. All acknowledge the complex interplay between individual and contextual factors—although the focus varies: Marshall explores the circumstances under which the links between individuals and their jobs may be broken. By contrast, Goffee and Jones are interested in the differing ways in which social relationships might bind people together. Somewhere between these two points sit Cadin and colleagues, who build a framework guided by two criteria: the number of firms individuals had worked for and their degree of dependence or social distance. Despite these differences, each of the contributors shares an ambition to account for career experiences in ways that properly reflect rather than diminish their complex, multifaceted nature.

Marshall's approach explores the narratives of women managers involved in significant career transitions or reviews. The shifting, incomplete, and sometimes contradictory nature of these accounts is revealed as individuals construct stories that place personal experience within the context of wider, dominant social values and expected paths of development (a process paralleled, as she points out, by academics theorizing careers). On the basis of a series of interviews and conversations, a variety of reasons for leaving or wanting to leave employment are presented: some search for different lifestyles following significant career achievement; others look for balance between work (or employment) and non-work; a significant number are moving on from work contexts where the personal costs and disappointments are no longer acceptable. Threading through these accounts are issues related to the 'survival' of women managers in male-dominated work environments and the strains involved in maintaining a sense of self. As Marshall points out, the stories are indicative of 'mid-life' work and they encompass a world that goes far beyond the boundaries of organizations, occupational choices, and employment.

Cadin and colleagues replicate the work of Arthur, Inkson, and Pringle in New Zealand within the French context to determine the extent to which new career trajectories and attitudes are present. As they point out, French society differs significantly from Anglo-Saxon cultures—from which much contemporary career theory derives. They draw attention in particular to differences in power distance, uncertainty avoidance, and masculinity values originally described by Hofstede; in employment relationships and occupational stratification; in divisions between public and private life; and in educational systems and labor markets. From interviews with a cross section of the French workforce, they build a taxonomy grounded in their data rather than existing concepts. Five categories emerge: *sedentaries* (traditional organizational careers); *migrants* (moves between employer but not between jobs); *itinerants* (frequent changes of employer to exploit personal expertise); *borderers* (moving between employment and self-employment); and *nomads* (the self-employed or those whose links to organizations are 'ephemeral'). It is only the last category that we might recognize as 'boundaryless', yet, as the authors point out, nomadism is not always freely chosen, nor is it always successful. There is more to nomadism than an elitist view of people with distinctive competencies. Linked to this it should not surprise us that the nomads are not confined to self-designing organizations. Nomadic trajectories are explored in more detail via Arthur, Claman, and DeFillippi's *knowing-whom, knowing-how, knowing-why* framework.

Goffee and Jones take as their starting point the need to conceptualize the social context of modern careers in a way that might reveal boundaries other than those conventionally captured through occupational, functional, or hierarchical distinctions. They develop a framework for differentiating the social architecture of distinctive work settings that draws upon an established sociological literature. The central dimensions are sociability—affective, non-instrumental relationships of friendship—and solidarity—instrumental, task-centered cooperation between individuals and groups. The framework that emerges is applied mainly to modern, large-scale corporations, but has potential applicability to career analysis within the context of professional groups, geographic regions, or national cultures. Three familiar themes from the career literature are explored here: the psychological contract; the relationship between work, family, and private life; and mobility and career development. In each case, differing social architectures suggest a distinctive set of career trajectories, development processes, employment relationships, and work/non-work dynamics.

There are no easy generalizations to emerge from these three chapters. To some extent, this may simply reflect the loss of certain boundaries that once framed career experience. But it also results from a determination by each of the contributors to work through divergent and contextually grounded examples and to resist the temptation of excessively neat categorization. As individuals negotiate transitions between different life stages and work contexts, we should anticipate diversity rather than uniformity; each of these chapters is suggestive of approaches and methods that can contribute to our understanding of that diversity.

Living Lives of Change: Examining Facets of Women Managers' Career Stories

Judi Marshall

Facet. A little face; *orig.* one of the small cut and polished faces of a diamond.

(The Shorter Oxford Dictionary, 1973)

In this chapter I shall explore various facets of women managers' career stories. I shall reflect on senior women managers' career patterns and decision making by examining content themes that appear in the stories of women who have experienced significant career transitions or reviews. I shall also look at what forms these accounts took and aspects of how they were told.

I am working critically with an interest in narrative. There is currently abundant attention to the notions of narrative and story and their relevance to researching people's lives (e.g. Rosenwald and Ochberg 1992; Mumby 1993; Lincoln and Denzin 1994; Lincoln 1997; Denzin 1997). Understanding narratives as constructions of truth generated through complex, active (individual, interpersonal, and social) processes of sensemaking, self-presentation, and interpretation is seen by many as a pathway beyond the social realism we can no longer claim in our research (Lincoln and Denzin 1994). I approve this general direction, but am also concerned that working with narrative can become as conventionalized and stylized as any other form of inquiry. I am especially interested in three aspects of this work: first, in how form (shape, pattern) arises in the accounts people give of their lives; secondly, in the reference points people use to create and legitimate the stories they tell (for example, whether these are externally/socially or internally/personally oriented or a combination of the two); and, thirdly, in how the telling of stories functions as a life process. In exploring these issues, I am seeking to keep notions of narrative open, to engage with *narrating as process* rather than with narrative as product.

These interests can all be applied also to the parallel process of career theorizing as an academic activity. As researchers, we too construct narratives, use established ideas as reference or counter points, and so on. I am interested in how form arises in academic theorizing. This chapter's process orientation allows this as a parallel attention, but only briefly because of space. However, it is highly germane to my own processes of narrative construction as I develop text and theory about women managers' lives for an imagined audience.

I have chosen the imagery of facets to name the multi-stranded analytic approach I am taking. For me it implies looking from different angles that constitute different types of analysis, and making no claim to encompass a whole in any one of these (in fact doubting whether there is coherence to reach for). I want to look at content, form, and processes of narrative generation and sensemaking. This chapter's approach is, therefore, offered as an exploration. Examining these different facets, moving between them and allowing incompleteness in any particular stream of attention, seems to provide a theoretical practice congruent with the subject matter of the chapter—people's life and career narratives and choices.

Theoretically I shall be exploring issues of career through stories told about career and life changes and decision making. I shall be suggesting that these articulations are often multiple, shifting, contradictory, incomplete accounts; that people are typically relating overtly or covertly in constructing their accounts to dominant social values and expected paths of development, with consequences for the storyteller; and that telling one's story fully, and being heard with respect, can be part of a process of life development.

The Study

The research engagement on which I draw is a qualitative study (reported in detail as Marshall 1995) into the experiences of women who had reached middle- and senior-level management positions and then left employment, been forced out, or considered leaving but eventually stayed. It was motivated by wanting to explore the *apparent* phenomenon of high-achieving women leaving or expressing ambivalence about senior positions, which has received some media and academic attention (e.g Taylor 1986; Rosin and Korabik 1992). I wanted to tell such women's stories from their own perspectives, to articulate their meanings in a world of organizational theory and media interpretations that seemed either unlikely to value what they had done or actively to devalue it.

I wanted to contact people who had felt that they *had* to leave employment or a particular job, rather than those who had moved for immediate career progression. Once I had set this parameter on participation, I let the

contacts I made inform me of the kinds of experiences people had. I eventually worked with sixteen women in depth, and spoke informally to others. I
had many other relevant conversations. Also I presented reports to practitioner and academic audiences and had the themes confirmed. So, while
sixteen stories provide the heart of the data, I have gained substantial confirmation that the issues the study raises for attention are concerns for many
women managers, those who leave organizations and those who stay. The
study's findings also align with those of North American statistical studies on
women's propensity to leave employment that suggest that lack of promotion opportunities, male-dominated corporate cultures, and organizational
politics are key factors (e.g. Rosin and Korabik 1991; Brett and Stroh 1994;
Stroh and Senner 1994). As this inquiry looks at a small group of people
intensively, it provides complementary data to larger-scale survey research.
It especially offers insights into some of the dynamics involved in career
reviews and transitions, and into how complex decision making, inter-
twining careers and lives more generally, happens.

As the enacted research approach is significant to the themes of this
chapter, I shall discuss this below. Before doing so I shall give some demographic details of the people studied.

Women managers moving on

The positions managers had moved or considered moving from were: Chief
Executive (1), Executive Directors (5), Senior Management Team Members or
Departmental Heads (4), senior managers (2), and middle managers or
professional staff (4). Their occupational roles were indicative of the areas
in which women have relatively more access to senior jobs (although against
a low base)—i.e. personnel, organizational development, general management, nursing, public relations, sales, community work, and training. Four-
teen were working in the UK, one in North America, and one in New Zealand.
They ranged in age from mid-thirties to early fifties. In terms of ethnic origin,
all were 'white'.

Demographic characteristics of the sample contradicted potential stereotypes that women might leave senior jobs mainly because of parenting (only
one person had young children) or because they could be financially dependent on a male partner to support them. Only four people were potentially in
the latter situation, and one of the partners heavily resisted his wife's intention to leave work, as he had married an independent career woman not a
potentially dependent homemaker. Some of the women with partners were
themselves the main family salary-earners. Other participants were single or
divorced. These were, then, mostly decisions with significant financial
consequences.

Most people moved from their jobs and organizations and then spent
some time out of employment. Many felt that they regained life energy as

they moved on. Several talked about returning to interests or levels of vitality which they associated with their youth. But a few people faced increased pressures and stress in at least the short term.

By the end of the study, a duration of approximately two years, most participants had re-entered employment or become self-employed. Their occupational positions were: Managing Director and other roles (1); Non-Executive Director and public speaker (1); Directors (2); senior managers (2); middle manager (1); consultants (6); academic and trainer (1); entrepreneur (1); and parent at home (1).

The participants had moved on to find or create life and career circumstances that they felt were more freely chosen. This contrasting of job positions at two points in time should, however, be treated with caution; it gives a misleadingly stable picture. The research participants had experienced much more change than is apparent in terms of their employment, life circumstances, attitudes, and perceptions—and their lives were continuing to change.

Is gender at issue in these data?

I am not suggesting that the experiences reported here happen exclusively to women. To what extent gender is at issue in these data is a matter of open debate, which must remain inconclusive. Some aspects seem likely often to be gender associated given the implicit if not overt gender cultures in organizations (Collinson and Hearn 1994), how much norms of management behavior are still shaped by idealized male sex role stereotypes, the relatively low percentage of women in senior jobs, and women's generally wider range of social roles than men. Some factors are more associated with the power dynamics of elite groups and how they exclude those defined as 'other', which could be on the basis of gender, race, or other factors. Some men would certainly report experiences of senior management and career that have similar or related themes to the stories told here.

Women managers who 'leave' as test cases

It is important to note that this research focused on privileged people, who are also unusual, atypical women. The majority of women are still concentrated in low-pay, low-level jobs and there is much occupational gender segregation. Women make up a high percentage of the part-time, flexible workforce. Many have limited career and pay prospects, job security, and quality of working life. So there is more to achieving gender-associated career understanding (and equality) than this chapter addresses.

And, if we remember this, it *is* worth looking in depth at this elite group, because its members are test cases in several senses, providing potential insights into organizational life, and careers more generally, as seen through a selective lens—the perceptions of relative newcomers to the territory of senior management. Most of those studied were pioneers for women in their organizations. They were highly visible, so that how they behaved was likely to be over-interpreted, treated as symbolic of all women (a potential trap in career theorizing also). They are difficult to understand against both dominant stereotypes of women and ideal images of management (which are still often male-associated despite the so-called feminization trend). We therefore need to analyze with a both/and framing, to see both these specifics *and* the more general picture.

I do not offer these data as a tale of woe or victimhood, but as issues that need to be engaged with, a sensemaking narrative that needs to be told frankly—and heard openly—within the field of women in management in order to move on in practice and theoretically. The field of gender theorizing is also an evolving story. If we can take stories such as these seriously, and listen to their forms and concerns *within their own registers* rather than seeing them only from dominant social or academic framings, we contribute to helping organizational life and theorizing become more malleable, accommodating of diversities, and available for revision.

Storying Lives—Attending to Form

How stories come to be told and how they undergo changes and reformulations as relatively routine life processes are significant issues when we want to treat such material as research data.

The research approach I adopted assumed a process and constructivist approach to storytelling. (And my use of the material here invites a sense also of critical theory.) This section is, therefore, offered as an exploration in processes of story-making, paying attention to narratives and their construction as an interactive inquiry process. My interest in working with subjective, unfolding notions of career has resonances with the approach of Parker and Arthur (Chapter 5). I provide less explicit methodological structure than they do, however, as I treat the way research participants express themselves as an additional source of data.

Initially I interviewed participants individually, taping our conversations. I asked them to discuss their career and life history, the job and organization situation they had left (or wanted to leave), the process of leaving, and their general views on being a woman in employment. The timings of the interviews in the person's career transition varied from some people anticipating a forthcoming event to others looking back a year or so after leaving a specific job, and so offered different aspects of the experience.

These interviews were mostly frank, direct, and self-reflective on the managers' parts. For some people they were cathartic events. The women wanted to be heard and accepted by someone, without having to distort or suppress 'truths' they felt about the experience. Sometimes it seemed that telling the story fully allowed their lives and the story of their lives to move on. Some reflected on what they found themselves saying in this permissive space. One noted with surprise and delight how much warmth she felt towards the experience; she felt she had learned from it despite the challenges. Another noticed how much the events still upset her, that she had not left them behind as she had thought. Telling her story to me allowed her to take further steps in doing so.

The women were telling their stories to another woman in private, with the purpose of later making them public. Some talked overtly about handing them over to my care. They believed that these stories should be told, because they reveal aspects of women's organizational lives that are seldom so frankly spoken. They thought women should speak out—especially to other women who may have similar experiences—to tell the less glamorous sides of success. But most did not feel they could do this personally.

I wrote their individual stories based on thorough and highly engaged qualitative data analysis (Marshall 1995). I then negotiated the stories with the women and revised them, to agree a story we could tell in public. (The names used are pseudonyms.) It was valuable that for various reasons it took some time (up to two years) before I reached this stage. Most people were more willing to tell their stories fully, because their lives had moved on and the accounts seemed to be of past selves. This was, however, certainly not true in one case, and the woman withdrew her crafted story from the research based on a diffuse sense of anxiety that it might prove recognizable and disrupt her recently re-established life (see Ruth below).

As the research neared a close, people told me about further developments in their lives and about revised perceptions of the career changes we had discussed. At some point I decided to stop integrating new information or insights into the data, needing to stop updating the stories in order to close the research engagement. But these further discussions gave me insights into how storying often shifts—that many lives are continually in process, and that asking participants to 'verify' research accounts is a complex endeavor. (I note that some people may want to hold more fixed, consistently replicable, versions of their life stories, and may be served by doing so.)

As the research progressed, I realized that my initial intention to tell the women's stories was not a straightforward process, especially as: there was no one truth to tell about any one person, but often multiple, sometimes conflicting, themes and issues; I expected readers to interpret the stories from different viewpoints, assumptions, and value positions (some probably highly critical and looking for weaknesses); and I might be making women vulnerable by being so open. Sensemaking in this area is contentious and highly politically loaded. I soon came to realize that addressing these issues was an integral part of the research process—that the research was as much about *finding an analogically suitable form* to represent the material as it was about the issues involved.

So the sixteen stories are at the heart of the resulting book, incorporating ambiguities, conflicts, and my voice occasionally with reflections and questions (Marshall 1995). Among them are sections of commentary that draw out issues for exploration. I sought to make choices and dilemmas of interpretation overt, rather than seeking to arrive at one truth about these women managers' lives. I wanted people reading this research material to engage with issues of sensemaking—and therefore valuing—for themselves. (In career—and all—theorizing, then, I suggest that the form of the academic presentation is as important as the content of the conceptual storyline.)

At a late stage in the project I held two workshops in which research participants met and commented on the themes that were emerging in analyses. This more interactive research engagement added another source of data to the study, a further perspective rather than a competing notion of truth.

Despite their richness as sources of data and forms of representation, narrative and story have potential disadvantages, especially in this type of research area. They may direct attention and analysis to the individual and deflect attention from systemic and cultural issues. As individual and organizational/social issues are intertwined, they often mirror each other. Often characteristics of the system as a whole are lived out by individuals—our story is seldom ours alone. When we seek to interpret, we may then individualize inappropriately, for example, either judging someone as incompetent without appreciating that much of his or her behavior (or how it is interpreted) is shaped by contextual factors, or thinking ourselves incompetent when we cannot find productive working strategies to deal with situations beyond our control. Thus we risk inappropriately assigning characteristics of the system as if they are characteristics of the individual. To overcome this possibility we need dual frameworks of sensemaking that recognize potential individual *and* contextual factors and take care if choosing one interpretation frame over the other. In working with the research material here, it is important, then, that we do not only turn the spotlight of scrutiny on women, as much research does, but also illuminate the organizational world through their experiences. Goffee and Jones (Chapter 12) offer similar reminders that career theorizing may easily over-individualize and under-conceptualize systemic influences.

Sources of plot lines

Rosenwald and Ochberg (1992) suggest that people draw from socially and culturally allowed themes in constructing their own lives and life narratives. This means they are constrained in the stories they can tell.

We assume that all stories are told and that all self-understanding is realized within the narrative frames each culture provides its members. These frames of intelligibility determine and limit the power of personal narrative. (p. 2)

Social influence shapes not only public action but also private self-understanding. To the degree that this is true, social control takes on a more ominous aspect. For now it appears that the alternatives one recognizes as possible or moral are constrained in the marrow of individual self-representation. (p. 5)

This was often the women's experience, and had significant consequences for their abilities to tell and affirm their own lives. Their decisions to pause in outwardly highly successful careers could not be readily understood *and valued* within most social (and academic?) frameworks of meaning about careers. Several noted that many colleagues in their organizations could not understand their decisions, and some would then note who had been able to do so or lines of explanation that had proved intelligible. (See Claire below.)

In public discussion it seems highly likely that women's decision making will be devalued. Women are sometimes portrayed as not tough enough, not willing to give the commitment considered normal in senior jobs and upward tracking careers. Several research participants had stayed over-long in difficult organizational settings because they did not want to concede to such interpretations of themselves, and of women more generally, appreciating that their behavior might be treated as symbolic.

It seems likely then that there are 'truths' and stories of lives that can and cannot be readily told. As senior women managers are currently still an atypical—some would say a contradictory—category, positive attributions for their behavior are not readily available in cultural frames of meaning. The themes from stories I present below are challenging in this sense. They can be readily dismissed as those of marginal voices who have not adjusted successfully to the realities of organizational life. Or they could be interpreted in the frames the women seek to articulate for them: alternative value bases and visions of possibilities, including taking life more generally as their base for career decision making. Emerging notions of career espouse related themes (e.g. Weick 1996). This chapter's stories offer potential insights into some of the dynamics and challenges people may experience as they live partly beyond organizational boundaries.

In addressing such themes this chapter is in related territory to that of Eaton and Bailyn (Chapter 9). In the powerful motif they use, what was ground (life as the background to career) becomes figure, to be paid attention to as a whole, so that notions such as purpose, achievement, and success are brought into question.

Rosenwald and Ochberg (1992) identify how the individual can live from alternative values:

We imagine that it is possible, though surely difficult, to enlarge the range of personal narrative. Individuals and communities can become aware of the political–cultural conditions that have led to the circumscription of discourse. If a critique of these

conditions occurs widely, it may alter not only how individuals construe their identities but also how they talk to one another and indirectly to the social order itself.
Discourse mediates between the fate of the individual and the larger order of
things.   (p. 2)

Those who would free themselves of their own culture's restrictions must find alternative conceptions of social engagement through which to develop their identities.
This too makes liberation difficult.   (p. 15)

Thus issues of society and control are always in the background (if not
featuring more prominently) when we articulate and hear life stories.

Leaving Journeys

Once I had set my core criteria for inclusion in the research—that people felt
they *had* to move from a particular job and were not doing so for promotion—I let the sampling inform me of different patterns people's lives took. I
identified suitable participants through contacts, a mailshot, and writing
about the research in a journal article inviting volunteers.

   It was characteristic of the research, and of my learning about women
leaving jobs, that there was no common pattern to people's leaving journeys.
Three people were forced to leave and two were placed under pressure to do
so. Most of these already wanted to leave of their own accord. The remaining
eleven more freely chose to leave, but then described pressing reasons for
doing so. Despite their dissatisfactions, not all the research participants
actually left employment. One contemplated leaving but then stayed in
her job temporarily; two others found new jobs before moving on. These
potentially different groups of people made very similar comments about
organizational life and career issues. The data, and other confirmatory
sources, therefore suggest that the issues they faced are more widely
relevant, and that leaving is one possible response. Given this sense of
resemblance, I treated the accounts as an array of related stories.

Multiple reasons

There was much diversity in the reasons people gave for wanting to leave
organizations, and there were typically multiple themes or issues in any one
story. This in itself was one of the study's main findings. Attempts to arrive at
simple explanations of women managers' behavior in this respect are therefore futile and inappropriate. Elaborating the themes that did appear, and
portraying the decisions as complex and multi-stranded, brought about a
major realization of the original research intent to portray experiences from
the women's perspectives. It was answering my original question and

answering back to potentially negative framings of women's decisions. Also, it soon became apparent that the women's stories were not about career alone but about life choices—and this too I sought to depict.

To be congruent with the stories told to me, I wanted to write accounts incorporating a mixture of voices and emotional tones; feelings of power *and* powerlessness; achievements *and* difficulties/stress. Narrative form can incorporate expectations of neatness, linearity, and singularity of plot line, coherence between past, present, and future. I suggest we need sometimes to recognize lives as more fittingly reflected by incongruence, multiplicity, or discontinuity of action and rationale, and not seek to tidy this up. We can instead look for aesthetic qualities of raggedness, incompleteness, and so on, if these are congruent to the tale told. In this research, for example, it was appropriate to write stories in which people identified multiple reasons for moving on, and would sometimes designate more than one as the 'main' reason, because this was the form of their narrative. This raises challenges for researchers about whether we can hear and tell multifaceted stories with incongruent aspects and not seek to close the gestalt.

Key Dynamics in Women's Accounts of Leaving or Wanting to Leave Employment

I am wary about overgeneralizing, about speaking as if there is more coherence and certainty in research material than is warranted, in order to smooth a theoretical narrative. I am seeking to honor the diversity in and process quality of the data. A summarized version is, however, necessarily selective. Below I examine themes in people's decisions to move on in their careers and lives. The typology offered is organized in terms of key dynamics represented in people's stories. It none the less fits my theoretical stance of holding ideas firmly but lightly, because it does not offer well-defined, mutually exclusive categories. Instead, stories placed under one heading share qualities or themes with those under other headings. The stories allocated to a particular grouping are more exemplars of their type. (And I appreciate that I could have adopted a different categorization initially, and so arrived at a different contribution to theorizing. Thus we come to tell selected theoretical truths about our research material.)

Within its frame, this is an initial but incomplete mapping of why women might leave senior management positions. It does not attend to issues of race or elder-care, for example, and I might expect a wider range of factors to emerge given a more extensive sampling. I shall describe each dynamic in some detail to show the complex of career/life decision making and the complex interweavings of individual and contextual factors to which the women paid attention.

Wanting different lifestyles

Four people in the sample come into this category and their stories have some relatively common characteristics. The women have shown much achievement and career success. Three had reached senior posts and had been highly committed to employment for many years. The fourth had developed career aspirations later in her work history. All now wanted to develop other aspects of themselves, which their working lives and who they had become as successful managers were not allowing them space to do. Kathy, for example, talked about wanting to 'go off in a completely new direction' (p. 54). (All page numbers quoted are from Marshall 1995 unless otherwise stated.)

Christina looked back at the organization in which, as Personnel Director, she had shaped several phases of significant change, and concluded:

In many ways it was a very repressive place to be, and I was sick to death of feeling compromised and had had enough of it. I'd put an enormous amount of work into my time there, had done everything I believed it possible for me to do.   (p. 62)

I really didn't feel I could be me, I had to be the person people expected me to be.   (p. 62)

Christina's story shows a strengthening sense of self-discovery, and increasing vitality and clarity of judgment, as she took more control of her career/life. Moving on, which was associated with several activities that helped make the transition to a reconnection with muted notions of self and interests, provided a release of energy and a sense of being a renewed person, which is at the heart of her account. 'One of the reasons I feel so youthful is that I recognize myself now as the person I was twenty years ago, and not the person I've been in between. The things that amuse me and the way I express myself are much more like they were then' (p. 62).

All four people wanted time and space to see what emerged. All were seeking a better fit between who they are and what they do, but needed an opening in their lives out of which fresh, more personally meaningful, possibilities might emerge.

Claire's story shows the complexity of multiple reasons for leaving, and the difficulties of trying to find a satisfactory explanation of one's behavior to give others in a social world of constrained images. She had been in her Personnel Director post for eighteen months. A major restructuring program was planned and expected to take two to three years. She realized that, while she was willing to help the organization make the first moves, she did not want to see this through:

I knew that I didn't want to go and do something else, I just wanted to stop. It's all I knew. I wanted out of the organization, corporate life, power, just to get out. I'd done it for twenty years and it was enough. But I had no clue about doing anything else. I just wanted to do nothing. And that was extremely hard for everyone I talked to to understand.   (p. 78)

She wanted 'to do all those things [she] hadn't done for the past twenty years', such as lunching with friends, going to exhibitions, getting up late, and handing her husband a gin and tonic when he arrived home from work. 'I wanted to switch part of my brain off for a while, so that I could feed another part of it' (p. 78).

Claire took charge of her life, and forced her decision through in the face of everyone's inability to understand. Some people thought, for example, that she would do something 'worthwhile' like study, expecting that she could not do 'nothing'. Her husband forcefully resisted her choice. He had married a professional woman and did not want her to become something else. Claire no longer wanted to do 'the right thing', as a received imperative from outside herself. She was determined to make a significant change, but noted how difficult it was for people to believe that she had had enough of high pressure living. 'I did feel some pressure to find a good reason, as opposed to just saying "I want to stop working because I've had enough and want a good rest". I had to find that good reason for everybody, including my husband' (p. 78).

Looking for an explanation to give others, Claire highlighted another factor in her decision making—that she was unlikely to be able to have a family given the busy life she was leading, was worried about time running out, and wanted to create space for this to happen. Saying this was 'embellishing a little', but ironically this stereotyped women's priority was the reason other people found easiest to believe. 'So then I had a ball for nine months. It was wonderful, just bliss' (p. 79). Claire thoroughly enjoyed herself, did not feel guilty, and regained her sense of vitality. Then she was enticed back by an invitation from an old friend to do some consultancy.

The four women in this category, and others, talked about 'no longer feeling driven' by internalized injunctions to work hard, prove themselves, do worthwhile things, and so on that had previously shaped their behavior. Instead, they were now in charge, generating their own directions, not working from received notions of success or career.

I noticed once I had grouped these stories together that all the managers were in Personnel (four of the five people in the study who were). Is this the nature of such women's jobs? The managers had lost touch with themselves and their needs, partly through being so responsive to other people's and their organizations' demands. Claire made this connection directly: 'Having been in a profession where you spend most of your time listening to other people, it was very important for me to feed myself and get some nourishment for me' (p. 81).

Wanting a more balanced life

There was only one person in the research sample who had young children and the extra life demands that this can bring. Her situation was especially demanding because of a long commuting journey; she often stayed away from home during the week. (When I was contacting potential participants for the research, I was told that many parents, especially those who have reached middle management levels and above, are using various forms of childcare and domestic help to manage combinations of employment and family lives, and so are less likely than might be expected to decide to pause their careers.)

Sarah was initiating a managerial function in a legal organization. The post had a limited timescale for her, because running the function would not have engrossed her sufficiently. So she saw this phase through and then left. But the primary reason for wanting to leave was that she could not balance the rest of her life with her job.

Undoubtably the most important factor for me was that I just wasn't seeing enough of my children and husband.   (p. 110)

I had two half-lives . . . and half and half didn't amount to one at all. It was a grey existence . . .   (p. 110)

The price was too much. The price is just loss of the rest of yourself, the rest of things that go to make up a civilized existence. A balance. I just couldn't balance any-thing.   (p. 110)

It sounds terribly undedicated or whatever, but I keep coming back to getting the balance right. I just felt I'd gone so far one way that I really needed to let the pendulum swing the other way for a while and then find the middle ground. (p. 113)

Sarah acknowledged that she had wondered whether delaying her return to employment might jeopardize her future choices, but also felt that life would change again: 'I'm quite happy to wait' (p. 113). Several people had been concerned that they might put themselves beyond the realm of employment for ever, but by the close of the study it was readily apparent that this had not been the case; that new, externally generated, opportunities or initiatives from them had emerged.

Leaving change roles that became untenable

Most of the research participants were involved in facilitating organizational change in one form or another and were successful in doing so. But for four people who had also previously been successful in these terms decisions to leave were made in extreme situations in which they were the leaders for significant change programs and the initiatives proved exceedingly difficult. Among these stories there were five interesting, although not wholly common, characteristics.

(a) The managers and the *change initiatives had initially been successful*, but then other powerful people had begun to mobilize against them, and to attack the woman manager as the figurehead. Patricia, a Nursing Director in a North American hospital, for example, had undertaken a major change program towards more participative decision making, enhancing the roles of nursing and other personnel. Improvements in patient care had resulted. Her Chief Executive Officer (CEO) asked her to disseminate such changes in other parts of the hospital. As she sought to do so, the doctors mobilized to resist the resulting shifts in power, in which their positions were threatened.

(b) *Senior figures*, who were advocating change in private, *did not support them in public*. Patricia reported this as a repeated dynamic, which she sought to challenge.

And through all this I was very supported by the CEO. When I would go back to him and say, 'In this meeting, when some of these things were questioned, you didn't really come out and support this, is this indeed what you still want to happen?', he would absolutely assure me that 'yes', it must go on, it cannot be stopped, they will come round to our way of thinking, but we must proceed ahead. And so there was a lot of encouragement to continue with this change process.   (p. 166)

But change was not being managed carefully organization-wide, and, despite her challenges, the CEO still failed to give public support: 'So in the back room I was very supported . . . but when it came to the open forum with the other administrators I always felt that I was being hung out to dry a little bit' (p. 166). When there was confrontation on a critical issue, the CEO sided with the doctors and let Patricia be used as the scapegoat. She was dismissed—with a compensatory settlement.

(c) *The women become isolated*. Relationships with their potential political rivals were already strained, but as the change initiatives became challenged many of their previous allies became unwilling or unable to support them. This is an interesting dynamic, as in several of these cases the women were acting on behalf of people with less organizational and social power than themselves. How much support it was appropriate for them to expect was, therefore, a challenging issue, as many of their allies were even more vulnerable than the change agents. For Patricia it was this withdrawal of support from those she had considered colleagues which was the most disappointing aspect of the events.

(d) *They became overcommitted to work*, losing other sources of perspective in their lives. Patricia noted with hindsight that she had funneled her life down to employment alone and so had eroded her own energy, becoming seriously tired as she sought to adjust her strategies and facilitate change in an increasingly unsupportive setting. She contrasted this with earlier challenging jobs, in which having a home life with teenage children had been a rich balancing factor for her.

(e) It was interesting, however, that the managers carried on, working actively, revising their change strategies, not being willing to be deterred. In doing so *they disregarded their own safety*. It seemed that this was an intentional or semi-intentional choice. When asked whether she had taken enough account of organizational politics in her activities, Patricia responded that she deliberately 'did not want to resort to playing politics'; she wanted to 'play it straight'. She wanted to model in her approach the revised image of organizational functioning that the change initiative was advocating. Patricia was too committed to the potential changes to heed her own concerns, to trust her gut reaction, which was telling her 'slow down, there's something wrong here'. But she also said that she did not want to be 'smart' enough not to try for what is sometimes unattainable. She had to be committed to her job and, as an organizational leader, to have thoughts on how the organization could be different, to make her working life worthwhile.

Patricia thought she probably knew two years before she left that the CEO's failure to support her publicly was dangerous. But she carried on trying to work through other sources of power and influence. Her focus was on the changes, not on her own security. 'I wanted to believe in what was happening. It wasn't that important to me to keep my job *per se*, but we were building something; it was important for both patient care and the profession of nursing . . .' (p. 168).

Patricia thought that women were more likely than men to disregard personal safety and push for goals they believe in: 'So, with any encouragement at all, we [women] will go forward and continue to pursue those goals. I think men are more political than women. We look at what the value is, and I think men look at whether this is going to fly. They're maybe not so committed' (p. 168).

These situations persisted until three of the women decided that 'the personal cost was too great' and to desist. One wrote a proposal for reorganizing her function that consolidated prior changes and made good organizational sense. She did not include a position for herself, thus making herself redundant. Patricia's CEO promised her support and the continuation of the change program until her penultimate day in the organization. He then dismissed her.

In these stories the women's value orientations are prominent, as is their willingness to work for visions of social change enacted through organizational processes.

Blocked promotion prospects

Two people in the sample especially reported not feeling fully stretched, having to push to achieve promotion, and seeing jobs go to other (male) people, some of whom they judged less competent than themselves. Mercedes had previously moved on to a new organization each time this had happened to her:

There are two things you can do if you're going to whinge [complain]. One, you can come to terms with what you're whinging [complaining] about and make the best of it and keep quiet. Or you can leave. And I go by the latter code really.   (p. 207)

She was in local government, making this more possible. She had moved organization three times during the previous eight years. But she had become too senior to do this easily. Her ambitions to be Director in her then authority had just been disappointed—and she could do her job 'standing on her head'. She had contemplated leaving, but by the time the interview came she had decided against. Her several reasons for staying, at least temporarily, were that she enjoyed her high salary and what it could buy, did not want to be beaten, and was determined to retire as a Director rather than as the deputy she then was. She was also watching her age (she was older than many new director appointees) and whether she would have to compromise and put on an act (of more masculine characteristics) at interview to gain consideration. By the end of the research she had moved organization again, taking up a Director post.

The other person in this situation, Stevie, was group manager in sales in a chemical company. Although there was little overt discrimination in her organization, she came to believe that covert processes were operating. 'For a long time I was of the opinion that . . . if you were good you'd make it. I hung onto this for about five years until the overwhelming evidence was that it's not enough to be good or better. There's accumulated stuff that's unconscious discrimination' (p. 212).

She described the 'general erosion' in career terms she later realized had been happening: she had not progressed as quickly as she thought she should, or as quickly as men recruited at the same time as her; she had had to push hard for promotions, and was not very stretched when they did come. Also she had to prove herself anew in each job; somehow her reputation did not accrue, as she saw men's doing. Stevie believed that her track record of achievement could not outweigh the fact that she did not fit the company's dominant cultural image of success.

People have an image of what a successful [company] manager is, how they behave, how they look and are, how they communicate and manage. And that is a [company] clone. Typically it's a man who has a wife who doesn't work, so he's geographically flexible. He probably has kids; if he hasn't he is a good sportsman and has a wonderful social life. He's one of the boys, he doesn't do anything excessively, he doesn't challenge or make waves. Pretty smart. A good guy. So when women come along they don't fit into any of those things.   (p. 215)

Stevie had already violated this image in more ways than being female. She had also talked back to a senior manager, following her own value of being blunt and honest but knowing that she challenged organizational norms, and had thus acquired him as a powerful enemy able to limit her progression opportunities.

No longer wanting to battle

The two people in this categorization were in the older age group in the sample. Their stories provide a conceptual sequel to those of limited career opportunities above. Both had achieved much in their careers and been pioneers as women in their occupational settings. But these achievements had had to be fought for, and the ground continually protected in order to maintain position and respect from others. Their energies for engaging in this added 'work' had eventually flagged.

Margaret was a manager in banking. She had spent over thirty years with one bank, and had had to fight every step of the way to be allowed necessary training or promotion. She was usually the most senior woman people had encountered: 'obviously, wherever I went I was a peculiar animal' (p. 242).

As Margaret felt that promotions had been given her on sufferance, to appease her and improve the bank's image, she had not developed faith in herself and her competence. This was despite her demonstrable successes in professional examinations and circles.

I always thought I got there because they thought 'It's a woman, so we'll just keep her quiet and we can say we've got a woman here,' not because of my ability. I never believed in my ability, and it's only since I've left the bank and seen people's reactions to me that I've begun to think maybe I wasn't so bad after all, and maybe I did get there on ability. But I never believed in myself during the job.   (p. 243)

Margaret could not discuss these issues with anyone directly, feeling isolated as a woman in a male-dominated environment and being preoccupied with maintaining her outward image and skills of professional competence. She could not, therefore, incorporate any alternative feedback she could trust into this picture of self-doubt.

Moving into senior management, she had relaxed more than usual after gaining promotion. She thought she had achieved her ultimate grade and was now weary of battling. Before she could find out whether this situation was temporary, pressures on banking because of recession had further eroded her energy and enthusiasm.

Reluctantly at first, she accepted an offer of early retirement. But moving on released her energy. After a pause of only a few months she had found a new job and was very successful, being promoted quickly—and she was able to have the confidence in her abilities, and positive feedback, that she had previously been largely denied.

Fighting for legitimacy

The following account is distinctive in the research for several reasons, not least because this person withdrew her carefully crafted story at a late stage and I had to write a skeletal version to include as data instead.

Ruth had been 'out' as a lesbian for several years, and had had to struggle to create a positive identity, acceptable to others. She was the departmental manager in an organizational context in which people were overtly committed to equality, but the atmosphere was charged and uncertain, with considerable ambivalence about authority. Ruth's attempts to take a managerial stance were sometimes undermined by her subordinates, and some senior managers were wary of her and of her department's work. Her ability to survive in this environment was further weakened by various incidents at work and by an unsettling experience in her personal life. Her vulnerability attracted people who had experiences of injustice or abuse to tell. Counseling them, and being unable to protect herself from feeling the issues they raised, was a further pressure. Looking back, Ruth believes her abilities to cope with these various demands were affected by internalizing devalued stereotypes of lesbians, undermining her feelings of competence and worth. She became defensive and excessively tired; the situation became too stressful. Eventually senior managers pressured her to leave and she negotiated a generous financial settlement to do so.

Ruth's experience shows how variable and conditional a lesbian manager's acceptability can be. It is an awkward sign that, while talking about gender and management is sometimes risky enough, there are issues that are mostly ignored, invisible, that point to dangerous territory for people to inhabit. There is little research in this area (Hall 1989 is an exception). Ruth's reasons for withdrawing her story mirror this sensitivity. The time with the organization and the experience of leaving had been traumatic for her. She had taken time to reorient her life. Two years later she was successfully in a middle management job, and accepted for who she was. Despite her wish to breach the relative secrecy about lesbian identities and politics surrounding sexual orientation, she experienced a diffuse anxiety that somehow people would recognize her even in a disguised account and that publication could threaten her current situation. That I should have partly to erase the story from the research therefore seemed very fitting.

Being forced or pressured to leave

Two women in the sample were forced out when new top managers took over their businesses. Both had intended to leave before this, but had wanted to do so in their own time. One was struggling to have her contribution accepted in an extremely male-dominated and quite unreformed (in these terms) organization. The other was highly successful in a female-dominated industry; unfortunately her success and public popularity did not endear her to her new boss. These two stories show some of the sharp end of interpersonal power dynamics at senior management levels that affect both men and women. I shall illustrate through Julia's account.

Julia was accepted for her competence in public relations, but otherwise felt consistently excluded and devalued by her senior management colleagues, all of whom were men. She had moved organizationally and geographically to take up her position, but soon felt some regret about this.

I've never come across such a chauvinistic environment in my life. (p. 279)

The men didn't want to know. They're all long-serving and didn't want their cozy 'club' disturbed. The only person who was half way decent to me was a fellow countryman . . . Basically they just couldn't cope with a woman in senior management at all. (p. 279)

By the end of her first year, Julia was already looking to move: 'I'd had enough, and wasn't happy. I wasn't going to fit in the environment. I'd actually done quite well by my own professional standards, but it was such an organization that you were basically lining yourself up to be hit with a big stick every day, no matter what you did' (p. 282). The political climate deteriorated further for Julia and for several other (male) senior managers when a new Chief Executive was appointed.

His view was that the way to manage a company was to create fear and have people bounce around. (p. 282)

The new Chief Executive . . . decided that my face didn't fit . . . Forget job descriptions and objectives and measuring any of that. He didn't like me in the role. He liked me, but not in the role. He told me that. (p. 283)

Some negotiations followed and Julia eventually left for another job. She was unusual in the sample in this, but she did not want the risk of leaving without financial security, explaining this as a significant and enduring aspect of her character and life pattern. She was subsequently very successful.

Three Cross-Woven Themes in People's Accounts

Through the stories there also ran three broader themes that appeared in different forms in different people's lives. These had significantly informed people's propensity for career/life transitions. They were: working in male-dominated environments; striving to maintain a viable sense of self; and experiencing stress and tiredness.

Working in male-dominated environments

Eleven of the women experienced significant dissatisfactions from working in what they termed 'male-dominated' organizational environments. They meant that men were strongly in the majority, that the *collective* dynamics of managerial life fitted negative stereotypes of masculine, adversarial, or exclusionary behavior, and that much recruitment was in 'like-image'. For most it was what happened after promotion or appointment beyond the organization's previous glass ceiling that mattered in their decision making. (The popular notion of glass ceiling can be a limiting metaphor. It implies that, once women are promoted beyond a previous barrier, much is resolved. But there are then challenges about inclusion, exercising power, having credibility, and so on that should not be underestimated.)

Interpersonal behavior at senior levels was described as often very aggressive, rude, territorial, status conscious, and hostile; with conflict, power struggles, politicking, bullying, and intimidation as common features. Research participants (variously) disliked the atmosphere of potential punishment and fear, 'the rough play of big boys', the 'hostile environment', and people running businesses on emotions and vindictiveness. They were shocked at these ways of operating, and thought them ineffective and energy wasting. They preferred working strategies they described variously as professional, effectiveness based, blunt, and honest.

The women felt 'at odds' in these organizational environments in several ways. They especially lacked available allies among their colleagues, reducing their potential job effectiveness and ability to influence decision making. It seemed that they were not accepted into informal networks despite their formal appointment and so had limited power bases; several became isolated.

It took me some time to realize that the women were describing the classic dynamics of tokenism—visibility, polarization effects, and assimilation to stereotypes—described by Kanter in 1977 as operating when there may be one or a few people who are in a relative minority in a group. She identified these dynamics in relation to gender among a company's sales force, but showed that they could operate across various sorts of socially salient differences. It seems from my research that they are now sometimes apparent at senior management team and Board levels.

Most managers' earlier careers had not prepared them for the dynamics of power and exclusion they encountered. They simply had not met such environments; they therefore had few coping strategies established and had to develop these in highly visible organizational positions. These processes pose many dilemmas of identity and effectiveness for the tokens (and are challenging for members of the dominant group who are under pressure not to 'break cultural ranks' and relate more authentically with tokens).

Several of the managers emphasized that they left not because they could not cope with these dynamics, but because they did not respect or want to be part of that way of operating. They wanted to work in more productive, less repressive environments.

Striving to maintain a viable sense of self

Many of the managers found it hard to maintain a viable sense of self, acceptable to themselves. They were especially experiencing significant, and for some increasing, incongruities between their internal and external images. Some of the processes involved were: invisibility, against which they had to assert themselves as senior managers; being judged against gendered images, which typically did not expect competence from women; finding success images to be those of men; and not liking what they had become as they adopted tougher, more adversarial, and masked styles to match their organizational environments and be effective. One woman described how the costs of acting 'out of character'—and the 'tremendous tiredness'—had become more evident. Another felt that she had lost a centered sense of self as she tried to meet the multiple expectations of work colleagues and family members. Another reflected: 'I guess, in the end, that was the fundamental thing which made me leave, because over a period of time it was just too difficult to hold together a coherent sense of self within all those competing expectations' (p. 143).

Some people may see such pressures as aspects of career accommodation for everyone (I would question this normality or its desirability), but they become more pointed when managers are also judged against idealized or devalued gender stereotypes.

Many of the women wanted to feel more authentic and coherent, and this was a major motivation in moving on. They wanted to work in organizational cultures in which they could be more fully 'themselves'. Some people would question whether coherence of self is possible in postmodern times. But this call was not for a romantic unity of personhood. Rather it was for full access to the multiple aspects of themselves, which they saw as the sources of their integrity, decision-making senses, and personal, and ultimately organizational, power. But it is difficult to maintain a viable sense of self in hostile environments—and so sometimes the powerful choice is to leave, releasing energy as a result.

Experiencing stress and tiredness

Many of the research participants reported excessive stress and tiredness, largely due to the additional work they undertook to present themselves and maintain job effectiveness in hostile cultures (rather than to job demands). Many also realized later that, as they had tried alternative strategies for being effective in these circumstances, they had become overcommitted to work and that the rest of their lives had been neglected, reducing further their bases of energy and support. Rather than casting doubt on women's capabilities, the data testify to strengths these people showed. Many had stayed over-long in highly demanding environments because of how 'tough' they were. Perhaps they were too tough for their own good.

This research material offers interesting insights into some dynamics that may underly some statistics of 'overworking' (Brett *et al.* 1998; Peiperl and Jones 1998). It shows especially that there may be complex interplays of individual and contextual influences prompting and sustaining such behavior.

In Reflection

In this section I shall relate the above material to career theorizing by exploring several selected themes and dynamics. These are usually not common to the whole group, but illuminated through different people's stories. Although I shall talk of women, because the data are grounded in women's lives, I do not expect all of these processes to be exclusive to women. However, they may often manifest differently in men's lives. The critical theorist in me maintains a watchfulness about whether gender inequalities might be replicated inadvertently in new conceptions of career.

One strong impression the collected stories give is of a senior organizational world that is often rejecting or hostile toward the women, in which they have repeatedly adjusted themselves and their behavior to seek effectiveness. This context is a major factor not only in prompting career movement, but also in challenging their attachment to employment and leading them to seek replenishing spaces that are 'outside' this world. A dilemma that has long been apparent in research on women in management is whether the adaptations of self many undertake to *survive* in organizations (Sheppard 1989) put their abilities to *thrive* in jeopardy. Many of the women in this study were making decisions based on the health of their whole lives to seek the places in which they might thrive, and many reported personal development as an aspect of the career transition process.

Issues of identity were highly significant in the research data; an inability to achieve a viable identity was a factor prompting movement. Despite the ways in which women had resisted pressures or shown their unwillingness to be molded, many had experienced personal erosion in their jobs that had become apparent to them in realizations that the costs they were paying were too great for the beneficial impacts they were having. They chose not to go on coping, in the hope that they could thrive elsewhere. The search to (re)gain sight of what was valuable in life or a centered sense of self was key for several people, leading them to set in train an evolving process of self-recovery and/or self-discovery.

It seemed that previously research participants had often been outer-directed—for example, internalizing received messages about achievement (these may well have been authentic for them at the time), or working on behalf of some notions of 'the greater good'. They had comparatively sup-pressed or subdued their own perceptions and needs. In deciding to move on, many shifted toward paying more attention to inner voices, wishes, and interpretations, sometimes prioritizing these in a highly focused way at key decision points (e.g. Claire). Some seemed, however, to find this difficult to justify, especially if they were then putting their own needs before those of others. They wanted to feel assured that they had tried sufficiently hard to address organizational issues before they could give themselves 'permission' to be more self-oriented. One important discrimination that many had to make was *when it was appropriate to persist* in a challenging environment and *when it was appropriate to desist*. The challenge of distinguishing this choice is most apparent in the change agents' stories. They pushed them-selves to stay in difficult situations as champions of the potential for change. They did not want to concede, partly unwilling to contribute to potential images of women as 'weak'. They had little if any feedback they could trust because they were isolated from colleagues. They pushed themselves beyond their limits.

So these career transitions are highly context influenced, but are simulta-neously strongly based in personal values and seeking self-realization. Again the form they took—of *multiple reasons* for moving on—is important. The stories give some glimpses into complex decision making that interweaves lives and careers. They show that factors other than women's reproductive roles figure significantly in shaping their careers. They show an openness to movement and change in the lives studied, and the continually unfolding nature of this. Here the research data are highly congruent with conclusions reached by Gunz, Evans, and Jalland (Chapter 2) that boundaries in career terms are now often valuably conceptualized as aspects of making sense of one's place in the world. With Weick (1996) I would see this as typically a continually evolving process, with enactment as a key aspect both emerging from life process and providing definition for its further development.

In the collection of stories offered above there are indications of what I would broadly call mid-life work. In Chapter 4 of this volume Boyatzis and Kolb offer a highly articulated mapping of potential modes of adaptation and growth. From my interest in storied lives I am both interested in this and wary about applying its categories and clarities to complexly unfolding lives. These women's stories could, none the less, be seen as explorations into different forms of generativity. In showing wide-ranging concerns and an active attention to legitimizing self-care alongside service to others, their meanings of generativity contrast with those advocated in Kanai *et al.* (1998), which have a narrower focus and a clarity of other-directedness. It would be inappropriate to over-interpret these apparent differences, given the many ways in which the databases and research approaches of the two studies vary. Sources such as Gallos (1989) would, however, suggest that notions of mid-life development are potentially gender associated.

Telling one's life

Telling their life narratives self-reflectively, to me or other people who would hear with respect, was part of many women's development. Their stories were grounded in personal (and often social and political) truths that needed to be told. (As stories are construction, I am not suggesting that there is an objective truth about a life. Rather, I believe that there are narratives that are 'true' to a person's experience at a particular time, and shape the life lived, that can be validated or not by interpersonal and social processes. Labeling such stories as outmoded 'social realism' or 'women's voices' is a dismissive, disparaging classification—paradoxically claiming a greater right to 'truth'.) The women were taking authority and power to assign meanings in their lives, and so challenging dominant social rhetorics, about women's life patterns and/or the value placed on hierarchic 'success' in employment, which were likely to devalue their choices. Stories *fully* told were part of them moving on.

Individuals may be able to go beyond career/life plot lines that are sanctioned in society's narrative 'frames of intelligibility' (Rosenwald and Ochberg 1992), toward developing alternative meanings. Whether the diverse stories then told, and enacted, can influence dominant value systems and theoretical frames is an interesting issue. Established forms of conceptualization and valuing are highly resilient and can be replicated in the incorporation of 'new' ideas. For example, flexible work notions are now sometimes associated with significant inequalities of control, pay, and opportunities, which are sometimes gender associated. Ideals of high commitment and overworking are still prevalent in organizational life.

Theorizing lives

With this chapter's material I am contributing to notions of women's flexible careers. But I do so only with great caution. This theoretical narrative has much potential value. Nicholson and West (1988), for example, argued that 'important differences in career paths and patterns of men and women' mean that, in these terms, 'men represent the past and women the future of organizational society' (p. 216). They identified two (of five) trends in women's career development as 'their more spontaneous and "existentialist" value-driven career orientations' (p. 216) and 'their retention of high levels of upward and radical career moves much later in their careers than men' (p. 216). The data above provide further confirmation for such patterns, but suggest that the prompting is not value driven alone. The contributions that gender/power patterns at senior management levels are making to career movement cannot be ignored, for example.

A theoretical contributor who gives a particularly appealing account of flexible careers/lives is Bateson (1989). She uses the core metaphor of 'composing a life', inviting us to see life as 'improvisations, discovering the shape of our creation along the way, rather than pursuing a vision already defined' (p. 1). Her ideas link with those of emergent career 'planning' I have developed elsewhere (Marshall 1989). She suggests that:

It is time now to explore the creative potential of interrupted and conflicted lives, where energies are not narrowly focused or permanently pointed toward a single ambition.   (Bateson 1989: 9)

Composing a life involves a continual reimagining of the future and reinterpretations of the past to give meaning in the present.   (Bateson 1989: 9)

Is Bateson's positive framing for discontinuous, changeful experience a viable discourse? It seems radical and holds much potential to honor data such as those presented above. And it may do us a disservice by painting a positive gloss on all experience, inviting us to make more virtue than is warranted out of challenging, sometimes stressful, necessity. Neither does it account for the stressful experiences of living at impasses that are apparent in several women's stories. The advocacy to hear multiple, potentially conflicting, voices in any one narrative I have presented here seeks to go beyond Bateson and incorporate her suggestions into a broader framing. With her, however, I think we need usually to conceptualize careers beyond the boundaries of organizations, occupational choices, and employment, so that lives provide the basic form, value base, and boundaries—which are then open to continuing revision.

In this chapter I have been seeking to hear the women's stories presented within their own registers, resisting temptations (internalized academic injunctions) to frame them from within established or emerging career theorizing. This is my academic parallel to telling a good enough life story, so that it (narrative and life) can then move on. How we theorize may be 'right' in its time, but it is always a construction. Women managers' stories are still trapped in a web of frames of meaning underpinned by notions of male/female differences. (I have not escaped them here.) We need a truly generative leap to tell life stories that are beyond gender themes altogether (glorifying women as different does not achieve this). So what we say can be considered true (against appropriate warrants of judgment) within a systemic, evolving process, rather than as definitive 'truth'.

References

Bateson, M. C. (1989), *Composing a Life* (New York: Plume).

Brett, J. M., and Stroh, L. K. (1994), 'Turnover of Female Managers', in M. J. Davidson and R. J. Burke (eds.), *Women in Management: Current Research Issues* (London: Paul Chapman).

—— Medvec, V., and Stroh, L. K. (1998), 'The Overworked American Manager', paper presented at Career Realities Conference, London Business School.

Collinson, D., and Hearn, J. (1994). 'Naming Men as Men: Implications for Work, Organization and Management', *Gender, Work and Organization*, 1(1): 2–22.

Denzin, N. K. (1997), *Interpretive Ethnography: Ethnographic Practices for the 21st Century* (Thousand Oaks, Calif.: Sage).

Gallos, J. V. (1989), 'Exploring Women's Development: Implications for Career Theory, Practice and Research', in M. B. Arthur, D. T. Hall, and B. S. Lawrence (eds.), *Handbook of Career Theory* (Cambridge: Cambridge University Press).

Hall, M. (1989), 'Private Experiences in the Public Domain: Lesbians in Organizations', in J. Hearn, D. L. Sheppard, P. Tancred-Sheriff, and G. Burrell (eds.), *The Sexuality of Organization* (London: Sage).

Kanai, T., Fujii, H., and Hirakimoto, H. (1998), 'The Impacts of Mentorship upon Middle Managers' Psychological Empowerment and their Leadership Behavior: Empirical Analyses of Direct and Indirect Impacts', paper presented at Career Realities Conference, London Business School.

Kanter, R. M. (1977), *Men and Women of the Corporation* (New York: Basic Books).

Lincoln, Y. S. (1997), 'Self, Subject, Audience, Text: Living at the Edge, Writing in the Margins', in W. G. Tierney and Y. S. Lincoln (eds.), *Representation and the Text: Re-Framing the Narrative Voice* (Alba New York: State University of New York Press).

—— and Denzin, N. K. (1994), 'Introduction: Entering the Field of Qualitative Research', in N. K. Denzin and Y. S. Lincoln (eds.), *The Handbook of Qualitative Research* (Thousand Oaks, Calif.: Sage).

Marshall, J. (1989), 'Re-Visioning Career Concepts: A Femininist Invitation', in M. B. Arthur, D. T. Hall, and B. S. Lawrence (eds.), *Handbook of Career Theory* (Cambridge: Cambridge University Press).

—— (1995), *Women Managers Moving On: Exploring Career and Life Choices* (London: International Thomson Publishing Europe).

Mumby, D. K. (1993), *Narrative and Social Control: Critical Perspectives* (Thousand Oaks, Calif.: Sage).

Nicholson, N., and West, M. (1988), *Managerial Job Change: Men and Women in Transition* (Cambridge: Cambridge University Press).

Peiperl, M. A., and Jones, B. C. (1998), 'Workaholics and Overworkers: Productivity or Pathology?', paper presented at Career Realities Conference, London Business School.

Rosenwald, G. C., and Ochberg, R. L. (1992), *Storied Lives: The Cultural Politics of Self-Understanding* (New Haven: Yale University Press).

Rosin, H. M., and Korabik, K. (1991), 'Workplace Variables, Affective Responses, and Intentions to Leave Among Women Managers', *Journal of Occupational Psychology*, 64: 317–30.

—— —— (1992), 'Corporate Flight of Women Managers: Moving from Fiction to Fact', *Women in Management Review*, 7/3: 31–5.

Sheppard, D. L. (1989), 'Organizations, Power and Sexuality: The Image and Self-Image of Women Managers', in J. Hearn, D. L. Sheppard, P. Tancred-Sheriff, and G. Burrell (eds.), *The Sexuality of Organization* (London: Sage).

Stroh, L. K., and Senner, J. T. (1994), 'Female Top Executives: Turnover, Career Limitation, and Attitudes Towards the Work Place', *Industrial Relations Research Association Proceedings* (Dec.).

Taylor, A. (1986), 'Why Women Managers are Bailing Out', *Fortune*, 18 Aug., 16–23.

Weick, K. E. (1996), 'Enactment and the Boundaryless Career: Organizing as we Work', in M. B. Arthur and D. M. Rousseau (eds.), *The Boundaryless Career: A New Employment Principle for a New Organizational Era* (New York: Oxford University Press).

Exploring Boundaryless Careers in the French Context

Loïc Cadin, Anne-Françoise Bailly-Bender, and Véronique de Saint-Giniez

In the past few years, research in careers has questioned the supremacy of the organizational career, and proposed a new concept to refer to the discontinuities and new forms of mobility experienced by an increasing number of people in their professional lives. This 'new career' has also been called the 'boundaryless career' (Arthur and Rousseau 1996) and the 'post-corporate career' (Peiperl and Baruch 1997). In a similar way to the 'protean career' (Hall 1976), the new career is no longer shaped by organizational needs but emerges from actions and choices of individuals, who act as inter-organizational players in the market for competencies (Arthur *et al.* 1999). They manage their careers in a more autonomous fashion, moving between jobs, companies, or professions, in order to accumulate competencies and increase their employment value.

The boundaryless-career concept has been used in various empirical studies, ranging from the analysis of regional labor markets such as Silicon Valley (Saxenian 1996), to the analysis of careers in professions (Chapter 8), or in activities where major organizational changes have already occurred, such as in film-making (Jones and DeFillippi 1996), and the study of individual careers in one country (Arthur *et al.* 1999). Arthur and his colleagues interviewed seventy-five New Zealanders about their career experiences in the period 1985–95, during which New Zealand's economy underwent massive deregulation and restructuring. Their study highlighted how people

We thank Michael B. Arthur, who proposed us to replicate in France the research he had led in New Zealand, who was a source of constant support, and who helped us to improve this manuscript. We gratefully acknowledge Adrian Bender and Danuta Liebig, who were kind enough to read our work and make suggestions to correct our English.

managed their careers in a more idiosyncratic way, experienced professional transitions, and developed new specific career competencies over the restructuring period.

Following the New Zealand study, we were interested to conduct similar research in France, in a very different economic and social context. France had not undergone such massive changes as New Zealand. The transfer of public-owned companies to the private sector had been more limited, the public sector had remained relatively unchanged, and the restructuring of firms had been more gradual, owing in part to social-oriented labor legislation that had not been as dramatically revised as New Zealand's. Under such circumstances, we were interested to see whether similar new professional trajectories and career attitudes could be found in France, and, if so, what forms and conditions characterized them.

We used the same methodology as our colleagues in New Zealand and conducted in-depth interviews with seventy-eight French nationals broadly representative of the French workforce. This chapter presents a typology of career patterns that emerged from the analysis of the interviews. The underlying hypothesis is that these categories 'tell something' about the structural and cultural contexts in which careers develop.

Careers have traditionally been studied under two different and sometimes conflicting perspectives: the subjective perspective, which focuses on the person, and his or her self-perceptions, motivations, and sense of personal competencies; and the objective perspective, which emphasizes the structural aspects of careers in relation to organizations, labor markets, or employment cultures (Schein 1984; Derr and Laurent 1989). Although these two streams of research have considerably increased our knowledge of careers, further research about the concrete aspects of the construction of careers needs to go beyond the subjective–objective duality (Bailyn 1989). Current economic and social transformations also mean that the social norms and models underlying objective career perspectives are being increasingly questioned (Hall and Mirvis 1996). Careers develop today in contexts that provide fewer guides to action, exercise less pressure for conformity, and allow more individual variations. As situations are 'weakened',[1] the old career models are less appealing and effective, and people are led to improvise and elaborate more idiosyncratic strategies (Weick 1996).

Weick notes, however, that this improvisation, although influenced by personality characteristics, occurs in social interactions during which people collectively elaborate new behavioral patterns. These may in turn become guides for action and lead to new institutionalized forms of careers and career management. The relationship between structure and action appears to be reversed, to the extent that structure originates from the micro-level of interactions, which comes to modify such institutions as the organizational vertical career and the traditional firm (see Chapter 6). Such processes occur in the long term and are difficult to grasp. However, as the current weakening of work situations leaves more space for the expression of subjectivity and idiosyncratic action, career analysis must shift to the study of social inter-actions. It must do so without neglecting the fact that such interactions do not take place in what is popularly called a 'social vacuum'.

Whereas social science has traditionally conceived of subjective and objective sides of social behavior as irreconcilable, recent sociological per-spectives (Giddens 1984; Barley 1989) propose to fuse these aspects. In doing so they turn the classical subjective–objective duality into a dialectical rela-tionship between the concrete level of situated interaction and the virtual level of institutions. According to these perspectives, individual actions are shaped by social contexts and at the same time contribute to produce and reproduce structural features of these contexts. Such views on social action allow for studies that take account of the structural and cultural dimensions of social systems in which people interact, without adopting an over-socialized conception of man (Wrong 1961). They allow for the study of how structural factors influence individual career strategies, as well as of how career strategies in turn reproduce or transform macro-variables such as rules of conduct and the distribution of resources.

In the first part of this chapter, we offer a brief presentation of the French economic and cultural context, as it stands out from the economic and sociological literature, along with some expected consequences of these macro-features on individual career strategies. We then present a taxonomy of five career patterns derived from the interview data we collected, and describe the elements that characterize these patterns. The taxonomy shows hybrid forms of career patterns between two 'ideal-types'—namely, the organizational career and the boundaryless career, which we call the *carrière nomade* in our French studies. Our study also highlights the mobilization of career competencies, some of them similar to the kind of competencies described by Arthur, Inkson, and Pringle (1999), others drawing more speci-fically on the structural and cultural features of French society and labor markets. Our conclusion deals with the possible implications of the research for the future nature of careers in France.

The French Context

We present below a summary of the literature about national features—social norms and employment practices—that may both encourage and constrain the construction of work careers in France.

Cultural aspects

The most extensive international comparison of work values so far made was conducted by the Dutch anthropologist Geert Hofstede, whose team analyzed over 116,000 questionnaires administered to IBM employees in seventy-two countries on five continents between 1967 and 1973 (Hofstede 1980; Bollinger and Hofstede 1987). The aim of the research was to highlight societal norms or value systems shared by the majority of people in a country. National cultures were conceived as 'collective mental programs', which account for the different ways of thinking between people of different countries.

Four dimensions emerged from the factorial analysis of the answers:

1. hierarchical power distance, measured from the questions about the perceived and preferred management style from the supervisor, as well as the fear of showing that one disagrees with one's boss;
2. avoidance of uncertainty, which relates to what extent the people of a given culture accept the uncertainty of the environment and worry about the future;
3. degree of *masculinity* of a culture, defined as the importance granted to promotion and financial success and to improving one's professional competencies; conversely, *femininity* values the quality of human relations at work and good working conditions;
4. degree of individualism, determined by the emphasis put on the satisfaction of individual needs at work, the preference given to individual decisions rather than collective ones, and a more utilitarian relationship with companies.

France does not differ greatly from Anglo-Saxon countries—which are the most individualistic countries in the survey—on the last dimension. However, France is characterized by high scores on the 'hierarchical power distance' and 'avoidance of uncertainty' dimensions, where the Anglo-Saxon countries have much lower scores. French culture is also considerably more feminine than Anglo-Saxon cultures. The implications of these results are that French people would generally tend to be risk averse, to prefer stable, rules-driven, and secure work situations, such as those provided by big companies, and to value professional achievement to a lesser extent than Anglo-Saxons. Such cultural features are consistent with the high proportion of people—one-third of the French working population—employed in either the civil service or state-owned companies.

Another cross-cultural study was conducted by the French sociologist Philippe d'Iribarne (1989), by means of document analysis and in-depth interviews with managers and employees of a French industrial company. The study covered three factories located in the USA, The Netherlands, and France. The author puts forward the hypothesis that the relationship between American workers and their supervisors is comparable to a commercial contract between peers, based on a fair exchange of the attainment of objectives against pay and promotion. D'Iribarne draws a parallel between the American culture of 'contract' and the foundations of the country by Protestant merchants. French workers tend to view their relationship with their boss in a very different way, which is less contract based than honor based. Workers expect trust and protection from their supervisor, whose legitimacy primarily derives from his or her technical expertise. In return, they commit themselves to do their best, following their own conception of what their professional duties are. According to d'Iribarne, the relationship between the supervisor and the workers can be described as a feudal exchange between a baron and vassals, whereby each party's conduct is ruled by moral codes of reciprocity, and where the relationship is long term and based on mutual fidelity. Although the author's methodology and historical analogies have been criticized, his analysis does account for French workers' resistance to formal objectives and for their emotional attachment to their employer. The latter was confirmed by a recent poll conducted in France and in the USA (Gibier 1997), which showed that 35 per cent of the French people interviewed feel attached to the company they work for, against 9 per cent of the US workers.

D'Iribarne also highlights the stratification of occupations among French workers, whereby some activities are considered to be more noble than others. Any professional field has its lower and upper jobs, with the status of the job defining the value of its incumbent. In France, the occupations involving services to individual clients are traditionally among the least valued. D'Iribarne relates this to the ancient contempt for servile behavior in feudal society. Again, although the historical explanation is controversial, there is little denying that French people look down on what they call 'little jobs' (*petits boulots*), which are chiefly in the booming service sector, and sometimes prefer to remain unemployed rather than accept such inferior jobs (d'Iribarne 1990).

A last cultural trait relevant to the theme of boundaryless careers is the traditional separation made between public and private life in French society. A distinctive aspect of the new career is the blurring of all kinds of boundaries, including those between organizational or professional communities and private networks of family members and friends. As people experience more work transitions and manage their careers more independently from firms, they come increasingly to rely on personal contacts for access into distinct arenas of activity and information (Raider and Burt 1996; Arthur *et al.* 1999). The French reluctance to use private networks in a utilitarian way for professional or business purposes has been little explored by empirical studies. However, signs of the legitimate frontier existing between private and professional matters can be seen in the particularly strong protection of the right of privacy in French law, which, for example, forbids the publication by the media of information or pictures regarding private lives (Kayser 1990). Political philosophy considers the differentiation between agora (public forum) and *for intérieur* (the inner thoughts and morale) as a condition for liberty and a protection against totalitarianism. French citizens also make a distinction between the public role and the private life of politicians and public figures. This distinction between the private and the professional sphere is echoed in the *savoir vivre* codes (informal rules of conduct), which prohibit *intéressé*[2] behavior with friends and family.

The functioning of French labor markets: institutional and economic aspects

A well-known characteristic of the French labor market is its emphasis on educational qualifications. French society has traditionally valued education, and selection by diploma has gained momentum since 1975, a period of growing unemployment (Vimont 1995). As more and more young people pass the *baccalauréat* (the equivalent of the A level[3]) and continue on to higher education, the increasing number of graduates makes it more difficult for unqualified people to find a job. This occurs even though a degree is no longer sufficient to guarantee a 'vertical' career (Goux 1991).

The French public and private sectors are famous for externalizing the detection and production of their elite to the *Grandes Écoles* (Bauer and Bertin-Mourot 1993). The importance of education received in defining the career path applies at all levels of the organizational hierarchy, as is shown in the comparative studies between France and Germany conducted by the LEST (Laboratoire d'Économie et de Sociologie du Travail) researchers based in Aix-en-Provence (Maurice *et al.* 1982). General education is much more valued in France than technical education, toward which people with lower academic performance are channeled. The stratification of jobs and careers by firms corresponds to the hierarchy established in the educational system. The education criterion is used as a means of segmenting the workforce between those who will have access to the better paid managerial and functional jobs and those who will remain in production. It also explains the wage differentials among production workers, other things being equal. The situation is different in Germany, where the two types of education appear complementary and are treated more equally than in France.

The same comparative studies highlight the following employment practices, which contribute to the predominance of organizational careers unfolding in just one or two firms. At the time of the French–German study (the 1970s), French technical education stopped before the *baccalauréat*. Production workers and employees were recruited at the bottom of the internal labor market and climbed up the hierarchy mainly through on-the-job training. These practices and the relatively poor quality of the training offered by the firms favored the acquisition of highly specific human capital, which did not encourage workers to change companies. In spite of recent efforts to promote professional education, there is still no such thing in France as the German dual system, which provides technical graduates with diplomas and qualifications valued by many firms and enables them to change employers more easily. A second factor is the emphasis put by firms on workers' seniority in the company and in the job. In contrast to Germany,

there is no immediate correspondence between the nature of the professional diploma and the job held in the firm, and a newly employed qualified
worker may have to start at a non-qualified job before being promoted. A
certain period of socialization in the company appears necessary before the
latter recognizes the qualification of the worker (Maurice 1993). Such practices, along with the fact that seniority is an important criterion in the
determination of wages, explain French workers' propensity to inscribe their
careers in firms' internal labor markets (Doeringer and Piore 1971).

Current economic realities accentuate the attraction of these internal
markets. Since 1975, France has been recording a persistently high level of
unemployment compared to Anglo-Saxon countries. French unemployment
stood at 9 per cent in 1983, and rose to 12.5 per cent by 1997, while what was
termed long-term unemployment stood at 36 per cent of the unemployed
population (DARES 1997). Economists generally attribute this situation to the
cost of French labor, especially for the less-qualified jobs, which accounts for
the reluctance of firms to employ new people when their business levels
improve (OECD 1992). A second factor is labor legislation, which restricts
workforce dismissals by imposing high financial costs on firms that lay off
more than thirty people at one time. In order to diminish the social cost of
massive redundancies, various government arrangements urged firms to
encourage the early retirement of their older workers. France now has one
of the lowest activity rates for workers above 55 among Western countries.[4]
Under such circumstances, French companies mainly adjust the level of
their workforce through early retirement and by sharply reducing their
recruitment, whereas US companies massively lay off and equally massively
employ when things are getting better (Fougère and Kramarz 1997). Although
some labor markets are more active than others—as is the case with jobs in
computing at the present time—employment is scarce in France. Moreover,
the best employment opportunities are reserved for young graduates and a
few experts with proven experience in a specific field.

The above forces caused inter-firm mobility to decrease between 1972 and
1985: 33 per cent of workers under 45 changed companies between 1972 and
1977, but only 23 per cent changed companies between 1980 and 1985. The
proportion slightly increased to 29 per cent between 1988 and 1993, but
chiefly as a consequence of the massive use of temporary work contracts,
which is another distinctive aspect of the French labor market since 1985
(INSEE 1994a). Other statistics show that 42 per cent of French workers—
excluding civil servants and people under short-term work contracts—have
been employed by the same company for more than ten years, this proportion rising to 56 per cent when considering only the people above 29 years
old (INSEE 1994b). All these elements draw the picture of rather closed labor
markets, whether internal or external, with high entry costs and especially
exit costs.

In conclusion, the cultural, economic, and institutional features of French
society appear quite unfavorable for the development of boundaryless

careers. People are rather risk-averse; they are reluctant to activate 'network-ing' strategies, define themselves by their occupation and hierarchical status, and still show some allegiance to their employers. The high level of unem-ployment is likely to increase the French workers' preference for 'safe' organ-izational careers and clearly accounts for the low inter-firm mobility. The large companies' practices contribute to this lack of mobility, as they dra-matically reduce their recruitment and base their hiring decisions on such criteria as the diploma, professional experience, and the age of the workers, which create new boundaries difficult to span for a majority of people

Yet, if the French context appears in many respects quite different from the New Zealand one, such a picture of national 'rigidities'—collective attitudes, norms, and market regulations—is oversimplified to the extent that it emerges in large part from comparative studies focusing on national differ-ences and cultural permanencies. In contrast, at the level of individual interactions, we may anticipate considerable variation in the way people deal with social norms and market constraints in constructing their careers. The preceding general characterization is also falsely static and does not take into account the cultural evolution undergone by France, like other Western countries, since the economic recession of the 1980s. A closer look at indi-vidual career strategies is thus likely to help us to refine these broad analyses, and suggest some dynamic processes that may now be underway in French society.

A Taxonomy of Career Patterns

Approach

Following the New Zealand study, in order to use a similar approach to study careers in France, we replicated the methodology used by the authors (Arthur *et al.* 1999). We randomly selected a sample comparable to theirs. We translated their semi-structured interview protocol and between March and July 1997 conducted interviews with seventy-eight persons, broadly representative of the French workforce. The sample's age range was between 25 and 60 (the average was 40) and 38 per cent of the sample were women.

We discovered that some French career patterns fit in perfectly well with established career models for boundaryless and organizational careers, but others could not be so labeled. We proceeded to construct a taxonomy following the methodology described by Demazière and Dubar (1997). First, we summarized every interview. We paid attention to the objective compon-ents of the career (number of employers, average seniority in different jobs, job components, reasons for changes, etc.) but also to the subjective aspects (such as people's explanations of the logic of their career patterns, and any reframing that was involved). After that, we sorted the interviews into categories created from a small number of interviews that we considered as typical and that had a 'function of attraction' (Demazière and Dubar 1997: 276) for the other interviews. That is, we worked from cases that seemed representative of the different career patterns we encountered.

Our taxonomy results from a trial-and-error process: 'the criteria are numerous and often vague at the beginning, but as the classification goes on, the criteria for definition of differences and similarities of the cases appear more and more clearly' (Demazière and Dubar 1997: 277). This approach led us to settle for a taxonomy grounded in the data, rather than a typology based on well-recognized concepts. Two criteria emerged as discriminants and guided us to establish this taxonomy. First was the number of companies people had worked for: some were faithful to one firm; others chose or were compelled to change employers several times. Second was the degree of dependence on any one firm: some people were highly dependent on their employing firms; others maintained greater social distance from their firms, or became self-employed.

Categories of the taxonomy

The taxonomy comprises five categories: sedentaries, migrants, itinerants, borderers, and nomads (Table 11.1). We first present those categories and their subcategories, from the most to the least dependent on organizations, illustrating them with the most representative cases. We then discuss the characteristics of each category.

Sedentary.   Sedentaries are people who follow a traditional track within an organization. Organizational careers are still not dead, especially in big firms. Mutations do not spare these companies. But effects on human resources are weak, as the following case shows:

> *Didier leaves school at 16 with a technical qualification as a lathe operator. He enters a small firm and leaves it a month later, when a big company offers him a more attractive wage. Ambitious and hard-working, his progression occurs without incident and he reaches a supervisory position. But then the unit he works for closes. He is offered three opportunities: redeployment, dismissal, or geographical mobility. For personal reasons he chooses the first option (his wife works nearby and they have just bought a house) and works in a design office. This job represents a regression, which leaves him frustrated. He warns his superior that he will leave as soon as possible, and asks him to let him know about alternative opportunities. The response happens four years later. Didier becomes responsible for studies concerning covering tubes for electrical cables and today is in charge of the same function for a larger department.*

Table 11.1. *Categories of the taxonomy*

Category	Sedentary	Migrants	Itinerants	Borderers	Nomads
Number of people	20	11	15	11	22
Characteristics	Organizational career	Extended organizational career (change of job but not of employer, or vice versa)	Frequent changes of employers in the same professional field	People who are, or were, their own employers, but keep links with one or more organizations	Radical or frequent job changes, with weak ties to organizations

This career is typical of an organizational one. Ambitious, Didier cannot imagine any mobility but vertical mobility. His career has been mainly managed by the organization. Didier occasionally expressed his will to change and asked for particular assignments, but his claims never fit with the opportunities available. Still, the only opportunities Didier ever considered were those offered by the firm.

'Sedentary' people are not only found in large firms:

> After obtaining his qualification as a hairdresser, Jérôme is hired in one of the six hairdressing salons of one of the most famous hairdressers in Paris. He spends more than five years there, following the in-house training of this organization. A new salon is opened with Jérôme's superior at its head. He asks Jérôme to follow him. Jérôme becomes the manager's assistant: he runs the salon during his chief's absence and trains the other hairdressers.

Usually hairdressers, after gaining experience in someone else's salon, hope to open their own salon or to run a franchised one. This is not Jérôme's wish. He strongly identifies himself with his organization and aspires only to become the manager of their salon(s).

Migrants.   Migrants are characterized by an extended organizational career. This term refers to changes of jobs or employers that occur within the boundaries of a large organization. Unlike the people who live the purest forms of boundaryless careers, they do not have to negotiate radical changes into unfamiliar environments, but experience rather safe and smooth professional transitions.

One example of the migrant is the civil servant 'on secondment'. These people take the initiative to suspend their employment contract for a time and work elsewhere. The most frequent form of this strategy is a leave of absence, sometimes for an extended period.

> Emilie passes an administrative examination for the Ministry of Finance. For three years she belongs to a pool of secretaries. She then takes a leave of absence from the civil service to work for a politician, a Minister who holds six different portfolios. After thirteen years she goes back to the civil service and works as the secretary of the Chief Treasury Inspector for seven years. Again she leaves the civil service and becomes the private secretary of the Minister of Finance. When he becomes Prime Minister, she follows him and works for him until his death. She goes back to the civil service in the Ministry of Finance.

This career is far from the routine one usually associated with civil servants. If such trajectories linked to political destinies are relatively uncommon, numerous civil servants manage to enlarge their career paths, as Elodie did:

> Elodie is the daughter of a civil servant and she has never seriously questioned the family tradition of serving the State. The level of studies that she

achieves enables her to enter the National Education School to train as a teacher. She spends several years in the school without qualifying as a teacher, which is unusual, and instead becomes an administrator responsible for the socio-cultural activities of the school. During her leisure time, she takes singing lessons. Following an institutional reform of the school, her job is suppressed and she asks to benefit from training in order to work in a library. She then becomes a librarian in a Music Center based in Paris (a state-owned facility that combines concert halls, a museum, and a school of music). In order to work in this environment, which corresponds to her passion, lyrics, she uses the possibility of a leave of absence from the administration that she belongs to. This device allows her to combine an idiosyncratic trajectory and a security that she is not ready to give up.

Itinerants.   This category comprises people who orient their careers around a specialization. It is similar to the notion of cosmopolitans that has been applied to professionals (Gouldner 1957). Here we enlarge this notion. This class incorporates all employees, whatever their profession and qualification, who stay in the same professional area. It includes secretaries and experts whose identity is not organizational but professional. Their changes of employers are generally motivated either by the prospect of a wage increase or by a wish to widen their experience.

Graduating as a clinical psychologist, Arnaud finds a job in a school for children with special needs. This kind of job is so demanding that it is difficult to do it for very long. He thus tries to join a private company, works here and there, going through periods of unemployment and fixed-term contracts. These experiences make him realize that the only work that really suits him is that of a psychologist. He focuses his employment research in this area and is finally recruited as a teacher for a limited period. After that, fear of unemployment leads him to reapply to the school he had worked for seven years before. But things have not changed and once more he resigns. By chance he finds a job as a juvenile delinquency prevention officer in a social center. Soon after he arrives, the director of the center leaves and Arnaud is promoted to this function. He likes this job and the responsibility it entails, but he wants to broaden his experience. He then finds a job as a psychologist in a center for the prevention of drug addiction.

Working as a psychologist is not easy. Most of the jobs are in hospitals, as civil servants with the national health service, but Arnaud cannot apply for those jobs as he does not have French nationality. He tried other jobs, which were not easy to find, even with his qualifications. Those experiences made him realize that he wanted work that included a social dimension, so he decided to search for jobs exclusively in his specialization, in, as he says, 'the world I was made for . . . the one I specialized in'.

Qualification and experience put people on a particular career path. Firms want people to become rapidly efficient. Recruiting companies have many candidates to choose from, and usually rely on demonstrable human capital, considered as a guarantee of competence and performance. Relying on human potential instead means taking risks and having confidence in someone. Employers are not keen to take this risk when they do not know with whom they are dealing. As potential is difficult to assess, employers trust objective signals.

> *Pascal spends all his youth traveling through Africa and the French Caribbean following his father, a police officer. Gifted for foreign languages and with a taste for human relations, he interrupts his studies after his* baccalauréat, *preferring to work instead. He starts in a human resource management department, specializing in administration and pay. He works as a payroll specialist for five companies in different industries within sixteen years: distribution, public services, communications, printing and manufacturing, increasing his pay and status with each move. He never stays more than four years in the same firm, always willing to change environment, to learn, and to broaden his experience. In 1992 he is contacted by a former boss and joins a non-profit organization. He is put in charge of HRM but also of communication and logistics. This experience gives him the opportunity to leave the payroll field. Nevertheless, with this new function he wonders how to position himself on the employment market, since, in his opinion, he is not seen as an HRM specialist any more.*

Pascal's specialization enabled him to change employers regularly. He liked his work but started to be fed up with the payroll function. Unfortunately, he could find jobs only in his specialist area. Only a former supervisor had enough confidence in him to offer him a broader function. He knew that Pascal would be able to learn and do something other than payroll.

Borderers.   Under this label, we find people who experience periods as employees and as self-employed simultaneously or alternately. Their relationship with the organization is a long-term one and they keep contact with their employers and colleagues. They lean on organizational resources to become self-employed, and, if that fails, depend on the same ties to enable them to rejoin the organization, as Geoffroy managed to do:

> *Geoffroy begins his professional life as a salesman in a sports shop and is regularly promoted until becoming a director. Once this is achieved, a second period of his life begins. He opens his own sports shops, first one, two, then three. But in the middle of the eighties, supermarkets specializing in sport retailing begin to capture market share. Geoffroy anticipates that this competition may be too tough for him and he sells out. At a sports show he runs into his former employers. He explains his situation and they propose that he rejoins the company. He thus becomes the director of a larger shop but this soon closes. He then joins another group after meeting*

*a friend of his former employer and is put in charge of the textile depart-
ment of a shop. He soon becomes manager of the shop in charge of several
product lines. At the time of the interview, he is thinking of a new self-
employment project.*

When Geoffroy resigned from his previous employer, there was no promise
of re-employment at a later date. The contact was loosely maintained and
enabled the new opportunity when he was once again job hunting. Another
example of a strategy that combines both personal projects and organizational support is Adolphe's story:

*Adolphe has a very short experience as an employee before running his own
jeans shop. After a few years, he enters a financial services company where
he spends twelve years and where, in his opinion, he learns a great deal.
This company is also tolerant with him during what turns out to be a
rather long transition to his next venture. Adolphe never tries to hide his
passion for someday starting a new business. He spends more and more
time buying and selling prestige cars and showing less energy at work.
Finally he sets up his own garage.*

The company is indulgent with Adolphe, and not only during the transition.
Of course, according to him, there would have been no possibility of returning to the company should his business fail, but one of his colleagues, whom
we also met, is convinced that the company would re-employ him.

Nomads. Nomads are people who experience frequent or radical professional transitions without being tied to any organization, either psychologically or economically. They are the sole managers of their careers and usually
cultivate a strong feeling of autonomy. They are particularly led to develop
idiosyncratic competencies as they break away from traditional paths and
have to seize various opportunities. We distinguished the three following
types of nomads:

(i) People who have only ephemeral relationships with firms, through time-
limited projects or short missions, as is often the case in cinema and information technology. We interviewed a cameraman, Tanguy, whose career in
the film and TV industry was a rather chaotic succession of achievements as
a director and more 'elementary' jobs as a cameraman or photographer.

(ii) Entrepreneurs, who create their own businesses totally independently of
firms. Abdel is a good example of someone with a classical 'entrepreneurial
anchor' (Schein 1978)—that is, a person with a strong inclination towards
creation and self-employment:

*Abdel, a Berber Algerian, has always known that he would never be an
employee but would manage his own business. In his country, it is highly*

valued to be an entrepreneur. After high school, Abdel has to leave Algeria for political reasons and moves to France to study computer science. One day, while playing music with some friends by the Seine, he attracts the attention of a businessman who asks him to come and play for his son's birthday. The two men become friends. Their friendship is based on a shared experience and common cultural identity (both are Berbers and political refugees). The man becomes Abdel's mentor and employs him first of all in his printing business. He then proposes that Abdel become his associate. Abdel agrees, leaves off his computer studies, and the two men together initiate various business activities. Having earned enough money to go it alone, Abdel starts buying restaurants and other firms in difficulty, then turns them around before selling them or putting a manager in charge of them. In a few years, he plans to launch a trading business exporting computer goods to Algeria.

(iii) If Abdel's entire professional life has been as an entrepreneur, others start this type of career much later. People in this third group go through a mid-life crisis, or they find themselves unemployed and have difficulty finding another job because of their age, their lack of qualifications, or both. The only way to subsist is to become their own employer.

Blandine starts her professional life as a clerk in a large retail bank. She is regularly promoted within the company, acquiring additional qualifications through internal training, but she does not engage in the complete training program to become a manager because she believes it to be incompatible with her family responsibilities. At 40, her children grown up, she becomes more ambitious, more involved in her professional life, and wants to climb the hierarchical levels. But opportunities are rare. Blandine arrives at a level where only people with degrees have a chance of being promoted. Given the increasing number of young graduates in the bank, she feels that her promotion prospects are limited. The bank goes through difficulties and has to cut down its workforce. Blandine seizes this opportunity and leaves voluntarily with quite a large amount of money. This money, added to the funds received by her husband who has also been dismissed, enables them to open a dry-cleaning franchise. They also benefit from legal advice paid for by Blandine's employer. Their new job does not leave them much spare time, but neither of them regrets the choice; they are achieving something together and do not depend on an employer any more.

The banking industry in France is undergoing important restructuring. Blandine suspected that this layoff would be the first of many. As she expected to be dismissed sooner or later, she felt that she should be proactive about the situation. The compensation funds offered were attractive and might be lower next time as other layoffs followed. At 40 years old, it would be difficult for her to find another job in this field. She thus decided to become self-employed, a situation that, even while it added certain risks, protected her from future dismissal.

Nomadism, especially when not a choice, is not always successful. Even some proactive people, with a high entrepreneurial identity, lack the specific skills that might predict success in this kind of career. Such people are caught in a vicious and precarious circle. They just cannot find a stable job, or at least a job that satisfies them, whether self-employed or not.

> *Gilles lives school at 14 and undertakes an apprenticeship in sales, which he does not like. During the 1960s, it is not too difficult to find another job. Gilles becomes a manual worker, learning on the job and changing employers when working conditions no longer suit him. After being dismissed, he passes an exam in welding and for the following eleven years is a contingent worker, finding jobs through temporary agencies. In 1988 Gilles wants to change and gains a license to drive trucks. For the next seven years he works for many different employers, mostly 'off the books'. Eventually, an accident compels him to give up this kind of work. After a year's unemployment, the job center offers him a training program and he decides to become an electrician. After this training he has been doing sporadic jobs in his new field for the past two years.*

Gilles is now confronted with several major employment barriers: age, low qualification, lack of experience as an electrician. He faces competition from young people whom employers consider more adaptable, more dynamic, and cheaper.

The French Model: Transformation and Continuity

The taxonomy that we have presented can be considered as a picture of the careers in progress in France between 1987 and 1997. We have classified these careers in categories, which we have tried to differentiate as clearly as possible. We now propose a 'horizontal' study of the table, focusing on the relations between certain categories of this 'panorama'. It is our contention that the careers of many of these people are signs and vehicles of current transformations in French society. In order to learn more about these processes, we propose to take a closer look at the interviewees' strategies. This will lead us to distinguish various individual capacities required to have subjective careers in Weick's sense (Weick and Berlinger 1989)—that is, to acquire skills, seize opportunities, and follow one's own guidelines, whatever the category. Such an analysis corresponds to a 'vertical' reading of the table (Figure 11.1), from objective careers at the bottom to subjective careers at the top. Finally, a study of the nomads will enable us to formulate propositions about the strategies of the people who practice, in a competent and successful[5] way, more boundaryless careers in France. This last step of our reflection

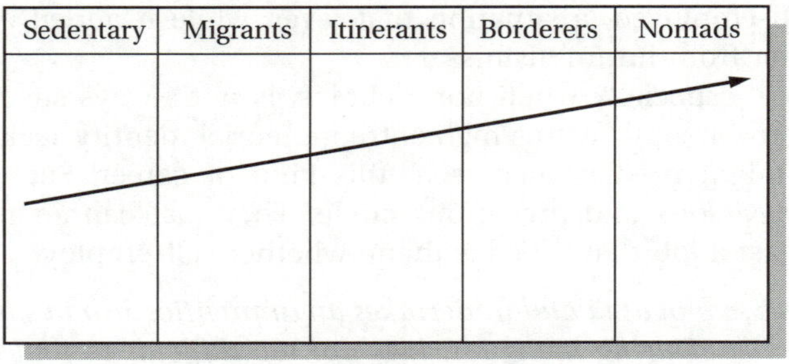

Sedentary	Migrants	Itinerants	Borderers	Nomads

Figure 11.1. **Increasing levels of boundarylessness, subjectivity, and change**

deals with the change dynamics illustrated by the diagonal arrow of the figure. It addresses the broad question of how the French could successfully adapt to the new economic era.

Some original categories

Three categories of the taxonomy are commonly found in the careers literature, although one has only recently been highlighted. Two further categories are more particular to our study. Thus, it is easy to see the similarity of *sedentary* with organizational careers, of *itinerant* with cosmopolitan careers and of *nomadic* with boundaryless careers. The remaining two can be considered as original extensions of the more classical categories, and call for further analysis.

The category of *borderers* comprises people who have alternated periods of self-employment with periods as employees of an organization. A simple view of these periods would see them occurring without continuity, and without connections in either the skills or relationships involved. However, closer inspection reveals something more, and supports our adoption of the *borderer* label. The more interesting cases that helped us build this category are those of people who have remained in contact with relations dating from previous work environments.

We have already spoken of Geoffroy, who, after having been employed, has tried self-employment and then become employed again; he was thinking of a new self-employment project when we met him. Typically for the *borderers* category, Geoffroy resigned from his employer with no promise of re-employment at a later date. However, the contact was loosely maintained and provided a new opportunity when Geoffroy was once again in search of a job. There was no formal contract, but an experience of one another, a confidence based on many years spent together, a reputation in a profession. In sum, there was an array of intangible elements that can provide a support for those, like Geoffroy, who experiment with self-employment. As for Adolphe, he extensively mobilized organizational resources, thanks to the indulgent behavior of his employer. Like Geoffroy, he may be re-employed should his business fail. In these two examples, employers do not resent the fact that their employees leave them; the relationship is not broken and employers prove more indulgent than pure economic logic would dictate.

In French, a popular expression summarizes this indulgent behavior: *être bon prince* ('to be a good prince'). This feudal connotation is consistent with d'Iribarne's (1990) analysis—namely, that the aristocratic tradition continues to dominate the daily relations in companies as well as in other institutions or spheres of society. Many observers of social behavior in French companies use the feudal metaphor intensively and regard them as federations of baronies or fiefdoms, each one extremely jealous of its autonomy when not fighting against another. In line with this metaphor, the newly hired person rapidly understands that he or she has to pledge allegiance to the local 'baron' or lord, and more generally to the hierarchical line upon which he or she depends. The hope is that one day the lord will grant his or her favors to those who have been loyal. It is a long-term tacit contract and an interpersonal relationship.

This kind of behavior is a feature of French human resource management (HRM). For example, a company may be interested in the identification of young high potential employees. A baron is very unlikely to cooperate in this detection process for fear of losing the best members of his or her team. Above all, the lord does not want his or her best performers to go to a rival. Perpetuating this relationship between lord and vassal even outside the boundaries of the organization is not a major problem, if this is the wish of the lord and of the vassal. If the lord has already anticipated giving the vassal his or her freedom, the cost is not unbearable. Moreover, the lord's debt is not extinguished and the vassal can expect some help in case of adversity or necessity.

The *borderers* category can be viewed as a transitional state toward the *nomads* category. Through the extension of the allegiance system found in many organizations, it limits the risk taken by those who experiment with self-employment. The risk reduction comes from a possible reintegration with the company and from the help of previous managers or employers.

It is interesting to look at the *migrants* category as contiguous with the *sedentary* one. Let us further consider the example of Elodie. When one looks at her career, the word that immediately comes to mind is 'boundaryless' although she originally seemed destined for a very bounded career. She used institutional devices such as leave of absence, professional training, and administrative exams in order to change jobs and employers. Her case is a particular one, but it highlights typical features of the public sector. Luc Rouban, a French sociologist, argues that the French *grands corps*,[6] who benefit from very protective employment rules, are a source of flexibility and adaptation in the public sector (Rouban 1996). The security provided by their employment status allows them to be innovative and to take risks. Of

course, it is a matter not only of security but also of quality of the recruitment, of the 'sense of the State' and of social prestige of these *corps*.

We emphasize civil servants, but the *migrants* category also comprises
employees from large private companies. The *migrants* could be included
in the broader category of organizational careers. However, we think it is
worth isolating, to present it as an extension of the *sedentaries* as a type of
nomadic trajectory within large administrative arenas. It shows a possible
evolution away from the strict organizational career model.

Making sense of careers

When we asked our interviewees to tell us about their lives over the previous
decade, we invited them to practice sensemaking. They tried to explain—or
to make sense of—what had occurred. In doing so they suggested who they
were (how their experiences reflected their individuality and idiosyncracies),
how their worlds functioned (what rules regulated their employing organizations and labor markets), and how they imagined the future (what implicit or
explicit projects they wanted to pursue). According to Weick, sensemaking
links people's sought identities with the activities they experience. Thus,
sensemaking (how people see the world) relates directly to enactment
(how people behave toward the world) (Weick 1996). At a general level,
everybody is continuously enacting their environments—but the environment can be positively enacted (influenced toward positive change) as well
as negatively enacted (influenced toward stasis)[7].

From enactment to subjectivity.   In the course of our interviews we developed the feeling that, independently of educational level, social status, or
personality type, some interviewees integrated more strongly and more
coherently than others the elements we discussed. That is, for some people
their work experiences, identity, relationship with the environment, and
projects undertaken all came together in a coherent whole. And the more
coherent the construction of sensemaking appeared, the more positive or
energized their enactment appeared to be.

Weick and Berlinger (1989) revisit the classical distinction between objective and subjective career. They propose a vision of subjective careers that
helps us to deal with the above-mentioned individual differences. In their
article, the authors shift rapidly from the classical distinction between the
objective career as a sequence of official positions and the subjective career
as subjective experiences to a slightly different conception. For them, the
subjective career underlies a sense of direction and identity building. 'The
subjective career emphasizes self-direction and greater personal responsibility for choices that are made' (Weick and Berlinger 1989: 321). This conceptualization enables us to classify our interviewees on a scale going from

objective to subjective careers and to speak of higher and lower levels of subjectivity.

We do not wish to conflate subjectivity with success, which would be contradictory, since social recognition belongs to the sphere of the objective career. Subjective values do not necessarily correspond to general social values or to the more particular social values in the career actor's environment. How, then, do we rate or classify the cases on a scale of subjectivity? We do not have strictly defined indicators, but take the following elements into account:

- clarity of self-concept, consciousness of one's talents and handicaps, as revealed by experience;
- reframing of the environment, reconstruction of concepts of true and good, in relation to one's own trajectory;
- questioning of taboos, definitions of new visions, projects, and perspectives;
- coherent integration of previous experiences, identity, environment, and project.

On this basis, we have divided our sample into two groups: relatively subjective and relatively objective ways of building careers.

Levels of subjectivity. Weick and Berlinger (1989) propose a relationship between careers and organizational paradigms. They set objective careers determined by traditional organizations against subjective careers that contribute to self-designing companies. Miles and Snow (1996) have subsequently developed this correspondence between organizational forms and career models. The suggested relationship between traditional organization and objective career, on the one hand, and new organizational forms and subjective career, on the other hand, is heuristic. However, the real organizations referred to in our survey are not so monolithic as these ideal-types. Most traditional organizations are going through transitions in order to adapt to a changing environment, and they include people who lead subjective careers as well as people with more objective trajectories.

Although our taxonomy is not a categorization of organizations—each category gathers individual trajectories that appear similar with regard to the relationship between the person and the organization—the organizations themselves and their HRM systems stand in the background. Our analysis confirms that the organizations that are the setting for most *sedentary* careers are nearer to traditional organizations and those that are the setting for *nomad* paths are more likely to be self-designing organizations. Each category, however, includes people who fit into the subjective career and people representative of the objective career.

The French National Education Service is often presented as an archetype of bureaucracy (the second in the world after the Red Army, according to some authors (Lesourne 1998)). Some of the most 'subjective careerists' we met were very active and happy in this organization and endeavored to elaborate adaptive answers, at their level, to the new problems the service faced. Highly subjective trajectories need not be *nomad* careers. In other words, companies could face serious problems if they were unable to attract, and retain, people whose subjectivity fitted into the organization.

Subjective and objective career patterns also coexist in the *nomad* category, as some are *nomads* by fate rather than by choice or personal creation of their environment. Their nomadism is imposed on them. Each of their attempts to have a long-term employment contract with a company is a failure, but they none the less dream of an organizational career.

A dynamic picture of the French model.   If we were to replicate this survey during the first decade of the twenty-first century, we would probably have some metrics against which to measure the transformations of career paths in France. However, as we do not currently have data giving the proportions and trends in each category, we have had to build hypotheses on the basis of simultaneous trajectories. The taxonomy in Table 11.1 can be read as a set of possible strategies in a context of profound organizational transformation. As 'strong' employment situations weaken, new strategies have to be invented, such as the ones adopted by the *migrants*, *borderers*, and *nomads*. A horizontal reading of the table enables us to grasp some sociological processes under way in French society—namely, how people tend to modify or reframe their relationship to organizations and invent new ways of dealing with both changing organizations and changing labor markets.

Current French economic transformations combine structural changes and more subjective careers in an interactive way. According to Weick and Berlinger (1989: 321), subjective careers are resources for self-design. Our survey shows how individuals transform or create their work environment through more subjective careers and how they become more *nomadic* in order to cope with more boundaryless organizations. These two directions correspond to the vertical and horizontal reading of the taxonomy. In physics, forces can often be decomposed into horizontal and vertical components. The question is thus: 'How is it possible to lead a more subjective and more nomadic career in French society?'

Nomad trajectories and the management of boundaries

What does a French person have to do to pursue a nomadic way of life? For an initial answer we refer to the trilogy of career competency arenas introduced by Arthur, Claman, and DeFillippi (1995): *knowing-whom* (relationships), *knowing-how* (skills and knowledge), and *knowing-why* (identity and motivation). First of all, we will present the relational strategies activated by the *nomads* with regard to individuals or organizations. Next we will turn to the functioning of skill-based labor markets, and finally we will deal with identity.

Knowing-whom, *or the art of interesting others.* Integration in a community (in the ethnic sense of the term) is an important card to play if you feel attracted by a nomadic trajectory and by self-employment. We have already spoken of Abdel, a Berber, and will now mention the case of Constant, who comes from the Aveyron region of France.

> *Constant, aged 26, strongly wishes to become the owner of a 'brasserie-restaurant'. The Aveyronnaise community is renowned for the number of its restaurants in Paris. People from this region were traditionally involved in the transportation of coal from the Aveyron to Paris. The coal was distributed by cafés. The accumulated capital was initially invested in cafés, and the more business oriented owners turned the cafés into brasseries and restaurants. The most famous brasseries in Paris are still in the hands of this community. An active network exists among the people of this region. They tend to spend each summer holiday in the Aveyron, where it is usual to exhibit one's signs of success, as in all emigrant communities. Young people who are interested in setting up a business in Paris can benefit from the help of the elders if they are considered to be serious and reliable. Constant is at the moment methodically developing his competencies through carefully selected and complementary work experiments; he receives advice and financial help from the community.*

To be born into an ethnic community is not, however, sufficient. One has to build one's network within the community and gain its confidence. The entrepreneurial project must be coherent and interest the network members. Weick (1996: 45) speaks of 'agency' ('The concept of enactment suggests that people are agents of their own development') and 'communion' ('People organize cooperatively in order to learn'); he explains that agency needs communion and vice versa: 'This continual mixing of agency and communion.' This can be applied to the example we are referring to. The Aveyronnaise community needs people who have a vocation for running brasseries, and tries in many ways to make the business attractive to the young generations. But the talented young people have to demonstrate that they are trustworthy and rich in 'agency'. What we describe here is not fundamentally different from what Jones and DeFillippi (1996) discuss in their article about the film industry. When we interviewed the aforementioned cameraman (Tanguy), he explained how he has built, and still continues to build, his network. This activity of networking is completely bound to the production of projects: possible projects arise from meeting someone new, and a new project brings new contacts.

Hirsch and Shanley (1996: 226) have already pointed out the importance of organizational position in developing personal networks: 'To have access to the best network positions required being employed in the firm.' They underline the point in criticism of boundaryless career rhetoric. However, there is no need to insist that organizational networks are essential. Our purpose here is to go beyond the opposition between organizational career and boundaryless career, and to show how organizations can help more nomadic trajectories.

There is a clear dividing line between public and private life in French society, which is echoed in the rules of *savoir-vivre*. A personal relationship (family, friends . . .) must be above utilitarian thoughts. It is not considered good taste to mix professional and affective relationships. This does not mean that interference between the private and public spheres never occurs, but that at least a minimal diplomatic taste must be displayed. *Sedentary* people have few problems in respecting the boundaries between the two spheres, especially in public bureaucracies, where the distinction is more or less codified (Bonis 1975). The concept of bureaucracy is based on a strict distinction of the function and the person; the person disappears behind the institutional role.

The people who stand on the right side of our table are less able to draw a line between the private and the professional spheres. They have to manage this social boundary as they pursue their career projects. These are so integrated with their identities, and absorb so much of their lives, that the distinction of spheres vanishes. Those people interest[8] their friends and relatives in their projects and transcend the stigma usually cast on utilitarian-based relationships.

Knowing-how, *or the quest for new territories.*   A nomad needs a territory to cover. Where are the territories open to nomadism, in a society that tends to build entry barriers to work, especially as far as professional matters are concerned? For example, many jobs in the services sector are looked down upon. In order to upgrade them, diplomas are created, employment rules are elaborated, and finally barriers are built to prevent job competition.

Our interviewees were fully conscious of the existing barriers—namely, diploma and age—and had completely integrated these norms in their career behavior. Legislation on continuing education and professional training, voted in to iron out the inequalities resulting from earliest scholastic selections in France, is already over twenty-five years old. Statistics systematically confirm that it is primarily the most qualified people who benefit from professional training (Dubar 1990). If we examine the lowest subjective profiles, it can be noted that those individuals who strategically seek post-scholastic qualifications are those who already hold diplomas. They are primarily on the left-hand side of the table, which is, to a large extent, an area of closed labor markets—that is to say, with high entry barriers, such as large firms and professional markets.

Among the people who lead the most subjective and nomadic careers, on the other hand, those who play the qualification card are a minority. Most of them are lowly qualified and adopt other strategies. They move to territories where entry barriers are lower, and thus show us where the *nomadic* areas are: the services sector, and fields indicated by the 'new career' literature as being boundaryless career arenas (culture, arts, cinema, software, and so on). These territories do not have high financial entry barriers. They are more innovation based and require a large range of *knowing-how* competencies (technical, commercial, and managerial, as mentioned by Allred *et al.* 1996).

Knowing-why, *or the creation of one's own rules of conduct.*   Weick (1995: 12) enquires: 'How can I know what I think before I see what I say?' Interaction with others helps people to become more conscious of themselves than soliloquy (see Chapter 10). Among the people we interviewed, those who manifested few signs of a subjective career led solitary lives or lived in a social environment where interactions were not really propitious to the discovery of oneself. Their job involvement was low (they granted more importance to their private life and leisure activities), and those who were classified in the *nomad* category were not *nomads* through choice.

When we study the interviews of people who displayed subjective-career behavior, we can observe two phenomena regarding their interactions with others.

- They were sensitive to others' opinions of them: the perceptions of others had obviously played a role in the definition of career projects and in the construction of their self-concepts.
- They did not necessarily take into account other people's advice or warnings. They hear what others say, but have sufficient autonomy to behave and live their lives through their own projects, even if this pre-supposes paying a certain price or taking a risk. The content of their interviews revealed that they had distanced themselves from stereotyped identities linked to classical definitions of professions. These individuals felt relatively independent from standard prestige scales and from the social images of activities. For example, Constant could have spoken of his time with Pizza Hut (one of his 'experiments') in more derogatory terms, but he reported that he had learned a great deal and that this experience was an important step in his trajectory.

An idiosyncratic trajectory is a path that makes sense to the person concerned rather than a curriculum that conforms to prestige scales and social norms. Weick and Berlinger write (1989: 321): 'the subjective career emphasizes self-direction and greater responsibility for the choices that are made.' The reframing activity involved in the subjective career helps us to understand how people can develop a more nomadic trajectory in a society whose dominant logic tends to restrict the areas opened to nomads. One recurring wish of many French families is to have a child who becomes a civil servant. Another recent example was a survey of youths who replied that their object-ive was to pass the Post Office exam and to marry a schoolteacher who would look after the education of the children. Our survey shows that the borders established by social norms are transgressed or bypassed by individuals or groups who are sometimes victims of the barriers or are strongly motivated by a personal project.

Conclusion

We have proposed a taxonomy, on the basis of interviews of a sample of the French working population, that provides a succinct view of career paths in France from 1987 to 1997. This taxonomy suggests that one should add intermediate categories to the canonical ones defined by career theory. Although the clarity and simplicity of the objective/subjective dichotomy is lost, the dualistic view of careers has perhaps already given all that it has to give. It might be the moment to consider more elaborate categories. Reality rarely provides for confirmation, or simplification, of conceptual models. It rather tends to produce hybrids. Mintzberg, a famous ideal-types designer, says that hybrids are more interesting than pure forms (Mintzberg 1982: 413). We suggest that our hybrid categories are not only the reflection of a com-plex reality, but also an image of the transformations occurring in French society. Accordingly we have tried to illustrate how actors develop strategies to tackle difficulties, and to escape or avoid blocked situations.

These hybrid categories may have some interest beyond the French case. They are likely to be adaptable to other contexts or countries. If so, they could be considered as transitional strategies or inventions. Should this be the case, it may be worth integrating them into a theoretical body of general propositions. Is this not, after all, the objective of international comparisons?

Notes

1. 'Weak' situations are ambiguous situations, which provide few guides to action and pressures to conformity. Conversely, 'strong' situations offer clear incentives, lead-ing most people to act in the same way whatever their personal preferences and representations (Mischel 1973).
2. To be *intéressé*, in this context, has a derogatory connotation in French. English–French dictionaries translate it as 'selfish', which does not capture its meaning. A closer meaning is 'utilitarian'.

3. The A level in the UK is roughly comparable to the high school diploma in the USA, although slightly more advanced.
4. The activity rate of male workers aged 55 to 59 dropped from 81.6% to 67.8% between 1975 and 1993 (INSEE 1994b).
5. We refer here to subjective success, according to one's own personal criteria.
6. Each year the best students of the École Nationale d'Administration enter five Grands Corps, which open the door to the most brilliant careers in the French public sector, considered the most desirable in France.
7. We are reminded of Seneca's dictum: 'We say that we do not dare because things are difficult. In fact they are difficult because we do not dare.'
8. We borrow this expression from Callon (1989), who uses it to explain the life of innovations. He shows that the technologies that become dominant are not necessarily the best or the most efficient but those that get the maximum support and interest from possible users, financial networks, economical and political actors, scientists, and so on.

References

Allred, B. B., Snow, C. C., and Miles, R. E. (1996), 'Characteristics of Managerial Careers in the 21st Century', *Academy of Management Executive*, 10: 4.

Arthur, M. B., and Rousseau, D. M. (1996) (eds.), *The Boundaryless Career: A New Employment Principle for a New Organizational Era* (New York: Oxford University Press).

—— Claman, P. H., and DeFillippi, R. J. (1995), 'Intelligent Enterprise, Intelligent Careers', *Academy of Management Executive*, 9: 4.

—— Inkson, K., and Pringle, J. K. (1999), *The New Careers: Individual Action and Economic Change* (London: Sage).

Bailyn, L. (1989), 'Understanding Individual Experience at Work: Comments on the Theory and Practice of Careers', In M. B. Arthur, D. T. Hall, and B. S. Lawrence (eds.), *Handbook of Career Theory* (New York: Cambridge University Press).

Barley, S. R. (1989), 'Careers, Identities and Institutions', in M. B. Arthur, D. T. Hall, and B. S. Lawrence (eds.), *Handbook of Career Theory* (New York: Cambridge University Press).

Bauer, M., and Bertin-Mourot, B. (1993), 'Quelle alternative à la tyrannie du diplôme initial?', *Education Permanente* (Mar.).

Bollinger, D., and Hofstede, G. (1987), *Les Différences culturelles dans le management* (Paris: Les Éditions d'Organisation).

Bonis, J. (1975), *Le Système humain des organisations* (Paris: Éditions Hommes et Techniques).

Callon, M. (1989), *La Science et ses réseaux* (Paris: La Découverte).

DARES (1997): Direction de l'Animation de la Recherche et des Statistiques, 'Conjoncture de l'emploi et du chômage au 1er trimestre 1997', *Premières informations*, 28/2: 1–6.

Demazière, D., and Dubar, C. (1997), *Analyser les entretiens biographiques: L'Exemple des récits d'insertion* (Paris: Nathan, coll. Essais et Recherche).

Derr, C. B., and Laurent, A. (1989), 'The Internal and External Career: A Theoretical and

Cross-Cultural Perspective', in M. B. Arthur, D. T. Hall, and B. S. Lawrence (eds.), *Handbook of Career Theory* (New York: Cambridge University Press).

D'Iribarne, P. (1989), *La Logique de l'honneur* (Paris: Seuil, coll. Sociologie).

—— (1990), *Le Chômage paradoxal* (Paris: Presses Universitaires de France).

Doeringer, P. B., and Piore, M. J. (1971), *Internal Labor Markets and Manpower Analysis* (Lexington, Mass.: D. C. Heath).

Dubar, C. (1990), *La Formation continue la découverte* (Paris: Reperes).

Fougère, D., and Kramarz, F. (1997), 'Le Marché du travail en France: Quelques pistes d'analyse', *Économie et Statistique*, 301–2: 51–60.

Gibier, H. (1997), 'Les Salariés français craquent. France, Europe, États-Unis: Les Cruelles Leçons d'un sondage', *L'Expansion*, 562: 96–101.

Giddens, A. (1984), *The Constitution of Society* (Berkeley and Los Angeles, University of California Press).

Gouldner, A. (1957), 'Cosmopolitans and Locals: Toward an Analysis of Latent Social Roles', *Administrative Science Quarterly*, 2.

Goux, D. (1991), 'Coup de frein sur les carrières', *Économie et statistique*, 249: 75–87.

Hall, D. T. (1976), *Careers in Organizations* (Glenview, Ill.: Scott, Foresman).

—— and Mirvis, P. H. (1996), 'The New Protean Career: Psychological Success and the Path with a Heart', in D. T. Hall and Associates, *The Career is Dead: Long Live the Career* (San Fransisco: Jossey-Bass).

Hirsch, P. M., and Shanley, M. (1996), 'The Rhetoric of Boundaryless—Or, how the Newly Empowered Managerial Class Bought into its own Marginalization', in M. B. Arthur and D. M. Rousseau (eds.), *The Boundaryless Career: A New Employment Principle for a New Organizational Era* (New York: Oxford University Press).

Hofstede, G. (1980), *Culture's Consequences: International Differences in Work-Related Values* (Beverly Hills, Calif.: Sage).

INSEE (1994*a*), *Mobilité professionnelle et mobilité géographique: Enquête sur la formation et la qualification professionnelle 1993* (Paris: INSEE Résultats, Dec.).

—— (1994*b*), *Enquête emploi 1993* (Paris: INSEE Résultats, Feb.).

Jones, C., and DeFillippi, R. J. (1996), 'Back to the Future in Film: Combining Industry and Self-Knowledge to Meet the Career Challenges of the 21st Century', *Academy of Management Executive*, 10: 89–105.

Kayser, P. (1990), *La Protection de la vie privée* (Paris: Economica; Aix-en Provence: Presses Universitaires d'Aix-Marseille).

Lesourne, J. (1998), *Le Modèle français: Grandeur et décadence* (Paris: Odile Jacob).

Maurice, M. (1993), 'La Formation professionnelle en France, en Allemagne et au Japon', *Entreprises et histoires*, 3: 47–59.

—— Sellier, F., and Silvestre, J. J. (1982), *Politique d'education et organisation industrielle en France et en Allemagne* (Paris: Presses Universitaires de France).

—— —— —— (1986), *The Social Foundations of Industrial Power* (Cambridge, Mass.: MIT Press).

Miles, R. E., and Snow, C. C. (1996), 'Twenty-First Century Careers', in M. B. Arthur and D. M. Rousseau (eds.), *The Boundaryless Career: A New Employment Principle for a New Organizational Era* (New York: Oxford University Press).

Mintzberg, H. (1982), *Structure et dynamique des organisations* (Paris: Éditions d'Organisation).

Mischel, W. (1973), 'Toward a Cognitive Social Learning Reconceptualization of Personality', *Psychological Review*, 80: 252–83.

OECD (1992): Organization for Economic Cooperation and Development, *Études économiques de l'OCDE: France, 1991–92* (Paris: OECD).

Peiperl, M., and Baruch, Y. (1997), 'Back to Square Zero: The Post-Corporate Career', *Organizational Dynamics* (Spring), 7–22.

Raider, H. J., and Burt, R. S. (1996), 'Boundaryless Careers and Social Capital', in M. B. Arthur and D. M. Rousseau (eds.), *The Boundaryless Career: A New Employment Principle for a New Organizational Era* (New York: Oxford University Press).

Rouban, L. (1996), 'La Réforme de l'appareil d'état', in V. Wright and S. Cassese (eds.), *La Recomposition de l'état en Europe* (Paris: La Découverte).

Saxenian, A. (1996), 'Beyond Boundaries: Open Labor Markets and Learning in Silicon Valley', in M. B. Arthur and D. M. Rousseau (eds.), *The Boundaryless Career: A New Employment Principle for a New Organizational Era* (New York: Oxford University Press).

Schein, E. H. (1978), *Career Dynamics—Matching Individual and Organizational Needs* (Reading, Mass.: Addison-Wesley).

—— (1984), 'Culture as an Environmental Context for Careers', *Journal of Occupational Behavior*, 5: 71–81.

Vimont, C. (1995), *Le Diplôme et l'emploi* (Paris: Economica).

Weick, K. E. (1995), *Sensemaking in Organizations* (Thousand Oaks, Calif.: Sage).

—— (1996), 'Enactment and the Boundaryless Career: Organizing as We Work', in M. B. Arthur and D. M. Rousseau (eds.), *The Boundaryless Career: A New Employment Principle for a New Organizational Era* (New York: Oxford University Press).

—— and Berlinger, L. (1989), 'Career Improvisation in Self-Designing Organizations', in M. B. Arthur, D. T. Hall, and B. S. Lawrence (eds.), *Handbook of Career Theory* (New York: Cambridge University Press).

Wrong, D. (1961), 'The Oversocialized Conception of Man', *American Sociological Review*, 26: 184–93.

12

Career, Community, and Social Architecture: An Exploration of Concepts

Rob Goffee and Gareth Jones

It is commonplace to assert that high rates of change and uncertainty within the industrial economies have buried, perhaps once and for all, the conventional notion of the career as an orderly, cumulative trajectory, organizationally bounded and marked by measurable shifts in status and social recognition. While some observers argue that the term should be disposed of altogether, others seek broader redefinitions that understand the career as 'the evolving sequence of a person's work over time' (Arthur *et al.* 1989). This sequence of experiences, it is often claimed, is increasingly owned and shaped by individuals. Personal intentions, aspirations, and abilities have become more salient determinants of career 'outcomes', however they may be defined—earning a living, achieving promotion, building a family, and so on. But one may embrace changing conceptions of careers without endorsing this increasingly individualist paradigm.

To see careers as increasingly the property of individuals is understandable given the disintegration of those familiar social and organizational structures that once 'housed' them. The redesign of corporate hierarchies and work processes, the growing diversity of family structures, and the disintegration of 'local' communities variously remove the conventional contexts within which career histories have been mapped and understood. For some commentators this means that careers—like organizations—are becoming 'boundaryless'—enacted more within shifting social and professional networks, demanding continuous learning and development and higher rates of mobility across employers and between employment and self-employment (De Fillippi and Arthur 1994; Arthur and Rousseau 1996).

It is not hard to find evidence that might support such a notion. At the organizational level (where after all the notion of boundaryless was first coined) a variety of forces—inter-organizational collaboration (strategic alliances, joint ventures, and so on); information sharing; customer responsiveness initiatives; cross-functional teamwork—have combined to reduce the sharpness of conventional boundaries within and between corporations. Wider political and economic trends may be producing similar effects—take, for example, the gradual erosion of borders within the European Union associated with a single currency, the development of more flexible labor markets, and so on.

But have these environmental shifts combined to produce boundaryless careers? It depends on where you look. Focus on knowledge workers and other skilled professional and technical groups and the answer is affirmative; concentrate on less fashionable occupations—middle managers in medium-sized manufacturing enterprises—and the world remains 'bounded' in recognizable ways. Think, too, of differences between regions—high growth, high tech, networked zones in California, Cambridge, or Northern Italy will produce a very different picture from that derived from Birmingham, Stuttgart, or Beijing. Then again, much turns on which of these regions, sectors, or occupations—if any—are taken as guides to the future.

In the light of these widely divergent patterns perhaps there are simply no easy generalizations; the picture is complex and dynamic. But if boundaries overlap, are more porous, and reconfigure more rapidly, this is not to say they have disappeared. Hierarchies and functions persist, although, arguably, they provide a less complete context for the analysis of careers.

If the social context of the modern career has become more complex and differentiated, then this, in turn, makes analysis more difficult—impossible perhaps within the rather static organizational frameworks that place discrete jobs, functions, and hierarchical distinctions center stage. Yet even the very recent literature tends to focus, as Cricitto points out, on 'explicit boundary passages' as a pragmatic point from which to explore new career environments. As she continues, 'Future research might focus on how implicit psychological boundaries change as the individual adjusts to multiple employers, projects and teams' (Cricitto 1998: 177–8).

It is our contention that, 'as work experiences unfold over time', individuals will continue to encounter boundaries—explicit and hidden, objective and subjective—that delineate contexts (and career phases) that must be worked through in distinctive ways and between which significant career transitions occur. Since career theory is concerned fundamentally with examining the relationship between individuals, their work, and the social context within which they work over time (Lawrence 1995), we argue that recent theory may exaggerate the 'protean' (that is, person-driven) career at the expense of social context (Hall and Mirvis 1996). Further, where social context is explored, regional and occupational factors are emphasized—perhaps at the expense of the immediate employment context. In this chapter we provide a framework for differentiating the social architecture of distinctive work settings. The typology we describe draws upon

well-established sociological concepts largely ignored in the career literature. However, as we show, these concepts can provide insight into several
familiar themes within the established body of career research. We illustrate
our framework mainly within the context of the large-scale corporation, but
it has application within other contexts: to smaller enterprises, occupational
networks, and professional associations as well as regional or even national
communities (Goffee and Jones 1998).

The Corporate Social Context of the Modern Career

Pressures for disintegration in the modern large-scale corporation have
grown. This is largely because processes of decentralization, de-layering,
and devolution towards complex sets of differentiated centers—focused
upon distinctive products, customers, regions, suppliers, or competences—
have made the task of integration more demanding (Hales 1993; Goffee and
Scase 1995). Differentiation—an inevitable concomitant of scale, complexity,
and innovation—must be balanced with a need for corporate integration.
But maintaining a balance between integration and differentiation is no
longer a matter of 'either/or'. Hence, in facing the issue of centralization/
decentralization, for example, designers of the modern 'transnational'
corporation attempt to combine the autonomy and flexibility of the local
business with the cross-unit integration necessary to compete globally
(Ghoshal and Bartlett 1997).

How is such flexible coordination achieved? Excessive reliance upon conventional formal mechanisms for organizational integration—hierarchies,
structures, systems—is regarded as inappropriate. Increasingly, vertical
integration mechanisms are replaced by lateral integration processes: teams,
project groups, social events, and networks of one kind or another, as well as
a range of development processes and value-shaping activities that promote
'appropriate' attitudes and behavior (Evans 1993).

The contemporary language and imagery of corporate integration are,
then, distinctive. 'Culture' or 'nervous system' is the preferred metaphor,
with internal organizational architecture described in terms of 'networks'
or 'clusters'. This is the social context within which the corporate career is
enacted: a world of relationships driven—according to those who promote
it—by collaboration, mutuality, interdependence, and reciprocity; a new
work context where the critical skills are those of 'referral', 'partnering' and
'relationship management'.

But what, precisely, is the nature of these relationships? How do networks
differ? How might 'reciprocity' vary in different work contexts? There is little
in the modern literature of work organizations to help answer these questions (although Parker and Arthur address some of them in Chapter 5).
However, there is a long tradition of analysis in the social sciences—

particularly sociology—that can provide insight. In the rest of this chapter we draw upon these traditions to look more closely at two conceptually distinct types of social relations—those of sociability and solidarity (Goffee and Jones 1998). We use this analysis as a means for understanding the distinctive social architectures of work communities and their implications for career experiences.

Analyzing Social Architectures

Sociability is an aspect of social life central to much sociological analysis. It refers to affective, non-instrumental relations between individuals who may regard one another as 'friends'. Friends tend to share certain ideas, attitudes, interests, and values and to be inclined to associate on equal terms. So defined, friendship groups frequently constitute a primary unit in socio-logical analysis of status groups and of social class (Gerth and Mills 1948). In its pure form, sociability represents a type of social interaction that is valued for its own sake (Simmel 1971). It is frequently sustained through continuing face-to-face relations typically characterized by high levels of unarticulated reciprocity; there are no 'deals' prearranged. We help each other with no strings.

Solidarity, by contrast, describes task-centered cooperation between *unlike* individuals and groups (Durkheim 1933). It does not, in other words, depend upon close friendship or even personal acquaintance; nor is it necessarily sustained by continuous social relations. Solidarity can be demonstrated instrumentally and discontinuously—as and when the need arises. In contrast to sociability, then, its expression can be both intermittent and contingent.

Although sociability and solidarity may be distinguished conceptually in this way, many discussions of organizational life confuse the two. Clearly, social interaction at work may constitute the sociability of friends, the solidarity of colleagues, both, or—sometimes—neither. Equally, when col-leagues socialize outside work, this may represent an extension of workplace solidarity, rather than an expression of intimate or close friendships. Few descriptions of organizational social life explicitly address these distinctions, though some provide sufficient ethnographic material to enable an informed guess and we draw on these later.

Clearly, to cooperate in the instrumental pursuit of common goals it is not necessary for individuals to like one another. Indeed, solidarity may often be exhibited among those who actively dislike each other. Equally, intimate forms of sociability may actually be less likely among those who 'must' act solidaristically as work colleagues.

The intensity of sociability may vary directly, independently, or inversely with the intensity of solidarity. As a starting point, it is useful to distinguish

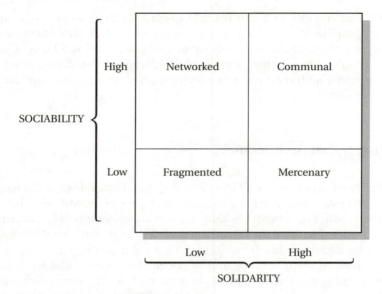

Fig. 12.1. **Four organizational archetypes**

organizations as exhibiting high or low levels of sociability and solidarity. In effect, this suggests four distinctive corporate forms: the *networked*, the *mercenary*, the *fragmented*, and the *communal* (Goffee and Jones 1996, 1998). The examples we use below are intended to illustrate each type of organization and are drawn from recent field research. For purposes of illustration the unit of analysis is the firm, but the model can be applied at various levels—the division or business unit, the function or the team, for example.

Networked organizations exhibit high levels of sociability but relatively low levels of solidarity. Such organizations are often characterized by long service, a 'family ethos' and work patterns regularly punctuated by social events and rituals of one kind or another. These help to sustain a strong sense of intimacy, loyalty, and friendship among managers. Patterns of sociability within the workplace often extend beyond it via leisure and sporting clubs and informal social contacts among families.

Levels of solidarity, however, are low. Ties of affection do not automatically translate into high levels of intra-organizational cooperation. Indeed, although social networks are characterized by well-established friendships, the culture of networked organizations can often be described as 'gossipy' and 'political'. Indeed, it is a mistake to assume that well-developed patterns of sociability will necessarily form the basis for solidaristic cooperation. In fact, the reverse may be true. Close friendships, for example, may limit possibilities for the open expression of difference, which is a necessary condition for developing and maintaining a shared sense of purpose.

At the level of the firm, the *networked* form may be indicated where:

- knowledge of local markets is a critical success factor;
- corporate success is an aggregate of local success (interdependencies are minimal);
- there are few opportunities for learning between divisions or units;
- strategies are long term (sociability maintains strategic intent when short-term calculations of interest would not).

In *mercenary* organizations, a heightened sense of competition and a strong desire to succeed—or at least 'protect territory'—is often a central feature of corporate culture. The dominant values are built around competitive individualism and personal achievement, but these do not preclude cooperative activity where this demonstrably produces benefits for both individuals and their organizations. In other words, colleagues display a solidarity that does not depend upon close friendships or ties of affection. Day-to-day relationships in such organizations are rarely characterized by high levels of collective cooperation—quite the reverse may be true. As we have pointed out, solidarity may be both *intermittent* and *contingent*.

The *mercenary* form is indicated where:

- capacity to act swiftly in a highly coordinated way is a critical source of competitive advantage;
- economies of scale and competitive advantage can be gained from creating corporate centers of excellence that can impose processes and procedures on operating units;
- the nature of the competition is clear—external enemies help to build internal solidarity;
- corporate goals are clear and measurable and there is little need for consensus building.

But what of organizations that exhibit low levels of both sociability and solidarity? Can these *fragmented* organizations survive or succeed? Although it seems unlikely, there is evidence that, at least in some contexts, these 'disintegrated' corporate communities can survive and grow. For example, organizations that rely heavily on outsourcing and homework and those that rely largely upon the contribution of individual, non-interdependent experts and professionals may be predominantly fragmented.

Thus, the major contingencies which indicate the *fragmented* form are:

- when innovation is produced primarily by individuals not groups;
- when standards are achieved primarily through input (e.g. professional qualifications) rather than process controls;
- where there are few learning opportunities between individuals (or when professional pride prevents knowledge transfer);
- where there are low levels of work interdependence.

Although, then, it is clearly possible for corporations to survive and prosper in their absence, it is perhaps not surprising that some see the *communal* organization—with high levels of both sociability and solidarity—as the ideal. Solidarity alone may suggest an excessively instrumental organizational orientation. In effect, cooperation may be withdrawn the moment that it is not possible for members to identify shared advantage. In such organizations, scope for 'goodwill', 'give and take', and general 'flexibility' may be absent. By contrast, organizations that are characterized primarily by sociability may lose their sense of purpose. Critics claim that such organizations tend to be overly tolerant of poor performance and possibly complacent.

No doubt, the *communal* organization has considerable appeal. Indeed, this model informs much of the literature on innovative high-performing organizations. However, it may be an inappropriate and unattainable ideal in many business contexts. Those businesses that are able to achieve the communal form frequently find it difficult to sustain. There are a number of possible explanations. High levels of sociability and solidarity are often formed around particular founders or leaders, whose departure may weaken either or both forms of social relationship. Similarly, the communal corporation may be difficult to sustain in the context of growth, diversification, and internationalization. More profoundly, there may be an inbuilt tension between relationships of sociability and solidarity that makes the communal corporation inherently unstable. In effect, friendships can undermine collective interests or vice versa (Homans 1951).

The *communal* form is indicated where:

- innovation requires elaborate teamworking across functions and locations;
- there are measurable synergies and opportunities for teamworking across organizational sub-units;
- strategies are long term and emergent rather than the sum of measurable milestones;
- the business environment is dynamic and complex—requiring multiple interfaces with the environment and high capacity for internal information synthesis.

Of course, many organizations will occupy more than one quadrant. This poses interface management issues. Two examples may illustrate this point. First, in highly innovative pharmaceutical companies, for instance, we might expect the R&D function to be *communal*, and the sales and marketing function to be *mercenary*. In such organizations a perennial issue is 'how and why, in the innovation process, should marketing be involved?'. Turf battles often follow as the *communal* R&D function protects its cherished 'values' from the perceived 'ruthlessness' of the *mercenary* marketeers. Similar interface issues arise in companies with cultural products—music, books, television programming. Again there are frequent clashes (rarely productive) between functions and activities with different social architectures.

Career Issues within Different Social Architectures

Having developed our framework we now apply it by reference to some familiar themes from the career research literature: (1) the psychological contract; (2) the relationship between work, family, and private life; (3) patterns of occupational and organizational mobility and associated career development processes.

The psychological contract

The relationship between individuals and their employing organization has been usefully conceptualized in terms of the psychological contract (Argyris 1964; Schein 1978; Rousseau 1995)—the exchange that, explicitly or implicitly, is negotiated when individuals join, remain with, and perform in organizations. Whereas some issues—working hours, job tenure, or pay, for example—may be negotiated explicitly, other issues—notions of personal worth, justice and loyalty, for example—may remain implicit. These mutual obligations between individuals and organizations are negotiated and re-negotiated as work histories unfold with different trades of commitment for reward (material and psychological).

These contracts vary according to a variety of factors: age, experience, and career orientation (see Chapter 4), on the one hand, and organizational context, on the other.

How, then, might the distinctive organizational architectures that we have described help us to predict differences in the psychological contract? In the *networked* form we would expect the psychological contract to be pre-dominantly implicit—with substantial elements of the relationship neither written down nor precisely articulated. Close social ties between individuals are likely to have been built up gradually over time providing the basis for relatively high levels of interpersonal trust. Heavy emphasis is placed upon nurturing of relationships that are flexible and long term—with the tacit assumption that immediate actions have consequences that may emerge much later.

As Kay (1995: 57) points out, this type of 'relational' contract 'works best when all parties recognize that they are bound into a repeated game. Life-time employment, seniority based promotion, generous pension schemes and other forms of deferred remuneration all serve this purpose'. He goes on to assert 'Many managers have come to see these as outmoded ways of doing business. This is often a serious error.' We agree. It is within the *networked* form that the traditional contract of employment security in exchange for loyalty and obedience has come under most severe attack. Under pressure to reduce costs, demonstrate 'value' from acquisitions, and focus on core capabilities, many employers have acted opportunistically to exploit the discretion granted by relational contracts and so to gain short-term competitive advantage. In the process, long-term trust relationships have been undermined.

In effect, organizational change processes in many larger, well-established corporations in the 1990s have involved a deliberate attempt to move from a *network* to *mercenary* social architecture—high in solidaristic pursuit of clearly defined, shared interests ('strategic intent') but rather lower in terms of sociability. In the *mercenary* context we would expect the psychological contract to be more explicit, specific, and transaction/project related. This process of change can be understood by reference to an expectancy-theory type analysis of the motivational links between effort, performance, and reward. Large-scale corporate restructuring—downsizing, de-layering, and so on—is an attempt to do more with less: to reduce labor costs and maximize work intensity or 'effort'. At the same time there has been an increasing emphasis upon the monitoring and measurement of 'performance'—particularly for those groups previously free of such external controls: managers and professionals—and the linkage of reward packages to such measures. Just as Braverman (1974) suggested, management is not itself free from processes of work rationalization. Managers have themselves become the objects of a tendency to increase the intensity of work. The nature of 'rewards' has also shifted, with processes of restructuring serving to undermine two significant (and often implicit) rewards: job security and promotion; to be replaced by differing mixes of intrinsic (challenge, growth, autonomy) and extrinsic (money, share options) alternatives. Whatever the mix, the trend is clear—rewards are more clearly contingent upon current, measurable contribution. This is a world where contracts are more closely defined and, apparently, 'equal' parties stay together for as long as it serves their respective interests and then renegotiate or break apart when it no longer works.

Gains in terms of clarity and mutual responsibility (rather than dependence) must be set against losses in terms of flexibility, rapid information flows, and more open-ended preparedness to help—all of which can characterize the network form at its best. It is also clear that the intended transition from *networked* to *mercenary* is not always successfully achieved. Whereas the latter form's explicit contract of 'interests' may be entirely consistent with the expectations of certain professional groups—those employed within highly competitive investment banks or consultant surgeons in hospitals, for example—it can appear as a peculiarly soulless place for those more used to high sociability workplaces.

The evidence suggests a number of patterns. Well-established patterns of social relationships can hijack change programs and ensure the persistence of the *networked* form. Alternatively, attempts to reduce long-established relationships of sociability can produce reactions that appear to undermine both sociability and solidarity, creating an apparently uncontrollable descent into the *fragmented* form. In effect, when employers opportunistically exploit relational contracts, they may provoke a similar response from employees. Some men in mid-career, for example, denied the job security and hierarchical progression implicitly promised at the beginning of their careers, may develop more calculative orientations to their work, their careers, and their employing organizations.

We have referred to these as 'reluctant managers . . . cautious about their commitment to employing organizations if only because of the greater risks of career 'failure', redundancy, and redeployment . . . feelings of psychological well-being can be sustained through limiting the extent of their occupational involvement and corporate attachment' (Scase and Goffee 1989: 179–80). Under these circumstances, individuals may deliver sufficient performance to ensure their jobs—but little more. Little time is wasted on building relationships with colleagues or expending energy promoting the organization. Again, as we have pointed out, the *fragmented* form may be appropriate in work contexts—particularly where there are low levels of interdependence between tasks—but organizations that drift towards fragmentation may have produced a psychological contract that severely damages their performance.

The psychological contract of the *communal* form has often been promoted as the ideal in much of the prescriptive management literature. In this form there is a powerful alignment of individual and organizational behavior. Employees become completely immersed in their work and workplace; there are high levels of 'identification' (Etzioni 1961). Here reciprocity is generalized—individuals give with no expectation of return (as in blood-giving); they do so because it is good for the organization. By contrast, reciprocity is balanced in the networked form (a return is expected but not immediately); negotiated in the mercenary form (the exchange is both more immediate and explicit); and negative in the fragmented form (members attempt to get help without giving anything in return). Relationships of general reciprocity may be more sustainable in not-for-profit or smaller organizations; there are few examples of larger business corporations that have maintained this form over time. Hewlett-Packard may represent one high-profile exception (Goffee and Jones 1998). But, in a similar sector, the parallel example of Apple's near-demise illustrates the high risks of disillusionment in this contract when ideals are seen to be transgressed or simply not delivered.

Work, family, and private life

Another persistent theme of the career literature is the relationship among work, family, and private life (see Chapters 9 and 10). Our argument is that these relationships too are played out in the context of the social architecture of the organization. This concern is part of a more general social-scientific focus on the relationship between work and non-work (Parker 1983). So far as managers are concerned, there has been, perhaps, excessive focus on the extent to which the nature of managerial employment conditions all other aspects of personal and social experience. This has arisen partly out of the gender-skewed sample from which this research has been drawn. For men it has been reported that family and private lives have relatively little impact on work lives except in times of personal crisis. For women, exactly the opposite relationship is described (see Chapters 9 and 10). They are portrayed (perhaps unintentionally) as preoccupied with personal, family, and domestic obligations in a way that leaks into their working lives (Scase and Goffee 1989). It is clear to see the ideological functions of such representations. Since women cannot give their all to their careers, they cannot expect such rapid rates of mobility as are achieved by their male counterparts. We, for our part, want to conceptualize the relationship between employment, family, and private life, as at least in principle being characterized by two-way causal direction.

Let us begin with the *mercenary* organization, perhaps the paradigm capitalist enterprise of the 1990s. Here we would expect the clearest separation between employed life and private life. Clearly focused managers devote as much time as it takes to success at work, pursuing measured targets in exchange for tangible rewards. The clarity of the psychological contract, it is alleged, allows an equally clear separation between work and private life. Managers in *mercenary* organizations may work hard, but when they stop their time is their own. Indeed, we can imagine that they conceive of the efforts they make at work as primarily instrumental—allowing them material possessions to be consumed in their private or domestic lives. However, this idealized portrayal of life in the *mercenary* organization may conceal as much as it reveals. Even if there is a sharp separation of work and non-work lives, the pressured executive carries work obsessions and anxieties home. The burgeoning research on executive stress is ample testimony to this (Quick *et al.* 1992). If separation is to be achieved it clearly requires considerable psychological work to police the divide, to insulate one world from another. This does not always work. There are at least two other relationships that might arise. First, the demands of the *mercenary* context may require so much of the executive that work and domestic lives become severely in conflict—so much so that negative consequences are generated for either or both spheres of life. This is picked up in popular cultural representations of the manager who arrives home unable to interact effectively with his or her family, drained by the demands of work to which they are unable to contribute. Secondly, to use Evans and Bartolomé's terms (Evans and Bartolomé 1980), home may be seen as *compensation* for the rigors of employment. Again, popular representations portray the home as a kind of dressing station for the damage inflicted by employment. Weekends become periods of intensive rest and recreation before managers re-enter the combat zone on Monday mornings. The extent to which any of these arrangements can be made to work may depend on the psychological characteristics of the key players, their individual agendas, and the inter-action of both of these with the corporate context.

By contrast, in the *networked* organization the division between work life and personal life is much more blurred. As we have already mentioned, *networked* organizations are characterized by high levels of sociability and part of this involves an inquisitiveness about colleagues' personal lives. Indeed, in order to operate successfully in such a context, it may be 'required' that one reveal aspects of one's private life. Further, organizational rituals, such as retirement parties, sales conferences, even birthday celebra-tions, may involve interaction including both 'work' and 'private' partners.

This brings an altogether different feeling to the relationship best described, again using Evans and Bartolomé's work, as 'spillover', where '[work] affects [non-work] in a positive or negative way'. Let us look at the possibilities in more detail. On the one hand, a partner may add to the resources at one's disposal in one's organizational life; partners may confirm one's positive attributes, complement weaknesses, or add required social capital. Indeed, in highly *networked* contexts, access to senior positions in the organization may depend upon not just the individual manager but his or her partner and wider family. When this happens, the organization may feel like family life, but at the same time family life is never quite separate from work. On the other hand, partnerships established early in life may prove a considerable impediment later on in one's career. In one highly *networked* organization where we have been carrying out research, the standard black humor is that when you join the elevated ranks of those senior executives who personally negotiate employment contracts it is *de rigeur* to change your partner!

When we examine the *communal* quadrant we can see some of the same patterns driven to their extreme case. Here work is so powerful that is subsumes everything—values, norms, rituals, obsessions. Managers may derive all of the satisfactions that they need from their employed life—material, emotional, and intellectual. Some have argued that, in this context, work relationships take on many of the characteristics of familial relation-ships (Kanter 1990), with all of the dysfunctions this may imply. It is certainly the case that when working in and with people from *communal* organiza-tions we have observed many behaviors that testify to the subsumption of all to working life and working relationships. For example, little account is taken of the measurement of time at work; it is simply assumed that time at work is time well spent. And, when away from work, members of such organizations are driven to talk and argue about work yet again. Even in recreation, the best people to be with are work colleagues. This obsessive quality may help to explain why maintaining commercial organizations in the *communal* quadrant is rather difficult, for in order to do this they need to meet a multiplicity of needs, not all of which are compatible. Hence the difficulty that such organizations face when they need to downsize: since work is all embracing, anything that threatens the working life of a colleague undermines the psychological infrastructure of the whole organization.

In the *fragmented* organization we may characterize the relationship between work and private life as entirely independent. Since one's value at work is entirely dependent on both outcome measures and the value of individual human capital, there is little or no interest in life away from work. In *fragmented* organizations characteristically individuals know little about the domestic or private lives of their colleagues (although even here we may find 'rogue cells' of communality). However, there is a complication. Even though individuals may have little concern for their organizational presence, they may have considerable concern for their occupational careers and this may require of them that their partners exhibit the requisite social skills. Think, for example, of the old professions of medicine and law; here occupational mobility may well be dependent not just on one's individual output but on the networks that one can build within the occupation, which may themselves be maintained through social relationships involving family. It is perhaps paradoxical in this context that the organizational form that offers most freedom at work may still implicate family and partners in processes of occupational career mobility.

Mobility and career development

When we turn more specifically to matters of occupational and organizational mobility and their connections with career development processes, we can see implications of social context rather clearly. First, it needs to be noted that questions of occupational and organizational mobility and matters of career development are different perspectives on the same general phenomenon. That is to say, while occupational and organizational mobility are closely connected to the dynamics of the labor market (see Chapter 11), career development processes are (particularly as managed by the human resource (HR) function) organizational responses to those same labor-market characteristics. Individuals find themselves occupying the space between the wider social and economic environment and the organization's responses to it. They may make use of this space, but it is one of the central contentions of this chapter that they can do so only within fairly tight limits.

In the *networked* organization, as we have already seen, there is an expectation that employment will continue and that career progression is possible, at least in principle. What then are the obsessions of career-development processes? Since these organizations place such high value on the establishment and maintenance of functioning social relationships, considerable attention is placed upon 'polishing' the social skills of those perceived to have high potential for career mobility. In rather subtle ways, aspiring individuals need to internalize ways of behaving that fit this organizational context well. Even the so-called 'high-flyers', moving rapidly up the hierarchy, will be counseled to avoid making too many enemies who might seek 'revenge' later in their career. They need to have enough enemies to indicate their intolerance of poor performance, but not so many that they cannot build effective teams in the future. Career development becomes focused on helping people to become 'the right stuff'. A further characteristic of career development in this quadrant arises when the *networked* organization is international. In this context, building the right networks involves moving not just between one function and another but also between one country and another. Unilever asks that its young 'high-flyers' manage outside their function and outside their culture by their early thirties. This is a very ambitious development target, but, when it works, it produces individuals ideally suited to the social context in which they must operate. Managers can move around the globe and between businesses, able to build effective social networks locally while maintaining their connections at head office. It is this capability that leads some to conclude that Unilever operates largely outside its formal control mechanism through a system of interlocking social networks (Bartlett and Ghoshal 1988).

Much of this polishing work may be accomplished by the HR function, which will aid in the identification of high-potential managers and devise training and development plans that inculcate the right behaviors. In this quadrant the key tasks of HR will be recruitment, talent identification, and careful management of the development process. If it is effective in these tasks, it will achieve considerable organizational legitimacy.

In the *mercenary* quadrant things are quite different. Clearly the psychological contract is more brittle. We know that key executives may leave if they get a better offer. Even here, however, there are career development processes, but they are much more like 'knock-out tournaments', where talented executives are pitted against each other to see who will win (Rosenbaum 1984; Sonnenfeld and Peiperl 1988). And there can be only one winner—in other words, career development is a series of zero-sum games. These games, however, can be useful to the organization only if the measures of performance are clear and tightly related to business objectives. Thus, in the *mercenary* quadrant much emphasis is given to the development of effective measurement systems that tie individual output to corporate objectives. Never mind how you do it—just hit your targets. In efficient *mercenary* organizations, these measures are themselves constantly reviewed in an effort to avoid goal displacement.

For the HR function operating in such a context, several issues force themselves to center stage. Of course, there has to be a concern with recruiting effective individuals, but this is less important, because, if they turn out to be only moderate performers, there is little impediment to letting them go. Much more important will be the design and implementation of effective measurement systems to ensure that 'winners' get through to the top. In addition, given the reality and immediacy of the labor market, considerable emphasis is given to retaining key executives. It is in this quadrant that the imagery of 'golden handcuffs' was first formulated, and much intellectual energy is given to tying in key executives or at the very least ensuring that the competition will have to pay a great deal to tempt them away. Here, then, the labor market drives career development.

In the *communal* quadrant career development is essentially concerned with practicing the core values of the organization. Whether it is the Hewlett-Packard Way or the Johnson & Johnson Credo, we are concerned with the behaviors that flow out of value statements. The credo audit at Johnson & Johnson is a central plank of career development; it measures not just what executives achieve but how they achieve it, and it is taken extremely seriously by all involved. Several key tasks must be performed if this process is to be effective. First, it must be possible to deduce behaviors from value statements. Motherhood statements like 'be creative' are insufficiently specific for effective career development in communal organizations; there is a need to know *what* has to be done and *how*. Secondly, behaviors need to be visible and recordable. There is a need to account for commitment to organizational values through observable behavior.

The HR function is often cast in the role of guardian of corporate values in this communal context. It is asked to recruit individuals who may become 'believers' and who will not in any event damage the integrity of the organization. It runs value-inculcation sessions that repeat central organizational messages. If it is very effective, it will apply these constantly to new contexts—thus avoiding any sort of 'mind-numbing' conformity. A further key role will be removing those who threaten the basis of communality.

In stark contrast, in the *fragmented* organization there is little explicit concern with matters related to organizational careers. Individuals are primarily concerned with their reputation in an occupational context and very often their employing organization merely supplies the means through which they advance their occupational career. That is not to say that in fragmented organizations there is no concern for human capital. On the contrary, it is a fixation. The success of *fragmented* organizations depends upon their ability to attract the 'best' and to retain them if they continue to perform very well (see Chapter 7). Elite *fragmented* organizations will be characterized by considerable concern with reputation in the wider occupational community. When individuals from fragmented organizations talk to each other, one of the questions they constantly ask of each other is: 'Is this a good place to work?' by which they mean: 'Would working at this organization add to my résumé and while I am here would I be allowed plenty of space to decide my own priorities and get on with my own work?'

If fragmented organizations have an HR function at all, it is concerned with meeting the demands of the 'prima donnas' who might add value to the reputation of the organization. In addition, some effort will be directed to scanning the labor market to identify rising stars in other organizations and tempting them to join with offers of even more freedom. It is in organizations such as this that the protean model of careers is most appropriate (Hall and Mirvis 1996).

Conclusion

In this chapter we have argued that, while there are powerful forces shaping and reshaping career patterns, it does not follow from this that we need to adopt an entirely individualist paradigm to explain the modern world. On the contrary, key issues in career theory are illuminated by focusing on the social architecture of organizations, which provides the context in which careers are worked out. We have tried to offer a model based on concepts drawn from classical sociological theory that allows us to describe these social architectures. We are drawn back to a suitably 'postmodern' uncertainty. We can agree that the old certainties of stable careers, in so far as they ever existed, are in decline, but we cannot agree with a picture of individual free choice that ignores organizational context, labor-market variation, and cultural specificity. There may be no general statements to be made about career, community, and culture. Rather, we may be faced with working through empirically divergent, contextually grounded examples (Goffee and Jones 1998). Generalizations, if they are to be found, are likely to be highly abstract. Individuals may make their careers, but they do not make them entirely under conditions of their own choosing.

References

Argyris, C. (1964), *Integrating the Individual and the Organisation* (London: Wiley).

Arthur, M. B., and Rousseau, D. M. (1996) (eds.), *The Boundaryless Career: A New Employment Principle for a New Organizational Era* (New York: Oxford University Press).

—— Hall, D. T., and Lawrence, B. S. (1989), *Handbook of Career Theory* (Cambridge: Cambridge University Press).

Bartlett, C., and Ghoshal, S. (1988), *Managing across Borders: The Transnational Solution* (Boston: Harvard Business School Press).

Braverman, H. (1974), *Labor and Monopoly Capital* (New York: Monthly Review Press).

Cricitto, J. (1998), review of M. B. Arthur and D. M. Rousseau (eds.), *The Boundaryless Career: A New Employment Principle for a New Organizational Era*, in *Academy of Management Review*, 23: 177–8.

DeFillippi, R. J., and Arthur, M. B. (1994), 'The Boundaryless Career: A Competency-Based Perspective', *Journal of Organizational Behavior* 15: 307–24.

Durkheim, E. (1933), *The Division of Labor in Society* (New York: Free Press).

Etzioni, A. (1961), *A Comparative Analysis of Complex Organizations* (Glencoe, Ill.: Free Press).

Evans, P. (1993), 'Dosing the Glue: Applying Human Resource Technology to Build the Global Organisation', *Research in Personnel and Human Resource Management*, 3: 21–54.

—— and Bartolomé, J. F. (1980), *Must Success Cost So Much?* (London: Grant McKintyre).

Gerth, H. H., and Mills, C. W. (1948), *From Max Weber: Essays in Sociology* (London: Routledge & Kegan Paul).

Ghoshal, S., and Bartlett, C. A. (1997), *The Individualized Corporation* (New York: Harper Business).

Goffee, R., and Jones, G. (1996), 'What Holds the Modern Company Together?', *Harvard Business Review* (Nov.–Dec.).

—— —— (1998), *The Character of a Corporation* (New York: Harper Collins).

—— and Scase, R. (1995), *Corporate Realities* (London: Routledge).

Hales, C. (1993), *Managing through Organisation* (London: Routledge).

Hall, D. T., and Mirvis, P. H. (1996), 'The New Protean Career: Psychological Success and the Path with a Heart', in D. T. Hall and Associates, *The Career is Dead: Long Live the Career* (San Francisco: Jossey-Bass).

Homans, G. (1951), *The Human Group* (London: Routledge & Kegan Paul).

Kanter, R. M. (1990), *When Giants Learn to Dance* (London: Unwin).

Kay, J. (1995), *Foundations of Corporate Success* (Oxford: Blackwell).

Lawrence, B. S. (1995), 'Career Theory', in N. Nicholson (ed.), *Encyclopedic Dictionary of Organizational Behavior* (Oxford: Blackwell).

Parker, S. (1983), *Leisure and Work* (London: Allen and Unwin).

Quick, J., Murphy, L., and Hurrell, J. (1992), *Work and Well-Being* (Washington: American Psychological Association).

Rosenbaum, J. E. (1984), *Career Mobility in a Corporate Hierarchy* (New York: Academic Press).

Rousseau, D. M. (1995), *Psychological Contracts in Organizations* (London: Sage).

Scase, R., and Goffee, R. (1989), *Reluctant Managers* (London: Routledge).

Schein, E. H. (1978), *Career Dynamics: Matching Individual and Organizational Needs* (Reading, Mass.: Addison-Wesley).

Simmel, G. (1971), *On Individuality and Social Forms*, ed. D. N. Levine (Chicago: University of Chicago Press).

Sonnenfeld, J. A., and Peiperl, M. A. (1988), 'Staffing Policy as a Strategic Response: A Typology of Career Systems', *Academy of Management Review* 13: 588–600.

13

Continuing the Conversation about Career Theory and Practice

Michael B. Arthur and Maury A. Peiperl

In Chapter 1 we issued an invitation to join in the 'conversation' among this book's contributors. We suggested four principal dichotomies that prevailed in the career studies field, and offered these dichotomies as a key for relating to the chapters to follow. The key, we anticipated, would allow for both following and joining the conversation among subsequent chapter authors from the reader's perspective.

In this brief closing chapter we offer a further invitation. It is to carry the conversation forward beyond the meeting ground that this book provides. As part of this further invitation, we reintroduce the four dichotomies covered in Chapter 1. However, we do so not to affirm the differences among intervening chapters, but rather to illustrate their level of potential agreement. As we probe what has been said, we see that the dichotomies on their own—while helping us to frame the points being raised—do not emphasize the connections the chapters make to one another.

Yet such connections abound. Although each team of authors adopts a different viewpoint, each also reaches out to acknowledge alternative views. Gone, it seems, are the days of taking classical vocational, or bureaucratic, or stage-driven views of careers as gospel without regard for other related perspectives. The study of careers and the benefits from studying careers, suggest our contributors, come from a broader, more appreciative understanding. It is an understanding about how different perspectives can influence and complement one another, rather than simply compete for the same explanatory space.

Moreover, in connecting our viewpoints it seems we increase our chances to better understand the connected world of career practice we seek to study. It is a world that engages people's essential human nature, their underlying affinity with national and institutional cultures, their potential for psychological growth, their propensity for social interaction, their attachment to communities, their identification with opportunities for promotion or other affirmations of self-worth, their involvement with the emergence of new knowledge, their contribution to the strategies of employer companies, their further investment in the prosperity of larger industrial sectors, their engagement with families, their expression of gender differences, and their exhibition of further 'facets' of their individual selves. This is no random list. It is a partial list of the concepts given serious attention in this book.

It is with the above list in mind that we return to our four dichotomies, although in a slightly different order, which reflects the thrust of the intervening chapters. We look now for links between the polarities stated, for the *and* of interconnection. In doing so we see many *and*s, each with different features, strengths, and limitations. They are *and*s that link between separate theories, as well as *and*s that link between theory and practice. The connections we describe below are intended to fulfill what various commentators have offered as a useful yardstick. That is, they are intended to help us bridge from practice to theory, or theory to practice, or both (see Lawler and Associates 1985; Bartunek *et al.* 1993; Wicks and Freeman 1998). In addition, we emphasize that the connections come into view only when one looks hard at the threads of individual *careers*—that is, at the unfolding sequences of people's work experience over time.

The Static *and* the Adaptive

On the one hand, career actors have been described in this book as 'the possessors of a defined human nature, genetically encoded and structurally embedded in the physical system of brain and body'. This essential human nature has been 'shaped over millions of years' but has remained virtually unchanged for at least a few thousand of the most recent years of our species' experience. Accordingly, human nature is untouched by 'communal dwelling in city-sized settlements, the nation state, and organizational structures for warfare, work, or worship' (Nicholson, Chapter 3, p. 55). These factors, all usually seen as critical to the nature of contemporary careers, are mere blips within the longer-term context in which our psychological make-up has evolved. The message is that we must look much further back in time if we are usefully to see ahead.

On the other hand, the 'changing landscape of jobs and careers' calls for our greater understanding of 'what excites and stimulates an individual toward growth and adaptation throughout life' (Boyatzis and Kolb, Chapter 4, p. 76) The idea of a career as a 'life path', 'evolving . . . with changes . . . [and] life experiences' (Eaton and Bailyn, Chapter 9, p. 192) adds a similarly dynamic aspect that needs to be reconciled with the static view. Where, then, to proceed in our search for connections?

One way forward is to appreciate the link between apparently static and adaptive viewpoints. Nicholson is reporting what is common to our distinctive evolutionary species as human beings. He is not, at that stage of the argument, reporting how our species' members can grow through and distribute themselves among the 'tribes' through which we organize our lives. Boyatzis and Kolb, in contrast, are looking hard at the individual tribal member, at his or her capacity for personal development beyond initial membership, and at the contribution that might be made to a tribe's further existence. There is room for each viewpoint to inform the other. There is also room for both chapters to converge in their views about the industrial age—since, say, the early middle 1800s—as a backdrop for observing career behaviour. Both suggest that the age was substantially ill-suited to, and inhibiting of, humankind's adaptive capabilities.

A different static perspective comes from the images of enduring culture, the mental programs or nervous systems that help us to appreciate the constraints on career behavior we see in particular countries (Cadin, Bailly-Bender, and Saint-Giniez, Chapter 11), or particular companies (Goffee and Jones, Chapter 12) that play host to work arrangements. Yet, both of these teams of authors see culture as the context in which career adaptation can be better understood. For the first team, understanding comes through a taxonomy of popular adaptations to national cultural circumstances. For the second team it comes through an appreciation of the interplay between established company levels of sociability and solidarity. Another author (Marshall, Chapter 10, p. 205) sees gender cultures entrenched in the career contexts in which both women and men engage. However, she uses this observation to highlight the process of narrating career stories, a process through which people are in turn better able to adapt to the career contexts in which they work.

Furthermore, the static view of our species and the adaptive view of its individual members come together in the models of career behavior they offer. There is much in common, for example, between Nicholson's evolutionary Motivation and Boyatzis and Kolb's personal-development mode with its related quest for meaning. These two conceptions may also be seen to overlap with the framework of personal career investments in motivational *knowing-why*, skill-centered *knowing-how*, and relational *knowing-whom*, adopted by several contributors to this volume. The framework helps us see how career adaptations to each of national culture (Cadin, Bailly-Bender, and Saint-Giniez, Chapter 11), professional service firm (PSF) strategy (Jones and Lichtenstein, Chapter 8), and mediating community attachments (Parker and Arthur, Chapter 5) may be better appreciated, and with what consequences for the host institutions involved.

Structure *and* Action

Static views of the world assume accompanying structures, but structures themselves need not be assumed to be static. The distinction is important to the way we view careers in general, and boundaryless careers (Arthur and Rousseau 1996) in particular. It is not that careers are conceived to unfold without constraint, and not that what are termed boundaryless careers imply an assumption of an unstructured world. Rather, the question is about what kinds of structures are emerging, and with what implications for the kinds of careers that they host. Gunz, Evans, and Jalland (Chapter 2, p. 25) contend that in the late twentieth century 'career boundaries [became] considerably more complex and multifaceted'. Even if certain organizational boundaries became more permeable, 'different kinds of boundaries [became more] salient' in the changing employment arena that was witnessed. Thus structures, although in many cases more changeable and more multifaceted than before, still play a role in shaping careers.

A contrasting response lies in the argument that it is theories of action, rather than theories of structure, that help us to understand the shift in the basic image of careers. It is a shift from a rising trajectory of hierarchical positions to an idiosyncratic sequence of experiences lacking 'external cues provided by strong, hierarchical structures' (Alvarez, Chapter 6, p. 127). For Jones and Lichtenstein it is the emergence of dominant logics through the actions (choices) of partners in architectural firms that determine career patterns within those firms.

One way to better connect different views of structure and action is to better understand the duration of the projects to which, for example, work in the biotechnology industry is attached. As two of the chapters in this volume would attest, the typical time to completion of biotechnology research and development projects is 'literally measured in decades' (Gunz, Evans, and Jalland, Chapter 2, p. 43). This stands in sharp contrast to the much shorter project durations typical in high technology (Saxenian 1996) or independent film-making (Jones 1996) that have been highlighted in the boundaryless-careers literature. Project duration can tie a senior collaborator to the company for a prolonged period, or it can prevent someone who seeks a flexible work schedule from becoming too deeply involved (Eaton and Bailyn, Chapter 9). The concept of career is especially helpful here, since it insists that we look at how work unfolds over time. We can see, as both Gunz, Evans, and Jalland, and Eaton and Bailyn, see, the time-linked insights that more limited conceptions of project 'jobs' or 'roles' would not provide. That is, structures of some duration may emerge as a function of long-term career 'actions' such as commitments to a fifteen-year-long project.

Thus, action may precede rather than succeed structure. The very importance of structure is attributed to careers 'that are bounded in ways that emerge from the striving of actors to make sense of their place in the world'

(Gunz, Evans, and Jalland, Chapter 2, p. 50). This relates closely to an action perspective viewing managers, for instance, as 'not merely the occupants of pre-established domains, but significant shapers through their actions of the tasks and positions in the structure, and, through these, of their organizations' (Alvarez, Chapter 6, p. 135). The point may be extended from the world of organizations to the larger world of occupational, industrial, and social institutions that also play host to careers (Arthur *et al.* 1999). Moreover, the structures that do emerge will be less constrained by physical space as the virtual, information-based organization (Nicholson, Chapter 3, p. 70) extends beyond that space.

Even in what appear, from a distance, as tightly defined and culturally reinforced structures, we can see, close up, the subtleties of individual action. Cadin, Bailly-Bender, and Saint-Giniez describe several examples in which existing structures (both within and beyond particular institutions) gave rise to individual actions (such as career transitions) that later led to structural adjustments (such as the creation of a new division) (Chapter 11). These subtleties do not deny the existence of structure, but rather offer a valuable, action-based complement to it. It is this complementarity that many of the authors in this volume have identified, and that allows us to take a more integrated—though not necessarily a more comprehensive— view of careers.

The Universal *and* the Particular

A comprehensive view of careers would require enough 'universal' concepts to subsume at least the majority of career experiences within them. In this volume, two approaches make particular progress in this direction. Nicholson's Motivation–Selection–Connection model and Goffee and Jones' four-cell model of careers in different corporate cultures set out, although in very different ways, dimensions along which careers, firms, and events may be calibrated. Drawing on principles of evolutionary biology and sociology, respectively, these two chapters map common career processes and attributes (recruitment, selection, fit, assignment, development, individual and group identity, mobility) in order to provide a systemic view of careers and the ways in which they evolve.

Turning to the 'particular' end of the spectrum, two further chapters stand out. The first is Marshall's, with its focus on the distinctive 'facets' of people's career stories. Looking at facets involves 'looking from different angles' but 'making no claim to encompass (any) whole' (Chapter 10, p. 203). Indeed, Marshall doubts that there is any wholeness to reach for, given the many contrasts among the stories she relates.

Marshall further suggests that the very act of storytelling contributes to the process of people's life development. One hears from Marshall more than a hint of 'new-science' thinking—namely, that the observer is a part of the action, inextricably influencing it (Wheatley 1992). As this book goes to press, the larger implications of chaos theory, complexity theory, and other new-science formulations are receiving fresh attention (Bird and Gunz, forthcoming). However, it is already clear that the careers researcher must shoulder a new accountability for the activity of data collection. It is an activity that may never fully meet the formal strictures of normal science. However, it is also an activity that, if carefully and considerately performed, may itself contribute to the effectiveness of the careers being studied.

Eaton and Bailyn extend Marshall's perspective by looking at 'the push to find a context in which one can experience one's whole self', but emphasizing that 'people are embedded in relationships outside work' (Chapter 9, p. 185). Their particular focus is on family relationships and the way these relate to the work structures in which careers take shape. The 'push' of women's careers is again emphasized, again not to exclude men but to highlight workers with children who 'were either single (parents) or had full-time working spouses with their own demanding careers' (p. 186). The authors observe that 'family and work conditions intersect in deciding the shape of these careers' (p. 186), and yet there is much 'unrealized potential' for work to be redesigned with 'employees' personal needs in mind' (p. 191). The problem is that universal assumptions about work still get in the way.

It is instructive that both the Marshall, and the Eaton and Bailyn, chapters focus on the nature of women's experience. A long-standing 'universal' complaint about career systems has been that they reflected a masculine bias, not only in their appeal to masculine 'agency' over feminine 'communion' (Marshall 1989), but also in their highly prescriptive models of success. These so-called objective models, and their intolerance for more personalized ideals, have weighed heavily on careers research. They are responsible, for example, for measuring personal development or mentoring programs by their participants' subsequent passage through company hierarchies, rather than by any more individualized measures of success (Ragins 1997). For Marshall's women, in contrast, personal success is more a matter of fit and integrity. For Eaton and Bailyn, it is a matter of integration and balance. Both of these reports are sensitive to people's particular career aspirations. It is universal 'masculine' assumptions, which even men have been shown to outgrow (Levinson *et al.* 1978), that are seen as the problem.

Yet the chapters in this book also begin to show us ways to link the universal and the particular, in part by reframing the universals. Eaton and Bailyn's focus on relationships is extended by Parker and Arthur into a larger picture of multiple community attachments, particularly those that people hold beyond their workplaces. People develop careers through combinations of career communities, which make the meaning of community particular to each career actor, yet the ten types of communities are more or less universally in evidence. Communities come alive for the way that they highlight rather than disguise people's separate career investments. This way of thinking about community finds encouragement in what Nicholson (Chapter 3, p. 70) sees as the genuinely new possibilities for virtual inter-action, and further reinforcement from what may be seen as genuinely different possibilities for occupational and other kinds of affiliation (Peiperl and Baruch 1997).

Institutional Knowledge *and* Individual Knowledge

A final set of connections can be drawn between what have so far been treated as largely separate constructs—namely, institutional and individual knowledge. The subject of organizational learning has been popular in recent years, but most of the writing has stayed at an aggregate level of analysis, so that the consequences for individual learning (and for the further effects of individual learning) have been largely neglected. The reverse may be observed for studies of individual learning—namely, that their contribution tends not to look at collective learning possibilities. We are caught in traditional thinking about levels of analysis. However, a prin-cipal argument stemming from this book is that careers transcend these levels of analysis. So too, it may be argued, does the learning that accom-panies careers. Beyond restrictive notions of simple disaggregation or aggre-gation, the relationship between the institutional and individual realms is rich in possibilities for further exploration.

Two chapters in this book embark on that exploration, as well as providing a rich contrast when each is seen in the light of the other. The first one is Morris' critique of traditional assumptions behind 'up-or-out' career systems in PSFs. Elaborating on the claim that 'knowledge in the firm is more than the existing professional knowledge base' (Chapter 7, p. 142) he proceeds to show that knowledge has both collective and tacit components. Yet both of these components are ignored in typical career arrangements, resulting in knowledge loss through the exit of unsuccessful candidates for promotion—a loss that goes unquestioned by career system administrators. Further questions, such as 'How is a firm to permanently capture knowledge from a transient workforce?' and 'In what form can captured knowledge be stored?' follow from the line of analysis undertaken. The conclusion is that career systems will need to become much more sophisticated if they are to avoid relative 'knowledge starvation' in the future competition to supply professional services.

The chapter by Jones and Lichtenstein travels in the opposite direction. Rather than focusing on the partnership's career system or policy, they focus on the individual partner's own career goals. It is a focus on the individual career that 'provides important insights into how competencies are acquired and developed in professional service firms', and in turn into how the domi-nant logic of those firms gets established (Chapter 8, p. 154). This logic emerges from the career motivation (*knowing-why*), professional skills (*knowing-how*), and relationships (*knowing-whom*) in which partners invest through their own careers. Jones and Lichtenstein's focus is on stayers rather than leavers, on gains rather than losses. The complementarity of the two chapters shows a two-way connection between the firms and their members' careers. However, it is a connection about which we have much still to learn. What these two chapters affirm is that we cannot learn what we need to without a clear focus on the careers of the players involved.

Parker and Arthur suggest other beneficiaries of knowledge accumulation—namely, the multiple career communities to which people attach themselves. In their view, the range of institutional knowledge-holders is much more diffuse, and the role of the firm assumes less significance. Their perspective raises questions such as 'Does it really matter if the occasional architectural or consulting practice goes out of business?' or 'Is displaced knowledge not safely held in the memories of associated professional communities?' or 'Might the delivery of professional services be more responsive to changing client needs through periodic decline of old and ascent of new provider firms?' However, to explore these questions will require studies of careers that measure the returns to employment mobility for people and firms, rather than assuming firm-based careers in which mobility is either an anomaly or an unwelcome necessity.

A final issue concerns the nature of tacit knowledge, and its generation, storage, and transfer through career behavior. The complexity of this issue is signaled by the fundamentally different views of tacit knowledge that the most recently cited authors take. For Morris, it is principally an attribute of the firm; for Jones and Lichtenstein, an attribute of the person; for Parker and Arthur, an attribute of the external career communities to which a firm's members also belong. It is clear that careers themselves are 'repositories of knowledge' (Bird 1996) and that career behaviors create shared spaces (communities) in which more collective forms of tacit knowledge are accumulated. However, there appear to be all manner of subtleties involved in how careers and tacit knowledge interact. This book offers some helpful pointers, but the larger questions still call for much deeper exploration.

Conclusion

The contributors to this volume, then, have not so much solved the debates outlined in Chapter 1 as they have extended and connected them in ways that bridge the polarities and pose challenging questions for our field. The new conceptions of working lives that result add not only richness but also rigor—the rigor not of normal science methodology, but of conceptual, integrated thinking about careers *as they are* and are likely to become.

It is a conversation well worth continuing—indeed, necessary to continue—as the frontiers of careers move on.

References

Arthur, M. B., and Rousseau, D. M. (1996) (eds.), *The Boundaryless Career: A New Employment Principle for a New Organizational Era* (New York: Oxford University Press).

—— Inkson, K., and Pringle, J. K. (1999), *The New Careers: Individual Action and Economic Change* (London: Sage).

Bartunek, J. M., Bobko, P., and Venkatraman, N. (1993), 'Toward Innovation and Diversity in Management Research Methods', *Academy of Management Journal*, 36/6: 1362–73.

Bird, A. (1996), 'Careers as Repositories of Knowledge: Considerations for Boundaryless Careers', in M. B. Arthur and D. M. Rousseau (eds.), *The Boundaryless Career: A New Employment Principle for a New Organizational Era* (New York: Oxford University Press).

Bird, A., and Gunz, H. (forthcoming), 'Careers and the New Science', special issue, *Human Relations*.

Jones, C. (1996), 'Careers in Project Networks: The Case of the Film Industry', in M. B. Arthur and D. M. Rousseau (eds.), *The Boundaryless Career: A New Employment Principle for a New Organizational Era* (New York: Oxford University Press).

Lawler, E. E., and Associates (1985), *Doing Research that is Useful for Theory and Practice* (San Francisco: Jossey-Bass).

Levinson, D. J., with Darrow, C. N., Klein, E. B., Levinson, M. H., and McKee, B. (1978), *The Seasons of a Man's Life* (New York: Knopf).

Marshall, J. (1989), 'Re-visioning Career Concepts: A Femininist Invitation', in M. B. Arthur, D. T. Hall, and B. S. Lawrence (eds.), *Handbook of Career Theory* (Cambridge: Cambridge University Press).

Peiperl, M., and Baruch, Y. (1997), 'Back to Square Zero: The Post-Corporate Career', *Organizational Dynamics* (Spring), 7–22.

Ragins, B. R. (1997), 'Diversified Mentoring Relationships in Organizations: A Power Perspective', *Academy of Management Review*, 22/2: 482–521.

Saxenian, A. (1996), 'Beyond Boundaries: Open Labor Markets and Learning in Silicon Valley', in M. B. Arthur and D. M. Rousseau (eds.), *The Boundaryless Career: A New Employment Principle for a New Organizational Era* (New York: Oxford University Press).

Wheatley, M. J. (1992), *Leadership and the New Science* (San Francisco: Berrett–Koehler Publishers).

Wicks, A. C., and Freeman, R. (1998) 'Organizational Studies and the New Pragmatism: Positivism, Anti-Positivism, and the Search for Ethics', *Organization Science*, 9/2: 123–40.

NAME INDEX

SUBJECT INDEX